D1614552

WITHDRÁWN

Democratic Theory and Mass Incarceration

Democratic Theory
and Mass Incarceration

Edited by ALBERT W. DZUR, IAN LOADER,
AND RICHARD SPARKS

OXFORD
UNIVERSITY PRESS

Oxford University Press is a department of the University of Oxford. It furthers
the University's objective of excellence in research, scholarship, and education
by publishing worldwide. Oxford is a registered trade mark of Oxford University
Press in the UK and certain other countries.

Published in the United States of America by Oxford University Press
198 Madison Avenue, New York, NY 10016, United States of America.

Library of Congress Cataloging-in-Publication Data
Names: Dzur, Albert W., editor. | Loader, Ian, editor. | Sparks, Richard, 1961– editor.
Title: Democratic theory and mass incarceration / edited by Albert W. Dzur,
Ian Loader, and Richard Sparks.
Description: First edition. | Oxford ; New York : Oxford University Press, 2016. |
Includes bibliographical references and index.
Identifiers: LCCN 2016004823 | ISBN 9780190243098 (hardcover : alk. paper) |
ISBN 9780190629144 (epub)
Subjects: LCSH: Imprisonment—Political aspects | Criminal justice,
Administration of—Political aspects. | Crime prevention—Government policy. | Democracy.
Classification: LCC HV8705 .D46 2016 | DDC 365.01—dc23
LC record available at http://lccn.loc.gov/2016004823

9 8 7 6 5 4 3 2

Printed by Sheridan Books, Inc., United States of America

CONTENTS

CONTRIBUTORS

Christopher Bennett is Reader in Philosophy at the University of Sheffield. He has published articles on various aspects of criminal law and criminal justice, and the nature of blame, forgiveness and retribution. He also has interests in democratic political theory, moral psychology, and the history of philosophy, especially German Idealism. He is the author of *The Apology Ritual: A Philosophical Theory of Punishment* (Cambridge, 2008) and *What Is This Thing Called Ethics?* (Routledge, 2010). He is a member of the Research Advisory Group of the Howard League for Penal Reform and is Chief Editor of the *Journal of Applied Philosophy*.

Thom Brooks is Professor of Law and Government at Durham University's Law School where he is also the Head of Durham Law School and Director of the Centre for Criminal Law and Criminal Justice. He has held visiting positions at the universities of Oxford, St Andrews, Uppsala and Yale Law School. Brooks advises the Labor Party on criminal justice issues and immigration law and policy. His books include *Hegel's Political Philosophy* (Edinburgh, 2ed 2013), *Becoming British* (Biteback, 2016) and *Punishment* (Routledge, 2ed. forthcoming).

Lynne Copson is Lecturer in Criminology at the Open University. Her research centers on utopian theory, the emerging perspective of zemiology and its relationship to criminology (particularly in terms of their respective implications for imagining and realizing "the good society"), and the sociology of contemporary knowledge production. She has previously held positions at the School of Law, University of Edinburgh where she served as co-director for the Centre for Law and Society.

Richard Dagger is E. Claiborne Robins Distinguished Chair in the Liberal Arts and Professor of Political Science and Philosophy, Politics, Economics, and Law at the University of Richmond. In addition to many essays on punishment, political obligation, republicanism, and other topics in political and legal philosophy, he is the author of *Civic Virtues: Rights, Republican Liberalism, and Citizenship* (Oxford, 1997) and coauthor (with Terence Ball) of *Political Ideologies and the Democratic Ideal* (Pearson, 2010). His *Playing Fair: Political Obligation and the Problems of Punishment* is forthcoming from Oxford University Press.

R. A. Duff is Professor Emeritus at the University of Stirling, and a former professor in the University of Minnesota Law School, where he helped to create the Robina Institute of Criminal Law and Criminal Justice. He works in the philosophy of criminal law, and has published on criminal punishment (*Trials and Punishments*, 1986; *Punishment, Communication, and Community*, 2001), on the structures of criminal liability (*Intention, Agency, and Criminal Liability*, 1990; *Criminal Attempts*, 1996; *Answering for Crime*, 2007), and on the criminal process (*The Trial on Trial*, co-authored, 2007). He recently led major research projects on *The Trial on Trial*, and *Criminalization*, and is currently working on a book, *The Realm of the Criminal Law*, arising from the *Criminalization* project.

Albert W. Dzur is Professor of Political Science and Philosophy at Bowling Green State University. A democratic theorist with an interest in citizen participation and power-sharing in criminal justice, he is the author of *Punishment, Participatory Democracy, and the Jury* (Oxford, 2012); *Democratic Professionalism* (Penn State, 2008); and numerous articles in journals such as *Constellations, Law and Society Review, Political Theory*, and *Punishment and Society*.

Roberto Gargarella is Professor of Law at the Universidad de Buenos Aires and the Universidad Torcuato di Tella and a researcher at CONICET (Argentina) and at the CMI (Norway). He has specialized in legal and political theory and comparative American Constitutionalism. His works include *The Legal Foundation of Inequality: Constitutionalism in the Americas, 1776-1860* (Cambridge, 2010), and *200 Years of Latin American Constitutionalism* (Oxford, 2013). He has also been awarded a John Simon Guggenheim scholarship (2000), a Fulbright scholarship (2010) and has taught at numerous universities, including the New School for Social Research, Columbia University, Bergen University, and Southwestern University.

David A. Green is Associate Professor of Sociology at John Jay College of Criminal Justice, The City University of New York. His main research interests involve the interplay between crime, media, public opinion, punishment, and politics, often through a comparative lens. Current projects focus on media consumption and the crime decline, public and state punitiveness, and the nature and extent of the changing penal climate in the United States. He is the author of *When Children Kill Children: Penal Populism and Political Culture* (Oxford, 2008), winner of the 2009 British Society of Criminology Book Prize. His work appears in *The British Journal of Criminology, Crime and Justice, European Journal of Criminology, Punishment & Society*, and *Crime, Media, Culture*, among others. He has been a Junior Research Fellow at Christ Church, University of Oxford, and a Fellow at New York University Law School's Straus Institute for the Advanced Study of Law and Justice.

Amy E. Lerman is an Associate Professor of Public Policy and Political Science at the University of California, Berkeley. She writes widely on issues of political engagement, public opinion, and public policy. Her recent work examines the ways that growing economic inequality, persistent racial bias, and the rise of the carceral state influence citizens' political beliefs, racial identities, and rates of political participation. She is the author of two books on criminal justice policy, *The Modern Prison Paradox* (Cambridge, 2013) and, with Vesla M. Weaver, *Arresting Citizenship* (Chicago, 2014). Professor Lerman's scholarship can be found in a variety of journals, including the *American Political Science Review, Perspectives on Politics, Journal of Politics, Public Opinion Quarterly, Political Psychology*, and *Punishment and Society*, among others.

Ian Loader is Professor of Criminology and Professorial Fellow of All Souls College at the University of Oxford. His research interests lie in the fields of policing, private security, public sensibilities towards crime, penal policy and culture, the politics of crime control, and the public roles of criminology. Ian is Editor-in-Chief of the Howard Journal of Crime and Justice.

S. E. Marshall is Professor Emeritus in Philosophy at the University of Stirling, and a former Research Scholar at the University of Minnesota Law School. Her main research interests are in issues that connect legal, political, and social philosophy. Recent publications include articles on privacy, on the family, friendship and community, and on criminal responsibility. She is currently working on theories of criminalization, on the idea of public wrongs and the criminal law, and on victims' duties and civic virtue. She was one of four collaborators on *The Trial on Trial* and *Criminalization* projects.

Lisa L. Miller is Professor of Political Science at Rutgers University. Her research interests are in law, social policy, inequality and crime and punishment, as well as in constitutionalism and democratic politics. Her most recent book is *The Myth of Mob Rule: Violent crime and democratic politics* (Oxford University Press). She has been a Visiting Fellow at Princeton University and the University of Oxford.

Peter Ramsay is Associate Professor of Law at the London School of Economics and Political Science. He is working on a theory of the penal law that explains its historical development as an aspect of the democratization and subsequent post-democratization of modern states. He is the author of *The Insecurity State: Vulnerable Autonomy and the Right to Security in the Criminal Law* (Oxford, 2012). He is Associate Editor, *New Criminal Law Review*.

Richard Sparks is Professor of Criminology and currently Head of the School of Law at the University of Edinburgh where he is also a co-director of the Scottish Centre for Crime and Justice Research. His research interests center on penal politics and institutions, especially prisons and imprisonment, and on the uses of criminological knowledge in public life.

Rebecca U. Thorpe is Assistant Professor of Political Science at the University of Washington. Her research focuses on political institutions and state development, with an emphasis on democratic accountability, political exclusion and state violence. She is the author of *The American Warfare State: Domestic Politics of Military Spending* (Chicago 2014), and she currently working on a project examining the development and expansion of the American prison apparatus.

Elizabeth R. Turner is a Lecturer in the Department of Sociology, Social Policy and Criminology, at the University of Liverpool. Her research is concerned with democracy, criminal justice and the public role of social science. Past research has focused on the generation and utilization of data on public opinion about crime and criminal justice. Current ongoing research projects include an ethnographic study of police discretion and an analysis of the media portrayal of specialist anti-gun and gang police units.

Vesla Mae Weaver is an Associate Professor of Political Science and African American Studies at Yale University and is the founding director of the ISPS Center for the Study of Inequality (I-CSI). Weaver is broadly interested in understanding racial inequality in the United States, how state policies shape citizenship, and the political causes and consequences of the growth of the criminal justice system in the United States. She is the author with Amy Lerman of *Arresting Citizenship: The Democratic Consequences of American Crime Control* and with Jennifer Hochschild and Traci Burch, *Creating a New Racial Order: How Immigration, Multiracialism, Genomics, and the Young can Remake Race in America.* She was awarded a 2016 Andrew Carnegie Fellowship for a new project that will map patterns of citizenship and governance across cities and neighborhoods, the *Faces of American Democracy.* Weaver's research has been supported by fellowships from the Russell Sage Foundation, National Science Foundation, the Ford Foundation, and the Brookings Institution. She currently serves on the Harvard/NIJ Executive Session on Community Corrections, the APSA Presidential Taskforce on Racial Inequality in the Americas, the Center for Community Change's Good Jobs for All initiative, and the Yale Faculty Senate.

Democratic Theory and Mass Incarceration

CHAPTER 1 | **Punishment and Democratic Theory**

Resources for a Better Penal Politics

ALBERT W. DZUR, IAN LOADER, AND RICHARD SPARKS

Introduction

On July 16, 2015, President Barack Obama toured El Reno Federal Correctional Institution near Oklahoma City and had a forty-five-minute roundtable discussion with six nonviolent drug offenders, a conversation recorded by HBO for a documentary on criminal justice. Mass incarceration, the president said during his visit, has become an unquestioned part of American life: "We have a tendency sometimes to almost take it for granted or think it's normal. It's not normal. It's not what happens in other countries. What is normal is teenagers doing stupid things. What is normal is young people making mistakes."[1] The president's El Reno trip was intended to build support for a significant shift in federal policy: reduction or elimination of mandatory minimum sentences, alternative sanctions for nonviolent offenders, restoration of voting rights to former prisoners, and "ban the box" rules to discourage employers from asking job candidates about their criminal records. The president's visit and his proposed reforms illustrate a departure from a dominant leadership paradigm in the United States, aptly characterized by Jonathan Simon as "governing through crime."[2] For over a generation few political costs were paid and many benefits reaped by elected officials for increasing sentences, ignoring racial disparities, and indeed considering mass incarceration to be "normal." President Obama's attempt to bring criminal justice into public view, to begin a dialogue on how to punish better and more fairly, is in itself a significant change in the political culture.[3]

The president's prison visit is a further sign that over recent years, in the wake of the crime drop and falling levels of public concern with and attention to crime, the seemingly inexorable upsurge in US imprisonment is slowing down, or being sent into reverse.[4] The recent publication and discussion of high-profile reports on the *problems* of mass incarceration and police racism and brutality are also indicators that the terms of debate about crime and justice may be shifting.[5] It is no doubt too early to tell to what extent, or how durably, the penal climate is altering and to know whether recent reversals signify a material change (in that climate), or simply a reversible fluctuation (in the penal weather). It would certainly be naïve to rely on simple optimism that things are taking a turn for the better, to assume that state austerity will alone be sufficient to produce significant penal change, or to underestimate the reach and embeddedness of the American carceral state.[6] In this regard, we should recall something else that makes the El Reno trip remarkable: Obama was the first sitting president to visit a federal prison, the first leader of America's democracy to visit the unfree world that has been constructed in that democracy's midst. What had been keeping these powerful men away for so long from the disempowered and disenfranchised? What was so repellent about the institutions over which the president has ultimate oversight? Why did it take the intolerable financial burden of massive public spending on incarceration at a time of deep economic recession to push criminal justice, slowly and hesitantly at first, on to state and federal executives' agendas?

These are important caveats: reminders of the invisibility of the prison within the life of modern democracies. It may nonetheless be the case that room is opening up for new forms of constructive thinking and strategic intervention in the penal field wherein we can bring to bear new intellectual resources in addressing questions of punishment.[7] But what concepts and arguments are available to us at this moment of possibility, after more than a generation of "normal" mass incarceration, to speak to its abnormality and to fix what is broken about a dysfunctional system that implicates all of us who have grown accustomed to it and in whose name it was assembled? What social and institutional resources exist for creating different futures for the penal arrangements of modern capitalist democracies? How—if at all—can criminology and related forms of knowledge make such futures more likely to be achieved? What are the best outcomes for which we can reasonably hope in penal politics?

In this introductory chapter we want to outline and develop the core idea that animates this volume: namely, that one underexploited resource for a better penal politics lies in investigating the ideals and institutions of democracy and thinking about how these ideals can be theorized and given practical effect in reshaping the criminal justice and penal arrangements of advanced capitalist democracies today.

The Long Shadow of Mass Incarceration

Over the last thirty years mass incarceration (especially in the United States) came to seem inexorable and unremitting. This was so not just in terms of chronically high levels of imprisonment. It was also registered in terms of massive racial disproportion and the demotic symbolic politics that made "the prison" appear a necessary, obvious, commonsense solution to problems of crime and violence. But the more immovable mass imprisonment came to seem, the more it imposed a block on our capacity to imagine alternatives to it. The major and urgent task became that of tracing the contours of this phenomenon and grasping its social, institutional, economic, and cultural impact.

The long shadow cast by mass incarceration over penal scholarship has generated much original work on this phenomenon and its wider consequences. We consequently now know a great deal about the structural *causes* of this phenomenon and about the political dynamics that have fueled and shaped it.[8] Of late, rather more sustained attention has been devoted to examining the *effects* of mass incarceration, not only in terms of its impact on crime,[9] but also in respect of how it has reshaped other institutions of American society from the economy, to families, to communities, to the political process.[10] This has been important work. But beneath the shadow cast by penal excess it is also possible to discern certain temptations and attendant pathologies that have informed both analyses of mass imprisonment and prescriptions for how best to respond to it. Our judgment is that these pathologies have become an impediment to our capacity to think not just about, but also *beyond*, mass incarceration.

Common among them, we suggest, has been nostalgia: a lament for a better and lost world in which welfare liberal social policies were ascendant, where these coincided with (or helped produce) imprisonment rates that were lower and more stable, and where the climate of social and penal policymaking was much "cooler" and more rational. As we have noted elsewhere, this lamentation for mid-twentieth-century welfare liberalism (or in European terms, social democracy) is often accompanied by the miserabalist premise that what gets bad is going to get worse.[11] In terms of intervention, the heating-up of the penal climate over recent decades has given rise to a situation in which countervoices of social science have tended to eschew spaces of public engagement for fear of being trashed by a febrile media, as well as adopting a certain defensiveness in the diagnosis of what is to be done. The result is that penal politics has come to be seen as a rear-guard action where the principal objective is damage limitation or the protection of the hard-won and fragile gains of the past.

Two points might usefully be made about these structuring orientations toward mass incarceration. The first is to ask why lament and defensiveness has become so prevalent in the social analysis of, and responses to, penal excess. One answer is that mass imprisonment has played to criminology's self-image (and, we should add, its strengths) as a "dismal science." Our most powerful and compelling stories of penal change are narratives of decline and disaster. They have variously documented, warned, alerted, and critiqued. In the process the field has spun or imported (and sometimes loosely deployed or overextended) certain now-familiar concepts—risk, populism, punitiveness, and neoliberalism being obvious cases in point. But the social analysis of punishment has much less frequently speculated, reconstituted, or imagined alternatives to the penal disasters that it describes or denounces.

The second is to bring more clearly into view one alternative world that is to be found (sometimes expressly, often implicitly) in dominant accounts of mass imprisonment. What holds these responses to mass incarceration together, we think, is an outlook that one might call penal elitism. This is the worldview which holds that so long as experts—government officials, justice professionals, lawyers, researchers, and so on—are given the predominant say over the shape of penal policies, or else reinstated to a position of dominance, better penal outcomes will follow—where "better" means something along the lines of more moderate, milder, rights-respecting, liberal, or principled. The flip-side of this warm embrace of expertise has been a certain "discomfort with democracy":[12] a fear of permitting the demos too great an influence over penal policy and a concern that too intimate a connection between the public and policymakers will lead to immoderately punitive measures. This discomfort with democratic practice (and the resultant tendency to neglect democratic theory)[13] has been one of the most striking analytic effects generated by the three decade long penal upsurge. It has come close to acquiring the status of orthodoxy among analysts and critics of mass incarceration—one that has made a return to insulated professionalism and technocratic governance seem an obvious antidote to "hot" issues such as criminal justice. Protecting punishment from democracy has, in short, become the default answer to the question of what we can reasonably hope for in penal politics. So much so that the problematic that animates and organizes this book may (initially) strike readers as counterintuitive, even decidedly odd.

Distrust of the public has first and foremost shaped thinking on how to explain the rise of mass imprisonment—and the "exceptional" character of penal regimes in the United States. Reflected in scholarship on so-called penal populism, but also in the day-to-day assumptions of politicians and sitting government officials, looms an image of the punitive public demanding tough sentences and resistant to progressive reform. This, the argument runs, has been coupled with "the radically extensive and extraordinarily decentralized quality of US democracy"[14]—porous state and local political systems that have given way to democratic pressures of uninformed electorates and frenzied media responses to dramatic criminal events.[15] The ability of penal bureaucrats to manage or fend off these pressures is, conversely, posited as the principal explanation for the relative mildness of punishment in Scandinavia and parts of Western Europe.[16] By extension, keeping the public at bay has become a central plank of several influential accounts of how to temper punitive excesses. Here the claim is that the only way to scale back imprisonment is to insulate criminal justice policy through more backroom decisions, more expert interventions in sentencing commissions, and fewer grandstands offered to politicians seeking office on the back of tough-on-crime promises. The attendant ambition is to defend existing institutions of mediation between public demands and penal outcomes (such as parole boards) or to create new expert authorities, operating at one remove from direct political pressure, in and through which rational penal policy can be formed.[17]

Such technocratic solutions have also loomed large in recent governmental thinking about how to navigate a route away from mass incarceration. Even as the current administration began to draw mass incarceration into focus as a policy problem, high-ranking officials continued to block broader critical thinking on the issue as a *public* problem. In 2013, at the beginning of the policy shift, US Attorney General Eric Holder, the nation's most visible criminal justice professional, proclaimed that his colleagues needed to be "smarter on crime," meaning more sensible about sentencing for nonviolent or low-level offenses and more conscious of the racial biases of current practice.[18] Though Holder applauded the professionalism of his colleagues standing at the gateway to prison—the police, attorneys, prosecutors, judges, wardens, probation officers—his "smarter on crime" remarks implied that status-quo tough sentences and racial bias do not lead to safer streets; they are "dumb." At a time when leading scholars increasingly see criminal justice as "the most dysfunctional of the major institutional accomplishments of the Enlightenment,"[19] Holder's framework suggests that the way forward is a return to Enlightenment rationality (rather than an immanent critique of it) to become more sophisticated criminal justice experts and professionals. Being smart on crime, on this view, means listening to the experts more and the electorate less.

Penal Politics and Democratic Hope

This volume takes issue with technocratic discourse and the attendant suspicion of the public—and its participation in political life—that is at its root. It is not entirely correct to say, as President Obama did, that "we," meaning "the public," think mass incarceration is normal. It may be more precise to say that we the public have not been provided many opportunities to think seriously about mass incarceration at all. Crime and punishment saturate news and entertainment media, to be sure. But we actually don't engage in much concerted public discourse about the process or the practices our taxes support. Indeed, institutions involved in policing, adjudicating, and punishing have successfully repelled critical public awareness and involvement. Criminal justice work is often physically removed from the lay public, as with prisons that tightly control communication and interaction with those outside. Probation and other postincarceration administrative decisions and programs too are normally conducted outside the public gaze, commonly attracting attention only when something goes very wrong. Even the court process leading to prison can hardly be called public, as backroom plea bargaining has drastically replaced trials, leaving a scant 1 to 4 percent of state and federal criminal cases in the United States for the courtroom.

The aim of this volume is to connect debate about the future of punishment to a wider conversation about ideals and institutions of democracy. We want to encourage research and reflection on the mutually corrosive relationship that occurs, but also on the mutually supportive associations that may be fostered, between penal practices and democracy. In so doing, our aim is to treat democratic values and commitments as an underexploited "resource of hope" for building a better—by which we mean more deliberative and inclusive—penal politics.[20] Doing this, however, means making connections between areas of scholarship that have long and puzzlingly been disconnected: namely, between the social analysis of punishment and political theory in general and democratic theory in particular.

The United States remains the "world champion" in incarceration, to borrow Nils Christie's words, and jurisdictions in the United Kingdom, though some distance behind, are persistently among the European countries with the highest per capita rates of imprisonment. Yet until recently Anglo-American political theory has hardly registered mass incarceration and has done little to analyze any incongruity with mainstream normative commitments.[21] This disconnect is puzzling, first, because of the powerful lines of argument present within progressive, liberal, and conservative traditions alike which draw limits to state coercion and demand strict scrutiny over threats to individual rights, human development, and civic dignity posed by institutionalized exclusion and stigmatization. It is puzzling, second, because of the common ground occupied by restorative justice advocates and political theorists concerned with deliberative democratic institutional design. It is puzzling, third, because of the available links to robust and sophisticated theoretical discussions within criminology by David Garland, Jonathan Simon, and other scholars on the state, citizen action, and efficacy of punishment.

But this general dissociation between punishment and political theory also holds for the more particular domain of theorizing about democracy. The disconnection that concerns us here is of a particular kind, and the allegation may at first sight appear somewhat puzzling. Of course legal and political theorists have long concerned themselves with problems about the relationship between systems of law and personal and political liberty, and with questions about the justification of coercion in general and the right to punish in particular. Our point is rather that it is just *because* these sorts of problems are of such central and permanent interest that the slow and hesitant extent to which scholars of those questions have taken note of a phenomenon of such scale and consequence as that of contemporary mass incarceration is so puzzling. Against this backdrop, this volume therefore also invites people whose primary focus is with the concept of democracy and the development of democratic practices to consider how mass incarceration bears upon their core concepts and fundamental arguments about how institutions function and how they might improve, or be supplemented, or replaced, or transformed. Contemporary democratic theorists have to date done considerably less to address the subjects of crime, punishment, prison, and re-entry than we might have expected, despite the massive social, political, economic, and moral reverberations of mass incarceration. At a time often referred to as a renaissance in democratic theory, the field has been eerily silent on punishment. We think this neglect—what Bernard Harcourt has called the "invisibility of the prison in democratic theory"[22]—has emaciated scholarship on power, social justice, political equality, citizenship, institutional innovation, and related topics. By avoiding the real world of mass incarceration, democratic theory has risked becoming less democratic, less relevant to political reform, and less able to contribute productively to public discourse.

So just how should we go about better acquainting democratic theory with the study of mass incarceration in particular and punishment in general? How might the former alter the ways in which we think about, research, and evaluate the latter? Why should the carceral state command the attention of democratic theorists? What questions open up if we examine punishment though the lens of democratic theory and practice? We want to suggest three main ways in which a productive interplay between punishment and democratic theory is being developed.

A first line of analysis seeks to extend the *critique* of mass incarceration by situating it within the frame of democratic ideals and practice, thereby extending and recasting our analysis of what is at stake in penal policy and politics. Much of the empirical research on American punishment in recent years has focused on the impact of political systems *on* punishment—whether in terms of the advent of governing through crime,[23] the rise of symbolic and populist political forms,[24] the incentive and opportunity structures created (or blocked) by different political arrangements,[25] or the mobilization of social movements in the penal field.[26] But thinking about punishment through the lens of democracy also calls for analyses of the impact of mass incarceration *upon* democratic politics.[27]

To think democratically—rather than simply in crime control terms—about punishment is not just to revisit longstanding questions about the claims of retribution, deterrence, or rehabilitation as penal aims, or about the grounding of the sovereign right to punish in general. Rather, in our current contexts, it is also to seek to ask sharper questions about the collateral effects of the transformations of the carceral state upon political participation, the formation of civic identities and the associational life of impacted communities. The recent body of work on felon disenfranchisement is most obviously of importance here. But the very particular and locally variable phenomenon of felon disenfranchisement is one that opens a much wider set of concerns. It has as such provided a jumping-off point for the emergence of broader research agenda on what Lerman and Weaver term the political consequences of the carceral state, for investigating and theorizing the ways in which American punishment "violate(s) the democratic imperatives of voice, responsiveness, and accountability."[28] The further development of this agenda entails, among other matters: demonstrating that how societies punish goes to the quality and reach of their democratic claims; problematizing the relations between (excessive) punishment and democratic legitimacy; and identifying the ways in which crime control institutions attend to, or breach, democratic principles.

A second—in some respects more established and well-trodden—path entails finding within penal and political theory arguments for *restraining* the reach of the penal state, whether via desert theory, penal communication, or republicanism. Democratic theory has, arguably, been an under-utilized resource in such normative thinking about justifying and limiting the scope of state punishment. It is a field that might usefully be mined further in order to make the numerous sage recommendations for penal moderation or parsimony more compelling and better grounded—and we and others have recently intimated that the concepts of legitimacy and citizenship might prove to be useful meeting grounds for extending that conversation.[29] In our view, such an extension of penal theory offers grounds for questioning the *democratic* credentials of a society that punishes its citizens in the way that the American polity currently does. Quite a few criminologists in the United States and elsewhere have taken steps in these directions,[30] sometimes in alliance with progressive administrators and practitioners, and those parties need to be both supported and challenged by democratic theory.

A third point of connection is to be found in the use of democratic theory as a resource for exploring strategies of penal reform and for more broadly *reconstructing* how democratic societies might respond to crime. This has been a lively but still nascent theme with a small body of literature on deliberative democracy and punishment. Work here has largely developed as a response to, and critique of, the orthodoxy of insulating criminal justice from political control. It has sought instead to explore the unfulfilled promise of the ideal of greater democratic participation in crime control, and to bring to notice and advance understanding of practical innovations that give effect to such public involvement, in respect of restorative justice, justice reinvestment, and beyond.[31] There remains a great deal more theoretical work to be done along these lines, not least in demonstrating that populism and technocracy are not the polarized ideologies they are typically assumed to be within criminology, but can be theorized instead as twin pathologies of our contemporary anti-political malaise,[32] both of which "disfigure" the ideal and practice of democratic government by neglecting the normative force of democratic procedures.[33] But there is also a rich agenda of research and theorizing entailed in furthering practices of "democratic experimentalism" in crime control and punishment[34]—that is to say, in fostering the development of, and learning lessons from, deliberative practices whose aim is to promote civic reintegration, emphasize mutual accountability for penal decisions, and foster proper recognition that those whom we punish are co-citizens.[35] In other words, we need greater reflection on what it would look like to impose sanctions without magnifying existing inequalities and in ways that maintain equality of concern and respect for all parties involved.

In our view, these points of intersection between democratic theory and penal practice offer a theoretically rich and politically promising agenda for thinking about punishment beyond mass incarceration. It is an agenda that focuses—via the three moments of critique, restraint, and reconstruction we have described—on the aims and practices of crime control institutions and asks from the standpoint of democratic theory what one tasks police, probation, and prisons to do. From this standpoint, the overarching question that emerges is how to produce criminal justice institutions that *contribute* to democratic development and *build up* civic capabilities and participatory resources. Can this democratic ambition for criminal justice be justified, and if so how? What might one require of different criminal justice institutions if we conceived of their purposes at least in part in these terms? How would such institutions have to be remade and reimagined if they are to become agents of a deeper democracy?

Organization of this Volume

This collection of original chapters seeks to catalyze an engaged, multidisciplinary discussion among philosophers, political theorists, and theoretically inclined criminologists about how contemporary democratic theory might begin to think beyond mass incarceration.[36] Rather than viewing punishment as a natural reaction to crime and imprisonment as a sensible outgrowth of this reaction, we frame these as institutions with deep implications for contemporary civic identity and that present unmet demands for public oversight and reflective democratic influence. What conceptual resources can be deployed to support decarceration and alternatives to prison? How might democratic theory strengthen recent efforts in restorative justice and other reform movements? How can the normative complexity of criminal justice be grappled with by lay citizens rather than experts or officials—from street-level policing decisions, to adjudication, to prison and probation policy? How, in short, might modern publics forge a creative alternative to an unreflective commitment to mass incarceration? In reflecting on these questions, the authors investigate how to better situate the prison in the discourse of reform, offer conceptual guideposts for thinking about incarceration, critically examine the methods and uses of public opinion regarding punishment, and suggest ways of reconceiving crime control institutions to enhance rather than thwart citizen capabilities.

One explanation for the *doxa* surrounding the normalcy of mass incarceration, and a problem facing any attempt at a more critical public discourse for reform, is social geography. As Rebecca Thorpe's chapter forcefully points out, prisons are out of sight, out of mind, and highly ambiguous for many people. The rapid growth of prisons since the 1970s, especially in rural America, has provided jobs and revenues in impoverished communities. This kind of public investment is an economic dead end, however. As prison areas are rarely sites of further growth or development, it represents the shortsighted triumph of penal policy over more constructive approaches to rebuilding the poor, urban, and racially segregated neighborhoods disproportionately filling the rural prison cells.

How to orient our normative thinking about reform is the subject of the next three chapters. Reform efforts targeting contemporary penal institutions need to take their bearings from some overarching understanding of the purposes served by criminal justice. R. A. Duff and S. E. Marshall draw attention to the ideal role of the criminal law in a democratic republic, understood as a political society made up of free and equal citizens. Criminal law in such a society would be recognized by citizens to be something they shared and took part in as a common law. Focusing in particular on citizens convicted of crimes, they discuss the civic roles related to punishment that emerge in a democratic republic and how these roles, considered as a matter of ideal theory, reflect just how far current punishment practices are from widely embraced political ideals.

Seeking a gravitational principle that can shed light on the core question of just how much punishment is enough, Richard Dagger calls our attention to the importance of fair play. When punishment is deployed justifiably it intends to pay back those who do not play fair and it communicates disapproval of rule breaking, thus shoring up a cooperative, law-abiding system. When used in excess, it is a symptom of dysfunction calling into question the fairness of the laws and the status of the polity as a cooperative enterprise. Honing in on the value of political equality, Peter Ramsay argues that taking this value seriously results in strict limits on the use of imprisonment as a sanction. It is a mistake, he argues, to see an incarcerated person as a full and equal citizen. Prison inevitably takes away the exercise of free association and free assembly, and it severely limits free speech. Prisoners are in no way able to take part on equal terms with their fellow citizens in the regular political process. Political equality demands radical decrementalism in penal reform and points the way toward the abolition of incarceration.

Chapters 6 and 7 consider what more widespread citizen participation might contribute to criminal justice institutions. Focusing on adjudication and sentencing, Christopher Bennett asks whether greater lay participation would help produce more moderate decisions than the professionalized, official justice that has done little to block the development of mass incarceration. Democratization efforts may prove less beneficial in this respect than some scholars believe, he argues, but could be normatively significant nonetheless if they held citizens responsible as co-owners for punishment enacted for the public good. One approach already available for involving citizens as stakeholders in criminal justice is the wide range of practices offered by restorative justice programs as supplements to or substitutes for traditional sentencing procedures. Thom Brooks discusses the advantages of restorative justice as an alternative to mainstream criminal procedures for both victims and offenders. To serve as an effective institutional reform movement, however, restorative justice needs to become a more routine part of the criminal justice system and expand to handle a wider variety of cases, including serious offenses. To do so, Brooks argues, it may need to include penalties like suspended sentences and short prison stays for cooling off or rehabilitation.

Chapters 8 through 10 approach the complicated and controversial relationship between public opinion—about criminal offenses, offenders, and proper punishment—and the development of public policy that undergirds mass incarceration. In response to what she sees as the limitations of mainstream academic discourse, Lynne Copson argues that any satisfying theory of criminal justice reform must move some significant distance from conventional assumptions about what the public wants from crime control measures and what victims and offenders require. Reform must be grounded in utopian thought: committed to posing large and general questions about the kind of society we wish to have and the kind of citizens we hope to become.

Taking up the debate over so-called penal populism, David Green and Elizabeth Turner reject the aforementioned elite-centered orthodoxy that points to the political success of "tough on crime" campaign rhetoric and advocates expert dominated sentencing commissions insulated from demotic electoral pressures as an antidote to penal severity. Like Copson, Green and Turner favor more direct and robust public involvement.

Decremental strategies that rely on stealth, Green points out, have had some modest success in the United States and United Kingdom, but they do nothing to build lasting support among the citizenry. It is better for governments to expand real opportunities for the public to contribute to criminal justice policy discussions, policymaking, and adjudication. One possibility Turner explores is the use of deliberative democratic techniques such as deliberative polls and citizens' juries, which have uncovered less public support for "get tough" measures than traditional public opinion polling because they typically provide context and promote discussion of multiple viewpoints. While it is a mistake to think that such methods disclose "real" public opinion, they do ask people to foster defensible positions, alert them to issues they may not have contemplated, and help participants see their connections to others' lives.

Rebuilding crime control institutions that can both respect and enable the civic capacity of regular citizens is an uphill struggle. Chapters 11 to 13 take aim at exclusionary practices in the penal system, policymaking process, and in the legal system. Amy Lerman and Vesla Weaver investigate the legal and institutional barriers to democracy inside prisons. An early twentieth-century reform idea, inmate self-governance through advisory councils thrived in the 1960s and 1970s, reflecting reform-minded idealism about creating more democratic prisons as well as pragmatic thinking about how to respond to inmates' demands for voice that had found violent expression in disruptive riots. Despite early positive evidence about the effects of inmate associations, courts have held that the state's interest in prison safety supported a tight rein on organizations such as unions. The prison was not a "public forum," the Supreme Court held in 1977, allowing administrators to override the associational rights of inmates and block organizations if they had the potential for disruption. Drawing on survey data from California prisons, Lerman and Weaver show that inmate participation in self-governance correlates with a decrease in prison violence. They advocate further democratic innovation inside one of our currently least democratic institutions.

Lisa L. Miller disputes the common view of the American political system as overly sensitive to democracy in its openness to popular pressure. She shows how the combination of federalism, separation of powers, multiple decision-making venues, and judicial supremacy produce a labyrinthine obstacle course with many veto points for those with the resources to block social policy. The public good of security from violence has close connections to poverty reduction, employment, education, and other social welfare measures, but the complexity of the American system—not to mention its counterdemocratic fixtures such as the Senate and Supreme Court—makes it extremely difficult for these to survive the policy gauntlet.

Drawing attention to relatively unexplored links between democratic theory and the criminal law, Roberto Gargarella suggests that criminal trials, sentencing, and penal decision-making can become both more democratic and more deliberative. Trials can treat offenders as active contributors to a moral dialogue about harmful action and the law, not as passive subjects of condemnation, while sentencing and justice policymaking can become more open to civil society. Rejecting both penal elitism and pure populism, a deliberative democratic approach to criminal justice seeks out ways of constructively welcoming citizen participation and action on criminal justice issues. Openness to public engagement, even when it takes the form of disruptive social protest, is needed to address the serious legitimacy problems facing the law in many countries.

This collection comes at an opportune moment when the onward march of mass incarceration has taken a pause, thus weakening the politically and intellectually convenient alibi of inevitability. Against this backdrop, the chapters in this volume offer an exciting agenda for theorization, empirical inquiry, and civic engagement. They present a new *political* mode of judgment and critique of actually existing penal practices, reminding us that criminal justice and punishment are always about more than just the regulation of crime. As the arguments presented in the pages that follow forcefully attest, issues of crime control are also inescapably entangled with the question of how to foster and sustain better democratic governance; the task that confronts us is not simply "downsizing the carceral state," but "strengthening the democratic state."[37]

Notes

1. *New York Times*, July 16, 2015.

2. Jonathan Simon, *Governing through Crime* (Oxford: Oxford University Press, 2007).

3. It is noteworthy that similar shifts in political leadership around prisons appear to be underway in the United Kingdom where the new Conservative Justice Secretary, Michael Gove, has publically signaled that he would like to see much less reliance upon imprisonment and to make productive changes to what happens inside prisons. See, for example, Gove's speech to the Prisoners Learning Alliance on July 17, 2015: www.gov.uk/government/speeches/the-treasure-in-the-heart-of-man-making-prisons-work.

4. David Green, "US Penal-Reform Catalysts, Drivers and Prospects," *Punishment & Society* 17, no. 3 (2015): 271–298.

5. We have in mind here the enquiry set up by the National Academy of Sciences into the causes and consequences of high rates of incarceration: Jeremy Travis, Bruce Western, and Steve Redburn (eds.), *The Growth of Incarceration in the United States: Exploring Causes and Consequences* (Washington, DC: National Academy of Sciences, 2014) and the *President's Task Force on 21st Century Policing*, whose final report was published in May 2015: www.cops.usdoj.gov/pdf/taskforce/taskforce_finalreport.pdf.

6. Amy E. Lerman and Vesla M. Weaver, *Arresting Citizenship: The Democratic Consequences of American Crime Control* (Chicago: University of Chicago Press, 2014) and Marie Gottschalk, *Caught: The Prison State and the Lockdown of American Politics* (Princeton, NJ: Princeton University Press, 2015).

7. A point also made recently by Jonathan Simon, "Editorial: Mass Incarceration on Trial," *Punishment & Society* 13, no. 3 (2011): 251–255.

8. On the former, see inter alia David Garland, *The Culture of Control* (New York: Oxford University Press, 2000); David Garland (ed.), *Mass Imprisonment: Social Causes and Consequences* (New York: Sage, 2001); Nicola Lacey, *The Prisoners' Dilemma* (Cambridge: Cambridge University Press, 2007); and Loïc Wacquant, *Punishing the Poor* (Durham, NC: Duke University Press, 2009). On the latter, key contributions have included Marie Gottschalk, *The Prison and the Gallows* (New York: Cambridge University Press, 2006); Simon, *Governing through Crime*; and Naomi Murakawa, *The First Civil Right: How Liberals Build Prison America* (New York: Oxford University Press, 2014).

9. Frank Zimring, *The Great American Crime Decline* (Oxford: Oxford University Press, 2008, ch. 3).

10. On the economy, see Bruce Western, *Punishment and Inequality in America* (New York: Russell Sage Foundation, 2007) and Devah Pager, *Marked: Race, Crime and Finding Work in an Era of Mass Incarceration* (Chicago: University of Chicago Press, 2007); on the family, Megan Comfort, *Doing Time Together* (Chicago: University of Chicago Press, 2007); on communities, Todd Clear, *Imprisoning Communities: How Mass Incarceration Makes Disadvantaged Neighborhoods Worse* (New York: Oxford University Press, 2008); on the political process, Jeff Manza and Christopher Uggen, *Locked Out: Felon Disenfranchisement and American Democracy* (New York: Oxford University Press, 2006) and Lerman and Weaver, *Arresting Citizenship*.

11. Ian Loader and Richard Sparks, "Beyond Lamentation: Towards a Democratic Egalitarian Politics of Crime and Justice," in Tim Newburn and Jill Peay (eds.), *Policing: Politics, Culture and Control* (Oxford: Hart, 2012), 11–41.

12. We borrow this coinage from Roberto M. Unger, who originally claimed it was one of the "dirty little secrets of contemporary jurisprudence." Roberto M. Unger, *What Should Legal Analysis Become* (London: Verso, 1996, 72). This terminology also plays a role in earlier work by Ian Loader and Richard Sparks; see especially their *Public Criminology?* (London: Routledge, 2010).

13. To take just one recent example: in a collection of chapters reflecting on the normative significance of public opinion in shaping penal policy and outcomes, those contributors who argue for limiting public involvement in such matters consistently defend that position with little or no reference to the underlying theory of democracy that is implicit in their argument. This results in a status-quo bias that is complacent about the operation of existing expert-dominated criminal justice while imposing stern tests of any

proposal to extend public participation. Jesper Ryberg and Julian Roberts (eds.), *Popular Punishment: On the Normative Significance of Public Opinion* (New York: Oxford University Press, 2014). See especially the chapters by Jan W. de Keijser and Roberts.

14. Nicola Lacey and David Soskice, "Crime, Punishment and Segregation in the United States: The Paradox of Local Democracy," *Punishment & Society* 17, no. 4 (2015): 461.

15. David Garland, *Peculiar Institution: America's Death Penalty in an Age of Abolition* (Oxford: Oxford University Press, 2010); Lacey and Soskice, "Crime, Punishment and Segregation in the United States."

16. See, for example, Michael Tonry, "Determinants of Penal Policies," in Michael Tonry (ed.), *Crime, Punishment and Politics in Comparative Perspective* (Chicago: University of Chicago Press, 2007) and Sonja Snacken, "Resisting Punitiveness in Europe?," *Theoretical Criminology* 14, no. 3 (2010): 273–292.

17. See, for example, Phillip Pettit, "Is Criminal Justice Politically Feasible?" *Buffalo Criminal Law Review* 5, no. 2 (2002): 427–450; Julian Roberts, Loretta Stalans, David Indermaur, and Mike Hough, *Penal Populism and Public Opinion: Lessons from Five Countries* (Oxford: Oxford University Press, 2003); Frank Zimring and David Johnson, "Public Opinion and the Governance of Punishment in Democratic Political Systems," *ANNALS of the American Academy of Social and Political Science* 605, no. 1 (2006): 265–280; and Lawrence Sherman, "Evidence and Liberty: The Promise of Experimental Criminology," *Criminology & Criminal Justice* 9, no. 1 (2009): 5–28.

18. Eric Holder, "Remarks at the Annual Meeting of the American Bar Association's House of Delegates," San Francisco, August 12, 2013, www.justice.gov/opa/speech/ attorney-general-eric-holder-delivers-remarks-annual-meeting-american-bar-associations.

19. John Braithwaite, "Between Proportionality and Impunity: Confrontation -> Truth -> Prevention." *Criminology* 43, no. 2 (2005): 283.

20. Raymond Williams, *Resources of Hope* (London: Verso, 1989).

21. There are of course key exceptions, especially among those who address the meeting points between penal theory and political theory. See, for example, John Braithwaite and Phillip Pettit, *Not Just Deserts: A Republican Theory of Criminal Justice* (Oxford: Oxford University Press, 1990); Barbara Hudson, *Justice in the Risk Society* (Maidenhead: Open University Press, 1993); and Matt Matravers (ed.), *Punishment and Political Theory* (Oxford: Hart, 1999).

22. Bernard Harcourt, "The Invisibility of the Prison in Democratic Theory: A Problem of 'Virtual Democracy,'" *The Good Society* 23, no. 1 (2014): 6–16. Harcourt's point, of course, is that the prison in not unseeable, just not seen.

23. Simon, *Governing through Crime.*

24. John Pratt, *Penal Populism* (New York: Routledge, 2007).

25. Lisa L. Miller, *The Perils of Federalism: Race, Poverty and the Politics of Crime Control* (New York: Oxford University Press, 2008) and Vanessa Barker, *The Politics of Imprisonment* (New York: Oxford University Press, 2009).

26. Gottschalk, *The Prison and the Gallows.*

27. Vesla M. Weaver, Jacob S. Hacker, and Christopher Wildeman, "Detaining Democracy? Criminal Justice and American Civic Life," *Annals of the American Academy of Political and Social Sciences* 651 (2014): 6–13.

28. Lerman and Weaver, *Arresting Citizenship*.

29. Ian Loader and Richard Sparks, "Unfinished Business: Legitimacy, Crime Control and Democratic Politics," in Justice Tankebe and Alison Liebling (eds.), *Legitimacy and Criminal Justice: An International Exploration* (Oxford: Oxford University Press, 2013), 105–126 and R. A. Duff, "A Criminal Law for Citizens," *Theoretical Criminology* 14, no. 3 (2010): 293–309.

30. Elliott Currie, "Consciousness, Solidarity and Hope as Prevention and Rehabilitation," *International Journal for Crime, Justice and Social Democracy* 2, no. 2 (2013): 3–11; David Brown, "Mapping the Conditions of Penal Hope," *International Journal for Crime, Justice and Social Democracy* 2, no. 3 (2013): 27–42.

31. For example, Archon Fung, *Empowered Participation: Reinventing Urban Democracy* (Princeton, NJ: Princeton University Press, 2004); Albert Dzur and Rekha Mirchandani, "Punishment and Democracy: The Role of Public Deliberation," *Punishment & Society* 9, no. 2 (2007): 151–175; Albert Dzur, "Trench Democracy: Participatory Innovation in Unlikely Places," *Boston Review*, October 11, 2013, www.bostonreview.net/blog/dzur-trench-democracy-1; David Brown, Chris Cunneen, Melanie Schwartz, Julie Stubbs, and Courtney Young, *Justice Reinvestment: Winding Back Imprisonment* (Basingstoke: Palgrave, 2015).

32. Pierre Rosanvallon, *Counter-Democracy: Politics in an Age of Distrust* (Cambridge: Cambridge University Press, 2008).

33. Nadia Urbinati, *Democracy Disfigured: Opinion, Truth, and the People* (Cambridge, MA: Harvard University Press, 2014).

34. Roberto M. Unger, *Democracy Realized* (London: Verso, 1998).

35. Albert W. Dzur, *Punishment, Participatory Democracy, and the Jury* (New York: Oxford University Press, 2012).

36. Some of the chapters in the book originated as contributions to a special issue of the *Good Society* journal on democratic theory and mass incarceration. *Good Society* 23, no. 1 (2014). Thanks to Joshua Miller for his early organizational work.

37. Lerman and Weaver, *Arresting Citizenship*, 237.

CHAPTER 2 | Democratic Politics in an Age
of Mass Incarceration

REBECCA U. THORPE

Introduction

Since the early 1970s, the prison population in the United States has
increased more than 600 percent.[1] With 5 percent of the world's population, the United States currently incarcerates 25 percent of the world's
prisoners—including seven out of every one hundred US adult residents.
While incarceration rates are comparatively high for whites, blacks and
Hispanics are significantly overrepresented in the nation's criminal justice system. If trends continue, one in three black men and one in six
Hispanic men are expected to serve time in prison or jail during their
lives.[2]

These startling figures raise several alarming questions about American
democracy. Why does the United States—a nation founded on a fear
of centralized power and resistance to institutions of state violence—
currently incarcerate more of its citizens than any other nation on earth?
And why is it that the system of criminal punishment disproportionately
affects poor communities of color? Finally, what do these trends suggest
for the long-term health and viability of American democracy?

The rapid and unparalleled growth of the US penal system and its disproportionate impact on minority groups spurred a large body of literature characterizing mass imprisonment as a hostile reaction to the 1960s
civil rights movement. Following Richard Nixon's "law and order" campaign, conservative Republicans pioneered strategies conflating crime
and disobedience with racial pathologies.[3] State and federal expansions
of harsh penal policies heightened inequalities concentrated among poor,

uneducated black men,[4] culminating in a new form of racial subjugation that replaced previous systems of slavery and segregation.[5]

Yet as John Eason points out, while slavery was a regional system of racial terror and oppression, mass incarceration is a national system that sweeps up large numbers of the poor and economically dispossessed.[6] It is also a uniquely bipartisan endeavor, garnering support from liberal and conservative lawmakers across both political parties. While conservative Republicans engineered the new law-and-order discourse, Democratic lawmakers competed to demonstrate their punitive credentials to voters.[7] Meanwhile, support for criminal penalties gained many unlikely adherents, including feminist movements who promoted harsh punishments for perpetrators in order to validate victims,[8] and liberal lawmakers and interest groups who built up an expansive federal law enforcement apparatus in order to protect blacks from violence and enforce procedural fairness.[9] Reliance on surveillance, regulations, and criminal justice procedures have permeated nearly every aspect of public life, including schools, the workplace, and the provision of social service,[10] while mobilizing few detractors.

While a large body of research reveals the disproportionate impact of harsh penal policies for poor uneducated black men excluded from the labor market,[11] the effects of prison expansion in predominantly white, nonmetropolitan communities are not as well understood. However, just as the extensive use of incarceration coincided with the loss of work among poor blacks, demand for prison development also emerged during a period of declining economic prospects among many lower-class rural whites. Further, while most prisoners come from poor urban communities that are isolated by race and class, prison facilities are increasingly concentrated in these impoverished rural areas.[12]

This chapter outlines a new framework emphasizing the spatial dimensions of poverty, joblessness, and mass incarceration in postwar American society. I argue that the growth of the prison apparatus can be more fully explained by the proliferation of isolated urban and rural spaces cut off from resources, investment, and opportunity. First, disproportionate numbers of young black and Hispanic men living in impoverished urban districts were taken off the streets and warehoused in prisons. Second, prisons became an economic development tool to bring jobs, revenue, infrastructure, and wealth transfers to economically desperate rural communities.

The first part of the chapter recontextualizes the nation's vast prison expansion in light of disinvestment and destabilization in black urban neighborhoods in the immediate postwar decades. Highway construction and housing policies that catered to suburban residents at the expense of inner cities exacerbated the flight of low-skilled manufacturing jobs from the urban core. These trends contributed to the geographic concentration of poor blacks during and after the civil rights movement. Policymakers not only exploited white racial animus following civil rights victories[13] but also reacted to sharp escalations in violent crime, moral panics over illegal drug use, and severe economic dislocations that created a jobs crisis for America's poor and working classes. In this context, the collapse of racial segregation in the Jim Crow South and rise of socially isolated urban ghettos in the North created new conditions encouraging an expansive law enforcement apparatus. An expansive criminal justice system allowed policymakers to uphold racial hierarchies, curb urban violence, and monitor, regulate, and remove economically superfluous, undesirable, or threatening populations shut out of an increasingly deregulated, globalizing economy.

The second part of the chapter recasts the geographic shift toward prison development in economically depressed, rural areas as an opportunistic attempt to counter rural poverty. While rural prison development provides limited economic returns, these investments do increase the size, clout, and immediate economic viability of otherwise declining rural communities that host prisons.[14] While many predominantly white, rural areas incur short-term, transitory advantages from prison development, the most debilitating costs of harsh sentencing laws and aggressive police surveillance are concentrated on a large and permanent class of incarcerated felons in urban neighborhoods of color and the families and communities they leave behind.

The spatial logic illustrates a particularly pernicious component of contemporary American democracy, where political elites exploit economically distressed, rural spaces as a source of cheap land and politically expedient "dumping grounds" to warehouse prisoners, and these districts come to rely draconian punishment strategies to bolster political representation, jobs and revenue.[15] The consequences are self-reinforcing: Prison development helps to sustain many economically vulnerable, rural spaces cut off from diverse labor markets, while the most deleterious social harms are imposed on predominantly poor black and Hispanic communities subject to disproportionate levels of surveillance and incarceration.

Warehousing the Urban Poor

In the decades following World War II, many segregated black neighborhoods in central cities became predominantly poor, urban ghettoes. Despite a long and sordid history of residential segregation and racially discriminatory housing policies, these communities did not transform dramatically until the 1960s and 1970s, when middle- and upper-class residents increasingly disappeared and the poor began to occupy a larger share of the population.[16] Areas that were already quite poor in 1970 became even poorer by 1980, catalyzing a sharp increase in the geographic concentration of poverty.[17] Despite civil rights gains, new urban ghettos became seedbeds for poverty and joblessness.[18] The national homicide rate doubled between 1960 and the early 1970s, and violence became more geographically concentrated within these poor, black communities.

At the same time, the criminal justice system became a revolving door between prison and parole for citizens of poor, urban neighborhoods and communities of color. Loïc Wacquant cites research revealing that 75 percent of inmates serving a sentence in the entire state of New York during the late 1980s came from only seven black and Latino neighborhoods in New York City.[19] The poorest areas in the city—including Harlem, the Bronx, East New York, and Brownsville—supplied roughly 25,000 inmates each year, while 23,000 were discharged, on parole, back to these impoverished districts. Given a statewide recidivism rate of 47 percent, he estimates that 15,000 of them were shipped back "upstate" behind bars within the span of one year.

While one in three African American and one in six Latino men in their twenties are in prison, on probation, or on parole nationwide,[20] these figures pale in comparison to deindustrialized cities in the Northeast, where approximately two in three African American men between the ages of twenty and twenty-nine are under some form of correctional supervision.[21] Scholars help make sense of this trend by emphasizing economic dislocations that limited the job stability of low-skilled workers, while devastating communities comprised of low-skilled black men—particularly in the Northeast and Midwest manufacturing belt. This line of research suggests that when economic restructuring made African American labor expendable in the 1960s and 1970s, penal institutions replaced social welfare provisions as a principal mechanism to manage black poverty and joblessness.[22]

While sociologists, criminologists, and political scientists commonly locate the disproportionate impact of mass imprisonment in the urban ghetto, these studies tend to eclipse important historical work documenting the origins of the urban crisis. The social and economic isolation of poor blacks was not simply a result of changes in policing and incarceration or broader patterns of economic restructuring; rather, the urban crisis can be more fully understood in the context of calculated public policy decisions made across federal, state, and local governments. From the

1940s through the 1960s, low-interest home mortgages encouraged up-
wardly mobile whites to migrate from cities to suburbs, while freeway
construction, slum clearance projects, and exclusive zoning laws isolated
urban neighborhoods by race and class.[23] Highways connecting central
cities to their outer suburbs routinely intersected poor, black neighborhoods, reducing property values and promoting out-migration of middle-
class residents.[24] Urban redevelopment and the relocation of public housing projects also shifted crime and instability from areas adjacent to white
neighborhoods to locations deeper in black ghettos.[25] Consequently, spatially concentrated black poverty, chronic joblessness, and violent urban
riots all metastasized on the tails of the civil rights movement, forging
perceptions of black criminality when support for federal law enforcement
capacity reached a historical peak.

While antipoverty programs and an extension of the welfare state
largely ignored structural problems that fueled the urban crisis, incarceration sought to expel its most destructive symptoms through harsh and
degrading forms of punishment. Since the 1970s federal, state, and local
governments passed new laws explicitly criminalizing behaviors likely
to flourish in areas plagued by poverty and joblessness, including harsh
criminal penalties for the sale and possession of narcotics as well as an-
tipanhandling and antiloitering ordinances.[26] Since the 1980s, criminal
punishments for both nonviolent and violent crimes became much more
severe with the passage of three-strikes laws requiring twenty-five-year-
to-life sentences for a third offense (including a drug violation or petty
theft); ten, twenty, and thirty-year minimum sentences for violent, firearms, and drug offenses; increased use of life without parole; and laws
permitting the prosecution of young people as adults. This ratcheting up
of penalties ensured that more people were incarcerated for a range of
violent and non-violent offenses, while a growing class of incarcerated
felons served much longer sentences without the possibility of parole or
early release.

Meanwhile, the costs of imprisonment extend well beyond the length
of a prison term. People who have served time in prison are less likely to
be eligible to vote, find stable employment, receive public housing and
educational benefits, and maintain family ties.[27] Further, predominantly
poor, urban neighborhoods where outsized numbers of young men have a
prison record are subject to chronic instability, heightened social isolation,
and greater levels of civic distrust.[28]

The aggressive use of punitive sanctions also coincided with decaying
commitments to a social safety net and reinvigorated efforts to deregulate

markets and reduce social service provisions.[29] Although neoliberal, free-market rhetoric suggests a commitment to limited government, proponents of deregulation have instead instituted an expansive, expansive, and invasive law enforcement apparatus in order to support unregulated markets.[30] Katherine Beckett and Bruce Western capture this change by highlighting a "regime shift" from social welfare to penal governance.[31] This pivot from a social welfare bureaucracy in the New Deal and Great Society tradition to an aggressive penal bureaucracy is not a process of deregulation but a shift in the subject of government regulation. As Naomi Murakawa argues, liberal Democrats' initial investment in federal law enforcement capacity as a means to enforce procedural fairness and protect blacks from arbitrary prejudice and lawlessness was quickly repurposed to legitimize increasingly severe forms of criminal punishment.[32] At the same time, the bipartisan emphasis on punishment as a means to quell unrest, satiate an anxious public, and manage surplus labor requires even more obtrusive government institutions than previous forms of market intervention.[33]

Since the 2008 economic recession, the unsustainable fiscal costs of incarceration have spurred demands for criminal justice reform from fiscal hawks and civil libertarians. Interest groups and politicians on both the right and the left have forged bipartisan initiatives to reduce prison populations. However, despite the mounting financial expense for states, the criminal justice system also discretely supports a deregulated, postindustrialized economy. Criminal justice procedures are used to monitor and physically remove young men locked out of formal labor markets,[34] while creating new sources of employment, revenue, and infrastructure for economically dispossessed rural communities. The focus on financial expense alone is unlikely to persuade detractors to prioritize costs over safety, security, or retribution, and may bolster narratives that militate against alternative investments in social services.

While most research understates the extent to which federal policies contributed to spatially concentrated crime, violence, and drug markets in nonwhite urban spaces, scholarship also underplays, and often ignores, the dual role for the criminal justice system in poor, rural communities.[35] As the next section will show, heightened poverty and social inequality are bifurcated not only by race, but also by geography. The most virulent manifestations of inner-city poverty are subject to surveillance and imprisonment, while white, rural poverty creates viable spaces for warehousing incarcerated populations.

Rural Dumping Grounds

While federal divestment, the outsourcing of production, increasing competition from transnational markets and sharp reductions in social welfare programs led to unemployment and high levels of poverty in urban settings, structural changes in the global economy also contributed to deep poverty within rural communities. Confronted with declines in historically dominant agricultural and mining sectors and reductions in social service provisions, many rural counties faced chronic poverty.[36]

The emergence of a rural prison economy coincided with these broader patterns of economic restructuring and dislocation. In the 1960s and 1970s, fewer than half of all prisons were located in nonmetropolitan areas.[37] However, rural communities developed hundreds of new prisons during the 1980s and 1990s, accounting for the bulk of overall prison growth.[38] By the mid-1990s, rural prisons constituted almost two-thirds of new prison development, even though most inmates came from metropolitan areas.[39] Meanwhile, the overall correctional population nearly doubled in size since 1990,[40] even while violent crime rates declined steadily throughout major US cities.

While projects such as prisons and nuclear power plants are often viewed as unattractive sites that decrease property values and deter more lucrative ventures, the traditional NIMBY ("not in my backyard") reaction is more likely to gain traction in "high-amenity," as opposed to "low-amenity," environments.[41] High-amenity communities, or "rural playgrounds," enjoy natural assets that attract wealthy tourists, artists, and intellectuals. Low-amenity communities, or "dumping grounds," lack tourist attractions and must compete for large corporate investments. For rural communities impacted by deep poverty, a weak economy, and diminished ability to provide social welfare relief, prison sitings offer a widely coveted opportunity to boost employment and draw revenue that is generally viewed as recession-proof.[42] The counties most likely to bid for and attract prisons to their communities routinely exhibit greater economic need, lower levels of social capital, fewer owner occupants, and more rural geography.[43]

The proliferation of rural poverty not only created viable dumping grounds for prisons, but also encouraged aggressive lobbying among more economically disadvantaged areas for the opportunity to host them. In the 1980s and 1990s, municipal governments competed to offer cheap land and large tax subsidies to promote prison development. Yet while rural communities clamored to compete for prison facilities that their urban counterparts typically reject, researchers overwhelmingly find that communities where prisons are built experienced limited economic improvements.[44] Although estimates suggest that prisons create an average of thirty-five jobs per every hundred inmates housed,[45] state prisons have strict union employment requirements and high training standards that often require skilled labor of individuals living outside of the community. While private prisons hire nonunion labor and have lower skill requirements, they typically pay much less than state and federal institutions. In addition, the main sources of economic development and job creation that prisons attract typically include low-paying service industries. Finally, prisons fail to build ties with the communities in which they are sited.[46] Instead, they engender a sense of fear and heighten concerns about community safety, which tend to reinforce punitive attitudes.[47]

Even though most research suggests that prisons do not draw additional social or economic capital in host communities, political and business elites still have powerful interests in promoting these investments. While the prison construction boom is currently in decline, lawmakers representing rural prison towns work to stave off closures and protect these assets.[48] Prison construction offers a sense of revitalization and crucial stimulus for otherwise desperate rural communities, including construction contracts, upgrades to infrastructure, and reliable employment and revenue streams. At the same time, a large, institutionalized population also has the potential to reverse long-standing trends of population loss in rural counties, while redistributing resources and political power from urban to rural voters.

According to US Census practice, imprisoned populations are counted as residents of their correctional institutions—as opposed to the hometowns where they previously resided—even though prisoners are denied the right to vote in forty-eight states. Accordingly, since prisoners are disproportionately incarcerated in nonmetropolitan counties where they are counted as local residents for census purposes, political power and funding are redistributed to rural communities where incarcerated populations are involuntarily confined.[49] Nearly two-thirds of the nation's prisoners are black or Hispanic and nearly half are from segregated urban neighborhoods like East New York and Brownsville—areas that routinely forfeit their share of government resources and representation.[50]

The practice of counting inmates as residents of correctional institutions also encourages lawmakers to draw legislative districts to include imprisoned populations in order to inflate local voting power and consolidate partisan advantage—a practice referred to as prison-based gerrymandering.[51] Given pronounced racial disparities within the nation's prisons and laws stripping felons of the right to vote, many legal scholars argue that prison-based gerrymandering not only violates the Voting Rights Act, but also reanimates the spirit of the Three-Fifths Clause by eroding African American political power and inflating the voting power of geographically proximate whites.[52]

Population counts in the decennial census are not only used to determine the number of congressional, state, and local representatives, but are also to derive formulas that the determine the amount of federal dollars that state and local governments receive for various programs, including social welfare assistance, Medicaid, foster care, adoption assistance, and Social Security block grants. At the state level, population counts from the census determine the level of funding for health services, transportation, public housing, local law enforcement, and public libraries.[53] As a result, many rural prison communities increase their share of state funding, while isolated urban communities lose resources and political standing.[54]

Democracy and Citizenship

The use of harsh criminal penalties and aggressive law enforcement tactics to combat problems endemic in low-wage labor markets highlights two bitter historical ironies: First, decades of racially exclusionary housing and transportation policies contributed to the destabilization of racially segregated urban neighborhoods; yet policymakers on both the left and the right ignored the government's role in creating conditions in which urban ghettos, social pathologies, and violence would metastasize, and instead attacked the most vicious symptoms through harsh and degrading forms of punishment. Second, and related, the rise of expedient prison development throughout economically distressed, rural areas created new, mutually exploitative structures that makes the penal system particularly difficult to dismantle.[55]

Criminalization strategies not only allow policymakers to claim credit for combatting violence, addiction, and social blight pervasive in impoverished communities,[56] but also gave rise to new actors and interest groups that lobby for carceral expansion.[57] The use of economically isolated rural

spaces to warehouse escalating numbers of presumably deviant, dangerous, or expendable members of society generated powerful interests in
maintaining imprisonment rates—despite dubious long-term social or
economic improvements and limited public safety returns.

Nonetheless, following four decades of persistent prison growth, incarceration rates are down 2.1 percent nationwide since the 2008 economic
recession. Politicians, interest groups, and advocacy coalitions of varying
political and ideological allegiances are building bipartisan coalitions to
address prison reform. While fiscal hawks are lobbying to reign in mounting financial costs, the left and libertarian wings are working to roll back
an excessively punitive and racially biased drug war.

However, reform may be more difficult than these trends suggest.
Rather, recent developments indicate that current reforms have merely
shifted fiscal costs in ways that mask larger underlying problems. Notably,
California's Public Safety Realignment initiative accounts for approximately 50 percent of the overall decline in state prisons.[58] However, while
California spent billions of dollars in legal fees on account of overcrowding and poor conditions in state prisons, the resulting Realignment initiative has largely imposed these problems on county jails where many state
inmates are transferred.[59] Since 2009 New York State Governor Andrew
Cuomo has closed thirteen state prisons, citing a $10 million budget gap
and unmanageable cost escalations. However, Cuomo spared many of the
largest prisons in the most remote regions of the state where lawmakers
warned of economic devastation if prisons were closed.[60]

As Marie Gottschalk argues at length, this unusual bipartisan issue
convergence centered on cost containment is unlikely to produce
meaningful and lasting reductions in the nation's incarceration rates—
at least not without a broader commitment to more systematic reforms
that cover a broader range of offenses.[61] Rather, the sole emphasis on
heightened fiscal discipline often leads to "leaner and meaner" incarceration strategies—including greater prison overcrowding, rising
inmate violence, and budget cuts targeting education, substance abuse,
and vocational programs.[62] At the same time, the exclusive focus on reducing sentences for drug offenders accounts for only a fraction of the
people in state prisons. Even while a number of states have softened
their marijuana laws, many have simultaneously heightened punishments for violent offenders as well as for other drug offenses including
methamphetamine. Meanwhile, increasing numbers of undocumented
immigrants and drug offenders are incarcerated in federal prisons (up
0.7 percent).

The framework outlined here illustrates a particularly pernicious component of American democracy, where the widespread use of incarceration is deployed to combat various social ills, while the transfer of inmates from urban to rural spaces for the sole purpose of confinement ties the political power and material wellbeing of a subset of lower-class, rural residents to the permanent social and political exclusion of predominantly poor urban minorities. A core subset of districts and lawmakers experience short-term gains, while the most devastating social costs are imposed on a largely invisible class of social, economic, and political exiles.

The nation's sprawling criminal justice system not only affects the 2.3 million individuals who are behind bars, but has also harms a large class of ex-felons who are permanently excluded from political, economic, and social life. Even upon parole, probation, or release, people who have served a prison sentence routinely lose the right to vote, face reduced access to employment, and experience a damaged sense of civic membership. More than 16 million Americans are permanently disenfranchised because they hold a criminal record, and millions more lack access to public housing, stable employment, and educational aid. This political and economic marginalization is particularly devastating within African American communities.[63]

Taken cumulatively, the scale and scope of the US criminal justice system, entrenched benefits that flow to a subset of districts, and disproportionate harm imposed on politically and economically marginalized populations suggest that meaningful efforts to dismantle the nation's punishment apparatus are likely to require more than cost-cutting measures or reduced penalties for minor drug offenses. Rather, a sustained movement to overhaul draconian sentencing laws across a wide range of offenses also requires a new civil rights movement for the twenty-first century—including mass mobilization, durable shifts in public opinion, and comprehensive policy commitments across legislative and executive institutions. A sustained civil rights initiative will also require a collective societal willingness to forfeit an urge for revenge or displaced anxiety that often fuels retributive sentiments, as well as a serious reassessment of the most effective, humane, and equitable strategies to promote public safety over the long run. Given that the perceived advantages of imprisonment are currently being called into question, it is time to refocus attention to a more robust commitment to civil rights, greater democratic inclusion, and humanitarian imperatives.

Notes

1. Jeff Manza and Christopher Uggen, *Locked Out: Felon Disenfranchisement and American Democracy* (Ann Arbor: University of Michigan Press, 2006), 95.

2. Bruce Western, *Punishment and Inequality in America* (New York: Russell Sage Foundation, 2006); Thomas P. Bonczar, *Prevalence of Imprisonment in the U.S. Population, 1972–2001* (Washington, DC: US Department of Justice, 2003).

3. Katherine Beckett, *Making Crime Pay* (New York: Oxford University Press, 1997); Velsa Mae Weaver, "Frontlash: Race and the Development of Punitive Crime Policy," *Studies in American Political Development* 21 (Fall 2007): 230–265.

4. Western, *Punishment and Inequality in America*, 2006.

5. Michelle Alexander, *The New Jim Crow: Mass Incarceration in the Age of Color Blindness* (New York: The New Press, 2010).

6. John Eason, "Extending the Hyperghetto: Toward a Theory of Punishment, Race and Rural Disadvantage," *Journal of Poverty* 16(3) (2012): 274–295.

7. Naomi Murakawa, *The First Civil Right: How Liberals Built Prison America* (New York: Oxford University Press, 2014).

8. Marie Gottschalk, *The Prison and the Gallows: The Politics of Mass Incarceration in America* (New York: Cambridge University Press, 2006); Kristin Bumiller, *In An Abusive State: How Neoliberalism Appropriated the Feminist Movement Against Sexual Violence* (Durham, NC: Duke University Press, 2008).

9. Murakawa, *The First Civil Right*, 2014.

10. Jonathan Simon, *Governing Through Crime: How the War on Crime Transformed American Democracy and Created a Culture of Fear* (Oxford: Oxford University Press, 2007); Loic Wacquant, *Punishing the Poor: The Neoliberal Government of Social Insecurity* (Durham, NC: Duke University Press, 2009).

11. Western, *Punishment and Inequality in America*, 2006; Wacquant, *Punishing the Poor*, 2009; Loic Wacquant, "Crafting the Neoliberal State: Workfare, Prisonfare and Social Insecurity," *Sociological Forum* 25(2) (2010): 197–220.

12. Calvin Beale, "Prisons, Populations and Jobs in Nonmetro America," *Rural Development Perspectives* 8(3) (1993): 16–19; Calvin Beale, "Rural Prisons: An Update," *Rural Development Perspectives* 11(2) (1996): 25–27; Ryan S. King, Marc Mauer, and Tracy Huling, "Big Prisons, Small Towns: Prison Economics in Rural America" (Washington, DC: The Sentencing Project, 2003); Heather Ann Thompson, "The Prison Industrial Complex: A Growth Industry in a Shrinking Economy," *New Labor Forum* 21(3) (2012): 39–47; John Eason, "Mapping Prison Proliferation: Region, Rurality, Race and Disadvantage in Prison Placement," *Social Science Research* 39(6) (2010): 1015–1028; Eason, "Extending the Hyperghetto," 2012.

13. Weaver, "Frontlash," 2007.

14. Peter Wagner, "Importing Constituents: Prisoners and Political Clout in New York" (Easthampton, MA: A Prison Policy Initiative Report, 2002). Peter Wagner, "Breaking the Census: Redistricting in an Era of Mass Incarceration," *William Mitchell Law Review* 38(4) (2011): 1240–1260; Jason Kelly, "The Strategic Use of Prisons in Partisan Gerrymandering," *Legislative Studies Quarterly* 37(1) (2012): 117–134.

15. Tracy Huling, "Building a Prison Economy in Rural America," in M. Mauer and M. Chesney-Lind (eds.), *Invisible Punishment: The Collateral Consequences of Mass*

Imprisonment (New York: The New Press, 2002), accessed at http://www.prisonpolicy.org/scans/building.html; Rebecca. U. Thorpe, "Perverse Politics: The Persistence of Mass Imprisonment in the 21st Century," *Perspectives on Politics* 13(3) (2015): 618–637.

16. Katharine Bradbury, Anthony Downs, and Kenneth Small, *Urban Decline and the Future of American Cities* (Washington, DC: Brookings Institution Press, 1928).

17. Douglas Massey and Shawn Kanaiaupuni, "Public Housing and the Concentration of Poverty," *Social Science Quarterly* 74(1) (1993): 109–122; William Julius Wilson, *When Work Disappears: The World of the New Urban Poor* (New York: Vintage Books, 1997).

18. Wilson, *When Work Disappears*, 1997.

19. Loic Wacquant, "Deadly Symbiosis: When Ghetto and Prison Meet and Mesh," *Punishment and Society*, 3(1) (2001): 95–134, at 114–115.

20. Rose M. Brewer and Nancy A. Heitzig, "The Racialization of Crime and Punishment: Criminal Justice, Color Blind Racism, and the Political Economy of the Prison Industrial Complex," *American Behavioral Scientist* 51(5) (2008): 625; Western, *Punishment and Inequality in America*, 2006.

21. Wacquant, "Deadly Symbiosis."

22. Ibid.; Wacquant, "Crafting the Neoliberal State"; Jamie Peck, "Geography and Public Policy: Mapping the Penal State," *Progress in Human Geography* 27(2) (2003): 222–232; also see Francis Fox Piven and Richard Cloward, *Regulating the Poor: The Functions of Public Welfare* (New York: Vintage Books, 1971).

23. Kenneth Jackson, *Crabgrass Frontier: The Suburbanization of the United States* (New York: Oxford University Press, 1987); Douglas Massey and Nancy Denton, *American Apartheid: Segregation and the Making of the Underclass* (Cambridge, MA: Harvard University Press, 1993); Desmond King, *Separate and Unequal: Black Americans and the U.S. Federal Government* (New York: Oxford University Press, 1995); Arnold Hirsch, *Making the Second Ghetto: Race and Housing in Chicago, 1940–1960* (Chicago: University of Chicago Press, 1998); Robert Self, *American Babylon: Race and the Struggle for Post-War Oakland* (Princeton, NJ: Princeton University Press, 2005); Robert Self, "'To Plan Our Liberation': Black Power and the Politics of Place in Oakland, California, 1965–1977," *Journal of Urban History* 26(6) (2000): 75; Thomas Sugrue, *The Origins of the Urban Crisis: Race and Inequality in Post-War Detroit*, Rev. ed. (Princeton, NJ: Princeton University Press, 2005).

24. Bradbury, Downs and Small, *Urban Decline and the Future of American Cities*, 1982; Nathaniel Baum-Snow, "Did Highways Cause Suburbanization?" *Quarterly Journal of Economics* 122(2) (2006): 775–805; Self, *American Babylon*, 2005.

25. Massey and Kanaiaupuni, "Public Housing and the Concentration of Poverty."

26. Doris Marie Provine, *Unequal Under Law: Race in the War on Drugs* (Chicago: University of Chicago Press, 2007); Kathleen Frydl, *The Drug Wars in America, 1940–1973* (New York: Cambridge University Press, 2013); Katherine Beckett and Steve Herbert, *Banished: The New Social Control in Urban America* (New York: Oxford University Press, 2010).

27. Bruce Western and Becky Pettit, "Incarceration & Social Inequality," *Daedalus* 139 (Summer 2010): 8–19; Amy Lerman and Velsa Mae Weaver, *Arresting Citizenship: The Democratic Consequences of American Crime Control* (Chicago: University of Chicago Press, 2014).

28. Weaver and Lerman, *Arresting Citizenship*, 2014.

29. Victoria Lawson, Lucy Ja1rosz, and Anne Bonds, "Articulations of Race, Poverty and Place: Dumping Grounds and Unseen Grounds in the Rural American Northwest," *Annals of the Association of American Geographers* 100 (2010): 655–677; Victoria Lawson, Lucy Jarosz, and Anne Bonds, "Building Economies from the Bottom Up: (Mis) Representations of Poverty in the Rural American Northwest," *Social and Cultural Geography* 9(7) (2008): 737–753; Peck, "Geography and Public Policy"; Wacquant, "Crafting the Neoliberal State."

30. Wacquant, "Deadly Symbiosis"; Peck, "Geography and Public Policy."

31. Katherine Beckett and Bruce Western, "Governing Social Marginality: Welfare, Incarceration & the Transformation of State Politics," *Punishment & Society* 3(1) (2001): 43–59.

32. Murakawa, *The First Civil Right*.

33. Wacquant, "Crafting the Neoliberal State."

34. For example see Peck, "Geography and Public Policy"; Western, *Punishment and Inequality in America*; Brewer and Heitzig, "The Racialization of Crime and Punishment"; Wacquant, "Deadly Symbiosis"; Wacquant, "Crafting the Neoliberal State."

35. For notable exceptions, see Anne Bonds, "Discipline and Devolution: Constructions of Poverty, Race and Criminality in the Politics of Rural Prison Development," *Antipode* 41(3) (2009): 416–438; Eason, "Extending the Hyperghetto."

36. Lawson, Jarosz, and Bonds, "Building Economies from the Bottom Up."

37. Beale, "Prisons, Populations and Jobs in Nonmetro America."

38. Eason, "Mapping Prison Proliferation."

39. King, Mauer, and Huling, "Big Prisons, Small Towns."

40. Lauren E. Glaze, "Correctional Populations in the United States, 2010" (Washington, DC: US Department of Justice: Bureau of Justice Statistics, 2011), www.bjs.gov/content/pub/pdf/cpus10.pdf.

41. Lawson, Jarosz, and Bonds, "Articulations of Race, Poverty and Place."

42. Bonds, "Discipline and Devolution"; Susan E. Blankenship and Ernest J. Yanarella, "Prison Recruitment as a Policy Tool of Local Economic Development: A Critical Evaluation," *Contemporary Justice Review* 7(2) (2004): 183–198.

43. Michele Hoyman and Micah Weinberg, "The Process of Policy Innovation: Prison Sitings in Rural North Carolina," *The Policy Studies Journal* 34(1) (2006): 95–112; Huling, "Building a Prison Economy in Rural America"; Thorpe, "Perverse Politics."

44. Ruth Gilmore, *Golden Gulag: Prisons, Surplus, Crisis and Opposition in Globalizing California* (Berkeley: University of California Press, 2007); Amy K. Glasmeier and Tracey Farrigan, "The Economic Impacts of the Prison Development Boom on Persistently Poor Rural Places," *International Regional Science Review* 30(3) (2003): 274–279; Christopher Setti, "Prisons and Their Effect on Local Economies: The Colorado Experience," Vol. XL VII, #3 (CPEC Center for Tax Policy Research: University of Denver, 2001); Gregory Hooks, Clayton Mosher, Thomas Rotolo, and Linda Lobao, "The Prison Industry: Carceral Expansion and Employment in U.S. Counties, 1964–1994," *Social Science Quarterly* 8(1) (2004): 37–57; Blankenship and Yanarella, "Prison Recruitment as a Policy Tool of Local Economic Development"; King, Mauer, and Huling, "Big Prisons, Small Towns."

45. King, Mauer, and Huling, "Big Prisons, Small Towns."

46. Glassmeier and Farragan, "The Economic Impacts of the Prison Development Boom on Persistently Poor Rural Places."

47. Ibid.; Blankenship and Yanarella, "Prison Recruitment as a Policy Tool of Local Economic Development"; David L. Myers and Randy Martin, "Community Member Reactions to Prison Siting: Perceptions of Prison Impact on Economic Factors," *Criminal Justice Review* 29(1) (2004): 115–144.

48. For example see Brian Mann, "Prison Closings Trouble Upstate New York," *National Public Radio*, March 4, 2008; Brandi Grissom, "In Two Cities, Opposite Reaction to State Jail Closing," *Texas Tribune*, August 2, 2013; Natasha Haverty, "Cuomo Cuts Corrections Budget, Closes Prisons," *North Country Public Radio*, January 22, 2014.

49. Sarah Lawrence and Jeremy Travis, "The New Landscape of Imprisonment: Mapping America's Prison Expansion" (Washington, DC: Justice Policy Center: Urban Institute, 2004); Wagner, "Importing Political Constituents"; Huling, "Building a Prison Economy in Rural America."

50. Huling, "Building a Prison Economy in Rural America."

51. Wagner, "Importing Political Constituents"; Kelly, "The Strategic Use of Prisons in Partisan Gerrymandering."

52. The Three-Fifths Clause was a provision of the US Constitution (Article I, Section 2, Clause 3) that counted slaves as three-fifths of a free person for the purposes of legislative apportionment and political representation. See John C. Drake, "Locked Up and Counted Out: Bringing an End to Prison Based Gerrymandering," *Washington University Journal of Law and Policy* 37(1) (2011): 237–263; Rosanna Taormina, "Defying One-Person, One-Vote: Prisoners and the 'Usual Residence' Principle," *University of Pennsylvania Law Review* 152(1) (2003): 431.

53. Lawrence and Travis, "The New Landscape of Imprisonment."

54. Huling, "Building a Prison Economy in Rural America"; Hooks et al., "The Prison Industry," 40; Wagner, "Importing Political Constituents"; Taormina, "Defying One-Person, One-Vote: Prisoners and the 'Usual Residence' Principle."

55. Thorpe, "Perverse Politics."

56. For example, see Wacquant, *Punishing the Poor*; Beckett and Herbert, *Banished*.

57. Gottschalk, *Caught*.

58. Ann E. Carson and Daniela Golinelli, "Prisoners in 2012—Advance Counts" (Washington, DC: Bureau of Justice Statistics Bulletin: US Department of Justice), www.bjs.gov/content/pub/pdf/p12ac.pdf.

59. Christopher Patrella, "Consequences of California's Realignment Initiative," *Prison Legal News*, June 12, 2014, www.prisonlegalnews.org/news/2014/jun/12/consequences-californias-realignment-initiative/.

60. Thomas Kaplan, "Cuomo Administration Closing Seven Prisons, Two in New York City," *New York Times*, June 30, 2011, www.nytimes.com/2011/07/01/nyregion/following-through-on-budget-state-will-close-seven-prisons.html?_r=0.

61. Gottschalk, *Caught*; Gottschalk, "Cell Blocks and Red Ink."

62. Gottschalk, "Cell Blocks and Red Ink," 67.

63. Lerner and Weaver, *Arresting Citizenship*.

CHAPTER 3 | Civic Punishment

R. A. DUFF AND S. E. MARSHALL

The Death of Socrates

Socrates had been sentenced to death by an Athenian court. In accordance with Athenian custom, a prison officer brought him a cup of hemlock, which he drank; this caused his death. There are three ways in which we could interpret such an action.

First, we could interpret it as a personal choice, made in order to avoid the more painful or less dignified death that a condemned person would otherwise face: the Athenians were "willing to let wrongdoers convicted to death use hemlock to commit suicide in advance of their execution provided they could afford to pay for the dose"; the alternative was a form of "bloodless crucifixion"—*apotympanismos*.[1] On this interpretation, drinking hemlock was a way of avoiding execution—of avoiding punishment.

Second, we could interpret drinking the hemlock as the obedient action of a deferential subject. The court commands me to drink the hemlock: mine not to reason why; mine but to do, and die. On this reading, the condemned man is the agent of his own execution; but his role is strictly subordinate, to obey the commands of a superior authority.

Third, we could interpret drinking the hemlock as a civic action, undertaken by a citizen who is playing his active role—the role assigned to him by a law that he has made his own—in what he accepts as a just execution. On this reading, his *is* to reason why: he recognizes why he has been sentenced to death, and plays his part not out of mere obedience to the law, but because he recognizes a duty to play his part in the law's enterprise.

On a less dramatic, contemporary note we can similarly distinguish three ways in which a person sentenced to "community payback" by an English criminal court might undertake the hours of work assigned to her.

She might, first, see it as an inconvenient material burden that she undertakes only because the alternative (imprisonment) is even less attractive. Second, she might undertake it in a spirit of passive obedience: this is what "they" tell me I must do, so I do it. Or third, she might undertake it as a punishment that she can see she owes it to her fellow citizens to undertake in order to make appropriate reparation for her offense: she sees herself as playing this active role in the formal legal response to her crime, and undertakes the role as a civic duty.

Our aim is not to recommend that we reintroduce capital punishment—let alone capital self-punishment. Nor do we suggest that the third way of undertaking punishment is one that is plausibly available, or recommendable, to many who undergo punishment in contemporary penal systems (especially those in the United States and Great Britain): it would be grotesque, to take an extreme example, to say to someone locked in solitary confinement in an American supermax prison that he should undertake his own punishment as a civic duty that he owes to his fellow citizens. What we will argue, however, is that we should aspire to a system of criminal justice in which that understanding of punishment, and that way of undertaking it, is both plausible and recommendable—one in which we can say, with a clear conscience, that that is the spirit in which offenders should undertake their punishment.

This will be an exercise in ideal theory: we will be offering a partial sketch of what a system of criminal law ought to be, and of the kind of political community within which the law could aspire to be what it ought to be. As we will see, even when engaging in such ideal theory, we must attend to the need to protect citizens against dangers that afflict any human institution; but we will not here address the question of how distant even such a qualified ideal is from where we are now, or of how we could try to get there from here. There are of course familiar dangers in ideal theorizing, in particular that it becomes an exercise in fantasy that lacks any serious connection to our actual world and its institutions. We hope to avoid that danger here, by offering an admittedly idealized account of what can nonetheless still be recognized as our own practices of criminal law (our practices as they could and should become), appealing to values that we can recognize as demanding our allegiance. Such ideal theorizing has an important part to play in a critical normative discussion of existing practices and institutions of criminal law and punishment: if we can see the ideal as one toward which we can and should aspire, we can also then use it as a standard against which to measure, and criticize, our existing practices. It will help us to see more clearly what is wrong with those existing actualities, but can also help us to see that a response to the manifold injustices of our existing institutions need not take the form of an abolitionist search for a future without punishment, or without the use of imprisonment as a punishment:[2] it can lead us to argue for the radical reform—rather than the replacement—of our penal practices (and of the political conditions on which they depend).

Before we embark on the discussion of punishment, we should provide some background about the larger project of which this discussion is part, and the ideas that we will presuppose here.

Preliminaries: A Democratic Criminal Law

The larger project to which this chapter belongs is an attempt to work out the proper role of criminal law in a democratic republic—a society that aspires to be a polity of free and equal citizens. Such a project requires a political theory of democratic republicanism, which we do not provide here. All we can say here is that the conception of democracy to which we would appeal is participatory and deliberative; that Dworkin's slogan of "equal concern and respect" nicely expresses what citizens owe to each other as well as what the state owes its citizens;[3] that part of such respect is a practical recognition of each other as responsible participants in the civic life of the polity; and that such a recognition can also be captured by an expanded version of Pettit's "eyeball test," according to which citizens must be willing, as well as able, to "look others in the eye without reason for the fear or deference that a power of interference might inspire."[4] Our question is this: what kind of criminal law would be appropriate for such a polity; what would a criminal law for citizens be like?[5] An initial gesture toward an answer to this question is found in the idea of criminal law as "common law":[6] not common law as opposed to statutory law, but law that is common in the sense that it is our shared law, not one imposed on us by a separate sovereign. The task then is to work out what this idea might amount to—what would make the law a genuinely common law?

To ask what a common law, a law for citizens, could be is also to ask how the citizens of a republican polity would relate to a law that was their law. There are for present purposes two crucial aspects of such citizenship. First, citizens will respect the law (it is their law), but their respect will be critical.[7] They will try to understand the law—the mischief at which laws are aimed, the reasons that were taken to justify making them; they will be ready to debate whether the law is apt for its purposes, and whether those purposes are apt; they will respect the law as aiming to specify norms that citizens are to recognize as, or make, their own; but they will not take it for granted that it succeeds in this aim. One question then is whether and when good citizens will be ready to break the law (and whether such breaches can themselves manifest respect for the law).[8]

Second, citizens of such a polity will be active: they will be ready to participate in the civic enterprise of a self-governing polity. They will be ready, in particular, to play an active part in the civic enterprise of the criminal law: for if the law is to be their law, as a common law, they must be its agents, not merely its obedient subjects. We can give more content to this idea of active citizenship by looking at the various roles that citizens may be called on to play in relation to the criminal law.

Citizens can play three kinds of role in relation to the criminal law. Some are official and professional: those who fill them are employed by the polity to do so, and are meant to bring professional skills to the job. Examples include police officers engaged in preventing and investigating crimes; prosecutors determining whom to charge with what, and bringing cases to court (or otherwise disposing of them); defense counsel; judges and other court officials; correctional officers. We must ask in each case how the role should be understood; what aims those who fill it should pursue, what rights and responsibilities they should have.[9] We must also ask whether the role should exist,[10] and, if so, how people should acquire it (whether, for instance, by election or by appointment).

Another kind of role is official in that it carries legal authority, but is filled by lay citizens rather than professionals. Obvious examples are the roles of juror and lay magistrate or judge. But we could also consider lay roles related to policing—special constable, for instance; and ask why we should not create lay roles in the administration of punishments—beyond such modest roles as that of prison visitor. One question that we cannot pursue here concerns the relationship between these first two kinds of role. How far should a democratic criminal law be controlled by professional officials, whether elected or appointed? How far should it be controlled by lay citizens?

A third kind of role is acquired by citizens who have, or are thought to have, a relevant connection to a particular alleged crime, and who therefore acquire distinctive sets of legal, or civic, rights and responsibilities. Examples are the roles of victim, of witness, of suspect, and of defendant. In what follows we will concentrate on this kind of role, and will argue that it also includes the roles of offender and convicted offender.

Roles are located within particular institutions or practices, and are to be understood in terms of their contributions to the goals of the practice within which they fall. They consist in patterns of responsibilities, duties, and rights, which together specify the distinctive activities proper to the role. To understand a role is therefore to understand the practice within which it functions: that is why we can understand criminal law better by studying the roles it creates. But we must begin with some idea of what the practice is—in this case, of what the enterprise of criminal law is in a democratic republic. We can here only note two main features, two central purposes, of criminal law as a distinctive kind of law.[11]

The criminal law is concerned with public wrongs—wrongs that are the business of all citizens in virtue of their membership of the polity. In its substantive dimension, the criminal law defines a set of such wrongs: these, it declares, are wrongs that merit such formal public recognition, and require a formal, public response. In its procedural and penal dimensions, the law then makes provision for such a formal response: it provides a system of criminal trials, at which alleged offenders are called to answer to the accusation of wrongdoing, and for that wrongdoing if it is proved that they committed it, and a set of penal institutions in which those who are convicted of criminal wrongdoing can be punished. The roles that lay citizens may be called upon to play can be understood in terms of their contribution to this enterprise. Before we discuss some of these roles, however, two points should be noted.

First, such roles have both civic and legal dimensions. The criminal law's institutions define roles for such figures as victims, witnesses, defendants, in terms of sets of legal rights and responsibilities. But such roles also figure in our extra-legal lives, and can be understood in terms not of what the law formally requires, but of our (we hope) shared civic morality, of what we owe to each other as citizens. As civic roles, they might involve responsibilities (and rights) that lack the formal force of law—responsibilities and rights that are nothing more (or less) than aspects of what we hope is a shared understanding of what it is to be a citizen; they are enforceable only by informal persuasion from our fellow citizens.[12] Our first concern in this chapter will be with the civic responsibilities that should attach to these roles, but a further question will be when civic responsibilities should be formalized in legal responsibilities that the law requires us to fulfill, on pain of public censure and punishment if we fail to do so. If a role involves a civic duty to ϕ, we have reason to impose a legal duty to ϕ, since failure to discharge a civic duty is a public wrong that in principle merits formal public censure; but that reason might, we will see, not be conclusive.

Second, in analyzing the normative content of such roles, we must examine both passive and active dimensions: not only what we may or should do to those who fill these roles, but what we can expect or demand that they do; not only what rights they should acquire, or what burdens they can suffer, but what active responsibilities they should bear. Discussions about victims and offenders, for instance, often focus on the passive. We talk of victims' rights, of what should be done for them, and of how we may or should treat offenders: we do not talk much about the active responsibilities of victims or offenders. This is, however, an important dimension of the criminal law as a republican common law: in a democratic republic, citizens will be active participants in the civic enterprise, including the enterprise of criminal law.

There is much to be said about the roles mentioned above that lay citizens play in relation to particular offenses: such roles as victim, witness, suspect, defendant. We can understand these as normative civic roles structured by both rights and responsibilities: we can ask what civic duties I incur if I become a victim of crime,[13] or witness a crime,[14] or am questioned as a suspect by the police, or am formally charged with an offense and thus become a defendant in the criminal process.[15] More precisely, we can ask in sociological tones how these roles are in fact understood in a particular polity at a particular time—by what sets of responsibilities and rights they are structured in the positive sociopolitical ethics of that polity; or we can ask in more avowedly normative tones how they *should* be understood (in the kind of polity in which we are theorizing). Our interest is in the latter kind of question: in what roles citizens of what aspires to be a democratic republic should be ready to play, and in how they should understand or define those roles. Answers to these questions are neither easy nor uncontroversial: as we noted above, the character and content of such roles (indeed, whether they should exist at all) is a matter for normative debate—for public deliberation by the members of the polity. But there is nothing puzzling in seeing these as civic roles that citizens may be called on to play, and should be ready to play, as their contribution to the enterprise of their criminal law.[16]

Our interest, however, is in two further positions that it might seem stranger to describe as civic roles—those of offender and convicted offender. In what follows, we will sketch an account of how those roles should be understood (and why they should be recognized as civic roles) in a democratic republic that takes citizenship seriously; in doing so, we will also be putting a little more flesh on the idea of a common law as a law that free and equal citizens can make their own.

Offenders and Their Civic Duties

One reason why it might seem odd to describe offender as a civic role is that committing a crime cannot be the exercise of a civic role:[17] it is a violation of civic duty. The other reason is that such a view of offenders is at odds with much of the penal rhetoric, policy and practice of contemporary Anglo-American penality. Offenders (or those who commit the wrong kinds of offense) are often portrayed, not as citizens with a role to play, but as dangerous outsiders or enemies—a threatening "they" against whom "we," the law-abiding, must be protected, and against whom the war on crime is fought. It is then easy to portray their place in the criminal justice system as purely passive: we ask what "we" may or must do to "them"; their role is to suffer whatever we may or must do. This is also a feature of too much recent penal theory. Some theorists explicitly argue that someone who commits a crime thereby forfeits his civic standing, his position as a citizen;[18] and even theorists who do not talk of forfeiture often cast the offender in a passive role as one to whom things are done or on whom they are inflicted.

Committing a criminal offense is indeed not usually a civic act, an exercise of one's role as citizen (unless it is an act of civil disobedience). But it is something that citizens do: so we can ask how citizens should respond to their wrongdoing (and to that of others) *as citizens*, which will be to ask what responsibilities offenders and convicted offenders incur. This is a feature of many roles: the responsibilities of the role (and the virtues proper to it) include the way in which role-holders should respond to their own failures or misconduct in their discharge of the role. An account of what makes for a good doctor, for instance, must include an account of how a doctor should respond to her own medical mistakes or malpractice, as well as to those of her colleagues. We can thus properly ask how someone who aspires to be a good citizen would respond not just to the criminal wrongdoings of others (as, for instance, a victim, or witness, or juror), but to her own criminal wrongdoing; our answer will show how offender can be a civic role, with its distinctive set of responsibilities.

Another reason for asking this question, and seeking to portray offender as a civic role, is to resist the exclusionary tendencies that characterize current penal practices.[19] A democratic republic would, we hope, display an inclusionary rather than an exclusionary spirit, both in its response to those who wish to join (its immigration policies, its treatment of refugees), and in the way its members respond to each other. It would foster and display a sense of solidarity: a sense that is not indefeasible (as we will see, the bonds of citizenship can be broken), but that is not so fragile that it breaks when a fellow citizen commits a crime—even a serious crime. If we can understand offender and convicted offender as civic roles, to be played by people who are still citizens, and who are to play the roles *as citizens*, we can then aspire to a truly inclusive criminal law—a criminal law that is a law for all citizens, not just for "law-abiding" citizens.

If we are to do this, we must focus on the active dimensions of these roles, asking not just what we may do to (convicted) offenders, but what we may ask of them or expect from them. Penal theory often attends to offenders' rights: what rights they forfeit, which rights may be justly infringed in virtue of their crimes, what rights they retain that constrain what we may do them. Such questions are important; but if we are to understand how being a (convicted) offender could be a civic role, we must attend to the responsibilities by which it is defined: what can a citizen who commits a crime be expected to do, as an active participant in the enterprise of a criminal law that is his law? (Skeptics might suggest that what we can expect, empirically, from those who commit crimes is that they will do their best to avoid detection and punishment. However, first, our concern is with normative, not empirical, expectations. Second, our concern is with what can be normatively expected or demanded of those living in a tolerably just system of law—not of those whose conviction and punishment would simply add to the injustices that they have already suffered. Third, a crucial aspect of our argument is that we should still see those who commit crimes, even serious and repeated crimes, as fellow citizens, and thus as bearers of civic responsibilities that we can expect them to discharge—even if we also have very good reason to believe that such normative expectations will often not be fulfilled.)

Suppose I know that I have committed a crime, and what crime I have committed. If the crime was (as crimes should be) a moral wrong, and especially if it had an identifiable victim, I uncontroversially acquire responsibilities of reparation and apology, independently of the criminal law; but what responsibilities could I acquire in relation to the criminal law? Do I, for instance, have a civic responsibility to report myself to the police, to cooperate in their investigation, to plead guilty if prosecuted? Should democratic citizens, that is to say, understand what it is to be an offender in these terms? The answer must, subject to crucial qualifications to be noted below, be that I do acquire such responsibilities in committing a crime. First, as a citizen of the polity whose law it is, I have a civic responsibility to assist the criminal law's enterprise, including the enterprise of calling criminal wrongdoers to public account. Second, I should recognize my crime as a wrong, and to recognize it as a wrong is to recognize it as something for which I should answer, to those whose business it is. As a public wrong, a crime is the business of the whole polity, and the criminal trial is the public forum in which criminal wrongdoers are formally called to answer; I have a civic responsibility to answer for my crime in that forum, which I can do by reporting myself to the appropriate authorities, and pleading guilty if I am sent to trial. We can now talk of an offender's civic virtue, as a virtue that involves recognizing and responding appropriately to one's criminal wrongdoing. As a civic virtue, it concerns our civic dealings with our fellow citizens, under the aegis of the criminal law that helps structure those dealings: the criminal law provides the appropriate, formal response to the wrongdoings it defines as criminal; the offender's primary civic responsibility is to collaborate in that response.[20]

Now for the qualifications. First, I can have this duty only if I live under a tolerably just system of law, which I can be expected to see as my law, and committed what is legitimately defined as a public wrong; and only if I face a tolerably just criminal process and punishment ("tolerably just" will need a lot of unpacking). The account we sketch here is an ideal account of the kind of criminal law and institutions to which we should aspire as would-be democratic republicans, and of the civic duties we would have in such a system; to the extent that we do not live in such a system, our civic duties must be qualified or revised. It would be grotesque to say to a young African American man who knows that he committed what the law defines as criminal drug usage that he has a civic duty to surrender to the police and plead guilty at trial. It is at best doubtful that we can say that he should see the law as his law—as the law of his polity, in which he is properly treated and respected as a citizen, and to which he can therefore be called to answer for his public conduct;[21] it is at best doubtful that drug usage is justifiably criminalized; and if a guilty plea would lead to a mandatory prison term, we cannot say that he has a civic duty to accept or seek such a disproportionate punishment. The point here is not that our account is so idealized that it cannot apply to our existing systems of criminal justice—although we suspect that, in relation to many of those with whom they deal, they are indeed marked by such pervasive kinds of injustice and harshness that we cannot talk plausibly of an offender's civic responsibility to seek his own punishment; it is rather that we can use such an account to bring out more clearly some of the ways in which and reasons for which these systems need radical reform. If the ideal—of a polity whose criminal law is such that we can plausibly say that one who commits a crime has a civic responsibility to report herself and to plead guilty—is a plausible political ideal, we must recognize the many ways in which our own polities fall short of that ideal, and begin to explore the steps (both political and legal) that might bring us closer to it.

Second, we do not suggest that, even in a just system, we should report ourselves to the police whenever we know that we have committed a crime. This is why it is better to talk of civic responsibility than of civic duty, to make clearer that this is something that requires the exercise of judgment and discretion. Officials, police officers, and prosecutors, who are responsible for investigating alleged crimes and bringing cases to court, exercise discretion in deciding which cases to investigate and to prosecute (rather than ignoring them, or diverting them to noncriminal processes); even under a well-designed criminal law, we can expect that conduct that formally fits the law's definition of an offense will often be more appropriately treated in other ways. Citizens who respect the law as their law will be willing and able to make such discretionary judgments for themselves: to decide, in responding to their own criminal conduct and to that of others, whether they should treat the conduct *as* criminal—as something that should be dealt with through the criminal process.

Third, we are talking here of civic responsibility, not of legal duty: we do not suggest that a civic responsibility to report oneself, to plead guilty, to cooperate in the criminal process, should be turned into a legal duty— that one who fails to discharge that responsibility should face conviction both for the original crime and for failing to report himself or to plead guilty, thus facing two convictions, two punishments, relating to the same underlying crime. He is guilty of two distinct violations of civic responsibility; compared to an offender who confesses his crime, he commits a further wrong. But a decent system of criminal justice leaves room for dissenting citizens to enact their dissent, and guards against its own fallibility. A dissenting citizen, who denies the authority of the law or the court, might for that reason refuse to play his allotted part in the process—refuse to cooperate with the investigation or trial. If we take the law seriously, we cannot allow that to bar his trial; but we can refrain from punishing him for his very defiance. We must also recognize that any human system will sometimes err, and that even if we set a demanding standard of proof for the criminal trial, some innocents will be mistakenly convicted: it is bad enough that they are then punished for crimes that they did not commit; it would be even worse to punish them as well for failing to confess (falsely) to those crimes.[22] Finally, we must recognize the oppressive potential of any human system of law, and the fallibility of human officials: a legal duty to cooperate or to plead guilty would give even more power to those who administer the criminal process—a power that could all too easily be abused.

Even given these qualifications, a civic responsibility to report one's own crimes, and to plead guilty at one's trial, might seem implausible, for two reasons. First, it might be agreed that someone who reports herself and pleads guilty displays an admirable civic virtue: but her action is super-erogatory, not dutiful; it goes beyond the call of any plausible civic duty.[23] We would certainly distinguish a set of relatively modest (though often demanding) civic duties from exercises of supererogatory civic virtue. But a responsibility to report and admit one's own crimes is not overde-manding; nor is such reporting and admission a supererogatory exercise of unusual virtue. We might naturally say to a wrongdoer, in various con-texts, "You ought to own up," or "You ought to face up to what you have done"—talking the language of duty, not of supererogation; and we owe it to those whom we wrong to apologies to them—which involves admitting our wrong to them.

In systems that are less than tolerably just, or in which wrongdoers face penal and further consequences that are oppressive or exclusionary, we admittedly could not plausibly assert such a duty. Insofar as we recognize a danger that those who admit their guilt will face oppressive or exclusion-ary consequences, or that those whom officials believe to be guilty will face improper pressure to admit their (supposed) guilt, we should also be slow to *assert* any such duty, and slow to blame the offender who gives in to the all too human temptation to try to evade rather than face justice: but that does not undermine our modest claim that a citizen of a tolerably just polity has a civic responsibility to admit her crimes and to submit herself to the judgment of her peers through the criminal process; a responsibility, indeed, to play her active role in that process.

This response to the first objection is likely to provoke a second, deeper objection: that in asserting such a civic responsibility we misportray the re-lationship between state and citizen, and the criminal process—misportray it not merely as it now is, but even as it ought to be in ideal theory. We portray state and defendant as engaged, ideally, in a cooperative enter-prise of criminal law: but we should instead see them as, if not enemies, competitors in which the state has vastly superior power against which the citizen needs protection. A radical version of such a view is found in the Hobbesian story that Ristroph reconstructs, central to which is a right to resist one's own punishment: not a claim-right against the state that it not punish me, since it coexists with the state's right to punish me; but a liberty-right which is clearly inconsistent with any duty to offer myself up for punishment.[24] On this view the state is a monster, a leviathan, that we create because it is the only way to protect ourselves against a Hobbesian state of nature: but it, the sovereign, is a threatening as well as a protective force, against which we may need, and have the right, to protect ourselves; in particular, if it sets out to injure us, by punishing us, we have no duty to take part in this process as compliant victims, and retain the liberty to resist.

There are less dramatically dystopian versions of this objection: one is expressed in the US Supreme Court's declaration that "the purpose of the jury trial . . . is to prevent oppression by the Government."[25] On this view we should understand the criminal trial, not as a practice in which citizens should cooperate as defendants who make the trial's aims their own: rather, it is an institution that serves precisely to protect citizens against the oppressive power of the state. Without such an institution we would be even more vulnerably at the mercy of the state as it seeks to control us; but the "due process" safeguards that structure the criminal process give us some protection against this power.

Now in one way we do not dissent from this conception of the criminal process: that process is rightly structured by a range of requirements and constraints—those signaled by the ideas of due process and a fair trial—designed to protect citizens against the dangerous power of the state; and our insistence that the civic responsibility to report oneself and to plead guilty should not be transformed into an enforceable legal duty amounts to insisting that citizens must retain a legal liberty-right to refuse to participate in the process. But if we ask *why* we should include such protective safeguards, the answer is not—we suggest—that this gives institutional form to the ideal of a criminal process; or that "the state" is, in essence, a leviathan that we created but against which we need protection. The answer is, rather, that this is what we should do to guard against some familiar pathologies of states and polities. "The state" should not be understood, from the outset, as an inevitably alien power set against the citizens whose state it is supposed to be; rather, it should be understood (in aspiration) as the set of institutional mechanisms through which we can govern ourselves efficiently—as, to revive a cliché, our servant, not our master. But we need safeguards against the state because, as we and Dr. Frankenstein know, such servants can be dangerous. What is true in the critic's account is that, if we did not need to protect citizens against the state's power, we would not have a criminal process structured by such procedural safeguards. What the account misses, however, is that we need such a process not because trials would ideally be (would serve their proper purposes if they were) such a contest between state and citizen, a contest in which it is no part of the citizen's role to help the state convict her; but because it protects us against the oppression and injustice that are likely to ensue if the institution malfunctions (as any human institution might).

Were the "contest" view of the criminal trial right, as an account of the trial's proper aim, then a defendant who pleads guilty is not "playing the game"—the guilty plea undermines the proper aims of the trial (just as giving one's opponent a walkover in a game undermines the point of the game). Now guilty pleas, especially in a system that depends on plea-bargaining, are indeed often something other than honest confessions of guilt by offenders who want to answer for what they know to be their wrongdoing; and, partly for that reason, even when a defendant insists on pleading guilty, the court should satisfy itself that he is indeed guilty of the offense charged.[26] Suppose, however, that a defendant pleads guilty not because he has been pressured into a plea bargain, nor on the basis of a prudential calculation of costs and benefits, but because he believes that he ought to make such a public admission of his own wrongdoing: he does not subvert the purpose of the trial; he behaves as a decent citizen—he does his civic duty.

We therefore maintain our claim that subject to the caveats discussed above, a defendant who knows he is guilty of a crime (and what crime he is guilty of) has a civic responsibility to report himself to the police, and to plead guilty if he is then prosecuted. In doing that, he displays his continuing (or renewed) commitment, as a citizen, to a law that he recognizes as his law, and to those whom he recognizes as his fellow citizens; and in accepting his plea and convicting him the court, speaking in the name of his fellow citizens, must also show that it recognizes him as a citizen—as a full member of the polity to whom respect and concern are owed, as they are to all citizens. The court might speak in censorial tones of the character and implications of his crime: but it must address him as a citizen who has in this respect erred, not as an enemy, or an outsider, or a person of lesser civic status.

On the basis of this account of the civic responsibilities of offenders, we can now turn to the other role that we need to discuss: that of convicted offender.

Convicted Offenders and Their Punishments

If prosecuted and convicted, an offender becomes a convicted offender. One difference that this new status makes is that it can bring in its train a host of "collateral consequences," which can have a serious impact on the person's life. We cannot discuss such consequences, which could be seen as attaching to the (dubious) role of "ex-offender," here, although they require more sustained critical attention than they have so far received:[27] we focus instead on punishment, to ask whether we can portray "convicted offender" as a civic role—as a responsibility-bearing role that a citizen could play.

It might seem odd to call "convicted offender" an active civic role, for two reasons that reflect common features of existing penal rhetoric, theory, and practice.[28] First, we are more used to thinking of convicted offenders as passive rather than as active: what may we do to them; what should they suffer?[29] We are not used to thinking of them as having active roles to play, and often see punishment simply as something done to those on whom it is imposed. Second, there is the tendency to see offenders as outsiders: as having forfeited their status as citizens. If that was an appropriate understanding of the implications of criminal offending, we could not ask what civic duties convicted offenders might have qua offenders, since theirs could not be a civic role. But as we saw in the previous section, those very reasons show why it is important to think about the civic duties of offenders: this is how we can recognize that offenders remain citizens (as they must in what aspires to be an inclusive republic), and how we can understand citizenship as an active matter of playing one's part in the civic enterprise —including the enterprise of the criminal law.

What then could the convicted offender's role be, if not just that of passively accepting his punishment? The answer is that his primary responsibility is to *undertake* the punishment as the formal, prescribed way to show his recognition of his crime and make reparation for it. The first point to note is that although the offender's role in punishment is usually discussed in passive terms, most punishments in fact require the offender's active engagement: they are to be undertaken, rather than simply undergone. This is most obviously true of noncustodial modes of punishment.

Even a fine is something that the offender is required to pay (although it may be exacted from him if he fails to do so), other modes of punishment demand more in the way of activity. Someone sentenced to "community payback" is required to undertake a specified number of hours of a specified type of work.[30] Someone sentenced to probation is also required to be active—to report to the probation officer as required, perhaps to undertake programs that address his offending. Imprisonment looks like a striking exception to this claim, and we will discuss imprisonment shortly: but it is worth beginning with noncustodial punishments, the most common sentences even in the most enthusiastically carceral systems, which can be portrayed as—in the familiar rhetoric—a debt that the offender owes the polity, and that it is (initially) up to him to pay. Of course, in our existing penal systems, distant as they are from the republican ideal, the convicted offender's activity might more often fit the first rather than the third of the ways of responding to punishment that we sketched at the start of this chapter: undertaking punishment will be a matter of prudence, tactically avoiding something even more onerous, rather than of genuine acceptance. But our aim here is to show how criminal punishment *could*, in a decent penal system, be understood and undertaken as a civic duty—not to claim that this is how those suffering punishments in our present systems should respond to them.

How far criminal punishment can be portrayed as an active civic duty that is required of the convicted offender depends on how we understand punishment and its aims. If we see it, for instance, simply as deterrence, or incapacitation, we will not give offenders an essentially active role. It is easier to operate a penal system if offenders cooperate; but incapacitation and deterrence are measures that we inflict upon people, not enterprises to which their own active cooperation could be integral. The same is true of those versions of retributivism that portray punishment as a matter of inflicting a quantum of deserved suffering on the offender: again, the offender is portrayed simply as the passive recipient of punishment. Such retributivists can argue that offenders should cooperate in their punishment—that they ought to recognize that the punishment is justified, and for that reason cooperate in its imposition. But there is nothing about the aims or meaning of punishment itself, on these accounts, that requires such cooperation: lack of cooperation does not undermine punishment's legitimacy, or frustrate its aims. However, if we are to portray punishment as an active civic duty, we must portray it as something that, ideally, requires the offender's active participation: the paradigm of the sentence must be not "This is what we will do to you," but "This is what you must do." Offenders who refuse to undertake their punishment will not thereby escape it; punishment will be imposed if it is not undertaken. But punishment that is merely imposed is on this view defective precisely as punishment: it is not something the offender undertakes as a citizen.

By contrast, a communicative view of punishment does make the offender's participation central, since it portrays punishment as, in intention if often not in fact, a two-way process of communication from polity to offender and from offender to polity. What the court says to a convicted offender in passing sentence is that this is what he must undertake as a symbolic reparation for what he has done (thus communicating to him an appropriate message about the character and implications of his offense); or, as Bennett portrays it, this is what he must undertake as a ritual of apology for what he has done.[31] But reparation and apology must be made by the offender, not done to him. Insofar as reparation involves material compensation, it can be exacted from an uncooperative debtor: but it then lacks the communicative character that it is intended to have as reparation for a wrong—as a way of giving material force to an offender's recognition of his wrong; and it certainly cannot constitute an apology. This is not the place to defend such an account of punishment, and we do not suggest that other accounts cannot portray punishment as a civic duty that falls on convicted offenders: our claim is only that if we hold that convicted offenders are still citizens, who acquire distinctive civic duties in virtue of this role, a communicative account of punishment seems especially apt.

This still leaves many questions about the form of a civic system of criminal punishment: about how punishment can treat those who are punished as citizens, and ideally itself express such a recognition of fellow citizenship between punishers and punished. A salient question concerns modes of punishment (a question to which penal theorists pay too little attention).[32] What modes of punishment can citizens properly demand of or impose on each other? What modes are consistent with, or even expressive of, a recognition of citizenship? This question concerns not just the material or psychological impact of punishment, but its meaning: what does each mode of punishment say about the offender or the crime, to the offender, the victim and the polity? We cannot discuss the different modes of punishment here, save to note that if punishment is to be a civic duty that the offender could be expected to undertake, the modes of punishment (and the spirit in which they are administered) must not be such as to degrade or humiliate those who must undertake them. Some theorists argue that punishment *should* demean or humiliate,[33] and those who design and administer punishments clearly sometimes intend just this: but this is inconsistent with a conception of punishment as something that is required of offenders as citizens to whom we still owe civic respect and concern. Punishment must be something that the offender can undertake without humiliating himself—and that his fellow citizens can respect him for undertaking.

That still leaves the question of imprisonment, which does not seem amenable to such an account. Surely the only plausible meaning of imprisonment is exclusion from ordinary civic life and fellowship; and it is simply imposed on offenders—it is not something that we could plausibly see as a punishment that they are required to undertake as active participants in the enterprise of criminal law. Imprisonment matters not just as a sentence that may be passed at conviction, but as a backup sanction of last resort on which other modes of punishment rely: when an offender keeps reappearing in court after a string of noncustodial sentences, sentencers often fall back on imprisonment; and imprisonment in fact often functions as a final sanction for breaches of the requirements of noncustodial sentences. If we cannot portray imprisonment as an appropriate punishment for citizens to require of each other, then our talk of criminal punishment as a civic duty will seem hollow: not simply because it cannot capture this salient and most serious mode of punishment,[34] but because the threat of imprisonment as a backup sanction must throw a less attractive light on the way in which offenders can be expected to undertake noncustodial sentences. If we cannot show imprisonment (at least in principle) to be a sentence that the offender could properly be required to undertake, or to be consistent with an inclusionary recognition of the offender as our fellow citizen, we must argue either that imprisonment cannot be justified in a democratic republic; or that some crimes or some criminal careers are such that those who commit or engage them should no longer be seen as citizens—that they can properly be excluded as wrongdoers whose citizenship is suspended or forfeited; or that imprisonment is, sadly, an injustice that necessity (the necessity of having such a final sanction to sustain the possibility of a generally inclusive criminal law) forces us to commit.

Imprisonment *can* be actively undertaken. Suppose that a convicted offender is sentenced to N months in prison, and is instructed (as happens in some systems) to report to a specified prison on a specified date to serve his term; suppose that the prison is an open prison, with no walls to prevent prisoners walking out. Imprisonment is then something that is required of the offender, as a duty that he must undertake.[35] However, critics will argue, such practices are sustainable only because there is always the prospect of coercive detention in a closed prison if one disobeys the requirements: remove that threat, and many of those required to undertake imprisonment will predictably fail to do so. Furthermore, active (self-) imprisonment, in open prisons, is implausible for more serious and violent kinds of crime.

One question is whether we must rely on imprisonment as the final backup sanction for all noncustodial punishments—indeed, whether we need a final backup sanction that can be simply imposed, rather than involving requirements that the offender can refuse to fulfill. It is tempting to think that we do: if there were no such final unavoidable sanction for breaches, there would surely be an increasing number of such breaches, and a possible collapse of the system. Perhaps—but perhaps not, especially if breaches led to the offender being required to appear in court each time, and being forcibly brought to court if he did not present himself;[36] perhaps we should recognize, in this as in other contexts, that people do not always fulfill their obligations and cannot always be forced to do so.

However, we still face the question of whether imprisonment in a closed prison could be justified as an inclusionary civic punishment that citizens could legitimately be expected to undertake. Of course, if we think about imprisonment as currently practiced in American and English prisons (and focus on the worst examples of those), the question is easily answered: this is not a punishment that treats those subjected to it as citizens, or that an offender could undertake as a mode of punitive reparation in which he retains his dignity as a citizen.[37] "The experience of the prisoner is, from the outset, an experience of being violently dominated, and it is colored from the beginning by the fear of being violently treated."[38] But prisons need not be like that, and we can ask how far they could become sites of genuine civic punishment.

Imprisonment in a closed prison can be undertaken, not merely undergone, if the prisoner approaches it in the appropriate spirit or with the appropriate demeanor. Those in prison can be active rather than passive—active in fruitful ways, if their prison is minimally decent (and their sentences tolerably just): they may be able to make the prison regime their own, rather than merely a set of alien rules that they must obey (a lot depends on the nature of the regime); to engage in reasonably fulfilling and productive work, or in educational programs. This will be possible, as something that a prisoner could undertake as his own self-respecting project, only given appropriate prison conditions and appropriate attitudes from prison staff. Furthermore, if prisoners should have toward the prison regime the kind of respect that citizens should have for the law (since the prison regime is an aspect of the law), they must be enabled and ready to take a respectfully critical stance toward it: they must be ready to object to what they see to be oppressive or unjust; and the prison must make such dissent possible, not merely as an ineffective letting off of steam, but as a way in which change can be sought, and achieved.[39]

We can then try further to rethink prison regimes in ways that would bring prisons closer to a condition in which they can be sites of civic punishment. We can think about what goes on inside the prison—its architecture, living conditions, how prison staff address and treat those who have been imprisoned, what kinds of work or activity are available, what kind of control they have over their daily lives, and so on.[40] We can think about how porous prison walls could be—what kinds of connection or engagement with the personal and civic world outside the prison could be allowed or encouraged. These are not issues that we can pursue here, save to note the symbolic importance of the right to vote while in prison:[41] denying that right is an obvious way of denying the citizenship of serving prisoners; maintaining it is an obvious way of making clear that they are still citizens.

Whatever such changes can be made, however, the brute fact of prison walls remains: the walls might be made more porous, but they will still be there. The question is, then, whether we can honestly say to a convicted offender that he is required, given his crime, to seclude himself from his ordinary personal and civic life for a specified time—to exclude himself, albeit partially and temporarily. If we can say that, we can see the prison walls as more like the locks we put on our houses: a method of preventing the offender from doing what he has a duty not to do—leaving the prison. We do not suggest that this could justify as extensive a use of imprisonment as we now make: indeed, since the message of imprisonment cannot but be exclusionary (however modulated and qualified that exclusion is), it must be reserved for that limited number of crimes whose seriousness and implications can be adequately marked only by the offender entering the kind of temporary and partial seclusion that prison provides. But, if reformed in the ways indicated here, imprisonment could be a civic punishment that offenders could be expected to undertake as citizens.

Concluding Comments and Qualifications

We should, finally, comment briefly on four points about the account of civic punishment that we have sketched here.

First, a human system of criminal justice will sometimes mistakenly convict and punish innocent people. If a convicted offender has a civic duty to undertake his punishment, what can we say to the innocent who is wrongly convicted? We noted above the injustice suffered by those whose release is delayed because they continue to protest their innocence:[42] but our account might seem to treat them no less unjustly, by requiring them to undertake punishment as if they were guilty. They do, we think, have a civic duty to undertake their punishment, *if* their trial was procedurally just, and *if* their punishment is appropriate to their alleged crime: for they have a duty to respect the institutions of the law, and although that respect should be critical, it must include a willingness to abide by the law's good faith mistakes. That is *not* to say, however, that they should apologize for their (alleged) crimes, or pretend to be guilty. If that is true of the civic duty of mistakenly convicted innocents, however, it has implications for the *legal* duty of all convicted offenders, whether innocent or guilty: that their duty is to undertake the ritual of punishment, but not to mean it as a genuine apology or expression of remorse, nor to pretend to mean it. An innocent who undertakes his punishment while still protesting his innocence fulfills both his legal and his civic duty. A convicted offender who undertakes his punishment while expressing his lack of remorse or of any respect for the law, has not fulfilled his civic duty: he owed it to his fellow citizens to make a genuine apology for his wrong, and to respect the law that is their common law. But we should not hold him in breach of any legal duty, since the law must leave room for dissenters to express their dissent, free from the threat of further sanctions.[43] This is one limitation that a liberal criminal law must respect—one way in which it must not intrude too deeply into its citizens' souls.

Second, it might be argued that our argument points not toward criminal punishment as a civic duty to be discharged by active citizens, but toward practices of "restorative justice." For such practices emphasize an active role for the offender and other parties; they address offenders as members of the community whose business the crime is; they seek to preserve, or restore, the bonds of community that would otherwise be threatened. Rather than trying to render such an essentially oppressive institution as criminal punishment consistent with—let alone expressive of—a recognition of fellow citizenship with the offender, should we not see our line of thought as a further reason for favoring "restorative" over " retributive" justice?[44] We cannot discuss here the role that different kinds of "restorative" process can play either as alternatives to a criminal process, or within a system of criminal punishment; nor can we discuss the viability of the contrast that is often drawn or assumed between "restorative" and "retributive" justice.[45] We would just make two points. The first is that, as we noted earlier, a choice must often be made (by citizens or by officials) about whether to mobilize the criminal process in response to what formally counts as a crime: some kinds "restorative justice" process are alternatives to a criminal process, and are sometimes appropriate; all we need claim is that sometimes, given the nature and context of the wrong, it will be more appropriate to invoke a formal criminal process. Second, once we understand crimes as public wrongs that concern the whole polity; once we recognize the importance of formal rituals in the civic life of a liberal polity, and the related importance in such a polity of not requiring citizens to engage in more intimate and self-revelatory encounters: we can see why the *required* response to public wrongs should often take the form of a criminal process as portrayed here.

Third, we have argued that we should aspire to an inclusionary, rather than exclusionary, system of criminal law and punishment, and to the kind of polity in which this could become a plausible aspiration. But, it might be objected, we surely cannot believe that it could ever be possible to treat *all* offenders as full citizens. That would make citizenship unconditional: but why should we suppose that when other normative human bonds (of marriage, of friendship, of collegiality) are breakable, those of citizenship are not? We might admire someone who treats the bonds of marriage as unbreakable—whatever she or he does, she or he is still my spouse:[46] but surely it is not plausible to take the same view of citizenship. We agree that there might be some crimes—or more plausibly some criminal careers—that are so destructive of civic fellowship that we are justified in thinking that we can no longer see or treat the perpetrator as a fellow citizen, but there will be very few such cases:[47] for the vast majority of offenses and offenders we can plausibly aspire to an inclusionary approach. As for those few, we must think about modes of exclusion, of detention, that still respect their status as moral agents and as fellow human beings: but we must also regard such exclusion as being only presumptively permanent. There must always be a way back, even if the onus is on the offender to show that he should be allowed back; his detention must include provisions for effective programs through which he could make his way back. The American sentence of "life without prospect of parole" is horrifying partly because it rules out, in advance, any prospect of such a return. English courts recognize this point: an Imprisonment for Public Protection (IPP) sentence "does not require the abandonment of all hope for offenders on whom it is imposed. They are not consigned to penal oblivion. To the contrary, common humanity, if nothing else, must allow for the possibility of rehabilitation."[48]

Even if IPPs could in principle be justified, their legitimacy in practice was undermined by a failure to provide access to the kinds of program that IPP prisoners needed to undertake if they were to persuade the Parole Board that they could safely be released; this rendered that "possibility of rehabilitation" a mockery.

Fourth, the account sketched here is incomplete, since it does not look beyond the formal completion of punishment. We must look critically at the range of "collateral consequences" that, in our existing systems, attach to conviction and punishment, making a mockery of any idea that offenders, having paid their debt to their fellow citizens, are restored to good civic standing;[49] we must also attend to the ways in which offenders' fellow citizens respond to them, during and after their formal sentences. If criminal punishment is to be an inclusionary enterprise through which offenders can make formal reparation to their fellow citizens, their fellow citizens must be ready to accept that reparation as adequate: they might not be ready to (re)build personal or intimate relationships with them, but must be ready to behave toward them, as fellow participants in the civic realm; in this as in other contexts, the civic realm is a realm of outward, often relatively formal conduct rather than of inner sentiment. This might often not require anything dramatic, especially for sentences served "in the community"; but, in the light of our discussion of imprisonment, it is worth asking whether, given its inevitably exclusionary character, we should not institute formal ceremonies of rehabilitation for those who complete a prison term.[50] That, however, is a topic for another essay.

We hope that we have shown that it is fruitful, first, to ask how punishment could operate in an inclusive, democratic republic; second, to look at the roles that democratic citizens can play in relation to their criminal law; third, to see "offender" and "convicted offender" as civic roles that can be actively undertaken by citizens; and fourth, to reconceptualize punishment (including even imprisonment) as something that convicted offenders could have a duty to undertake as a way of discharging the civic duty of apologetic reparation that they incurred by committing their crimes. We should again emphasize, however, that we are not claiming this to be a possible or plausible way to view criminal punishment as it is typically practiced on, and suffered by, many of those convicted in our courts: our claim is rather that we ought to aspire to a penal system in which punishment could be thus understood, and to the kind of society in which such a penal system would be possible. Our account is thus not intended to rationalize, or make good normative sense of, the penal status quo. Nor, however, is it simply an exercise in ideal theory (in philosophical fantasy) that can have no connection to and no implications for that status quo. If the ideal is, as we have argued, a plausible ideal for republican democrats, it provides a standard against which we can assess current practice, and in whose light we can see more clearly some of the ways in which it is inadequate and unjust—some of the reasons for which we cannot now say that offenders have a civic duty to undertake their own punishments.[51] It also shows us the directions in which we need to seek to reform our practices and institutions, and the political structures in which they are grounded, so that our criminal law could become at least something more like what it ought to be: a law that the citizens of a democratic republic could properly make their own.[52]

Notes

1. Danielle S. Allen, "Punishment in Ancient Athens," in *Dēmos: Classical Athenian Democracy*, March 23, 2003, 5 www.stoa.org/projects/demos/article_punishment?page =5&greekEncoding; see also Danielle S. Allen, *The World of Prometheus: The Politics of Punishing in Democratic Athens* (Princeton, NJ: Princeton University Press, 2000), 232–237.

2. For a recent example, see Allegra M. McLeod, "Prison Abolition and Grounded Justice," *UCLA Law Review* 62(5) (2015): 1156; see further the section here titled "Convicted Offenders and Their Punishments."

3. See Ronald M. Dworkin, *A Matter of Principle* (Cambridge, MA: Harvard University Press, 1985), 190; Dworkin is concerned only with what a state owes its citizens.

4. Philip Pettit, *On the People's Terms: A Republican Theory and Model of Democracy* (Cambridge: Cambridge University Press, 2012), 84: Pettit treats the ability to look others in the eye as a criterion of republican freedom as nondomination.

5. We should emphasize that this is not to apply Jakobs's notorious distinction between "citizen criminal law" and "enemy criminal law" (Günther Jakobs, "Kriminalisierung im Vorfeld einer Rechtsgutsverletzung," *Zeitschrift für die gesamte Strafrechtswissenschaft* 97 [1985]: 751); and that while an account of the criminal law must begin with citizens, it must also explain how the criminal law respects noncitizens who fall within its jurisdiction. See further R. A. Duff, "Responsibility, Citizenship and Criminal Law," in R. A. Duff and Stuart P. Green (eds.), *Philosophical Foundations of Criminal Law* (Oxford, Oxford University Press, 2010), 125, 141–143.

6. Compare Roger M. Cotterrell, *Law's Community* (Oxford: Oxford University Press, 1995), ch. 11.

7. Compare William A Edmundson, "The Virtue of Law-Abidance," *Philosophers' Imprint* 6(4) (2006): 1.

8. Compare Kimberley Brownlee, *Conscience and Conviction: The Case for Civil Disobedience* (Oxford: Oxford University Press, 2012).

9. See Kimberley Brownlee, "Responsibilities of Criminal Justice Officials," *Journal of Applied Philosophy* 27(2) (2010) 123.

10. Would a decently democratic system include the role of executioner, for instance? Compare Christopher J. Bennett, "Considering Capital Punishment as a Human Interaction," *Criminal Law and Philosophy* 7(2) (2013): 367.

11. See further R. A. Duff, Lindsay Farmer, S. E. Marshall, and Victor Tadros, *The Trial on Trial III: Towards a Normative Theory of the Criminal Trial* (Oxford: Hart, 2007); R. A. Duff, "Relational Reasons and the Criminal Law," *Oxford Studies in Legal Philosophy* 2 (2013): 175.

12. The substantial existence of such roles thus depends on the existence of genuinely shared understandings of civic life and of its institutions. Pessimists might question whether we—whoever "we" are—actually have such shared understandings: perhaps all we have left are mere "simulacra" of morality, and of the practices that would give material form to a shared conception of a civic enterprise. See Alasdair MacIntyre, *After Virtue*, 3rd ed. (London: Duckworth, 2007). We cannot discuss such skepticism here, but it must be met if law is to be possible.

13. See further S. E. Marshall, "'It Isn't Just About You': Victims of Crime, Their Associated Duties, and Public Wrongs," in R. A. Duff, Lindsay Farmer, S. E. Marshall, Massimo Renzo, and Victor Tadros (eds.), *Criminalization: The Political Morality of the Criminal Law* (Oxford: Oxford University Press, 2014), 291.

14. See Miriam Gur-Arye, "A Failure to Prevent Crime—Should it be Criminal?," *Criminal Justice Ethics* 20(2) (2001): 4.

15. See further R. A. Duff, "Pre-Trial Detention and the Presumption of Innocence," in Andrew J. Ashworth, Lucia Zedner, and Patrick Tomlin (eds.), *Prevention and the Limits of the Criminal Law* (Oxford: Oxford University Press, 2013), 115.

16. The matter is less straightforward in the case of defendants, given the common conception of the criminal trial as a contest between defendant and prosecutor, in which "the law" is easily seen as being on the side of the prosecutor: we would appeal to an alternative conception of the trial (see n. 11), as a process in which the defendant should ideally play a more collaborative role; see further at nn. 24–26.

17. Unless it is an act of civil disobedience: see at n. 8.

18. See, e.g., Alan H. Goldman, "Toward a New Theory of Punishment," *Law and Philosophy* 1(1) (1982): 57; Christopher W. Morris, "Punishment and Loss of Moral Standing," *Canadian Journal of Philosophy* 21(1) (1991): 53; also Christopher Wellman, "The Rights Forfeiture Theory of Punishment," *Ethics* 122(2) (2012): 371.

19. At least in the United States and Great Britain—though we are sure that these penal systems are not uniquely exclusionary.

20. Suppose I am unsure about whether I have committed a crime, or what crime I have committed (thanks to Carol Steiker for this question)? If the argument we sketch here is right, I still have a responsibility—to be exercised with discretion—to report myself, to seek clarification, and if necessary to face trial.

21. See Amy E. Lerman and Vesla M. Weaver, *Arresting Citizenship: The Democratic Consequences of American Crime Control* (Chicago: University of Chicago Press, 2014); also R. A. Duff, "Blame, Moral Standing and the Legitimacy of the Criminal Trial," *Ratio* 23(2) (2010): 123.

22. Compare the wrong done to a mistakenly convicted innocent whose release from prison is delayed because he persists in asserting his innocence, and thus has not "faced up to his crime."

23. Thanks to Garrett Cullity for this objection.

24. Alice Ristroph, "Respect and Resistance in Punishment Theory," *California Law Review* 97(2) (2009): 601.

25. *Williams v Florida* 399 US 78 (1970), at 100; see further Duff et al., *The Trial on Trial*, 94–96.

26. See generally Richard L. Lippke, *The Ethics of Plea Bargaining* (Oxford: Oxford University Press, 2011). What we say here applies to systems of adversarial trials: a different story would be needed for more inquisitorial systems. We think a story could be told that is consistent with our overall argument—but not here.

27. See Margaret C. Love, Jenny M. Roberts, and Cecelia Klingele, *Collateral Consequences of Criminal Convictions: Law, Policy and Practice* (New York: Thomson West, 2013); Zachary Hoskins, "Ex-Offender Restrictions," *Journal of Applied Philosophy* 31(1) (2014): 33; R. A. Duff, "Who Must Presume Whom to be Innocent of What?" *Netherlands Journal of Legal Philosophy* 42(3) (2013): 170, 185–192.

28. See at nn. 17–18.

29. For two exceptions see Jacob Adler, *The Urgings of Conscience* (Philadelphia: Temple University Press, 1992); Victor Tadros, *The Ends of Harm* (Oxford: Oxford University Press, 2011).

30. See Criminal Justice Act 2003 (ss. 177, 199–200).

31. See R. A. Duff, *Punishment, Communication and Community* (New York: Oxford University Press, 2001); Christopher J. Bennett, *The Apology Ritual: A Philosophical Theory of Punishment* (Cambridge: Cambridge University Press, 2008).

32. But see David Garland, *Punishment and Modern Society* (Oxford: Oxford University Press, 1990) chs. 9–10; Peter Young, "Putting a Price on Harm: The Fine as a Punishment," in R. A. Duff, S. E. Marshall, Rebecca E. Dobash, and Russell P. Dobash (eds.), *Penal Theory and Practice* (Manchester: Manchester University Press, 1994), 185; Richard L. Lippke, *Rethinking Imprisonment* (Oxford: Oxford University Press, 2007).

33. See notoriously D. M. Kahan, "What Do Alternative Sanctions Mean?," *University of Chicago Law Review* 63(2) (1996): 591 (on which see Stephen P. Garvey, "Can Shaming Punishments Educate?," *University of Chicago Law Review* 65(3) [1998]: 733). See also Jean Hampton, "Correcting Harms versus Righting Wrongs: The Goal of Retribution," *UCLA Law Review* 39(6) (1992): 1659—although it is not clear whether her talk of "humbling" or "bringing low" the offender is best understood as involving a kind of demeaning that is at odds with a recognition of his equal citizenship. Braithwaite's distinction between stigmatizing and reintegrative shaming (John Braithwaite, *Crime, Shame and Reintegration* [Cambridge: Cambridge University Press, 1989]) is important here; but we do not have the space to discuss in further detail the kinds of emotion that civic punishment may (or may not) properly seek to induce, or express.

34. We leave aside here capital punishment, and other possible modes of punishment (torture, for instance) that could not be portrayed as inclusive punishments that offenders may be required to undertake. Socrates's example reminds us that an offender could be active in his own execution; but we do not aim to justify such modes of punishment.

35. We leave aside here the role that might be played by such sanctions as home detention.

36. And such coercion can be justified, as preventing the offender from carrying through the criminal wrong of failing to answer the summons to appear in court. See also Rob Allen, *Reducing the Use of Imprisonment: What Can We Learn from Europe?* (London: Criminal Justice Alliance, 2012).

37. Compare McLeod, "Prison Abolition and Grounded Justice," n. 2; but she recognizes the extent to which her argument is less about imprisonment in general than about American imprisonment in particular.

38. Robert M. Cover, "Violence and the Word," *Yale Law Journal* 95(8) (1986): 1601, at 1607; quoted by Allegra M. McLeod, "Confronting Criminal Law's Violence: The Possibilities of Unfinished Alternatives," *Unbound: Harvard Journal of the Legal Left* 8(3) (2012–2013): 109, at 109.

39. Compare the activities of KROM, the Norwegian Association of Penal Reform: Thomas Mathiesen, *The Politics of Abolition Revisited* (London: Routledge, 2015); McLeod, "Confronting Criminal Law's Violence."

40. See Lippke, *Rethinking Imprisonment*; also, on the example of Norwegian prisons, Thomas Ugelvik and Jane Dullum (eds.), *Penal Exceptionalism? Nordic Prison Policy and Practice* (London: Routledge, 2011); John Pratt and Anna Eriksson, *Contrasts in Punishment* (London: Routledge, 2012).

41. Taking a dogmatic stand on a controversial issue: see Claudio Lopez-Guerra, *Democracy and Disenfranchisement: the Morality of Electoral Exclusions* (Oxford: Oxford University Press, 2014).

42. See n. 22.

43. See text at n. 22.

44. Thanks to Jovana Davidovic and Meira Levinson for pressing versions of this point.

45. See R. A. Duff, "Responsibility, Restoration and Retribution," in Michael Tonry (ed.), *Retributivism Has a Past: Has it a Future?* (Oxford: Oxford University Press, 2012), 63.

46. Compare the character of Stephen Blackpool in Dickens's *Hard Times*.

47. It might be thought that terrorist crimes are of this kind, since a terrorist precisely defines himself as an enemy, not as a citizen: but that raises the question of whether we can deal with (avowed) terrorism under domestic criminal law.

48. *R (on the application of Wells) v Parole Board for England and Wales* [2010] 1 AC 553, para. 105 (Lord Judge LCJ); see the European Court of Human Rights decision on the same case, *James v United Kingdom* (2013) 56 E.H.R.R. 12. IPPs were introduced Criminal Justice Act 2003, ch. 5, and replaced by more limited provisions for extended sentences for "dangerous" offenders by the Legal Aid, Sentencing and Punishment of Offenders Act 2012 ss. 122–128: see Harry Annison, *Dangerous Politics: Risk, Political Vulnerability, and Penal Policy* (Oxford: Oxford University Press, 2015). See further Duff, *Punishment, Communication and Community* (n. 31), 164–174.

49. See at n. 27.

50. See Shadd Maruna, "Reentry as a Rite of Passage," *Punishment and Society* 13(1) (2011): 3.

51. The nature and extent of these inadequacies and injustices will of course vary as between different systems of criminal law, as will therefore the extent to which we can or cannot plausibly talk of a civic duty to undertake one's own punishment: in the systems

that we know best, those in Britain and the United States, the distance between the actual and the ideal seems considerable; we can hope that there are some other polities in which it is narrower.

52. We are grateful to for helpful comments received in discussions of ancestors of this chapter at Cardozo Law School, the Universities of Edinburgh and Nottingham, King's College London, Harvard Law School, the Society for Applied Philosophy, and from the editors of this volume.

CHAPTER 4 | Playing Fair with Imprisonment

RICHARD DAGGER

Introduction

This chapter rests on two assumptions, at least one of which is controversial.[1] The first is that something is wrong when a society imprisons as many people as the United States now does. According to a widely published columnist, George Will, the rate of imprisonment was about 100 per 100,000 Americans until the 1970s. Since then the rate has shot up, to the point where "700 per 100,000" are now in prison; "America," Will reported in 2013, "has nearly 5 percent of the world's population but almost 25 percent of its prisoners."[2] It is possible, of course, that these figures are just where they ought to be, or even too low. When a professed conservative such as Will takes them to be alarming, however, there seems little need to defend the assumption that something is amiss.

The second assumption is that the principle of fair play underpins the justification of legal punishment. This assumption is clearly controversial, for only a few scholars nowadays justify punishment in terms of fair play.[3] For present purposes, however, I shall simply point to the defenses I have offered elsewhere and respond to criticisms of the fair-play approach only in passing.[4] In effect, I shall be presenting an oblique defense of this approach by demonstrating how it provides a helpful way of addressing the problem of excessive incarceration. In doing so, I shall also address the concern that democratic societies are especially prone to this problem because of their tendency to foster what has come to be known as *penal populism*. My argument is that democracy leads to mass imprisonment only when an otherwise democratic polity neglects what Albert Dzur calls the "moral dimension" of democracy: "Because citizens are lawgivers as well as law abiders, they have a special obligation in a republic to be vigilant to the possibility that their laws are unfairly burdening some over others, that their laws are exclusionary or discriminatory."[5] Dzur makes no explicit reference to the principle of fair play here or elsewhere in his book, but I hope to show that the vigilance he calls for requires attention to that principle.

Analyzing Excessive Incarceration

From a purely analytical point of view, there seem to be four possible reasons for excessive incarceration. These are:

1. Too many people are committing crimes.
2. Too many activities count as criminal.
3. Too many criminals are imprisoned.
4. Too many prisoners are imprisoned for too long.

Any one of these reasons, or any combination of them, could account for overimprisonment, as a brief elaboration should make clear.

First, there is a sense in which the statement "too many people are committing crimes" is self-evidently true: even one crime is a crime too many. If we proceed from some sense of what a normal or tolerable level of crime is, however, we can make realistic judgments of whether we have reason to worry that too many people are committing crimes. If such judgments are warranted, we then need to ask why so many are engaging in criminal activity, and one possibility is that some kind of social failure is at work. This could be a failure of prevention in the straightforward sense of not putting enough police on the streets, for example, or not training them properly. Or it could be a failure to cultivate the appropriate attitudes of respect for law and other persons through family discipline, civic education, and other forms of socialization. Or it could be a failure to provide sufficient opportunities for people to live a decent life without resorting to crime. In any or all of these ways, a society may unwittingly contribute to the high crime rates that lead to high rates of incarceration.

The second analytical possibility—and probably the one scholars most frequently cite—is that too many activities are classified as criminal. The leading example of this tendency "to criminalize too much and to punish too many," as Douglas Husak contends, is "the crime of illicit drug possession."[6] "Nearly one of every five prisoners in America," he notes, "is behind bars for a nonviolent drug offense."[7] Simply repealing the laws that make the possession of various drugs illicit would apparently lead to a significant drop in the rate of incarceration. But repealing such laws is not a simple matter. In addition to the problem of persuading legislators to take steps that may make them appear to be "soft on crime," there is the difficulty of determining exactly what the law ought and ought not to proscribe. This is a difficulty, though, that anyone who attributes mass incarceration to excessive criminalization must face. At the least, we should acknowledge that the spirit of fair play cannot countenance much harsher sentences for the possession of a relatively inexpensive drug, such as crack cocaine, than for its possession in purer and more expensive forms.

To be sure, conviction of a criminal offense need not entail a prison sentence. There are alternatives, such as probation, community service, and restitution to the offender's victims.[8] That is why the third possible reason for excessive incarceration is that too many criminals are imprisoned. Instead of locking up so many of them, perhaps we would do better to punish offenders in another way.[9] Here, though, we face the difficulty of determining what kinds of crimes warrant what kinds of punitive responses—of how to make the punishment fit the crime, in the standard phrase. Hardly anyone would say that supervised community service is proper punishment for a serial killer or that a prison term is fitting for someone who steals an apple from a store (setting aside possible three-strikes-and-you're out complications).[10] There are plenty of hard cases between these extremes, however, and some principled means of sorting them out will be required if we are to reduce incarceration.

Similar considerations bear on the fourth possibility. If we believe that excessive incarceration is largely the result of too many prisoners being imprisoned for too long, then we will need to find some way to determine the proper length of the sentences that attach to the various crimes warranting imprisonment. We will also need reasons for deciding whether determinate sentencing or mandatory-minimum sentences or three-strikes-and-you're-out laws, all of which may boost the length of prison terms, are justified. We will need, in short, a theory of criminal law and punishment.

Such a theory will not provide straightforward answers to every practical question that arises with regard to mass incarceration. No theory can tell us exactly how many days, months, or years is condign punishment for a certain criminal. Theories do provide necessary guidance, however, perhaps most notably by focusing our attention on a certain consideration, such as one or the other of those venerable rivals, deterrence or retribution, or by promising a harmonious blend of the two. In the remainder of this chapter, I shall try to show how the principle of fair play provides such guidance. In particular, I shall try to show how it grounds a theory of criminal law and punishment that is broadly retributive, communicative, and sensitive to democratic considerations. This last point is important because of the previously mentioned worry that democracy, in the form of penal populism, is somehow to blame for mass incarceration. Indeed, all but the first of the four analytical possibilities I have traced may well stem from the popularity of "get tough" policies as responses to crime.[11] If so, then it will be necessary "to educate democracy," as Tocqueville said, in order to resolve the problem of mass incarceration.[12] Reinforcing the value of fair play is essential to this education.

Crime, Punishment, and Fair Play

As children are quick to learn, any activity that requires cooperation is likely to give rise to complaints of unfairness. Sometimes the complaint will be about the unfairness of those who do not do their part; at other times it will focus on the supposedly unfair distribution of the benefits that cooperation produces. In either case the core idea is that cooperative activities provide benefits to the participants, with the benefits ranging from the pleasure of playing a game to those of sharing in the profits of a commercial enterprise or enjoying the protection afforded by a system of mutual defense. These benefits are not without costs, however, and those who participate in the activity are expected to bear a fair share of its burdens. Punishment enters the picture because cooperative endeavors usually produce the desired benefits even if some of the participants shirk their responsibilities. To prevent these potential free riders from taking advantage of the cooperative efforts of others, the participants invoke the threat of punishment. When the threat is not successful, then actual punishment is justified because the offenders have violated the principle of fair play.

For this account of fair play to provide a plausible theory of legal punishment, we must be able to conceive of a polity as a cooperative enterprise— in John Rawls's words, as "a fair system of cooperation over time, from one generation to the next."[13] To some extent this is to conceive of the polity as an ideal, and some countries will fall so far short of the ideal that we cannot reasonably judge their oppressed and exploited subjects to be participants in cooperative practices that entail duties of fair play. To the extent that the rule of law is in force, however, we can hold that a country's people are receiving the benefits of a cooperative enterprise and owe it to their fellow citizens to bear a fair share of the burdens of the enterprise—that is, to obey the law.[14] Everyone will find that obeying the law is at least occasionally burdensome, but good citizens will not leave it to others to shoulder this burden while they ride free. To assure these citizens that their cooperative efforts will not be in vain, those who break the law should be punished.

Much more needs to be said to fill out and defend this sketch of fair-play theory, but I can touch on only two points here. One is that violations of the law are not equal in weight or character. There is a difference between civil and criminal disobedience, for instance, that any theory of punishment should recognize. There is also a significant difference between offenses that are straightforward failures to play fair, such as tax cheating, and crimes such as murder, rape, and robbery. Fair-play theory can acknowledge these differences, however, while insisting that every crime is in part a crime of unfairness—a failure to restrain one's conduct in ways necessary for the success of "a fair system of cooperation over time, from one generation to the next." Although the severity of the punishment should match the gravity of the crime, it is the offense against fair play that justifies the legal authorities in administering the punishment. Some wrongs are wrongs regardless of what the law says, of course, and others are wrong only because the law says so. We need law and legal authorities to define and pronounce wrongs of both kinds, however, lest we face the "inconveniencies" of the state of nature, with its "irregular and uncertain exercise of the power every man has of punishing the transgressions of others,"[15] or the hazards of a society riven by blood feuds and the private enforcement of unsettled norms.

The second point to note is that fair-play theory is both retributive and communicative. It is retributive because punishment is a way of paying back those who do not play fair. Beyond retribution, fair play also calls for the communication of disapproval to the offender, in part as a way of reinforcing the importance to all participants of respecting the rules, but also in hopes of encouraging the offender to regret the wrong done and repair the damaged relationship with the law-abiding participants in the practice.[16] This is to say that fair-play theory not only has the backward-looking aspect characteristic of retributive approaches to punishment, which insist that punishment should be imposed only on those who have broken the law; it also has a forward-looking aspect usually associated with consequentialist approaches. That is, fair-play theory holds that punishment must serve to maintain the polity as a fair system of cooperation under law—or, more likely, to move the polity closer to that ideal.

That is a point to be elaborated shortly. First, though, it will be useful to apply this sketch of the argument from fair play to the four analytical considerations set out in the previous section. In doing so, I will be relying on the example of fair play in sports. Whether games and sports are suitably analogous to politics and law is a topic I turn to in the following section.

Regarding the first consideration—that is, the possibility that too many crimes are being committed—the straightforward application of the principle of fair play suggests that crimes are like violations of the rules of a game. If we find that the play of the game is suffering because too many players are in the penalty box, or suspended, or outright expelled from the sport, then we may want to know why so many players are opening themselves to sanctions—and jeopardizing the sport as a whole—by violating the rules. If it seems that they are simply cheating in order to gain an unfair advantage for themselves by free-riding on the cooperative efforts of others, then we will need to take the kinds of preventive steps I mentioned earlier—that is, stepped-up policing of the game and efforts to cultivate the sense of sportsmanship or fair play on which the game depends.[17] But we should also consider whether there may be something wrong with the rules themselves. There may be some rule, for example, that works systematically to the advantage of some players or teams, and the disadvantage of others, but is not important to the game itself. A case in point could be a game in which the players must equip themselves and only the wealthy can afford the most advanced equipment, thus giving them a significant advantage while playing. If we find that violations of the rules increase because less affluent players or teams are trying to compensate for their disadvantage, we should consider whether a change in the rules regarding equipment may be in order. Fair play is largely a matter of respecting the rules, to be sure, but we should not overlook the possibility that rules may be more or less encouraging of fair play.

In the case of the second analytical consideration, we may think of the possibility that too many activities are counted as criminal by way of an analogy with a sport that imposes too many rules on its players. Sports leagues and associations typically regulate the kind of clothing and gear players may wear, for example, and they do so in some cases for reasons closely related to the play of the game itself—not allowing football players to wear clothing studded with metal spikes or baseball pitchers to wear mirrors that reflect light into the batters' eyes—and in other cases for reasons that have little or no bearing on its play. Some clothing regulations aim at insuring that players project what the league officials think is the proper image; others ban clothing that advertises a product not approved by, or contributing to the coffers of, the league. Players who break these rules have been penalized in various ways for their activities, even though the activities seem to have no bearing on the play of the game. Is this fair? Are the nonconformist players taking unfair advantage of the players who conform to the regulations? Or would the sport benefit if rules that are not truly necessary to the play of the game were eliminated? Is it possible that an excess of rules—especially rules that seem petty, trivial, or pointless—will in fact undermine the sport by leading players to lose respect for the rules of the game? If the answer to these last two questions is "yes," then the rules in question should be abolished.[18]

What of the third analytical consideration—that is, the possibility that too many criminals are being imprisoned? In this case the analogy with a game raises questions about the severity of offenses and penalties. There are many offenses that occur inadvertently in the course of play, usually called "fouls," and in some cases players are allowed to accumulate fouls until they reach a set number, at which point they have "fouled out" and are expelled from the game. But some fouls are considered worse than others, such as intentional fouls, and some intentional fouls—flagrant fouls, in particular—may be cause for immediate ejection from the game and perhaps suspension from future games. There are also offenses against the referees, umpires, and officials who supervise the play of the game to make sure that the rules are followed—offenses that can pose a direct threat to fair play. It is no surprise, then, that those who govern sports leagues and associations devote considerable attention to determining the appropriate penalties for the various offenses that arise in the course of play. Nor is it surprising that the gauge they typically employ is the tendency of the penalty to assure the fair play of the game.

This same point carries over to the final consideration, which is that too many prisoners may be imprisoned for too long. In the case of sports, the question is not only whether some rule breakers are treated unfairly but also whether they are punished too severely for the good of the sport itself. Gambling presents a case in point. Both players and spectators need to believe in the fair play of the game, but it is difficult to sustain that belief when there are reasonable suspicions of "point shaving" or attempts to "throw"—that is, deliberately lose—a game or match in exchange for money from gamblers. As a result, sports organizations typically have rules that limit the gambling of those involved in the sport, or even prohibit contact with gamblers. Violations of these rules have led to suspensions for lengthy periods, even to the point of banishment for life. The result may be to promote confidence in the fair play of the game, but there also may be reason to question the justice of the sanctions imposed on people who may have failed to understand or appreciate what they were doing—as in the case of "Shoeless Joe" Jackson of baseball's notorious Chicago "Black Sox" Scandal of 1919. There are also reasons to question the wisdom, and fairness, of penalties that remove excellent players from competition. Surely those who grievously violate the rules deserve punishment; that is the retributive aspect of fair play. But they should be punished in a way, and to an extent, that holds the promise of restoring the offenders, when possible, to the status of full participants in the game. That is part of the communicative aspect of fair play.

This last point suggests a direct connection to one controversial question about what constitutes fair or unfair treatment of criminal offenders. I refer here to the question of whether convicted felons should lose their voting rights while serving their sentences, and perhaps even forever. Fair-play theorists may differ on the justice of disenfranchising felons while they are in prison, but they will hold that fairness requires the restoration of voting rights to those who have served their time. Again, this is in keeping with the communicative aspect of fair-play theory. Those who have paid their debts to society—and presumably learned to appreciate the importance of respecting the rule of law—should be restored to full citizenship in the polity. I return to this point below, when I defend disenfranchisement while imprisoned as an appropriate form of civic punishment.

This one example, however, is hardly typical of what the fair-play approach to the four analytical considerations reveals. In most cases, the principle of fair play does not supply a clear and distinct answer to the questions that follow from these considerations. But it does provide a unified approach to these questions that concentrates on the need to establish and enforce rules, and punish those who break them, in order to secure the fair play of the game. This still leaves us, though, with the question of whether this approach has any real bearing on law and punishment in the world beyond the sports arena.

Fair Play and the Polity

The question, in short, is whether the analogy between games and legal systems is sound. After all, one might object, the polity is not a game. The kinds of games I have been discussing take place within the larger framework of a legal order, which means that the legal order cannot be understood simply as a game itself. If someone playing ice hockey stabs an opponent with a knife, he has certainly failed to play fair; but we will not be content with sending him to the penalty box or even expelling him from the game. Justice requires a legal response in this case, not one governed by the rules of hockey. Moreover, the paradigm cases of crime—assault, robbery, rape, murder—are not simply violations of the rules or failures of fair play. To think of them as analogous to cheating in a game is to misunderstand them altogether.[19]

These are serious objections. Before responding to them directly, though, it is important to note the ways in which the analogy is illuminating. One way is that respect for the rules is vital to both the play of a game and the survival of a polity. There may be political and legal systems in which brute force seems to be the prevailing cause of obedience, but even tyrants rely on some degree of respect for their authority. Besides, in any system that professes to follow the rule of law, respect for the rules themselves is necessary. They need not be regarded as sacred or immutable, but neither should the citizens dismiss the rules out of hand as nothing more than arbitrary commands or regulations. When laws encourage that kind of attitude, they stand in need of reform.

A second strength of the analogy between games and legal systems is that the communicative aspect of rules and rule enforcement is vital to both. Laws are guides to conduct, and they cannot serve that purpose if they are not communicated to the people whose conduct they are supposed to guide. That is why Thomas Aquinas included *promulgation* among the defining features of law.[20] Punishment, too, serves a communicative function, as I have noted. So much is as true of polities as it is of games.

A third point of analogy—and one with particular significance for democratic theory—is that both games and legal systems rely on the ideal of equality. In competitive games, we do not expect that the competitors always will be equally matched. We do want them to have an equal chance to display their talents, however, as the familiar metaphor of the level playing field attests. The same is true within legal systems, where the ideal is for everyone to be equal before (or in the eyes of) the law. In neither games nor legal systems is the ideal always achieved, to be sure, and in some cases the actuality is a travesty of the ideal. But we can only recognize it as a travesty if we have the ideal to animate and inspire us.

These points connect to the principle of fair play in two ways. First, they represent aspects of that principle. To play fair is to treat participants as equally worthy of respect qua participants in a cooperative, rule-governed enterprise and to communicate to them both what the rules are and the consequences of violating them. Second, the three points of analogy indicate the *public* aspect of fair play. Rules and laws are matters of public concern. They cannot guide conduct and contribute to the play of the game, or the good order of a polity, if they are not made public. Furthermore, they benefit from being *made publicly*—a point I return to in the conclusion to this chapter.

But what of the two objections to the analogy on which fair-play theory rests that I mentioned earlier? The short answer—I have offered longer ones elsewhere[21]—is that the analogy need not be exact. It is true that the political and legal system must be larger and more encompassing than any of the games that take place within its boundaries. But that means that we should think of the polity as a special kind of game—that is, as a *super-* or *meta*-game that encompasses and governs other games and activities. It is a cooperative practice nevertheless, even though we may occasionally need to think of it as a meta-practice that is a necessarily public matter.[22]

The second point in defense of the analogy has to do with the nature of crime. Some crimes, according to the objection, are indeed violations of fair play. Tax evasion is a standard example, and some would include *mala prohibita* offenses in general.[23] For *mala in se* offenses, however, considerations of fair play are simply beside the point. My short answer is to concede that fair play does not capture the full wrongfulness of murder, rape, robbery, and assault, but to insist that it need not do so. What fair play does is to justify the *legal* punishment of the wrongdoers, whose actions not only injure their specific victims but threaten the cooperative order in general. That is why punishment is in the hands of "the authorities." Moreover, considerations of fair play can also help us to understand how some failures to play fair are more serious than others. The basketball player who intentionally fouls an opponent deserves a penalty; the player who flagrantly fouls an opponent deserves a harsher penalty; the player who pulls a gun on an opponent deserves not only an extremely harsh penalty from the game's officials but also punishment under the laws of the meta-practice. There is a violation of fair play in each instance, but the violation is progressively more serious in the latter two instances because the offender acts in such a way as to make it difficult or impossible for his opponent to continue to participate in the game—or even in the meta-practice of which the game is a part. Fair play may not tell us everything we need to know about an offense, but it tells us enough to justify legal punishment and to give us some sense of why some crimes are worse than others.

Democracy, Fair Play, and Imprisonment

What, though, does this talk of games and fair play have to do with the topics of this volume, democratic theory and excessive incarceration? One answer is that fair-play considerations help to explain why we are right to worry about the rates of imprisonment in the United States, and perhaps elsewhere, these days. For we have reason to believe that we are falling short of the standards implicit in the principle of fair play. When rates of incarceration are as high as they have been recently, we must ask how reasonable it is to regard the United States as a cooperative practice. Fair-play theory contains critical and aspirational elements, in other words, that point toward an ideal of a fully fair practice and demand attention to the ways in which a practice, including the meta-practice of the polity, falls short of that ideal. Mass incarceration is evidence that there is much to criticize in the current practice of criminal law in the United States.

Such criticism should lead us back to the four analytical possibilities I raised earlier. My claim is that fair play can help us to formulate responses to the problems that arise in all four cases. Are too many crimes being committed? Yes, certainly, but it is far from clear that spending more money on policing is the only answer. More needs to be done to encourage potential offenders to play fair by obeying the law and to provide them with opportunities to participate more fully, and fairly, in their society. Before we punish someone, as the philosopher T. H. Green long ago remarked, we should be sure that "the social organization in which a criminal has lived and acted is one that has given him a fair chance of not being a criminal."[24] Among other things, steps should be taken to reduce recidivism; for if it is true that too many crimes are being committed, it is also true that the same people are committing many of them. From the standpoint of fair-play theory, a particularly promising effort to reduce recidivism is the "social enterprise approach" sponsored in the United Kingdom by the Royal Society for the Arts, which aims to engage prisoners in paid work for social enterprises while they are in custody, then to continue their employment in a supervised Transition Zone before their full release into society.[25]

What of the other analytical considerations? Are too many activities classified as criminal? Yes, certainly, to the point where the criminalization of activities that do not amount to violations of fair play is probably undermining respect for law. Laws against gambling are a case in point, and especially so when they exist alongside state-sponsored lotteries. If we want to discourage people from risking their money on wagers, we should rely on education rather than coercion—and avoid the hypocrisy of encouraging them to take their chances in public lotteries all the while. Hypocrisy and unfairness also come quickly to mind with regard to drug laws, and their highly unequal enforcement, in the United States.[26]

Are too many convicted criminals imprisoned, as the third consideration asks? Yes, because there are other forms of punishment that are likely to do more to help criminals comprehend the cooperative nature of society and their duties of fair play. Community service is especially worthy of consideration, as is service that can provide some restitution to the particular victims of an offender's crimes.[27] And finally, are too many prisoners imprisoned for too long? Yes again, because of mandatory-minimum sentences and laws such as three strikes that do little or nothing to restore criminals to the status of law-abiding citizens—and less than nothing to promote fairness in the form of keeping the punishment in proportion to the offense. There is more, obviously, to be said to clarify and defend every one of these responses, but the point for now is that fair play provides the orientation we need as we work toward the answers.

This orientation is complementary, moreover, to democratic theory. Worries about penal populism have some basis in fact, in my view, but only to the extent that a society is democratic in a simplistic and perhaps corrupt way. On the simplistic view, democracy is merely a matter of majority rule, no matter how majority opinion is formed or what course it takes. Taking this view to its extreme, today's majority could vote to deny the franchise henceforward to those in today's minority, or even to enslave them. No democratic theorist endorses this simplistic view, however, because it fails to respect the fundamental democratic commitment to equality, here understood as a right to the equal consideration of everyone's interests.[28] If the problem of mass incarceration is in large part the result of penal populism, it is because those who make the laws are playing to an audience that is insufficiently concerned with equal consideration—and therefore with playing fair. In these circumstances, it is reasonable to speak of the corruption of democracy.

A well-functioning democracy, in contrast, is a cooperative enterprise. It must have rules, and it must have means of dealing with those who break the rules, including punishment. But the rules must be fair and so must the punishment. One sign of their fairness is that they must aim to do only what is necessary to secure and strengthen the cooperative enterprise. That means, among other things, that punishment must proceed in a manner that is likely to restore the offenders to full participation in the democracy. Those who have paid their debts to society by undergoing punishment that communicates to them and their fellow citizens the importance of abiding by the laws of a cooperative society ought to be able to regain the status of full citizenship. Mass incarceration and high rates of recidivism are signs that democracy in the United States is not proceeding in this manner—and is not, therefore, the cooperative practice it ought to be.

This claim turns on a distinction between two conceptions of democracy. One is the conception on which I have been drawing, which takes democracy to be a cooperative venture aiming to realize a common good; the other conception, and perhaps the more familiar and apparently realistic one, takes democracy to be a kind of machine for aggregating the personal preferences of the populace. The two conceptions share a commitment to equality and fairness, but what counts as fairness differs from one conception to the other; and only the first generates a sense of fair play robust enough to make clear the undemocratic character of mass incarceration.

The preference-aggregation conception of democracy is well known from the writings of Joseph Schumpeter and others who draw an analogy between economic and electoral competition.[29] As they see it, individual citizens bring their preferences into the political arena in much the same way that consumers enter the economic marketplace, with the primary difference being the kind of currency in use. Otherwise, candidates and parties compete for the voter's attention and support much as producers of goods compete for the consumer's money. Once in office, successful candidates do what they can to satisfy those who voted for them and to attract new supporters whenever possible, all in the hope of being returned to office at the next election. Not every voter wins, of course, in the sense of seeing her preferred candidates elected to office; but everyone eligible to vote at least has a chance to register her preferences, which the political system aggregates first by way of electoral results and second by way of the policies and laws enacted by those who win office.

What makes this preference-aggregation view a conception of democracy is its commitment to regarding everyone's preferences equally. You may care enough to go to the polls and vote while I do not, but your vote would count for no more than mine were I to cast one. Besides, my failure to vote is itself a statement of my preferences: you prefer voting to other activities available at the time, but I prefer other activities to voting. To be sure, you may exercise more influence over the outcome than I do even if I cast my vote, but that is probably because you expend more of your other resources—time, persuasive power, and perhaps money—than I do in the attempt to influence how others vote. So far as votes themselves are concerned, in a majority-rule system you and I are equal not only to each other but to every other potential voter.[30] In that sense, the preference-aggregation conception is clearly democratic.

It also reflects a sense of fairness. Just as fraud, theft, collusion, and other violations of fair competition in the economic marketplace must be guarded against, so must electoral fraud and political corruption. If the system is to aggregate personal preferences in a way that treats everyone equally, then someone will have to hold the authority to proscribe cheating and to punish those who do not play fair. Fair play in politics thus requires neutral officials to ensure that the competition takes place on the equivalent of a level playing field. Political competition shares this reliance on fair play with competition in both the marketplace and the sporting field.

What, then, are the implications of this preference-aggregation conception of democracy for the understanding of mass incarceration? The answer turns entirely on the preferences of the voters. Whether rates of incarceration are or are not excessive, according to this conception, will depend upon what the voters hope to accomplish by imprisoning offenders. Economic considerations surely will come into play here, for anyone who believes that prisons are necessary or desirable responses to crime will want them to operate efficiently. Other things being equal, the voters will prefer not to go to the extra expense of building more prisons to accommodate more prisoners. But they may also decide that the perceived gains in personal safety or the satisfaction of exacting retribution are worth the extra expense. These preferences may well lead them to vote for politicians who continue to insist on the tough-on-crime policies that lead to mass incarceration. Penal populism is thus fully at home within the preference-aggregation conception of democracy.

Taking democracy to be a cooperative venture in pursuit of a common good, however, produces a much different result. On this conception, the voter is expected to act as a citizen rather than a consumer, and democracy is less a matter of eliciting personal preferences than of evoking civic judgments. The two considerations, however, are not mutually exclusive. Like the preference-aggregation conception, the cooperative-venture understanding of democracy holds that everyone's interests are to be accorded equal consideration, and every member of the polity should have opportunities to express his preferences. But the cooperative-venture conception also holds that citizens should look beyond their personal preferences to what is good or best for the polity as a whole. This conception thus accords with the belief that every citizen holds office or, as John Stuart Mill put the point, stands in a position of public trust.[31]

Both conceptions share, as I have noted, a commitment not only to equality but to fairness. On either conception, democracy requires electoral competition, and that competition must proceed in accordance with regulations that ensure the fair conduct of elections. However, the cooperative-venture conception does not stop at this point; for competition itself must be understood as an element of what is a fundamentally cooperative enterprise. We may be tempted to think of competition in the marketplace or the sporting arena as a matter of winning at all costs, but it is nevertheless true that unbounded competition will lead to the destruction of both the market and the sport. If all that matters is winning, then there is no reason not to cheat and steal at every opportunity, and even to dispense with those whose office is to protect personal property or to uphold the rules of the game. In such cases, though, property rights will count for nothing and the game will no longer be recognizable as baseball or cricket or football. In such cases, both markets and sports will degenerate into something resembling Hobbes's state of nature. To avoid this outcome, the participants must find ways to underpin their competition with a cooperative commitment to playing fair—a commitment that includes the appointment of officials whose duty is to elaborate and enforce the rules of fair play.

This cooperative commitment also includes a commitment to regard the other participants as contributors to a common enterprise. We have a duty to treat them fairly, therefore, and encourage reciprocity on their parts. In a democracy, according to the cooperative-venture conception, there is a corresponding duty to regard every member of the polity as a potential contributor to the cooperative enterprise of self-government. There is also a duty to encourage reciprocity and to promote the virtues of citizenship among the members. In Rawls's terms this is "a natural duty of civility," which requires citizens, among other things, "not to invoke the faults of social arrangements as a too ready excuse for not complying with them, nor to exploit inevitable loopholes in the rules to advance our interests."[32] In order to sustain the cooperative enterprise, in other words, we must play fair even when personal advantage would have us do otherwise. Because we cannot count on everyone always to play fair, we need the police and judges and other officials to provide the security necessary to assure those who are willing to abide by the rules that their cooperative efforts will not be wasted. But we also need to do what we can to promote Rawls's natural duty of civility. Other things being equal, willing cooperation is better than coerced.

Another implication of the cooperative-venture conception of democracy has to do with the rules that govern the enterprise. In a democracy, these rules are themselves a matter of public choice, and the duty of civility extends to the framing of these rules. Before we enact a law, then, we must be sure that it is a law that does not impose an unfair burden on other members of the polity. In the context of this chapter, this means that we must determine what is to count as a crime in this light. The answer is clear enough in the standard cases of assault, murder, rape, and robbery, for we do not impose unfair burdens on our fellow citizens when we proscribe those actions. Indeed, the unfair burdens would fall on the victims of those crimes, whose suffering would make it difficult, at best, to continue to play the part of the cooperative citizen. There are many other activities, however, that democratically elected legislatures have outlawed even though these activities fall outside the standard cases. Whether they should or should not be outlawed is a matter to decide, on the cooperative-venture conception of democracy, in light of their bearing on fair play and civility. Some of these cases should be easy to settle. Suborning witnesses and threatening judges are actions that strike at the rule of law, and any burden that anyone suffers as a result of their proscription is hardly an unfair burden. *Mala prohibita* offenses, such as those involving traffic and environmental regulations, are likely to be justified as a means of ensuring cooperation in a collective enterprise; but if it becomes clear that the proscription in question places an unfair burden on some members of the polity, then either the proscription should be altered or the activity in question should be allowed.

From the standpoint of the cooperative-venture conception, in short, the question is not whether the aggregated preferences of the people, either directly or through their elected representatives, should or should not designate a certain activity as criminal. The question, instead, is whether the activity in question inhibits the fair play of the democratic game. If it does, then the question becomes one of efficacy—in other words, whether the criminal sanction is the best way to deal with those actions that interfere with democratic fair play or whether there are better alternatives. If the activity in question poses no threat to democratic fair play, then it should not be proscribed. In some cases this approach leads to straightforward decisions. For instance, anyone who proposes to make a crime of some form of sexual activity between consenting adults would have to show that the activity in question poses a serious threat to democracy understood as a cooperative venture, and that will be a difficult case to make. In many cases, though, the decision will not be at all straightforward. One could argue, for instance, that the production or consumption of any drug that renders people incapable of fair play or of carrying out their duties of civility should be a crime. Couched in those terms, the proposal is perfectly acceptable under the cooperative-venture conception of democracy. But those who are charged with determining what is to count as a crime would then have to make an informed judgment as to which drugs, if any, do in fact have those antidemocratic and unfair propensities. Once they have identified such drugs, if any, they would then have to make the further determination of whether the criminal sanction is the appropriate way to deal with the problem and, if it is, whether a blanket prohibition or a more limited response is better. In the case of alcohol, there is little doubt that its consumption at some point inhibits civility and the sense of fair play. Laws against public drunkenness and enhanced punishment for those who harm or endanger others while drunk, though, seem likely to address the problem more effectively than outright prohibition of the production, sale, or consumption of alcohol. Nor would such laws place an unfair burden on anyone, such as those who consume alcohol without endangering anyone or threatening democratic fair play. Extending this reasoning to drugs that are widely proscribed at present would almost certainly result in a dramatic reduction of drug crimes and a similar reduction in the prison population. Such a change by itself would not be enough to solve the problem of mass incarceration in the United States, but it surely would be a major step in that direction.

In this way the conception of democracy as a cooperative venture reinforces my earlier point about the connection between fair play and the reduction of the number of actions and activities that should be designated criminal. The conception also speaks to the concern that too many criminals are being imprisoned and too many are being imprisoned for too long. If the polity is a cooperative venture, then it is perfectly reasonable to discourage its members from engaging in actions that harm those whose law-abiding conduct sustain the venture or otherwise threaten to undermine it. It is also reasonable to punish those who have, despite the discouragement, committed such acts. Except in extraordinary cases, however, the aim should be to restore the offenders to full participation in the democratic venture, not to banish them forever. Again, there will be difficult judgments to make about whether imprisonment is the proper sentence for certain offenses and, if it is, how long the term should be. Even so, there is little doubt that the lengthy sentences that have contributed to the explosion of the prison population in the United States cannot be justified under the cooperative-venture conception of democracy. Such sentences unfairly burden those on whom they are imposed, and they do nothing to restore the offender to a place in society as a full participant in the cooperative venture.

With that point in mind, I return briefly to the controversy over the disenfranchisement of felons.[33] One issue here concerns whether imprisonment for a criminal offense should ever carry with it the loss of the offender's vote. In my view, as I stated earlier, it should. There are some cases—treason, electoral fraud, and attempting to bribe officers of the law are clear examples—in which loss of the vote seems appropriate because the offender has directly threatened the cooperative venture of the polity. But depriving the offender of the franchise is also fitting in the case of any offense serious enough to be considered a felony. Even if the offense is arson or burglary or some other crime that has no direct bearing on the conduct of elections or the functions of the government, it nevertheless constitutes a significant violation of fair play and civility. In addition to his imprisonment, then, the criminal should suffer a loss of status. He has breached a civic trust, and it is only fair that he surrender his vote as a result. This is not to say that the convicted criminal should be treated as an outcast who is altogether excluded from the polity. But neither should he be regarded as a member in good standing. In keeping with the communicative aspect of punishment, this diminution of his civic status should be reflected in the temporary loss of a fundamental civic or political right. Once again, however, the aim should be to restore him to full participation in the democratic venture, which entails the restoration of the franchise when he has completed his sentence. To do otherwise would be to impose an unfair burden on him while doing nothing to promote the spirit of democratic fair play among others.[34]

Fair Play and the Educated Democracy

Earlier in this chapter I quoted Tocqueville's remark, in his introduction to the first volume of *Democracy in America*, that it is necessary to educate democracy. By this Tocqueville meant that, if we are to live in a society governed by the common people—as he thought was inevitable—then it behooves the leaders of society to take measures that will prepare the people to govern democratically. Put simply, this education must comprise not only the standard subjects taught in schoolhouses but also education in the responsibilities of democratic citizenship. For this latter sort of education, the schoolhouse would be insufficient. Other venues, such as the town meeting and the courthouse, where citizens would sit in jury duty, would help to complete this education in democracy.[35]

Another way to put Tocqueville's point is to say that democracy is a matter of self-government in two senses of that word. It is, first, self-government in the sense that the people rule. But this is not to be the kind of rule in which the people, as a collective, simply do whatever they please, so that democracy becomes the tyranny of the majority that Tocqueville feared. It must also be self-government in the sense that the people *govern* themselves—that is, exercise self-restraint—in a thoughtful, prudent manner. In the terms of this chapter, that self-restraint, or self-government, is largely a matter of respecting the rule of law—laws that are to be made publicly, to serve the public good—and the principle of fair play. But that is not to say that self-government is a kind of altruism. Every citizen has a right to care for her own interests and to demand equal consideration of those interests from her fellows. That much the cooperative-venture conception of democracy shares with the preference-aggregation model. But equality of consideration requires her to extend this same consideration to all of the others. When she votes or otherwise contributes to the making of laws and policies, then, the citizen is to do so in a way that accords this equal respect to all citizens. She must, in short, act on the principle of fair play by bearing her share of the burdens of social cooperation and imposing no more than a fair share on others.

Republican theory also contributes to an educated democracy through its traditional emphasis on vigilance. As Philip Pettit notes in an essay that brings republicanism to bear on issues in criminal law, a vigilant citizenry has long been held to be necessary to the health and safety of the body politic; for "the citizenry should be ever vigilant of public power and be ready to contest and challenge it at the slightest suspicion or sign of abuse."[36] To Pettit's observation I would add that the citizens' vigilance ought to be aimed not only at those who hold positions of formal authority but also at themselves. Citizenship itself is a kind of public office, and failure to play fair with one's fellow citizens should count as an abuse of public power. An educated democracy is one that takes the task of encouraging this kind of civic vigilance seriously. It will look, therefore, to its political, legal, and educational institutions—to these and other *civic* institutions— to foster a citizenry that is vigilant in maintaining fair play within the polity. In particular, to return to a passage of Albert Dzur's quoted at the beginning of this chapter, citizens must "be vigilant to the possibility that their laws are unfairly burdening some over others."[37] Their laws, that is, and the forms of punishment that support and follow from them, must respect the principle of fair play, and the citizenry must be self-policing in this regard.

As the evidence of excessive incarceration suggests, the United States is not the educated democracy it should be. There is reason, though, to hope and work for improvement. Particularly encouraging in this regard are the results of a "deliberative poll" on issues in criminal justice that James Fishkin and his colleagues conducted in England—results that showed an overall shift from simple get-tough-on-crime attitudes toward the more flexible and less harsh responses that criminologists tend to favor.[38] If this small experiment in educating democracy is truly indicative of what more thorough efforts could achieve, then there is reason to believe that penal populism need not be a lasting curse of democracy in America.

Another reason to be hopeful is the simple recognition that there are plenty of other democracies in the world, few of which seem to be following the United States' example with regard to mass incarceration. In 2006, for example, incarceration rates "across the developed world ... ranged from 36 per 100,000 (in Iceland) to 737 in the USA, with England and Wales, at a rate of 148, ... having one of the highest incarceration rates in the EU."[39] Exactly how to account for these differences is a matter I must leave to social scientists. But there are two points worth noting here, for both connect rather directly to fairness. The first is the single-member, simple-plurality system of electing representatives to most offices— national, state, and local—in the United States. This is not only a respect in which the United States differs from most other democracies; it also seems to be related to higher rates of incarceration than those found in democracies that employ proportional representation.[40] The single-member system also plays a large part in the artful redistricting that makes representation in the United States less than democratic or fair.[41]

The second point to note is that economic inequality in the United States is generally greater than in other advanced democracies—and the gap between rich and poor continues to grow.[42] Whether there is a direct connection between economic inequality and mass incarceration is not clear. It is clear, however, that the poor in the United States account for a disproportionately high percentage of both the victims of crime and of those who commit crimes.[43] If nothing else, these figures suggest that there are likely to be better ways to address the problems of crime—ways that speak to the fairness and cooperative nature of the polity—than that of locking up as many offenders as possible.

There is, of course, something paradoxical in taking the existence of proportional representation and lesser degrees of economic inequality in other democracies to be a hopeful sign for the United States. There are, after all, great obstacles in the way of the adoption of proportional representation or a reduction of economic inequality in the United States. Nevertheless, they provide focal points for those who would work to educate democracy in America. They also indicate that the fair-play approach has something to contribute to the practice as well as the theory of criminal justice.

Notes

1. For helpful comments on previous drafts of this chapter, I am grateful to R. A. Duff, S. E. Marshall, and the editors of this volume.

2. George Will, "Seeking Sense on Sentencing," *Richmond Times-Dispatch*, June 7, 2013, A11. Will's unattributed data are consistent with those published in the *Sourcebook of Criminal Justice Statistics* (www.albany.edu/sourcebook/pdf/t6132011. pdf). Will also notes that "African-Americans are 13 percent of the nation's population but 37 percent of the prison population, and one in three African-American men may spend time incarcerated." For more recent but no less alarming figures, see Jed Rakoff, "Mass Incarceration: The Silence of the Judges," *New York Review of Books* 62 (May 21, 2015): 14–17, at 17.

3. For example, Michael Davis, *To Make the Punishment Fit the Crime: Essays in the Theory of Criminal Justice* (Boulder, CO: Westview Press, 1992); John Finnis, "Retribution: Punishment's Formative Aim," *American Journal of Jurisprudence* 44 (1999): 91–103; Herbert Morris, "Persons and Punishment," *The Monist* 52, no. 4 (1968): 475–501; and George Sher, "Deserved Punishment Revisited" in his *Approximate Justice: Studies in Non-Ideal Theory* (Lanham, MD: Rowman & Littlefield, 1997), 165–180.

4. See my "Playing Fair with Punishment," *Ethics* 103, no. 4 (April 1993): 473–488, and "Punishment as Fair Play," *Res Publica* 14, no. 4 (2008): 259–275. Note also R. A. Duff, "The Incompleteness of 'Punishment as Fair Play': A Response to Dagger," *Res Publica* 14, no. 4 (2008): 277–281; and Matt K. Stichter, "Rescuing Fair-Play as a Justification for Punishment," *Res Publica* 16, no. 1 (2010): 73–81.

5. Albert Dzur, *Punishment, Participatory Democracy, and the Jury* (New York: Oxford University Press, 2012), 87.

6. Douglas Husak, *Overcriminalization: The Limits of the Criminal Law* (Oxford: Oxford University Press, 2008), 16.

7. Ibid., 16.

8. Whether restitution ought to be regarded as a form of punishment or as an alternative to it is a controversial matter. I defend the former position against advocates of the latter in "Restitution: Pure or Punitive?," *Criminal Justice Ethics* 10, no. 2 (1991): 29–39.

9. For the purposes of this chapter I ignore arguments holding that something other than punishment—therapy, perhaps, or a system of pure (rather than punitive) restitution to crime victims—is the proper way to treat criminals. For a leading example of the first sort of argument, see Karl Menninger, *The Crime of Punishment* (New York: Viking

Press, 1968); for the second, see Randy Barnett, "Restitution: A New Paradigm of Criminal Justice," *Ethics* 87, no. 4 (1977): 279–301.

10. It is also important to recognize that not all forms of incarceration are equivalent—for example, a year in solitary confinement in a "supermax" prison is hardly the same as a year in a minimum-security prison. The difference will not bear on the rate of incarceration, however, unless it turns out that some forms of imprisonment are more likely to encourage or discourage recidivism than others.

11. Even the first possibility may relate to penal populism. This could happen, as Ian Loader has remarked to me, if crime rates rise because get-tough policies soak up resources that might otherwise fund preventive work and agencies.

12. Alexis de Tocqueville, *Democracy in America*, trans. George Lawrence, ed. J. P. Mayer (Garden City, NY: Doubleday, 1969), 12.

13. Rawls, *Political Liberalism*, expanded ed. (New York: Columbia University Press, 2005), 15.

14. Whether this duty of fair play extends to matters of crime and punishment, especially with regard to those living in disadvantaged or unjust conditions, is a much-discussed question. For different responses from within the broad framework of fair-play theory, see Jeffrie G. Murphy, "Marxism and Retribution," *Philosophy and Public Affairs* 2, no. 3 (1973): 217–243, and Michael Davis, "Criminal Desert, Harm, and Fairness," in Davis, *To Make the Punishment Fit the Crime*, esp. 219–221. For more broadly retributive positions, see Okeoghene Odudu, "Retributivist Justice in an Unjust Society," *Ratio Juris* 16, no. 3 (2003): 416–431, and Stuart Green, "Just Deserts in Unjust Societies: A Case-Specific Approach," in R. A. Duff and S. P. Green (eds.), *Philosophical Foundations of Criminal Law* (Oxford: Oxford University Press, 2011).

15. John Locke, *Second Treatise of Government*, §127.

16. The importance of this communicative function to punishment, and to criminal law in general, is a point many philosophers have emphasized in recent years, notably R. A. Duff in his *Punishment, Communication, and Community* (Oxford: Oxford University Press, 2001). Other noteworthy statements of this point include Herbert Morris, "A Paternalistic Theory of Punishment," *American Philosophical Quarterly* 18, no. 16 (1981): 263–272, and Jean Hampton, "An Expressive Theory of Retribution," in W. Cragg (ed.), *Retribution and Its Critics* (Stuttgart: F. Steiner, Verlag, 1992).

17. Strictly speaking, those who seek an unfair advantage may be *parasites* rather than free riders. That is, the cheater is not only trying to *take advantage* of those who abide by the rules; he is also trying to *gain an advantage* over them. If successful, the cheater's actions will worsen the situation of his opponents in the game, whose fair play makes them vulnerable and his parasitical efforts possible. Free riders, by contrast, do not directly worsen the condition of others. On this distinction, see David Gauthier, *Morals by Agreement* (Oxford: Oxford University Press, 1987), 96. The cheater's situation in my example is complicated, however, in two ways. First, his cheating may not worsen the situation of his rule-following teammates; and second, his cheating may fail to worsen the situation of his opponents, who may win despite his violation of the rules. In these cases, it seems proper to refer to him as a free rider.

18. There will be cases, of course, in which clear answers to these questions will be hard to find, such as the one that led to the US Supreme Court's ruling in favor of Casey Martin in *PGA Tour, Inc. v. Martin* (2000). The initial question was whether Martin, a

professional golfer whose congenital leg disease made it painful for him to walk, should be allowed to use a golf cart while competing in the Professional Golf Association Tour, thereby exempting him from the requirement that competitors in these events walk from hole to hole throughout the course. Whether Martin's use of a cart would constitute an unfair advantage over the other competitors or fair compensation for his disability became a controversial question. The case also raised questions about the nature of golf itself. For discussion, see Michael Sandel, *Justice: What's the Right Thing to Do?* (New York: FSG, 2009), chap. 8.

19. This seems to be why Victor Tadros finds it "very difficult to believe that just punishment is based on unfairly benefiting from a system of rules"; see his *The Ends of Harm: The Moral Foundations of Criminal Law* (Oxford: Oxford University Press, 2011), 27. For perhaps the best statement of this objection, see R. A. Duff, *Trials and Punishments* (Cambridge: Cambridge University Press, 1986), 211–217.

20. According to Aquinas's definition, law is "an order of reason for the common good by one who has the care of the community, and promulgated"; *On Law, Morality, and Politics*, trans. R. J. Regan, 2nd ed. (Indianapolis: Hackett, 2002), 15.

21. See my "Republicanism and the Foundations of Criminal Law," in R. A. Duff and S. P. Green (eds.), *Philosophical Foundations of the Criminal Law* (Oxford: Oxford University Press, 2011), 61–64, and "Punishment as Fair Play," esp. 269–273.

22. Avihay Dorfman and Alon Harel make a similar point when they refer to government as an "integrative practice" in "The Case against Privatization," *Philosophy & Public Affairs* 41 (Winter 2013): 67–102, at 84.

23. But cf. Husak, who holds that fair play can "ground the wrongfulness of pure *mala prohibitiva* offenses" in only "a small number of cases" (*Overcriminalization*, 118–119).

24. Green, *Lectures on the Principles of Political Obligation*, §189 (Ann Arbor: University of Michigan Press, 1967 [1882]), 190.

25. See Rachel O'Brien, *RSA Transitions: A Social Enterprise Approach to Prison and Rehabilitation* (November 2011); available at www.thersa.org/globalassets/pdfs/rsa_transitions_report.pdf.

26. As noted, e.g., in Ekow N. Yankah, "Legal Vices and Civic Virtue: Vice Crimes, Republicanism, and the Corruption of Lawfulness," *Criminal Law and Philosophy* 7, no. 1 (2013): 80–81.

27. On this point, see my "Restitution, Punishment, and Debts to Society," in J. Hudson and B. Galaway (eds.), *Victims, Offenders, and Alternative Sanctions* (Lexington, MA: Lexington Books, 1980), 3–13.

28. For the link between democracy and the "principle of intrinsic equality," see Robert Dahl, *On Democracy* (New Haven, CT: Yale University Press, 1998), esp. chap. 6.

29. Schumpeter, *Capitalism, Socialism, and Democracy*, 3rd ed. (New York: Harper & Row, 1950), esp. chaps. 21–23.

30. Here I set aside the various complications of electoral systems in representative democracies, such as first-past-the-post elections and districts composed on something other than a one-person, one-vote basis, that give greater weight to some votes than to others. I also ignore eligibility requirements that prevent some people from voting at all.

31. Note in this regard Mill's claim that the citizen's vote "has no more to do with his personal wishes than the verdict of a juryman." Indeed, Mill went so far as to oppose

the secret ballot on the ground that every citizen should stand ready to take public responsibility for how he or she voted. Mill, *Considerations on Representative Government*, in Mill, *On Liberty and Other Essays* (Oxford: Oxford University Press), 353–355 (354 for the quoted passage).

32. Rawls, *A Theory of Justice*, rev. ed. (Cambridge, MA: Harvard University Press, 1999), 312. For development of this and related points, see my "Citizenship as Fairness: John Rawls's Conception of Civic Virtue," in *A Companion to Rawls*, ed. J. Mandle and D. Reidy (New York: Wiley, 2014), 297–311.

33. See, e.g., the symposium on "Crime and Citizenship," *Journal of Applied Philosophy*, 22, no. 3 (2005): 211–273.

34. The position I take here is identical in most respects to that which Mary Sigler advances in "Defensible Disenfranchisement," *Iowa Law Review* 99, no. 4 (2014): 1725–1744. Sigler, however, takes the disenfranchisement of imprisoned felons to be "a means of regulating electoral eligibility in a liberal-democratic polity" (1728) that serves as "a regulatory counterpart to the institution of criminal punishment" (1744); but I regard disenfranchisement itself as a form of punishment.

35. For elaboration of this argument, see Dzur, *Punishment, Participatory Democracy, and the Jury*, chap. 4: "The Jury as a Civic Schoolhouse."

36. Pettit, "Criminalization in Republican Theory," in R. A. Duff, L. Farmer, S. E. Marshall, M. Renzo, and V. Tadros (eds.), *Criminalization: The Political Morality of the Criminal Law* (Oxford: Oxford University Press, 2015), 136.

37. Dzur, *Punishment, Participatory Democracy, and the Jury*, 87.

38. Robert C. Luskin, James S. Fishkin, and Roger Jowell, "Considered Opinions: Deliberative Polling in Britain," *British Journal of Political Science* 32, no. 3 (2002): 455–487.

39. Nicola Lacey, *The Prisoner's Dilemma: Political Economy and Punishment in Contemporary Democracies* (Cambridge: Cambridge University Press, 2008), 27.

40. Ibid., 76. For the anomalous case of New Zealand, where the rate of incarceration increased after it switched from the single-member system to proportional representation, see Lacey, "The Prisoner's Dilemma and Political Systems: The Impact of Proportional Representation on Criminal Justice in New Zealand," *Victoria University of Wellington Law Review*, 42, no. 4 (2011): 615–638.

41. For evidence in support of this conclusion, see Douglas Amy, *Real Choices/New Voices: How Proportional Representation Could Revitalize American Democracy*, 2nd ed. (New York: Columbia University Press, 2002), passim.

42. Green, "Just Deserts in Unjust Societies," 374, cites several studies to this effect.

43. Ibid., 354–355.

CHAPTER 5 | A Democratic Theory
of Imprisonment

PETER RAMSAY

Introduction

There are many normative theories of state punishment. Almost none of
them derive a justification of the practice from specifically democratic
premises.[1] The need for a democratic theory of punishment is pressing because electoral politics has, in recent times, involved a race to the bottom
in criminal justice policy, resulting in more punitive penal rhetoric, more
criminal laws and more severe penalties for breaking them. It appears that
democratic politics has resulted in true mass incarceration in the United
States,[2] and unprecedentedly high levels of imprisonment in the United
Kingdom.[3]

The association between rising penal severity, populism and democracy is misleading. The phenomena of penal populism have occurred at a
time of falling political participation both in elections and more generally.
It is, therefore, a mistake to understand contemporary criminal justice
policy as being politically popular. It is better understood as one among
many symptoms of the unpopularity of politics and a decline in participation in public life.[4] Since penal populism is one aspect of the decline of
ordinary citizens' participation in the life of the state, its baleful effects
are unlikely to be improved by further excluding citizens from political
decision-making.[5] On the contrary, as others have persuasively argued,
there is good reason to think that penal severity will be moderated in
practice by encouraging greater citizen participation both in the criminal process,[6] and in the broader political deliberation about crime and
punishment.[7]

The potential of greater popular participation in criminal justice to lessen penal severity in practice is an important subject, but it is not my direct concern here. I want instead to explore the relation of democratic government and imprisonment *in principle*. I offer a sketch of a theory of justifiable imprisonment that adopts some of the insights of liberal penal theory but democratizes them by putting political equality at the heart of its penal rationale. It is only a sketch. It will need much more work to secure its claims. However, it is worth sketching this democratic theory because its implication is that the more seriously a society takes the idea of political equality as its guiding principle, the more limited will be its use of imprisonment, and the more it will move to eliminate imprisonment entirely. By the same token, the weakening of political equality, such as we have experienced in recent times, will tend to increase penal severity. The strengthening of political equality is, therefore, the key to reducing imprisonment.

In the first section, I indicate the core proposition of what I take to be the dominant school of *liberal* penal theory, and I identify the key problem it has in setting limits to the severity and extent of punishment. In the next section, I argue that all imprisonment constitutes an interference with political equality, an interference that amounts to a suspension of the political citizenship of the prisoner. In the following section I outline the very limited conditions in which such a suspension of political citizenship is nevertheless consistent with political equality. I provisionally call this theory of punishment "democratic retributivism." In the next section, I argue that democratic retributivism contains an inherent tendency to reduce and even to eliminate the need for imprisonment, a tendency that is lacking in liberal theory. The argument up to this point will be abstract and will seem merely idealistic. After that, therefore, I seek to show that appearances notwithstanding, democratic retributivism offers a realistic explanation of our recent experience of rapidly rising incarceration. The democratic theory only appears unrealistic in so far as we take for granted the recent de-democratization of our public life. In the last section I respond to two normative arguments that might be raised against the democratic theory I have outlined. First, I show why the democratic theory imposes the same limitations on the punishment of noncitizens as it does on the punishment of citizens. Second, I respond to a criticism of retributive theory in general, specifically the argument that retributivism is unjust because it judges concrete particular individuals by the standards of abstract universal citizens. I will argue that democratic retributivism, precisely because it is a theory of criminal justice, cannot escape this criticism entirely, but that a democratic penal system would not only radically mitigate its force, but also offer a solution to the problem that the criticism draws our attention to. In the final section, I suggest that a more precise name for this theory is "democratic retributive abolitionism." I outline democracy's logical tendency to bring the practice of incarceration by the state to an end, and the significant obstacles to realizing this tendency in practice. My focus throughout will be on how a democracy can justify *imprisoning* its citizens, although the theory has wider implications for state punishment in general that I will not explore here.

The Liberal Claim to Penal Minimalism

Liberal penal theories are dominated by the concerns of moral philosophy. They tend to set out from liberalism's most fundamental proposition: that individuals enjoy an equal dignity as moral agents which constitutes them as ends in themselves, as persons who cannot rightly be used or coerced as a mere means to collective social ends. Since the 1960s, penal theorists have moved away from utilitarianism, which justified punishment on the grounds of its good consequences in reducing future offending by deterrence, rehabilitation, or incapacitation. Utilitarian justifications claimed to be committed to the principle of parsimony—that there should be no more punishment than the amount necessary to maximize social welfare. However, utilitarian justifications encompassed the possibility that the status of individual persons as ends in themselves could be overridden for the greater good of society as a whole. The liberal commitment to respect the individual's dignity has led penal theorists to seek to ensure that the distribution of punishment is not unfair to the individual.[8] The dominant trend in recent moral philosophies of punishment has, therefore, been to limit punishment to only that which is proportionate to the seriousness of the offense,[9] or at least to punishment that is not disproportionate.[10] The seriousness of the offense is generally thought of as some combination of the harm done to victims and the culpability of the offender.

These retributive theories seek to ensure that the state respects the rights of offenders as persons, enjoying the status of an end in themselves, by giving them no more nor less than what they, as a result of their own conduct, deserve. By doing this, the law addresses offenders as rational moral agents capable of conforming their conduct to the law. Although the idea of moral desert continues to be criticized by some theorists,[11] while, by contrast, some others eschew any role for consequential justifications,[12] most contemporary penal theorists try to combine the two types of justification, seeing the idea of proportional punishment as a constraint on the pursuit of the consequential, utilitarian purposes of punishment. The precise shape of the combined theories varies, but the idea that punishment should be proportional to what the offender deserves remains at the core of the attempt by liberal theorists to respect the dignity and rights of the individual person in the practice of state coercion.

The problem with this approach is that proportionality to moral desert, although it is respectful of the dignity and rights of the individual in the abstract, cannot by itself limit the severity of punishment. The proportionality of punishment consists of two different aspects: ordinal proportionality and cardinal proportionality. Ordinal proportionality means that offenses of similar seriousness receive punishments of similar severity and that the punishments increase in severity as offense seriousness increases. Cardinal proportionality concerns the severity of the entire scale of ordinally proportionate punishments. The problem for penal theorists is that while it is possible to devise ordinally proportionate sentencing regimes, there is no obvious answer to the question of how severe the punishments in that regime should be overall. The cardinal severity of the scale of ordinally proportionate punishment appears to be a contingent question. As John Braithwaite and Phillip Pettit put it:

> The eighteenth-century judge who sentences the burglar to torture followed by death, the judge from Alabama who sentences him to ten years, and the judge from Amsterdam who sentences him to victim compensation all pronounce that they are giving the offender what he deserves. There is no retributivist answer as to which judge is right. On the retributivist's view, so long as they are all handing down sentences for burglary that are proportionately more than those for less-serious crimes and proportionately less than those for more-serious crimes, they could all be right.[13]

The indeterminacy of the idea of proportionality leaves the scale of proportional punishment open to the possibility of relatively severe sentencing scales where, for example, the death sentence or multiple life without parole are possible for murder, permitting mandatory incarceration for minor crimes all the while maintaining ordinal proportionality. The idea of proportionality in itself does not contain any inherent restraint on the cardinal scale of proportionate punishment,[14] which appears to be a contingent question of social convention.[15] Should social convention, for whatever reason, come to regard the actions of offenders in general as constituting more serious wrongdoing than was previously thought, then the retributive idea of proportionality seems in itself to have no capacity to resist that. Although liberals generally claim to prefer state coercion to be minimal, their penal theory lacks an inherent restraining mechanism on the severity of punishment.

This problem is not necessarily fatal to liberal penal minimalism. Liberal theorists have responded to the problem of cardinal proportionality with various proposals as to how the overall scale of proportional punishments could be restrained.[16] The point being made here is simply that the liberal idea of just punishment is not immune to tendencies toward penal severity. Moreover, as I shall argue below, the understanding of crime as a relation between an offender and a victim, an understanding that is influential in both the moral philosophical theory of punishment and contemporary political discourse, will tend to construct any particular offense as a more serious wrongdoing than will the political understanding of crime that is maintained by the democratic theory, to which we now turn.

Democratic Sovereignty and Political Equality

The democratic theory I will set out has much in common with the liberal retributive theory, both in its sensitivity to individual rights and commitment to the proportionality of punishment. I will argue, however, that democracy contains an inherent tendency to reduce the cardinal scale. The more successful a democracy is in its own terms, the less imprisonment it will impose and vice versa.

A democratic theory of punishment is necessarily a political theory of punishment. As Corey Brettschneider observes, the problem for democratic theory is not what the offender morally deserves, but what the state has a right to do to its citizens.[17] Recently, Alan Brudner has contributed a sophisticated and detailed liberal political theory of punishment inspired by Georg Hegel's *Philosophy of Right*, a theory that precisely reformulates the problem of punishment as one of the proper limits of state power. I have argued elsewhere that, in its own liberal terms, Brudner's theory ultimately fails to explain or to restrain the expansive penal regime that we have.[18] Nevertheless, I think a more promising theory of punishment can be constructed by democratizing Brudner's liberal argument, and that is what I am going to do in what follows.

The main reason to set out from Hegel's penal theory is that it offers a solution to an otherwise perplexing problem that imprisonment poses to democratic theory. The problem is that in a democratic state citizens all enjoy an equal status as *rulers*, but, as I shall explain below, imprisonment entails depriving a citizen of that status. Hegel's theory precisely identifies circumstances in which the imprisoned citizen is herself the source of the authority for her loss of the status of ruler. This allows the democratic state to suspend the citizen's rights as a ruler in a way that is consistent with that status. In the process, Hegel's theory alights on the tension between citizens as we currently are and our potential to be participants in true collective self-government, and this tension provides another reason to set out from the Hegelian theory. The theory allows us to understand democracy not as a fixed institutional model or ideal-type of government but as a dynamic historical process through which actual living human individuals are more or less engaged in their own self-government. As a result, this penal theory is not merely a normative aspiration for criminal law. It also identifies the political mechanisms through which imprisonment can be reduced and helps to explain why our recent experience has been the opposite, one of rising incarceration. For these reasons, I will rework the elements of Brudner's Hegelian penal theory, deriving them not from the movement of reason through history, as Brudner does, but from what is practically necessary for the achievement of political equality.

Brudner sets out from the proposition that criminal law is coercion by a sovereign with a monopoly on legitimate coercion.[19] He argues that coercion is only legitimate *sovereign* coercion if the state coerces in the public interest, which is to say in the pursuit of interests that are *necessarily* shared by all the law's subjects. For Brudner, the public interest, or "public reason," in a liberal state is individual freedom, since individual freedom is the interest that *is necessarily* shared by the citizens of a state that claims to be a liberal state. The penal law of a liberal state and the limits on its use of coercion are therefore set by the public reason of individual freedom.[20]

Following the same logic, a democratic criminal law is coercion by a democratic sovereign. The interest that is *necessarily* shared by all the subjects of a democratic sovereignty is political equality. The raison d'etre of democracy is the rule of the people and this entails the equal right of all citizens to participate in and to influence both the making of laws and the exercise of executive power. Political equality might, therefore, be called democracy's public reason, since political equality is the interest necessarily shared by the citizens of a society that defines itself as democratic.[21]

Liberalism has good reasons to limit the use of imprisonment because imprisonment entails a deprivation of individual liberty. However, the deprivation of liberty entailed by imprisonment also supplies democracy with good reason to limit its use. Every time a citizen is deprived of their liberty by a democratic state there is a loss to democracy since depriving a citizen of civil liberty is also a denial of political equality. To understand why this is so, it is necessary to spell out two particularly significant normative commitments entailed by the pursuit of political equality.

The first implication of political equality is that to be committed to it requires making the assumption that ordinary citizens are normally competent to participate in the life of the state; that they are competent to rule themselves collectively.[22] Political equality is a rational way to go about political decision-making only if citizens are ordinarily competent to rule themselves collectively. What this means is that to be genuinely committed to political equality is to have no objection to collective self-government in so far as citizens have the will to govern themselves. This implies in turn that, as Brettschneider points out, the citizens of a democracy have the formal status of rulers. The law must address citizens as rulers, and the law must be consistent with its subjects enjoying that status.[23] Political equality, however, implies more than formal recognition of every citizen's status as a ruler. It is also a substantive condition in which upholding formally equal rights to participate makes possible a degree of equality of actual political influence that amounts to collective self-government.[24] Formal political equality does not guarantee collective self-government,[25] but collective self-government is both the ultimate normative ground of formal political equality and its immanent potential.

Note that this argument about actual self-government takes *formal equality* very seriously, and in no way implies that formal political equality is somehow unreal. On the contrary, the legal rights that guarantee the political equality of citizens as rulers—detailed in the next paragraph below—are the *form* taken by the *political activity* of collective self-rule. Without the forms of political equality, there can be no collective self-rule in substance. Substantial self-rule can only be achieved *if the formal rights are upheld.*[26] Political equality can, therefore, be more or less realized according to the extent that the formal rights of political equality are respected in practice by executive agents and other citizens, and to the extent that the citizenry exercises these rights to exert more or less influence over the making of law and the execution of policy. (Note that the word "rights" is used here to refer to the legally protected liberties or entitlements that are necessary to political equality, rather than to moral or human rights.)

The second implication of political equality is that to have an equal influence over public policy and the making of the laws that we will obey, citizens need more than equal *political* rights. Of course we must have an equal right to offer ourselves as political representatives, and an equal say in the choice of political representatives at elections.[27] However we also need very extensive rights against the executive to ensure that we are free to discuss with prospective representatives what they should do; to express our opinions; to try to change the opinions of others, and to have our opinions changed by the arguments of others; to associate with others in both public and private for this purpose; to assemble with others to debate and promote our political ideas; to enjoy sufficient privacy to develop and exercise the capacity for independent judgment.[28] Without these civil liberties, actual legislative and policy proposals, and their promotion, will depend on more or less shadowy networks of citizens whose influence comes from private connections with existing legislators or the executive branch. Even if citizens outside those networks get to express a preference in a vote at the end of the process, much of the political deliberation will have taken place in the absence of most citizens who will be rendered dependent on the laws authored by others rather than being the independent authors of the law. Such a regime could be more oligarchy than democracy precisely because it would frustrate political equality. True political equality, therefore, requires that the entire political process is open to all citizens on an equal basis, and this entails civil liberties in addition to narrowly political rights.[29]

Civil liberty is then an essential characteristic of political equality, and this explains why each and every act of imprisoning a citizen deprives that citizen of political equality for the duration of their imprisonment. At minimum, it strips the citizen of the right to move, assemble, associate, and enjoy a private life. While imprisonment does not deprive citizens of their nationality, or necessarily prevent them from exercising a right to vote or stand in elections, it does entail executive coercion that prevents a prisoner from participating in the political process *on equal terms with other citizens*. Imprisonment deprives a citizen of an essential aspect of democratic citizenship—formal political equality. The dependence on executive discretion that is entailed in imprisonment is simply inconsistent with participating in collective self-government on an equal basis. Imprisonment is not inconsistent with participating in political life as such—prisoners may be politically active and wield considerable political influence. Imprisonment is inconsistent with formal political equality. In a regime of political equality, prisoners have their political citizenship *suspended* for the duration of their imprisonment.[30]

This conclusion runs against the grain of an influential view among penal reformers that the rights of prisoners should be recognized *because* prisoners are citizens too.[31] Whatever the motivation for this argument, its logic is subversive of democracy. Since prisoners lack civil liberties, to insist on their citizenship is to discount the civil liberties as an essential component of democratic citizenship,[32] thereby undermining the conditions of collective self-government. Moreover, from the point of view of penal moderation, the argument that prisoners are citizens is perverse because it constructs imprisonment as consistent with a person's continuing citizenship. It therefore implicitly normalizes imprisonment and undermines arguments against mass incarceration.[33] From the democratic standpoint, by contrast, imprisonment can only be an exceptional condition precisely because imprisonment entails loss of political equality to a citizen, and so suspends their citizenship.[34] And here we come up against the core problem of imprisonment for a democracy. Imprisonment represents such a fundamental infringement of the rights of democratic citizenship that we need to ask how a democracy can imprison its citizens at all.

Democratic Retributivism

There are some limited circumstances in which upholding the norm of political equality allows for the possibility of suspending the political equality of particular citizens. As we have seen, political equality presupposes the equal right of all to influence the making of the laws, which is to say that in a democracy citizens enjoy the formal status of rulers. The ultimate political authority, therefore, lies with the citizens themselves. It follows that the only source of the political authority that would permit a citizen to be deprived of their share in ruling, and to have their citizenship suspended, is that citizen herself. To deprive a citizen of her formally equal share in political authority without that citizen's permission would be to discount her status as a ruler and violate political equality. In what circumstances does a citizen provide the state with the authority to imprison her?

We have seen that certain rights are essential to democratic self-government: the rights that we commonly refer to as civil liberties. However these civil liberties are in turn dependent on the existence of certain rights of personhood, rights to the control of one's own body and personal property, without which the civil liberties would be nugatory. These rights of personhood are the rights that are upheld by the ordinary criminal law. They are not unique to democratic societies but they are nevertheless a necessary component of them. There would be no civil liberty to speak one's mind, or to assemble with others in order to hear such speech, if others could attack, kill, or imprison the speaker or her audience with impunity. Speakers and audience would have to assert their rights to speak and assemble as natural rights in the Hobbesian sense, or as revolutionary acts. They would have to enter the political debate armed and ready for action. The underlying legal rights of personhood are, therefore, essential to the protection of political deliberation *as a civil liberty*. They are such a fundamental aspect of the existence of a state that we rarely think about them in the context of democracy.[35] It is here that democracy recognizes the insight of Hegelian political theory that a citizen may violate one of these rights in such a way as practically to deny the existence of such rights, and it is in such circumstances that a citizen can provide the authority for her own detention.

When a citizen commits a criminal offense against the personhood of another, then, providing that conviction for the particular offense requires proof that its commission was *deliberate*, the citizen does something that constitutes a practical denial of the existence of the rights of personhood.[36] Deliberate attacks on another's person or deliberate interferences with another person's property are the classic form taken by such rights denials. For example, if a person deliberately assaults another, she acts in a way that implicitly claims that her actions are not limited by the other's rights.[37] The attacker's action in such a case is, therefore, not only a violation of the particular victim's rights; it is also necessarily a denial of the existence of rights as such.[38] It is important to keep in mind that this denial is not a matter of the particular attacker's subjective opinions or motives in violating the rights of another. An attacker may have no opinion about rights at all. It is an assessment of the attacker's action from the objective standpoint of her political equality with others. Since the rights denied by the attacker are rights essential to the exercise of democratic citizenship, the attacker is in practice denying the existence of rights essential to citizenship. When a citizen denies the existence of the rights of democratic citizenship in this way, she is, therefore, denying them to herself also. If the state then suspends her rights and her political equality by imprisoning her, the state will only be acting on the principle underlying her own actions: the principle that our actions are not limited by others' rights.[39] In other words, the state is taking its authority to suspend citizenship rights only from the citizen whose rights are to be denied.

This relationship between democratic rights and the need for proof of deliberation in criminal offenses explains why the modern conception of *mens rea*, that requires proof that a defendant intended or at least knew there was a risk that they would commit an offense, came to influence the doctrines of the criminal courts only as formal political equality advanced over the course of the nineteenth and twentieth centuries.[40] Without proof of *mens rea* there is no proof of deliberation, and, therefore, no proof that a citizen has by her actions denied the existence of rights and authorized the suspension of her citizenship by imprisonment. This theory of punishment therefore only justifies imprisonment for the so-called true crimes that require proof of subjective *mens rea* (generally including homicides, assaults, sexual assaults, thefts, robberies, criminal damage to property). The theory does not justify imprisonment for offenses committed negligently or without proof of any fault. Negligence and strict liability are common in so-called regulatory public welfare offenses. The public welfare offenses raise controversial issues of their own for democracies that I am not going to deal with here.[41] Suffice it to say that as far as public welfare offenses are legitimately used by a democracy to deter activity that negligently creates an excessive risk of harm, the penalties that can be legitimately attached are limited to interferences with property rights—fines.[42]

This authorization to punish, that the citizen gives when she commits a deliberate rights denial, is generally implicit. Many offenders would not recognize that they had given it. The authorization is nevertheless real, in the sense that it is a logical implication of the citizen's own action, *in so far as we treat citizens' actions as the actions of citizen-rulers and political equals*. The giving of this authorization by the offender is a necessary condition of imprisonment in a society where all citizens are equal in their formal status as rulers.[43] Treating an offender's action as the action of a rational citizen in this way involves abstracting from the offender's concrete personality and situation. I will return to democracy's reasons for engaging in this abstraction in the section "Two Normative Objections Answered."

Like any retributive justification of punishment, democratic retributivism is limited to punishments that are proportional to the rights violation committed by the offender. Any particular offender's criminal denial of rights is specific; it only goes so far. A particular offense will involve a different degree of rights denial according to whether the offender intended or merely risked the particular rights violation. Moreover, the extent of any particular rights violation also varies according to the amount of harm done to the victim. The reason for the importance of harm is that the personhood of persons exists in embodied creatures that have needs and desires. Participation in self-government therefore depends upon various "agency goods" (such as life and limb, health, personal property, and so on) that are necessary to the satisfaction of these needs and desires. The denial of the rights of personhood can, and often does, involve harm to these essential agency goods, and the extent of this harm affects the extent to which the offender acted without regard to the rights of others.[44] In other words, a murder is a more serious and determined denial of rights than nonintentional homicide; homicide is more serious than causing minor bodily harms; and they are in turn more serious than thefts and so on. Since the offender's specific practical denial of rights only goes so far, it only permits a proportional response. A disproportionate deprivation would be in excess of the authority granted to the state by the citizen-ruler and, therefore, a violation of political equality.

The argument presented so far explains why a democracy can punish and imprison some of its citizens. However, it leaves this democratic account with the same problem faced by liberal justifications of punishment: the contingency of the cardinal scale of its proportional punishments.[45] What is to stop democratic punishments being harsh and extensive while maintaining ordinal proportionality?

Democratic Decrementalism

The first part of the democrats' answer is that, so far, we have only established that in certain circumstances a citizen-offender authorizes the democratic state to impose a proportional deprivation of her rights. This identifies the source of the democratic state's *authority to punish*, but it does not tell us what reason a democratic state would have to act on that authority or how severe any punishment should be, other than it must be ordinally proportionate. Even where imprisonment has been authorized by a citizen, the citizen's equal status will be suspended by imprisonment and she will be excluded from equal participation in the process of collective self-government. A state that is committed to political equality will therefore need good reason to maintain a cardinal scale of punishment that includes deprivations of liberty as a penal response to criminal rights-denials, reasons going beyond the mere fact that the citizen-offender has authorized a penal response.

The one compelling reason for a democratic state to act on the citizen-offender's authorization to interfere with her rights is that such a punishment would serve to uphold political equality in general, even as it interferes with it in the particular case. Imprisonment and other forms of penal hard treatment can do this in so far as they are necessary in order to realize the rights of citizenship. Here too we can democratize Brudner's theory. The offender has denied the existence of rights not merely in the form of expressing an opinion that people have no rights (which is permissible from the point of view of political equality), but in practice, by *acting* on the principle that she is not limited by others' rights. State punishment, by turning the offender's own principle back upon herself, "acts out" the self-contradictory character of this "criminal principle" and in so doing it restores the rule of law.[46] In this way, state punishment realizes (gives reality to) the authority of democratic rights. When a democratic state removes the offender's rights, it demonstrates in practice that the offender's denial of democratic rights was a nullity. Or, to put the point the other way around, punishment (and imprisonment as a punishment) will be necessary in a democracy only in so far as the failure by the state to punish a criminal rights-denials would, by leaving the offender's rights denial unchallenged in practice, tend to reduce the rights of citizens to mere fictions.

This political theory of punishment does not deny the familiar idea that crimes are often moral wrongs perpetrated by the offender against a victim. It does deny that censuring or condemning that moral wrong is the business of a democratic state.[47] Rather, a moral wrong only becomes a truly *criminal* wrong, a public wrong, when it amounts to a denial of the existence of rights, because the business of the state in wrongdoing is the realization of rights.[48] The specifically criminal aspect of a true criminal wrong is its denial of the existence of rights.

In a democratic regime the cardinal scale of punishment is, therefore, set by whatever is necessary to realize those rights that protect citizens' political equality, which is to say their equal status as rulers. How much punishment will that be? The answer to that question will depend on how potent the challenge of any criminal act is to the reality of democratic rights. The critical point here is that citizens' rights, and citizens' status as rulers, are not realized only, or even primarily, by negating criminal challenges to them by means of state punishment. In a democracy, citizens' status as rulers will be realized to the extent that practical respect for their rights is at the core of the everyday practice of both state agents and citizens. The more that state officials and other citizens are respectful of each others' status as corulers, and the more that state officials are practically dependent on the citizenry for their day-to-day power and authority, the more fully realized will be the rights of democratic citizenship and the stronger the authority of the democratic legal regime. And the stronger is the authority of these rights of democratic citizenship, the less significant any particular criminal denial of the rights of citizenship will be. The less potent is the offender's denial of rights, the less severe is the punishment that will serve to negate that denial. In other words, the more that the state is characterized by the political equality of its citizens, which is to say, the more democratic is the state, the less the challenge that any particular offense will represent to the rights of citizenship. As a consequence, the better realized are democratic rights and the stronger the democracy, the lower will be the cardinal scale of penal proportionality, and the more room there will be for leniency, since not every criminal rights denial will require a penal response for the regime of democratic rights to enjoy effectively unchallenged supremacy.[49]

This is a radically decrementalist theory of the cardinal scale of proportional punishments. To understand the decrementalism of this penal rationale, it is necessary fully to grasp the potential that dwells within the concept of political equality. The democratic rationale for political equality is the shared capacity for self-government. Liberating that potential, so that citizens actually become self-governing, by rendering the state dependent on those citizens' vigilant exercise of their rights, which is to say democratizing the state, tends to diminish the potency of the specifically *criminal* aspect of criminal acts—their denial of the rights of persons. As rights are strengthened in every other aspect of the relation of state and citizens, the specifically criminal aspect of criminal acts diminishes in relative significance, and so too does the need for severe punishments such as imprisonment. In so far as criminal denials of rights persist in a democratic regime that has become so strong that those offenses no longer present a significant challenge to the reality of democratic civil rights, then something like restorative methods involving interested parties can be substituted for incarceration.[50] Such a wholesale substitution of restorative methods for state punishment would be mediated by something like what Albert Dzur calls "thick populism": the development of a political way of life in which the citizenry organizes itself, through the exercise of its political rights, to carry out the process of government in collaboration with experts.[51]

There are numerous potential objections to this democratic theory. The first and most important is that the argument made so far is obviously abstract, and deliberately so. It is trying to establish some logical relations between the normative ground of political equality, the criminal laws of political equality and the practice of imprisonment by the state. It might appear to be unrealistic. In the process of elaborating it, I have imagined a society in which serious crimes might acquire a significance that is so limited as to no longer make imprisonment a necessary response to them. This is, of course, the opposite of our recent experience, in which the state's penal responses have become more severe. However, it is precisely this contemporary reality that indicates that the democratic theory is not merely idealistic. The recent expansion of incarceration has occurred over the same period in which Western societies have retreated away from the conditions of political equality toward a condition often now referred to as "postdemocracy."[52] There is reason to believe that the relationship between the two trends is not merely coincidental but causal.

Postdemocratic Punishment

The period since the 1970s, the period in which incarceration rates have risen, has also been a period in which the idea of collective self-government has been eliminated from the content of electoral politics. The decisive shift occurred when left-of-center political parties retreated from longstanding commitments to intervene in the market economy to guarantee full employment and to negotiate deals between employers and trades unions. The acceptance that "there is no alternative" to the market removed the basic economic and social questions about the organization of the production and distribution of goods and services from political contestation. This process necessarily marginalized the underlying normative basis of political equality, the idea that the political sphere was one through which the citizenry as a whole could gain collective control of their circumstances, and approach collective self-government. "Government by the people for the people becomes meaningless unless it includes major economic decision-making by the people for the people."[53]

Electoral politics was eviscerated. The parties of the left abandoned their traditional constituencies, and, without the threat of socialism and social democracy, the political mobilization of traditional conservatives also lost its rationale. Participation in electoral and representative politics has since suffered significant decline, with electoral turnouts falling and party membership falling further.[54] Politics has become a spectator sport: "a tightly controlled spectacle managed by rival teams of professionals expert in the techniques of persuasion, and considering a small range of issues selected by those teams" in which "the mass of citizens plays a passive, quiescent, even apathetic part."[55] These changes have been accompanied by a broader "de-democratization" as citizens have withdrawn from other forms of public life in addition to formal party politics.[56]

In other words, the emergence of populist penal policy during this period only tells us that the popularity of punishment is more or less proportional to the unpopularity of politics. On the one hand, as Ian Loader puts it, crime is "the preoccupation of a world no longer enchanted and animated by political vision(s)."[57] On the other, as Bernard Harcourt argues, in a society in which the large majority of citizens is not very engaged by politics and the public sphere, the widespread exclusion of citizens from democratic life by imprisonment seems unremarkable. Mass incarceration can arise without much controversy when our democracy is "virtual," and self-government is more a "potential" of our political institutions than it is their "actual" practice.[58] The dismal contemporary politics of crime and punishment have emerged as democracy has declined. Moreover, the rising severity of punishment, and the increase in prisoner numbers, can be understood as a function of this decline in political equality. We can grasp the connection between declining political participation and rising imprisonment if we consider the way in which the meaning of citizenship has been transformed over the same period.

Citizens of contemporary Western democracies are no longer integrated into the political community by virtue of their political role as corulers, even in theory. Citizens have been redefined as consumers: consumers in markets for privately provided goods and services, consumers of public services, and indeed consumers of politics.[59] For the consumer-citizen, autonomy lies in being able to realize her identity from the plurality of available lifestyles in the consumer society.[60] The consumer process of personal differentiation is quite different from, and in some respects opposed to, the process of ideological contestation that characterizes political citizenship, the political process through which shared and conflicting interests are identified and disputed or reconciled.[61] While political citizenship constructs the individual as a part of the process of collective self-rule and self-control, the individual consumer-citizen's autonomy, by contrast, is intrinsically vulnerable to forces *beyond her control*, as I have argued elsewhere in detail.[62] This intrinsic vulnerability of the consumer-citizen to harm is particularly sharply focused in criminal justice, which has also been transformed into a "public service" to be consumed by citizens. As consumers of the state's criminal justice services, citizens have been redefined as potential victims of crime.[63] Jonathan Simon points out that because the *representative* subject of law is conceived as a victim in this way, the vulnerability of the victim to criminal harm comes to "define the appropriate conditions for government intervention."[64]

Reimagining criminal justice as a matter of providing a service to the vulnerable potential victims of crime conceives crime itself as a moral relation between victim and offender. This tendency of the official mind to construct crime as a moral relation between victim and offender is, as we have seen above, different from the democratic conception of crime, in which crime is a denial of specific rights of citizenship. The "moral" conception of crime has an inflationary tendency on penal severity for at least three reasons.

In general terms, any particular offense, when it is viewed *from the standpoint of a victim*, as a moral wrong that has been done to that individual victim, necessarily appears to be more potent than it appears from the standpoint of the state, as a practical denial of the existence of rights.[65] The more that criminal offenses are understood and constructed as wrongs to victims, as opposed to denials of rights in general, the more the cardinal scale will tend to rise. It is striking that the major cause of the rising prison population in England, at a time when crime rates have been declining, is increasing sentence severity, with a higher proportion of convicted offenders receiving custodial sentences and the average length of those sentences increasing.[66]

A further tendency to penal escalation arises from the way that reconstructing the justification of punishment as a service to potential victims tends to reorder the relationship of retribution and incapacitation. When citizens are defined by their vulnerability to crime, their perception of their security becomes a vital interest because their freedom will be limited in so far as they are not secure from potential victimization. As a result of this, the criminal law of consumer-citizenship increasingly protects a "right to security," and it does so by constructing *dangerousness* as both a moral and penal wrong.[67] From this standpoint, simply *being dangerous* is a violation of citizens' right to security, and once dangerousness itself is considered a wrong deserving of punishment, then incapacitation becomes a proportionate response to the wrong of dangerousness.[68] In this precautionary understanding of criminal justice, not only does preventive incarceration acquire a new retributive rationale, but the scope of the criminal law will also tend to expand to cover "pre-inchoate" conduct that involves no practical denial of the rights of personhood but rather attracts liability to imprisonment because it provides evidence of criminal intentions, or at least of a willingness to increase the risk of future criminal wrongdoings.[69] More prisoners and longer sentences are the result.

Thirdly, as a precautionary construction of criminal justice has established itself, the regulatory public welfare offenses acquire a new significance. Although they involve no violation of a particular victim's rights, and no immediate harm caused, commission of these offenses will typically increase downstream risks of harm (the supply of drugs or possession offenses, for example). From the precautionary standpoint, failing to cooperate with harm prevention policy in the form of committing these offenses is a more serious wrong than it is from the democratic standpoint.

The populist tough-on-crime policies and the penal severity that has caused prison populations to rise have proved electorally necessary in societies in which citizens have come to vote as individuated and vulnerable political consumers rather than as politically organized aspirant corulers. Instead of being addressed by the penal law as rational persons capable of self-rule, citizens are addressed as victims and dangerous offenders instead. Markus Dubber points out that when converted into legal identities in this way, the "victim" and the "offender" have something in common. Both are no longer treated as persons.[70] This transformation of the meaning of citizenship subverts the legal recognition of personhood that democracy presupposes. In the same moment, it both occludes the normative basis of political equality in the potential for collective self-government, and creates powerful tendencies to penal severity.

Political equality has been denuded of its ideological content and lost the force that animated it—the popular engagement of a wide spectrum of citizens in the task of collective self-government through mass political parties. As the form of political equality has been emptied of life, so the form itself is proving vulnerable to decay. In recent years, the protection of civil liberty that we saw was essential to political equality has slowly given way to ever-wider restrictions on the freedoms of expression, association, and assembly, and very extensive state surveillance of private communications.[71]

The tendency toward penal severity and mass incarceration is the inverse of the tendency toward political equality. Logically, mass incarceration is a sign that political equality is poorly realized; practically, the rise in imprisonment in recent years is a symptom of the retreat of political equality in our public life. The only sense in which mass incarceration in the present could be laid at the door of democracy is the sense in which it arises from the failure of the citizenry to achieve democracy's end, to realize political equality and collective self-government. Though my emphasis here is more on ideological change and the historical decline of the old representative politics, the conclusions of this argument closely parallel the observations of Vanessa Barker's detailed comparative political sociology of American jurisdictions. As she puts it: "at the aggregate level, depressed civic engagement, withdrawal from public life, and lack of public participation in the political process may underpin mass incarceration in the United States."[72] They also support Barker's "counterintuitive claim" that "increased democratization can support and sustain less coercive penal regimes."[73]

Even if the democratic theory outlined here does offer a realistic account of recent experience, there are other potential objections to it. I will briefly consider the two most obvious criticisms: first, that a political theory of punishment based on the relation of state and citizen might permit discriminatory treatment of noncitizens; second, that as a retributive theory of criminal justice, it will fail to achieve social justice.

Two Normative Objections Answered

It might be thought that since democratic retributivism justifies state coercion on the basis of political equality among citizens, rather than the needs, dignity, or equality of human individuals as such, it would leave noncitizens at the mercy of an unrestrained sovereign power. However, as we noted at the outset, the normative assumption of a theory founded on political equality is precisely that *human individuals* are together capable of achieving collective self-government. This democratic theory is not based on any particularistic notion of the moral unity of a particular ethnic group or nationality. Once personhood, as opposed to national or cultural identity, is recognized as the basis of democratic citizenship, then *all persons become potential citizens*. A democracy that takes its virtues of political freedom and collective self-determination seriously will therefore protect and coerce both citizens and noncitizens with penal law on an equal basis.

To answer the social justice criticism of democratic retributivism, we should begin by recalling that democratic retributivism is not a theory of moral retributivism, but of what Brudner calls "legal retributivism." In the democratic version of legal retributivism, the legal structure of criminal offenses, containing clearly specified conduct elements and requiring proof of *mens rea*, is intended to ensure not that punishment by the state is morally deserved, but that it has the offender's authority behind it so as to be consistent with political equality. However, it is true that this authorization is in a large majority of cases implicit. If asked about this, many actual offenders who have been convicted and punished are unlikely to agree that they have given permission for their own punishment. These legal forms of punishment treat concrete particular individuals as if they had the abstract and universal characteristics of democratic citizens; they hold offenders to a standard of conduct that takes little or no account of their concrete personalities or the broader social circumstances in which their choices to violate others' rights are made.[74] The very idea of personhood, of individuals as rational agents, on which the democratic theory relies, is an aspiration as much as a description. Individual rational agency is not something that we are born with. Rational agency is an emergent property of embodied creatures with needs as well as the capacity to reason.[75] There are many ways in which a human's needs may not be met, and this failure can inhibit the development of the self-control that characterizes the abstractly rational person. Rational agency is, therefore, a property that is more or less fully realized in concrete human individuals.

The consequence of this abstraction lying at the heart of criminal justice is that the burden of the enforcement of formal equal rights by legal retributivism will fall most heavily on the most disadvantaged, those who for one reason or another are least able to conform their behavior to the requirements of equal rights. This means that doing criminal justice may continue to be an aspect of a broader injustice.[76] It will be those who most lack the economic, social, and psychological resources conducive to participation in self-government who will in practice be more likely to go to prison, and democratic punishment will be one more mechanism for the political and social exclusion of those who have the least control as individuals over their lives. To put it mildly, that seems to be in tension with democratic aspirations. At first glance, democratic legal retributivism appears to be as vulnerable to this criticism as any other retributive theory.

Democratic legal retributivism does not achieve social justice. It does not achieve it because social justice is not its purpose or rationale. The rationale of democratic legal retributivism is to realize more basic conditions of political equality—the formal rights essential to political equality. However, there is an intrinsic connection between formal political equality and bringing to an end the systemic material and social deprivation that is suffered by those citizens most likely to end up in prison.

As we have already seen, political equality is, like individual agency, an emergent property. The emergence of a significant degree of real substantive equality of influence over the state and society, which is to say the emergence of actual collective self-government, is the normative ground and immanent potential of formally equal political rights and civil liberties. Democracy upholds these formal rights of political equality in advance of the achievement of the collective self-government that is their potential; and it does so *in order to achieve that potential.* Real collective self-government cannot be achieved without a jealous attachment to the rights of formal political equality. By the same token, democracy upholds the rights of persons in advance of the full achievement of the rational agency among concrete agents that these rights formally declare, and it does so in order to foster that agency. When an offender is punished on democratic retributive grounds—that is, because the citizen-offender has given implicit permission—the state communicates both to the particular concrete offender and to the world in general that it takes all its citizens, the offender included, seriously as potentially rational agents and as rulers. Moreover it does this in order to realize democratic rights. In this process, the state institutionalizes its commitment not only to fostering rational agency among its citizens severally, but also to achieving self-government collectively (since without fostering that individual agency, collective self-government cannot be achieved). This commitment of democratic legal retributivism in turn shapes the form taken by the democratic state's penal response, and it does so in a way that not only radically mitigates the force of the social justice criticism of retributivism, but contributes to resolving the problem that the social justice criticism raises.

Firstly, and most obviously, realizing political equality is among other things a mechanism for eliminating criminogenic social and economic conditions. In realizing political equality, the majority of citizens gain access to the state's wider powers to reorganize, regulate and coerce, allowing them to democratize society's system for meeting human needs. The burden of crime and punishment falls overwhelmingly on the most economically disadvantaged sections of the population, the sections of society least likely to be engaged in the political life of the state. However, the more that a society seeks to realize political equality's normative content, the more it will seek to universalize the exercise of democratic rights. Citizens who respect themselves and each other on the grounds of their political equality, who respect each other's status as corulers, will seek to use their political influence over the state to eliminate the relatively poor social conditions that contribute to criminal wrongdoing and make it less likely that individuals will contribute to collective self-government. Such efforts will be a key element of a democratic criminal justice policy since the more that citizens are moved by their formal rights to achieve the content of political equality—to make themselves, and all of themselves, the real authors of the law—the less interest they will have in denying the conditions of their collective self-government, either by engaging in crime or by tolerating the persistence of the relative deprivation and inequality in which ordinary crime flourishes.

This argument too will appear idealistic, but only for as long as we take our present circumstances of de-democratization for granted. A key part of the process of democratization being described here is realizing the political equality of the relatively disadvantaged sections of society, those that have a much greater interest in preventing crime by improving their economic lot than they do in punishing the offenders among them. As Lisa Miller puts it: "When lawmakers are made to answer to people who are likely to experience violence and collateral consequences of a wide range of social and economic insecurities, there are fewer political incentives to rely on imprisonment as the sole or primary policy response."[77] Moreover, this tendency of political equality to eliminate criminogenic conditions will also tend to reduce the incidence of criminal rights denials, and in this way reduce the challenge to the authority of rights that crime represents, decreasing the scale and extent of imprisonment in the process.

Secondly, since democratic legal retributivism in theory eliminates moral blame from criminal justice, it is open to a much more constructive penal regime than that maintained in most Western prison systems. To a democracy, criminal punishment consists in a loss of civil liberties or fines because it is these particular official responses that serve to deny the criminal denial of democratic rights. Loss of civil liberties and fines deprive the offender in the same currency as that of the democratic rights that the offender has herself denied: either liberty (imprisonment or disqualifications or some "community sentences") or agency goods (money). Democratic criminal punishment requires no hard treatment in any other way. Indeed, the offending citizen of a democracy has not given permission for other forms of hard treatment, including prison conditions that are below ordinary standards of housing, nutrition, educational provision, healthcare, and so on. Moreover, in so far as society considers the question of moral blame for criminal offending, and to whom that blame should be attributed, a democracy cannot pretend that the conditions in which citizens are socialized do not contribute to crime, or that all the responsibility can be laid at the offender's door. As a regime that lays claim to the tasks of collective self-government, a democratic sovereignty cannot deny responsibility for the social condition of the population. In general, the moral blame for offending must be shared between offenders and society as a whole.[78] As a consequence of these aspects of democratic order, society as a whole acquires responsibilities to the offender, and the offender acquires concomitant rights. Within the constraints of proportionality and respect for the personhood of the offender, democratic retributivism implies a vigorous reintegrative approach to punishment, one in which prison conditions would need to be better than merely decent, and much better than they are now.

Democratic retributivism necessitates significant reform of prison regimes, but penal reform is not its primary purpose. Democratic reforms to prison regimes are necessary only as one subordinate aspect of democracy's broader tendency to reduce the use of imprisonment with the ultimate aim of ending it entirely.[79] Democratic retributivism is an abolitionist theory of state punishment and this is its most important contribution to resolving the problem of the injustice of imprisonment.

Democratic Retributive Abolitionism

A democratic state may continue to require imprisonment, but only for so long as it is weak because actual involvement of citizens in their own self-government remains limited, and their political equality little more than a formality. As we saw above, the more that the relation of state and citizens is one practically governed and organized by the exercise of citizens' democratic rights, the less imprisonment will be needed, and vice versa. Political equality contains an inherent tendency to the abolition of state punishment that liberalism lacks. The realization of political equality is a process that engages people in their own collective life in a way that reduces the necessity for imprisonment. Individual rights in a state that was in reality nothing other than the collective political action of its citizens would need no imprisonment to realize them.[80]

The virtue of democratic retributivism is that although it favors and tends toward abolition, it does not pretend that imprisonment can simply be abolished. Nor is it content with a simple antithesis between retributive state punishment and restorative procedures. Rather, it identifies the specific weakness of a democratic society that necessitates the persistence of criminal justice and state punishment. That weakness is our failure fully to recognize ourselves, and each other, as the rulers of our collective life, and the related inability to know how to act like corulers. This failure deprives democratic societies of their essential moral force: us.[81] In the same moment, democratic retributivism identifies political equality as a basis on which broadly restorative and rehabilitative methods can be progressively substituted for state punishment, and especially for imprisonment.

Democrats have no reason, therefore, to be defensive about the relation between democratic politics and state punishment. Democracy and imprisonment are antithetical. The increasing imprisonment of recent decades is a result of democracy's retreat over the same period. The democratic theory of state punishment may appear to be unrealistic only because democracy has been in retreat for decades, and the politics of popular sovereignty have been marginalized. The decremental and abolitionist tendency of political equality will not materialize in actual abolition simply as a result of the existence of universal suffrage. Practical political equality is an achievement of the democratic political process. Achieving it depends on the will of individuals and collectives, and there is nothing inevitable about it. In recent decades actual electoral majorities have turned away from eliminating criminogenic conditions, away from reducing imprisonment, and toward blaming and incapacitating. But this has occurred because practical politics has become dominated by a subtly antidemocratic ideology that presents citizenship not as an essential element of collective self-government, but as a promise of protection from the harms to which individual consumers are vulnerable. In practice, political equality has been eclipsed as a political ideal along with popular sovereignty. In other words, the source of the appearance of the democratic theory's utopianism is the proof of the theory's realism: the increase in imprisonment has arisen from democracy's decline. What this negative proof means, however, is that even though democrats have no cause to be defensive about the growth of imprisonment in recent decades, we nevertheless confront an enormous intellectual and political challenge.

We have become accustomed to very low horizons with respect to the possibility of true democratic self-government. Even the language used to describe the contemporary process of de-democratization constructs democracy as a thing of the past. Western democracies are now frequently described as "postdemocratic," notwithstanding the fact that in the past these societies never fully achieved even formal political equality, let alone the extent of popular participation that characterizes a truly self-governing population. The citizenry of these countries is marked by depoliticization and its accompanying outlook of distrust, anxiety and vulnerability. To reverse the depoliticizing trends of recent decades will require large numbers of ordinary citizens to be inspired once again to take responsibility for our collective social life and to seek to realize political equality. This is not going to be easy. Nevertheless, one among the many reasons to try is that democracy provides a way out of the carceral state.

Notes

I am grateful to Alan Brudner, Henrique Carvalho, R. A. Duff, Roberto Gargarella, S. E. Marshall, Alan Norrie, Mike Redmayne, Craig Reeves, and Charlie Webb for their comments and criticisms of the argument. I am especially in debt to Zelia Gallo, Jeremy

Horder and Nicola Lacey for their detailed comments on and criticisms of an earlier draft, and to Jo Murkens for our many discussions of democratic theory and for access to his unpublished research on democratic theory. The usual disclaimer definitely applies.

1. Nicola Lacey, *The Prisoners' Dilemma: Political Economy and Punishment in Contemporary Democracies*, The Hamlyn Lectures 2007 (New York: Cambridge University Press, 2008), 6. Penal theorists with an interest in democracy have generally relied on existing moral or utilitarian theories of punishment rather than directly deriving the penal theory from democratic premises (see, for example, the work of R. A. Duff or Nicola Lacey, *State Punishment* (New York: Routledge, 1994)). A recent exception is Corey Brettschneider, who derives some elements of a democratic theory of punishment from a broader democratic theory (see Corey Lang Brettschneider, *Democratic Rights: the Substance of Self-Government* [Princeton, NJ: Princeton University Press, 2007], ch. 5). Although I will adopt some aspects of Brettschneider's democratic theory here and note where our accounts of punishment coincide, our accounts of democratic public reason and public wrong differ significantly.

2. The Sentencing Project, "Trends in US Corrections," 2013, http://sentencingproject.org/doc/publications/inc_Trends_in_Corrections_Fact_sheet.pdf.

3. Ministry of Justice, "The Story of the Prison Population: 1993–2012, England and Wales," 2013, www.gov.uk/government/uploads/system/uploads/attachment_data/file/218185/story-prison-population.pdf.

4. Ian Loader, "Review Symposium: The Anti-Politics of Crime," *Theoretical Criminology* 12, no. 3 (August 1, 2008): 399–410; Albert W. Dzur, *Punishment, Participatory Democracy, and the Jury* (New York: Oxford University Press, 2012), 33.

5. Dzur, *Punishment, Participatory Democracy, and the Jury*.

6. Ibid.; Vanessa Barker, *The Politics of Imprisonment: How the Democratic Process Shapes the Way America Punishes Offenders* (New York: Oxford University Press, 2009).

7. Ian Loader, "For Penal Moderation: Notes towards a Public Philosophy of Punishment," *Theoretical Criminology* 14, no. 3 (August 1, 2010): 349–367.

8. H.L.A. Hart, *Punishment and Responsibility Essays in the Philosophy of Law* (Oxford: Oxford University Press, 1968).

9. Andrew von Hirsch, *Censure and Sanctions* (Oxford: Oxford University Press, 2000).

10. Richard S. Frase, *Just Sentencing: Principles and Procedures for a Workable System* (New York: Oxford University Press, 2013).

11. See, for example, Nicola Lacey, *State Punishment* (New York: Routledge, 1994); Victor Tadros, *The Ends of Harm: The Moral Foundations of Criminal Law* (New York: Oxford University Press, 2011).

12. See Michael S. Moore, *Placing Blame: A Theory of the Criminal Law* (New York: Oxford University Press Oxford, 2010); R. A. Duff, *Punishment, Communication, and Community* (Oxford: Oxford University Press, 2003).

13. John Braithwaite and Philip Pettit, *Not Just Deserts: A Republican Theory of Criminal Justice* (Oxford: Clarendon Press, 1993), 178.

14. Nicola Lacey and Hanna Pickard, "The Chimera of Proportionality: Institutionalizing Limits on Punishment in Contemporary Social and Political Systems: The Chimera of Proportionality," *Modern Law Review* 78, no. 2 (March 2015): 216–240.

15. Andrew von Hirsch, "Proportionate Sentences: A Desert Perspective," in *Principled Sentencing* (Oxford: Hart, 2009); Duff, *Punishment, Communication, and Community.*

16. See, for example, Andrew von Hirsch, *Censure and Sanctions* (Oxford: Oxford University Press, 2000); Richard L. Lippke, "Anchoring the Sentencing Scale: A Modest Proposal," *Theoretical Criminology* 16, no.2 (November 2012) 463–480.

17. Corey Lang Brettschneider, *Democratic Rights,* 102; compare Markus Dirk Dubber, "'Criminal Police and Criminal Law in the Rechsstaat,'" in *Police and the Liberal State* (Redwood City, CA: Stanford University Press, 2008) 95–96.

18. Peter Ramsay, "The Dialogic Community at Dusk," *Critical Analysis of Law* 1, no. 2 (2014): 316–322.

19. Alan Brudner, *Punishment and Freedom* (Oxford: Oxford University Press, 2012), 21.

20. Ibid., 22–23.

21. Note that political equality is the interest that is *necessarily* shared in so far as the legitimacy of the sovereign's coercion of subjects rests on the sovereign's claims to be democratic. Political equality may be an interest that is not *contingently* shared by all the actual citizens of any actual democracy—some citizens may be antidemocrats. Equally, on Brudner's account individual liberty is the public reason of a liberal state even though some of its citizens may be antiliberal and reject individual freedom.

22. Robert A. Dahl, *On Democracy* (New Haven, CT: Yale University Press, 2000) 74–76. Of course this assumption precisely assumes away the fact that some particular individuals may be barely competent or in fact lack this competence entirely. It is likely that those who are particularly disadvantaged in this respect will make up a substantial proportion of the prison population. I return to this problem in the section titled "Two Normative Objections Answered."

23. Brettschneider, *Democratic Rights,* 33.

24. Note the careful formulation: collective self-government implies a high degree of substantive political equality but does not aspire to a flat distribution of political influence. There is no space to discuss it in detail, but the theory here assumes that collective self-government can be achieved through representative government (see n 27), a process in which some will have more influence than others at any one time.

25. To approach substantive political equality, actual collective self-government, citizens will need to exercise their political and civil rights and to develop sufficient knowledge of their circumstances to deliberate effectively, see Peter Ramsay, "Democratic Limits to Preventive Criminal Law," in A. Ashworth, L. Zedner, and P. Tomlin (eds.), *Prevention and the Limits of the Criminal Law* (Oxford: Oxford University Press, 2013) 229–231; Franz L. Neumann, "The Concept of Political Freedom," in William Scheuerman (ed.), *The Rule of Law Under Siege: Selected Essays of Franz L. Neumann and Otto Kirchheimer* (Oakland: University of California Press,1996).

26. Note the emphasis here. It is *upholding* formal equality—not restricting it—that makes possible a greater substantive equality. As Giovanni Sartori put it: "From liberty we are free to go on to equality; from equality we are not free to get back to liberty." (Giovanni Sartori, *The Theory of Democracy Revisited—Part One: The Contemporary Debate: Contemporary Debate v. 1,* first edition [Chatham, NJ: CQ Press, 1987], 389).

27. On political representation as a means to collective self-government, rather than an obstacle, see David Plotke, "Representation Is Democracy," *Constellations* 4, no. 1: (April 1997) 19–34; Nadia Urbinati, *Representative Democracy: Principles and Genealogy* (Chicago: University of Chicago Press, 2008); Ramsay, "Democratic Limits to Preventive Criminal Law," 230–231.

28. The civil liberties set out here are among formal rights that cannot be compromised for the sake of substantive equality (see n 26). Note that they do not include a generic right to property. Some rights to *personal* property are a precondition of civil liberty, but no rights to property in the means of production are entailed by the commitment to democratic self-government.

29. Robert A. Dahl, *On Political Equality* (New Haven, CT.: Yale University Press, 2007) 12–18. See also Neumann, "The Concept of Political Freedom".

30. Note that on this account political citizenship is only suspended. Imprisoned citizens do not lose their nationality, and only lose their political status for the duration of their imprisonment. Political equality provides no rationale for the practice of "felon disenfranchisement" after release from prison. See Peter Ramsay, "Voters Should Not Be in Prison! The Rights of Prisoners in a Democracy," *Critical Review of International Social and Political Philosophy* 16, no. 3 (2013): 421–438; compare Brettschneider, *Democratic Rights the Substance of Self-Government*, 99.

31. Baroness Vivien Stern, "Prisoners As Citizens: A Comparative View," *Probation Journal* 49, no. 2 (June 1, 2002): 130–139; Joint Committee on the Draft and Voting Eligibility (Prisoners) Bill, "Draft Voting Eligibility (Prisoners) Bill Report" (London: The Stationery Office Limited, 2013); Cormac Behan, *Citizen Convicts: Prisoners, Politics and the Vote* (Manchester: Manchester University Press, 2014).

32. Peter Ramsay, "Letting Prisoners Vote Would Undermine the Idea That Civil Liberties Are Fundamental to Democratic Citizenship" (London: Democratic Audit UK, 2013). Available at http://www.democraticaudit.com/?p=1765.

33. Ibid.

34. It does not follow from this that prisoners have no rights in a democracy, only that their rights do not arise from their suspended political citizenship but from other duties owed to them by a democratic state. See Ramsay, "Voters Should Not Be in Prison! The Rights of Prisoners in a Democracy," 431–433; and text at n 78.

35. L. L. Miller, "Power to the People: Violent Victimization, Inequality and Democratic Politics," *Theoretical Criminology* 17, no. 3 (August 1, 2013): 285.

36. Here "deliberate" implies intentionally or recklessly in the sense that the offender knew that there was a risk that they might violate rights (for a full account, see Alan Brudner, *Punishment and Freedom*, ch. 2, esp 38–41).

37. Unless of course they can claim that one of the general defenses recognized by the criminal law applies to justify or exculpate their action.

38. Brudner, *Punishment and Freedom*, 76–81. This claim is not affected by the fact that much violent offending is a consequence of a failure to resist momentary impulses toward a particular other person. In so far as the act of violence is nevertheless deliberate, it constitutes a denial *in practice* of the existence of rights.

39. Ibid., 41.

40. Peter Ramsay, "The Responsible Subject As Citizen: Criminal Law, Democracy And The Welfare State," *Modern Law Review* 69, no. 1 (2006): 29–58.

41. For a discussion of the specifically democratic limits to the scope of the criminal law, see Ramsay, "Democratic Limits to Preventive Criminal Law." For the basic connection between democracy and strict liability, see Peter Ramsay, "The Responsible Subject As Citizen: Criminal Law, Democracy And The Welfare State," *Modern Law Review* 69, no. 1 (2006): 29–58.

42. The logic is the same as that of Brudner, *Punishment and Freedom*, 177–178. It is not the case that existing formal democracies abide by this limitation.

43. This Hegelian limitation appears to be more specific, and may be more demanding on the state, than Brettschneider's requirement that to be treated as rulers, the state must treat "individuals as rights-bearing citizens" (see Brettschneider, *Democratic Rights*, 104–105). But, as we shall see in the section "Two Normative Objections Answered," it limits the form taken by the state's penal response in ways broadly similar to those proposed by Brettschneider.

44. Brudner, *Punishment and Freedom*, 138–139.

45. It also endures the difficulties associated with establishing an acceptable ordinal scale of proportionality. But unlike some moral desert theories, this difficulty is ameliorated by legal retributivism's commitment only to not imposing disproportionate punishment, to a "limiting retributivism" (see Brudner, *Punishment and Freedom*, 55; Richard S. Frase, *Just Sentencing: Principles and Procedures for a Workable System* [New York: Oxford University Press, 2013]).

46. Brudner, *Punishment and Freedom*, 45–48.

47. Democratizing Brudner, ibid, 49. See also text before n 78 and compare Brettschneider, *Democratic Rights the Substance of Self-Government*, 102–105.

48. As we noted earlier, in its regulatory function the state also has a role in deterring the creation of excessive risks of harm. However, from the democratic point of view, legal protection from excessive risk of harm is in any case a species of "social right" (see Ramsay, "The Responsible Subject as Citizen," 48–52). Violations of these regulatory laws in the form of public welfare offenses amount to public wrongs because they are violations of these social rights. In any case, as we also noted earlier, where causing or increasing the risk of harm involves no practical denial of the existence of these rights, imprisonment is ruled out as a penal response to violations of the law.

49. Again democratizing Hegel and Brudner, see Alan Brudner, "The Contraction of Crime in Hegel's Rechtsphilosophie," in Markus D. Dubber (ed.), *Foundational Texts in Modern Criminal Law* (New York: Oxford University Press, 2014), 160–161.

50. Ibid., 161.

51. Dzur, *Punishment, Participatory Democracy, and the Jury*, 36.

52. Colin Crouch, *Post-Democracy* (Malden, MA: Polity Press, 2004); Jacques Ranciere, *Disagreement: Politics and Philosophy*, trans. Julie Rose (Minneapolis: University of Minnesota Press, 2004); Jurgen Habermas, "Europe's Post-Democratic Era," *The Guardian*, 2011, www.theguardian.com/commentisfree/2011/nov/10/jurgen-habermas-europe-post-democratic.

53. Jimmy Reid, "Rector's Inaugural Address," Glasgow University, 1972, Reprinted in *The Independent*, August 13, 2010.

54. Peter Mair, *Ruling The Void: The Hollowing Of Western Democracy* (London: Verso, 2013), 20–44; Colin Hay, *Why We Hate Politics* (Cambridge: Polity Press, 2007).

55. Crouch, *Post-Democracy*, 4.

56. Vanessa Barker, "Prison, and the Public Sphere: Toward a Democratic Theory of Penal Order," in David Scott (ed.), *Why Prison?* (Cambridge: Cambridge University Press) 131.

57. Loader, "Review Symposium."

58. Bernard Harcourt, "The Invisibility of the Prison in Democratic Theory: A Problem of 'Virtual Democracy,'" *The Good Society*, 23, no. 1 (2014): 11–12.

59. Crouch, *Post-Democracy*; Wolfgang Streeck, "Citizens as Customers," *New Left Review* II, no. 76 (August 2012): 27–47; Keith Faulks, *Citizenship in Modern Britain* (Edinburgh: Edinburgh University Press, 1998), 102–105.

60. Anthony Giddens, *The Third Way: The Renewal of Social Democracy* (Malden, MA: Polity Press, 1998), 37; Anthony Giddens, *Modernity and Self-Identity: Self and Society in the Late Modern Age* (Cambridge: Polity Press, 1991).

61. Streeck, "Citizens as Customers."

62. Peter Ramsay, *The Insecurity State : Vulnerable Autonomy and the Right to Security in the Criminal Law*, Oxford Monographs on Criminal Law and Criminal Justice. (Oxford: Oxford University Press, 2012); see also Jonathan Simon, *Governing Through Crime: How the War on Crime Transformed American Democracy and Created a Culture of Fear* (Oxford: Oxford University Press, 2009), 86–89.

63. Simon, *Governing Through Crime*, 76; Ramsay, *The Insecurity State*, 103; Alison Young, *Imagining Crime* (Thousand Oaks, CA: Sage, 1996), 55.

64. Simon, *Governing Through Crime*, 76.

65. Bear in mind that we are speaking here of an official construction of the citizen as victim, just as democratic political communities construct citizens as persons. Actual victims may be very robust in their response to an offense or very forgiving toward the offender. However, even from the standpoint of such concrete victims, an offender's wrongdoing is going to be more potent as a violation of their rights than it will be to the state as a denial of rights as such.

66. Ministry of Justice, "The Story of the Prison Population: 1993–2012, England and Wales."

67. Peter Ramsay, *Imprisonment under the Precautionary Principle* (Oxford: Hart Publishing, 2012); Ramsay, *The Insecurity State*.

68. Jean Floud and Warren Young, *Dangerousness and Criminal Justice* (London: Avebury, 1981), 46; Ramsay, *Imprisonment under the Precautionary Principle*, 204–205; Douglas Husak, "Lifting the Cloak: Preventive Detention as Punishment," *San Diego Law Review* 48 (November 2011): 1173. That incapacitation could be a proportionate retributive response to the wrong of dangerousness should not surprise us since proportionality as such "is virtually indeterminate in its substantive implications" (see Lacey and Pickard, "The Chimera of Proportionality").

69. Peter Ramsay, "Pashukanis and Public Protection," in Markus D. Dubber (ed.), *Foundational Texts in Modern Criminal Law* (New York: Oxford University Press, 2014), 199–218.

70. Markus Dubber, *Victims in the War on Crime: The Use and Abuse of Victims' Rights* (New York: NYU Press, 2006), 154–155.

71. Keith Ewing, *Bonfire of the Liberties: New Labour, Human Rights, and the Rule of Law* (Oxford: Oxford University Press, 2010).

72. Barker, *The Politics of Imprisonment*, 12.

73. Ibid.

74. Alan W. Norrie, *Law, Ideology and Punishment: Historical Critique of the Liberal Ideal of Criminal Justice* (Dordrecht: Kluwer Academic Publishers, 1990), 83–85.

75. Craig Reeves, "Retribution and the Metaphysics of Agency," unpublished paper (2014).

76. Alan W. Norrie, *Punishment Responsibility and Justice* (Oxford: Oxford University Press, 2000); Barbara A. Hudson, "Beyond Proportionate Punishment: Difficult Cases and the 1991 Criminal Justice Act," *Crime, Law and Social Change* 22, no. 1 (1994): 59–78.

77. Miller, "Power to the People," 285.

78. Norrie, *Punishment Responsibility and Justice*, 220–221.

79. Despite significant differences between democratic retributivism and other abolitionist perspectives, it shares with them this framing of penal reform as merely one moment on the road to abolition. See Thomas Mathiesen, *The Politics of Abolition* (London: Martin Robertson 1974), 210; Allegra McCleod, "Prison Abolition and Grounded Justice", *UCLA L. Rev.* 62 (2015) 1156, 1207–1218.

80. In other words, the radical democratization of the penal state entails its withering away (see Robert Fine, *Democracy and the Rule of Law* [Caldwell NJ: The Blackburn Press, 2002], 169).

81. Albert W. Dzur, "Repellent Institutions and the Absentee Public: Grounding Opinion in Responsibility for Punishment," in Jesper Ryberg and Julian V. Roberts (eds.), *Popular Punishment* (Oxford: Oxford University Press, 2014), 207–208.

CHAPTER 6 | Why Greater Public Participation
in Criminal Justice?

CHRISTOPHER BENNETT

Introduction

In this chapter I aim to clarify and further the debate over public participation in criminal justice. On one side of this debate are those who argue that the impact of public opinion has distorted criminal justice policy, giving politicians an incentive to introduce harsh policies of dubious effectiveness, and that the solution lies in removing criminal justice policy from direct political—and hence public—control. On the other are those who argue that the public has to have a decisive role in criminal justice policy, and that the problems arising from "penal populism" show not that public participation is bad as such, but simply that the way that electoral politics engages the public in decision-making can be highly problematic. On this latter view, we should agree that electoral politics is not a meaningful or constructive form of public participation, but we have grounds to be skeptical whether "expert" decision-making, uncoupled from public scrutiny and input, will always lead to optimal outcomes; furthermore, it is an evasion of citizens' responsibilities toward the "dirty business" of criminal justice if we leave experts to make decisions from which we can then avert our gaze. The lesson, according to this latter view, is that we need to think harder about the way the public are empowered to engage in decision-making.

One important point at issue between the two sides is whether insulating key policy decisions in criminal justice would be undemocratic, and whether it matters if it is. Answering this question will require us to say something about the nature and value of democracy, as well as saying something about the kinds of decision-making institutions that democracy requires. To this end, I aim in this chapter to provide a number of reasons we might have for approving of public participation. Once these reasons are articulated, we can use them to inform the question of how we might reform and rebuild criminal justice institutions to give the public a more productive role. My aim in this chapter is mainly to give a clear articulation of the ground on which this debate should proceed, and to show how we can begin to assess the strength of these arguments. While a (critical) friend of the pro–public-participation side,[1] I do not regard the argument as being settled, and I aim to show some of the challenges that lie ahead in making the case for this side of the argument.

The chapter proceeds as follows. In the next section I outline the view that we need a mechanism whereby criminal justice policy can be insulated from certain forms of public input. I look at the concern that this move might be undemocratic, as well as some responses to this concern. Next, I move to the other side of the debate, looking at the work of Albert Dzur. Dzur argues that the real solution to penal populism is *greater* public input. I then try to clarify the grounds of the debate between Dzur and his opponents, and I put forward eight theses that might be advanced by Dzur in defense of his claims; doing so allows us also to see how Dzur's opponents might respond, and therefore how the debate might be pushed forward. After some evaluative discussion of these claims, the final section concludes with some further reflections.

Is the Weakening of Public Control Over Criminal Justice Policy Undemocratic?

Reviewing the twelve "indices of change" within contemporary (Anglo-American) criminal justice systems that David Garland lists at the outset of *The Culture of Control*, the reader cannot help but see an overall picture emerge. According to this picture criminal justice policy has altered over the past thirty or forty years (for the worse?) as a result of the increased assertiveness, or at least the increased influence, of a criminologically unsophisticated public.[2] "The decline of the rehabilitative ideal," "the re-emergence of punitive sanctions and expressive justice," the changing "emotional tone" of criminal justice policy, and "politicization and the new populism": the suggestion, at first glance at least, is of untutored retributive public sentiments usurping the role previously occupied by penological experts, emotion replacing reason. Garland expresses this view of the rise of penal populism as follows:

> There is now a distinctly populist current in penal politics that denigrates expert and professional elites and claims the authority of "the people," of common sense, of "getting back to basics." The dominant voice of crime policy is no longer the expert or even the practitioner but that of the long-suffering, ill-served people—especially of "the victim" and the fearful, anxious members of the public. A few decades ago public opinion functioned as an occasional brake on policy initiatives: now it operates as a privileged source. The importance of research and criminological knowledge is downgraded and in its place is a new deference to the voice of "experience," of "common sense," of "what everyone knows."[3]

Garland is careful to leave it ambiguous whether the group that has usurped the criminal justice agenda is the public itself, or rather some elite group that *claims* to speak on behalf of the people—perhaps for its own ends.[4] For instance, does the appropriation of the criminal justice system by "the public" represent genuine popular control, or is the appeal to the public simply a device employed by politicians—and those in whose interests they act—to win votes and further specific political ends? Are the public really subject to the fear of crime and the retributive passions that appear, on Garland's picture, to be driving the political agenda?[5] We will come back to these questions later.

However we should understand the deeper significance of what is going on, the phenomena that feed this analysis seem to be reasonably clear. Greater use of imprisonment and longer prison sentences; prison conditions that arguably violate human rights; the widespread denial to prisoners of basics of citizenship such as a right to vote; three-strikes-and-you're-out policies that have the effect of bringing more people into the criminal justice system as a result of minor criminality; victim impact statements at sentencing; Megan's laws; civic and employment restrictions on those with a criminal record—measures of questionable impact on real public safety are introduced in the apparent hope of satisfying a perceived public appetite, while experts, evidence, and experience are neglected or even denigrated and ridiculed.[6] Furthermore, one key driver of this nexus between assertive public punitiveness and political power has been the electoral system.[7] Politicians have found that appealing to simple messages about crime control and individual responsibility—protecting "us" against "them" who would threaten us—has led to electoral success, and whatever the complexities that lie behind this fact, it has prevented the development of a serious and evidence-sensitive debate about crime in countries like the United States and the United Kingdom. Those at the sharp end of mass incarceration—often those who are already the most vulnerable in our societies—have been the needless victims of this rise in the temperature of the public mood and its political expression.

In the face of this problem, what is to be done? A characteristic liberal response is to try to take criminal justice off the political agenda. For Nicola Lacey, for instance, a way out of the toxic mix of criminal justice and electoral politics

> will be possible only if the two main political parties can reach a framework agreement about the removal of criminal justice policy—or at least of key aspects of policy, such as the size of the prison system—from party political debate. This might be done by setting up an initial Royal Commission, or something of yet wider scope, in an effort to generate an expanded debate that takes in not only the widest possible range of social groups but also a broad range of the non-penal policies and institutions on which criminal justice practices bear ... A further important condition would be the re-constitution of some respect for expertise in the field. As such it would be important not only to have the Commission serviced by a substantial expert bureaucracy but also, following implementation of its conclusions, to consign the development of particular aspects of future criminal justice policy to institutions encompassing both wide representation and expertise. In other words, the removal of criminal justice policy from party political competition would open up the possibility of the kind of solution to fiscal policy implemented through the Monetary Policy Committee (MPC) ... By conferring the task of setting interest rates to an independent body of experts located in the Bank of England, making this body's deliberations transparent, and setting up robust mechanisms of accountability to parliament, Gordon Brown crafted a strategy which has commanded remarkable public and political support [8]

So should we seek to create a criminal justice version of the UK Monetary Policy Committee into whose hands responsibility for key policy decisions should be placed, rather than having them made by politicians who are more directly accountable to the electorate?[9] The problem that we will be looking at in this chapter is that this might look undemocratic. After all, two large (but in principle attractive) principles might suggest that such a move would involve taking decisions away from the public that they have a right to make: first of all, that the rationale of institutions like the criminal justice system is to serve the public, and so the formulation and execution of criminal justice policy has to remain in the end the public's business; and secondly, that the ultimate source of authority in the state is the people as a whole—so no institution can legitimately act in the public's name without the public's say-so. These two claims seem to speak in favor of ultimate control over public policy resting in the hands of the public.

Lacey is careful, however, not to argue that democracy is unimportant. Democracy is important, in her view, but it is simply not the only thing that is important. Also important are values such as inclusivity and respect for rights—values, to be sure, not unrelated to the values of democracy, but which can come into conflict with some of the claims that are made for democratic procedures of transparency, popular choice, and accountability of public decisions. Furthermore, given that democracy encompasses a wide and variable set of values and claims, the answer to the question of which model of democracy is appropriate for a given political community at a given time will depend not simply on abstract ideal theorizing (although that will also have its place), but on the structural socioeconomic conditions faced by a particular polity at a particular moment in history. In other words, the implementation of a set of procedures for popular control that may be perfectly appropriate in one set of political circumstances might lead to intolerable violations of other important values when implemented willy-nilly in a quite different set of circumstances. Democracy, in a nutshell, is a value, but a value representing a weighty responsibility that needs to be used wisely. Where a demos has proven itself unable to exercise it wisely—perhaps for structural reasons as much as any moral or volitional failure—it can be the best thing to do, all things considered, to take some of those responsibilities away. As Lacey has it:

> While accountability and responsiveness are, in different guises, constants in democratic theory, they are in potential conflict with other values such as the aspiration to foster an inclusionary criminal justice policy. And this conflict may be accentuated by the particular institutional constraints under which different sorts of democratic governments operate.[10]

There are, therefore, a number of broad lines of response to the charge that taking criminal justice policy out of direct political control in the way that Lacey suggests is undemocratic: 1) We might reject the importance of democracy outright—on the basis, say, that the demos is lacking in the key expertise necessary to make decisions about criminal justice, and that it is crazy to put the fools in charge of the ship when there is a qualified captain at hand. 2) More sympathetic to democracy, we might nevertheless argue that it is not the only game in town. For instance, values of democracy might come into conflict with values of inclusion or basic rights and interests. 3) Even more sympathetic to democracy, we might nevertheless say that there are various conceptions of democracy, and that it is not clear that taking some decisions away from the people *is* undemocratic, at least where the decisions that are made are transparent and there is some manner of accountability. Another example, besides the Monetary Policy Committee, is of course the judiciary, in particular the institution of a constitutional court the authority of which is supreme over legislators. Many would say that democracy has to consist in more than just popular sovereignty, at least if this is construed as the idea that any policy affirmed by a quorate majority vote is legitimate. Democracy is at least in part grounded in a belief in the basic equality of each citizen, and this has led many to think that a political system in which the popular vote is constrained from passing laws that would violate that basic equality (e.g., laws that would deny some citizens a basic standard of treatment, as in an apartheid system), for instance by a constitution containing a bill of fundamental rights, is not undemocratic.

Furthermore, finally, 4) we might argue that there is no incompatibility, in principle, between democracy and the delegation of powers to representative or expert bodies to carry out particular functions—including functions of policy-setting.[11] The MPC would not be illegitimately usurping any functions that should belong to the demos, it might be said, as long as the demos has authorized it to carry out that job. Democratic authorization is a bit like a collective version of consent—a transfer of rights from one party to another, or an endowment of rights on one party by another. Your taking my property without my say-so would be an illegitimate denial of my authority over it, and hence theft; but once authorized by me to take it, you are within your rights to do so. Similarly, it might be said, there is no conflict with the authority of democracy if an expert body is democratically authorized to make those decisions. There is no incompatibility between delegation and democracy. If there were nothing more to democracy than the importance of collective authorization then this would definitively answer the charge that insulating sentencing policy from popular control is undemocratic.

A Dissenting Voice: In Favor of Greater Public Participation

In his book *Punishment, Participatory Democracy and the Jury*, and a series of articles, Albert Dzur has argued for a different view.[12] On Dzur's alternative, it is not public participation in criminal justice as such that is the problem. Rather the problem is a democratic deficit in criminal justice, and it is greater and more meaningful democracy that is required to get us out of it.

> The criminal justice discourse on the penal state views populism in a negative and monochromatic light, overlooking the constructive tendencies of populist movements historically and neglecting the possibility that public involvement could lead to less rather than more punitive policy in contemporary politics.[13]

Calling Lacey's suggestion "the technocratic response to penal populism" (29), Dzur claims that it faces a number of practical and normative problems. First of all, he worries that there is a "lack of will or political capital to launch such reforms"; indeed, this practical problem is implicit in the diagnosis of the problems to which this response is meant to be a solution, namely, the decline in public deference to expert bodies (31). Secondly, even if such a committee could get off the ground, it would be unlikely to be effective in the long-term because it fails to engage the public and hence engender the support and understanding that are necessary for any public body to command allegiance (30). Thirdly, and fundamentally, policies such as that suggested by Lacey "imply that the public is unable to self-regulate, unable to own up to a more measured approach to criminal justice, to punish but in a more thoughtful, consistent and humane fashion without strict elite guidance" (31). Dzur acknowledges that Lacey might respond in the way we have considered above: that there is no incompatibility between democracy and insulating protection of fundamental rights, or between democracy and delegation. But he makes three points: 1) that it is not clear that an insulated sentencing committee would be making only technical decisions, and that the political part of their decision-making should in a democracy be the business of the public; 2) that crimes are thought of, in Blackstone's terms, as "public wrongs," and hence as acts the nature of which the public is intimately concerned; and 3) it is to treat the public, from whom we can and should expect more, as legitimately "careless regarding the lives of others."[14]

By contrast, Dzur argues that the problems of penal populism have come about not because of too much democracy or public input, but rather because of insufficient or inappropriate forms of public input. The solution to this problem is not to sacrifice the demands of democracy to the more urgent demands of inclusivity and human rights, but rather to increase or improve the way the public are involved in the formulation and implementation of criminal justice policy. Dzur points out that concerns about penal populism emerge at the same time as social theorists started worrying about the decline of social capital and the "hollowing out" of the public sphere: thus there seems to be a contradictory movement of too much public control at the same time as not enough public engagement.

> How to make sense of this paradox of too much popular participation albeit concentrated on a specific set of issues, and too little at the same time? The best way is to see penal populism as a case of democratic deficit not surplus, a popular movement without the kind of social capital that would lead to constructive engagement in criminal justice policymaking. How the public was mobilized and what it was mobilized to accomplish are critical ... [Penal populism] is best understood, then, not as a failure to protect the system from public participation but as a failure to incorporate it in a constructive, dialogical way.[15]

An important illustration of Dzur's point here is a distinction that he draws on the basis of work by Harry Boyte between two ways of engaging the public: a mobilization strategy; and an organizing strategy. Quoting from Boyte in this passage, he explains the difference as follows:

> Mobilization strategies, in the form of signature drives, door-to-door canvassing operations, or protest marches, are potent but toxic. As Boyte points out, "they expect very little of the citizen; they depend upon caricatures of the enemy; and they are forms of citizen participation in which professionals craft both the message and the patterns of involvement." Organizing strategies, by contrast, stress "patient, sustained work in communities," "face to face horizontal interactions among people," and "respect for the intelligence and talents of ordinary, uncredentialed citizens" (35).

Unlike mere mobilization, genuine citizen organization gives lay people the opportunity—and indeed requires of them—to engage in making key decisions themselves, bringing their particular skills to bear and hence contributing to a wide-ranging collective pool of experience and knowledge, engaging in debate and thinking things through together, and thereby making both the resultant policy itself and the public support it can command more robust.

On the basis of this distinction between the potentially toxic "mobilization" strategy and the more participatory, deliberative and robust "organization" strategy, Dzur's claims about penal populism can therefore be reconstructed as follows. The ramping-up of criminal justice policy is the result of a particular form of public engagement characterized by a situation in which policy is formulated by political representatives competing for votes. This situation allows for, and even encourages, a lack of care and responsibility on the part of the public who are voting for one policy or another. Rather than having the weight of the fate of particular individuals on one's hands, one is rather expected to respond to caricatures and broad claims that it becomes impossible to verify. Politicians are adept at finding a message that will portray the issues in a particular way, and which will maximize the number of votes they can get. In such a way the public need not be seen as acting stupidly: they may be reacting appropriately given the way the issues are portrayed to them. But that is not the same as increasing public understanding of complex and many-sided situations and encouraging careful examination of the issues. If the public in these circumstances ends up voting for policies that reflect simple retributivist stereotypes, this is not because the public are incapable, if put into a situation that requires it, of dealing with many-sided complex problems.

The question is, then, what forms of public organization (as opposed to mobilization) could work in the realm of criminal justice. While some theorists of participatory democracy are resolutely anti-institutional and antigovernment, Dzur is less pessimistic, seeing institutions including government as *products* of collective endeavor rather than its enemies (34, 52–56). While institutions can become dysfunctional in the absence of public involvement, this does not show them to be fundamentally corrupt and corrupting; participatory democracy properly understood, on Dzur's view, takes place through public participation in preexisting institutions. It is therefore not necessary for democracies to constantly reinvent the wheel by dealing with each social problem afresh each generation, since institutions can, at their best, be repositories of collective wisdom that serve the public by laying down procedures, and by training experts, that provide efficient ways to solve or ameliorate such problems—though of course democratic input can be instrumental in stimulating institutions to reinvent themselves to meet the demands of new social conditions. For Dzur, the ideal comes about where institutions are "rationally disorganized" by the introduction of lay members. Rational disorganization is an apt phrase for two reasons: first because lay participation makes institutions operate less efficiently, and thus demands that the make-up of institutions builds in the recognition of procedural values other than efficiency; and secondly, because lay participants are more likely to bend standards of procedural correctness and generalization in favor of substantive justice and attention to the particulars of the individual case. However, to repeat, Dzur's ideal is not that lay participation should overwhelm or trump bureaucratic rationality and its formalization of expert knowledge, but rather that lay and professional input should complement one another in a complex harmony or balance; institutions on his view "are diminished when either professionals or laypeople become dominant." (58)

Of course, in common-law systems there already exists an institution of rational disorganization in the field of criminal justice, namely the jury, and it is this that Dzur recommends as a model for the kind of lay participation he has in mind to overcome the crisis in criminal justice. "Institutions like courts need rational disorganization as an antidote to rigidified, professionalized and remote practice." (57). As we will see, there is an argument that both institutions and citizens—and, indeed, the relationship between them—benefit from lay participation. However, what Dzur thinks of as the core importance of the jury lies elsewhere, in an elusive but suggestive thought not often articulated in mainstream Anglo-American political theory (again, we will have more to say about this later). This goes back to his view that "to be a good citizen is to work together and bear responsibility for the public sphere and for the institutions that shape social life" (34). He quotes from Chesterton's reflections on the trial and draws from this a crucial idea:

> Chesterton's main point, that the jury "allows fresh blood and fresh thoughts from the streets" to infuse courtrooms that otherwise become the mundane "workshops" of court professionals all too accustomed to the job, is well known. Equally important, I think, is its underappreciated flip side, namely, that the jury allows, indeed presses, ordinary citizens to take ownership of the "terrible business" of criminal justice ... In a democracy, citizens are not ever left off the hook of moral and political responsibility for punishment (40).

Some Reflections on the Debate: What Counts in Favor of Public Participation?

What we have done so far is to set up a debate about the proper response to those indices of change noted by Garland. Either side of the debate has to hand a diagnosis of the problem that these changes represent and a prescription for how to address it. According to one side, the problem lies with the extent of involvement of public opinion—opinion which, given social structural realities, is not particularly tractable at present; this diagnosis leads to the prescription that we should insulate criminal justice policy from public involvement. On the other side, by contrast, the problem lies rather in the disconnect between policymakers and the public, where representatives create policies that can gain public assent on the basis of superficial engagement, and the prescription is, rather than creating a formally insulated but actually inherently fragile panel of experts (fragile because it cannot gain popular support), to increase meaningful public participation.

This debate raises a number of questions that are beyond the remit of the chapter. For instance, if it were unrealistic to think that there would be either the political or popular will—or structural space—to undertake the kind of participation that Dzur recommends, his view would be more of a long-term aspiration than a live option. How realistic a proposal it is is not something I will attempt to address here.[16]

However, some aspects of the debate rest on key disagreements in political theory regarding the nature and value of democracy. That is: what does a system have to be like to deserve the epithet "democratic"; what is important about democracy; and what institutional forms are required to put what is important about democracy into action? Of course, insofar as Lacey and Dzur are offering us prescriptions as to how to get out of the crisis, they must be drawing on some view of practical priorities and values; but even their diagnoses of the nature of the problem that we face are underpinned by different conceptions of the apt division of responsibility between citizen and state, conceptions grounded in some view of the value of different forms of arrangement.

While I will not attempt to settle this debate in this chapter, I want to do some work clarifying the ground on which the argument will take place. So in this section I will set out a number of conceptions of the nature and value of democracy, and comment briefly on the strengths and weaknesses of these in relation to the debate we have been discussing. One of these will be the view of participation that Dzur finds in

Chesterton, and which I think has been underrepresented in recent discussions of democracy.

First of all, let us set the scene by drawing a distinction between what David Held has called "protective" and "developmental" conceptions of democracy.[17] While both of these conceptions accept basic democratic values of 1) equal liberty to live according to one's own lights, 2) equality of control over the exercise of political power, 3) state power being exercised only for the common good, and 4) authority resting ultimately with the people collectively as a whole—values that can be thought of as implicit in the description of democracy as "rule of the people, by the people, for the people"—the two conceptions give these features importantly different interpretations. According to the protective conception, democratic procedures are instrumentally justified as the best available means by which the individual rights can be protected from abuse by government and by other fellow citizens. Democracy may not be intrinsically just, on this conception;[18] rather the justification is that a system that accommodates a degree of popular sovereignty, applied by representatives and constrained by a constitution, is a powerful way to create a social scene marked by the stable protection of rights and freedoms. According to the developmental conception, however, democracy *can* have something of intrinsic value to it: democracy is necessary, not only, as a contingent matter, for the protection of individual rights, but also, noncontingently and constitutively, for something like "the education of an entire people to the point where their intellectual, emotional and moral capacities have reached their full potential and they are joined, freely and actively in a genuine community."[19] The developmental conception need not reject constitutionalism, or representative democracy, or the rule of law, or those other elements that serve to constrain the untrammelled exercise of popular will—or at least, it need not reject them entirely; nevertheless, on the developmental conception, some form of active engagement in the political life of one's community is an aspect of the good human life, and life is to some extent impoverished where this is absent.

It may in the end prove too simple to say that Lacey takes the protectionist view in which the key role of the state lies in the establishment and maintenance of a regime of stable protection of the rights of all those individuals who make up the polity, while the conception defended by Dzur sees citizen involvement in the state as a necessary part of a genuinely human life; but that will be a reasonable starting point for our discussion. Furthermore, should Dzur be able to back this developmental claim up, it will give his position some room for manoeuvre in the following sense.

Even if it were the case that democratic institutions with a high degree of public participation were not the best available means to creating a stable regime where the interests of all can be protected—if, for instance, as Lacey suggests, a better route might be to create an insulated expert committee immune to direct public participation and control—there may be some further values that make these otherwise deficient outcomes in some way *worth it*. In other words, the fact that certain developmental values are served might make it the case that outcomes that are deficient in other respects up to a certain degree can and should be tolerated. Of course, this may not be the case, and it may be that public participation will make the system function more accurately than otherwise. We will consider some arguments for this conclusion later. But even if it were to turn out that this is not the case, it would not necessarily follow that Dzur's argument was defeated. Politics is always a function of balancing and of gain and loss— the idea of a perfect state in which all values can be reconciled without moral loss is a figment of Isaiah Berlin's imagination (though of course, he took this as a target to argue against rather than to endorse). The main point, however, is that we should wait to see what case can be made for those developmental values before we conclude that the only thing that matters is "what works" in protecting basic rights and interests.

With this by way of preamble, let us turn now to a review of reasons that favor public participation. I will set out eight claims that might be put forward, separately or, more likely, jointly, and which are relevant to Dzur's case in favor of greater public participation. Having presented each, I will consider some complexities and possible responses. This will in no way amount to a comprehensive discussion, let alone the establishing of Dzur's case. This review will rather, I hope, serve the purposes of clarifying the nature of the debate and setting out the ground on which the arguments will have to take place. Nevertheless, it will also help to show, I hope, the argumentative resources that Dzur has on his side.

It might also be useful to say something about the organization of the following theses. A through C can be considered as grounds for thinking that at least some of the things that count in favor of Lacey's model will also count in favor of Dzur's: so the lesson from these theses is that Lacey's model has not been proven to be the better one. Theses D and E then point to problems that might arise from Lacey's model, and hence advantages of Dzur's. Then with F, G, and H, we get to the heart of Dzur's case—these are the key questions that will need to be worked through in order to decide how compelling his conclusions are. For instance, if F (the Correction thesis) is true, or at least partially true, then all the other theses would become immediately more appealing as a package; if it is not true, we face difficult choices.

A. The Defusion Thesis

"The most urgent need is to take criminal justice off the agenda of electoral politics. But this could be done equally well by having key decisions made by a jury, or a commission on which there would be significant lay membership, as it would by the institution of a commission of experts."

The question critics would ask is what is meant by "could be done equally well." On the one hand, it means merely that the use of the jury is another option for insulating key decisions from electoral politics. That is true. But is it an equally good, or even a better option than a sentencing commission? That, of course, depends on what further values are served, either by having the jury make the decisions, or having a commission do so. So this thesis cannot be persuasive until we have said some more on that front.

B. The Legitimacy Thesis

"The source of ultimate authority is the people, so they should have the final say over the exercise of collective coercive power. Therefore criminal justice policy cannot be legitimate without there having been a prior act of collective authorization by the body with ultimate authority: that is, the people. Authorization via plebiscite is impractical for anything beyond the very basic principles of sentencing policy. Given that more detailed authorization is needed, and that seeking such authorization through electoral politics have proven so damaging in other ways, an alternative source of authorization would be assent from a majority vote amongst a jury of citizens who can, by virtue of random selection, stand for the people."

The burden of this thesis is to suggest that the decision of a randomly selected jury can be a source of democratic legitimacy. If successful it would answer those who assume that democratic legitimacy can only come through the decisions of elected officials (or those appointed or endorsed by such officials). However, to answer this question decisively would require a theory of what legitimacy consists in and how it can be gained. Furthermore, it is not clear that this thesis has an answer to one of the initial responses we considered to the charge that insulating criminal justice policy is antidemocratic: the response that says that something like a sentencing commission would be perfectly legitimate and democratic if appointed by a democratically elected legislature. To undermine that claim we would need a further argument to show, for example, that elections do not really confer legitimacy on decisions made by the elected.[20]

C. The Fairness Thesis

"Where there is continuing and fundamental disagreement regarding political decisions amongst people who are not obviously incompetent or merely careless, the fairest response to such disagreement is to allow the decision to be made in such a way that each person has exactly the same say as any other—that is, through one person one vote."

This kind of thesis has been advanced in a different legal context by Jeremy Waldron.[21] It claims that regardless of the expected quality of the decision, there are grounds for submitting controversial political decisions to a democratic process, for in that way a fair procedure is used to make the decision. This thesis can be used to explain why it can be appropriate to submit issues to democratic decisions even if it were the case that democratic decisions were more likely to get it wrong than other available methods: for democratic decisions have the virtue of fairness, or of treating each person as mattering equally with everyone else when it comes to deciding how to make the decision. This is not quite the developmental theory of democracy considered by Held—since there is not the claim that democracy is inherently good by virtue of developing valuable characteristically human capacities—but there is the claim that there is something inherently valuable in a decision procedure that treats each participant equally; as a result, this thesis explains why there might be something important about allowing decision-making by public participation even where it is not an optimal pursuit of the state's protective functions.

One criticism of the Fairness thesis might be to ask whether it does not lead to the unpalatable conclusion that even complex empirical matters, if they bear on questions of the exercise of political power, can only fairly be resolved by means of one person one vote. Let me explain this briefly. First of all, the Fairness thesis has a restricted scope: normally we don't think that all decisions should be made by equal voting—expert decision-making has some role (a doctor should decide which medicine you are to take, for instance). So the question is what its scope is. The most obvious way to distinguish which decisions are subject to the Fairness thesis and which (like the doctor's) are not is to point to the exercise of collective political power (i.e., the power of the state, seen as an agent of the people). The procedural fairness of a decision becomes important in circumstances where it is the exercise of power that should in principle belong to all of us that is at issue. The issue is then, not just whether that power is exercised wisely, but whether it is exercised fairly. However, the problem arises if there are questions about the exercise of state power that can only be answered with reference to complex evidence that only experts can properly assess. Take for instance the question whether longer prison sentences reduces crime. This bears on the exercise of political power. Is there something to be said for the fairness of opening this question up to public decision? Surely this is a conclusion that should be left to those competent to assess it. If the Fairness thesis implies otherwise, this suggests that the Fairness thesis is false.

Nevertheless, the conclusion that we should draw from this criticism is not that the Fairness thesis fails, but that an argument needs to be provided to tell us which types of decisions considerations of fairness apply to and why. The Fairness thesis does seem to succeed in establishing that fairness as well as accuracy counts in the assessment of at least some decisions, in some contexts.

The overall thrust of A through C, then, is that there are some democratic values that could be compatible with Lacey's proposal of democratic delegation, but that could be served just as well, or even better, by public participatory mechanisms. But can we go further in support of Dzur?

D. The Efficacy Thesis

"Public support is necessary for the effective functioning of the criminal justice system, and is best brought about by having the public participate within that system."

This thesis makes two controversial claims that would need further support. First of all, that public support is necessary, and secondly that it is best brought about through public participation. In support of the first, one might point to the fact that officials themselves need to some extent to believe in the values of the system; and public input and cooperation is needed at many stages. In support of the second, one might point to the distance that can open up when the system becomes (or is perceived to have become) autonomous. However, it is also true that modern citizens have become quite used to centralized agencies as well as large private companies taking care of much of the business of everyday life. Of course, there is a large debate about whether such a state of affairs allows "insulated" institutions to have great power without accountability. But at least sometimes, it might be said, autonomy from public opinion is clearly no bad thing, since it enables public institutions to practice moral leadership—which they have done in the United Kingdom for instance by prohibiting capital punishment in the face of public opinion. So the argument over the Efficacy thesis is not settled—though it may be strengthened by combination with some of the theses that follow.

E. The Civic Schoolhouse Thesis

"Having greater public participation in decision-making in institutions like criminal justice helps to increase civic virtue in two important ways. First of all, it confronts citizens with the genuine difficulties and complexities of decision-making, and hence leads to a greater understanding of the challenges faced by representatives and officials, and helps to reduce disillusionment and disconnection between the two. And secondly, it makes citizens more adept at the kinds of skills of civic political thinking that officials need to employ, skills that are essential for the day-to-day business of (self-) government."[22]

With this thesis we broach one of the sources of the view that political participation is part of the human good—and hence the source of the developmental conception of democracy canvassed earlier. Political participation enriches human life, in part due to the acquisition of new and important skills, and in part by increasing one's awareness of the complexity around one. One of the main charges that could be made against this point is naïve optimism about the transformational potential of political engagement. Are citizens really likely to be shaken out of apathy and mutual suspicion by being given serious responsibility? Or is that simply to hand over the fate of those being decided about to people who simply won't take it seriously? Evaluation of juries is of course controversial.[23] Two things that might count in favor of the Civic Schoolhouse thesis, but about which we would need more evidence, are a) whether the imposition of responsibility can, in favorable circumstances, have the effect of encouraging people to deliberate seriously, and b) whether the fact that jury responsibility is one-off (or at any rate occasional or episodic) prevents it from becoming routine, and hence leaves jurors sensitized to the responsibility they bear. Some evidence about this might come from the literature on restorative justice.[24] However, the last word at present might perhaps be given to Lord McCluskey:

Now before this discussion began, if the Lord Chancellor will permit me, he said that many people—members of the public—they want to hang and they want to castrate and cut off the hands of thieves and things like that. My experience is that that may be what the people in the street think about crimes they read about in the papers but once they come into court and sit for several days, or even several weeks, they see the accused person, listen to the evidence, they discover the multi-faceted aspects of the case. Then they emerge as rational, judgemental human beings, and not the people who are screaming for the scaffold.[25]

F. The Correction Thesis

"Contrary to the claim that the public lack expertise, there is a clear role for nontechnical evaluative decisions at every stage of the criminal process, and there is no reason to think that the public would be less accurate in making such decisions than public officials. Indeed, a group like a jury may be more likely to be able to come up with accurate decisions for a number of reasons having to do with the biases that can affect those who operate within institutions. These may include: i) the fact that expert discretion and judgment are often exercised individually, whereas the jury would benefit from explicit collective deliberation involving a range of perspectives, and where one person's view can be challenged by others and improved, allowing a decision to be reached in which that range of perspectives are taken into account; ii) the fact that experts may become desensitized to the human reality that they are dealing with, as individuals become 'cases' or 'clients,' assimilated to a short-cut or stereotype that allows for efficient but distorting treatment, whereas a jury of one's peers may be more likely to deal with the case through fresh, untainted eyes; iii) the fact that experts are constrained by institutional procedures that have to meet demands of generality, simplicity, clarity, and may therefore have to artificially leave important elements of the situation out of consideration—e.g. to align the present decision with authoritative decisions in prior cases—whereas a jury could have the freedom and will to ignore such procedural constraints and attend to the essence of the matter in hand."

This argument says that public input into decision-making can correct for biases in official-made decisions arising from individual discretion, routine desensitization and procedural distortions. How could this thesis be established? The argument requires a) some criterion of correctness for decision-making; and b) comparative evidence regarding the performance of experts in institutions and the performance of lay people, controlled to ensure that only the relevant variables are being tested. It is probably unlikely that we have such evidence, or could get it.[26] However, the thesis relies on claims about the kinds of distorting forces that are at work on those who fill institutional roles. And it must also rest on a certain assessment—again hard to imagine how we would verify—of the moral competence of the average member of the public. Set against the Correction thesis, one would have to consider a more positive view of institutions as in principle progressively learning repositories for good practice regarding social needs and challenges. This might in turn require a wider consideration of professions and their role in a democracy.[27] Dzur does not reject this more positive view entirely—his view is that public input needs to take place under the aegis of institutions, and that juries should not be free to disregard institutional constraints altogether. Even if the thrust of the Correction thesis is accepted, on the question of exactly where to find the just balance between institution and lay input, the devil will be very much in the detail.

G. The "Rule of Men Not Law" Thesis

"This thesis reverses the traditional dictum trumpeting the rule of law.[28] The idea of the rule of law is that the role of individual discretion should be reduced and replaced by the determination of outcomes by general rules that apply to everyone. The 'Rule of Men' thesis holds that if the removal of discretion goes too far then the only rights that can be claimed are those that meet purely institutional criteria of desirability (for instance, that they can be stated in a clear and generalizable rule that is not subject to counterexamples). This can distort the honest and open-minded appreciation of the relevant features of the individual case. The Rule of Men thesis therefore has an epistemic aspect to it, according to which being free from procedure can make it more likely that an accurate decision will be arrived at. But there is also a normative component, concerning the quality of interaction between the representative of the institution and those with whom they deal. A person who is treated a certain way because the rules so determine may feel that their situation has merely been treated as an instance of a rule, and that their individuality has been undermined. There is some value in a type of authentic human interaction in which the members of a jury are asked to respond directly to the humanity of the other—and asked, not merely to follow the rules, but also whether the rules do justice to the nature of the case. They are therefore asked to take responsibility for an appreciation of the person's situation in such a way as to put them in a more direct—and more valuable—relation to that person than would be possible for an official whose conduct is mediated by rules and routine."

The Rule of Men thesis is connected with a theme of pro-democracy theorizing that has not been common in recent Anglo-American political theory but which flourished at the time of the New Left: the theme that institutions had become impersonal and bureaucratic, that some of our key relations and decisions are carried out automatically, efficiently, but with a sacrifice of those human characteristics that make them valuable—characteristics to do, not so much with getting the right outcomes as with having the right sorts of interactions.[29] The epistemic aspect of this thesis is connected to F(iii) above and claims that what is wrong with automatic, rule-mediated interactions is that they get the wrong answer. But another part of the thesis claims that, even were it to be the case that merely following the rules would be more likely to get you to the right answer, there would still be independent value in the decision being made by authentic human scrutiny. This is one aspect of the developmental democracy thesis—that there are some specifically political decisions the making of which through genuine scrutiny and care and the exercise of epistemic and moral virtues is inherently valuable.

The Rule of Men thesis argues—to some extent at least—against the rule of law. One advantage of the rule of law is of course that it means that people have rights that can be claimed in a court of law and are not subject to the gift or arbitrary say-so of a party who has power over the individual. The rule of law, it might be said, means that there is justice and not mere charity. However, the Rule of Men thesis argues that this argument for the rule of law presents a false dichotomy between either domination (in Pettit's republican terms) or else formalism.[30] Rather what individuals coming before some public tribunal or decision-making body have a right to is an unfettered and honest consideration of their case, guided by all and only those considerations relevant to its just resolution: consideration, in other words, structured by the employment of epistemic and moral virtues such as honesty, conscientiousness, imagination, and so on. Leaving room for this possibility means leaving room for discretion and judgment rather than taking the possibility of such judgment out of the tribunal's hands.

H. The Special Role Responsibility Thesis

"In the context of certain valuable relationships, it is inappropriate to delegate certain activities or tasks to others, even if it is the case that those others will carry it out better. For instance, if paid nurses would care better for my elderly mother than I would myself, it is not enough if I simply leave it to them, or even if I supervise what they are doing. To some extent I have to be there, actively involved. This is partly because of the effect that my being there will have on my mother; but it would still apply even were she comatose or demented or otherwise unable to recognize me. Sometimes you just have a responsibility to do some things yourself rather than passing them off on to other people. Similarly this can happen in the case of democratic politics. Being a good citizen involves sharing the responsibility of maintaining social life. There can therefore be a limit to the extent to which we the people can ask delegated technical experts to do our business for us—rather there are some things that (with the help of experts) we have to do for ourselves. That is part of being a good citizen. This particularly applies to those most challenging and difficult decisions that a society has to make—its 'dirty business,' if you like—such as crime. If as a society we are going to set up rules, enforce them, and punish those who break them, we should be prepared to deal directly with the consequences of doing so. Leaving it to a bureaucracy to deal with would be an abdication of responsibility."

This thesis and the last attempt together to get at the point Dzur draws from Chesterton's response to the jury. For Dzur this is a point about responsibility and the need for nonevasion. The thesis rests on a view of citizenship as a role in a valuable relationship, a role that brings responsibilities the fulfillment of which can be part of a viable conception of the human good.[31] To defend this thesis we would need to explain in what way citizenship is indeed an inherently valuable relationship—for instance, by reference to the particular value and achievement of self-government. We would also need to defend the second part of the thesis, namely, that some responsibilities are such that one cannot pass them on but must carry them out oneself. This has the ring of truth in certain cases—but how far does it generalize? Does the thesis show that there should be wide public participation in the health service, for example, or in other essential public services in the way that Dzur argues there should be in criminal justice? Again, however, this thesis is part of a dissatisfaction we can associate with the New Left regarding the moral quality of our interactions in modern society—that we are misled by the attractions of efficiency and convenience and fail to appreciate the way in which a richer conception of relations and responsibilities is leaching away.

Concluding Remarks

We opened this chapter with a consideration of the argument over the compatibility with democracy of a concrete policy proposal—the setting up of a sentencing commission staffed by legal and criminological experts. We looked at Lacey's argument that such a proposal would not be problematically in conflict with democratic values. In opposition to Lacey, we saw that Dzur claims, effectively, that such a response would misread the problem of penal populism, and that it would fail to solve the problem and may even exacerbate it. For Dzur, we need greater public engagement rather than less. In the third section of this chapter, I have argued that Dzur's argument can be read as having something like the following structure: allowing for greater public engagement is more likely to solve the problems termed "penal populism" than would Lacey's proposal of the commission of experts; however, even if it does not, it will have independent value. I then listed eight claims that Dzur might make in backing up this argument. I do not claim to have defended Dzur's view—indeed, in some cases I have shown that there are important counterarguments that would need to be addressed before Dzur's claims could be established. My main concern has been to clarify the ground on which the arguments have to proceed.

I have also sought to articulate two theses—the "Rule of Men not Law" and "Special Role Responsibility" Theses—that might be used in defense of some kind of participatory democracy, and which have, I think, been overlooked in the recent revival of interest in Anglo-American democratic theory. These are theses associated with the New Left and its concern that the dominance of instrumental, economic or bureaucratic rationality in contemporary society is leading to the decline of other, richer forms of human interaction. This is a theme that I have not developed in any detail in this chapter, but which it seems to me would repay further inquiry.

Before concluding, I would briefly like to illustrate this point with reference to what Feeley and Simon have called "the New Penology."[32] The New Penology, Feeley and Simon claim, involves a move away from traditional legalistic forms of criminal justice resting on culpability and sanction—as well as more humanitarian forms of criminal justice based in care for the offender and rehabilitation—and toward a penology based more on a) assessing and managing high-risk offenders, in short quantification, and b) systemic and formal rationality.[33] Without going into detail about Feeley and Simon's claims, we might ask: if they are correct, what would be wrong with this shift? My thought is that the position Dzur is articulating—in particular the developmental theses G and H—can explain why this form of criminal justice represents a kind of degradation of an important form of interaction that we have a responsibility to maintain between our fellow citizens. Rather than being treated as individuals, offenders and potential offenders are treated as risk factors to be managed and taken account of. It is a long way from being called to answer to a tribunal of one's peers.

Although this chapter has been concerned with the debate over penal populism, it is possible to see penal populism as only one of the problems currently facing the development of criminal justice, and perhaps not the most important one. Attempting to solve the problem of penal populism by further removing criminal justice from the ideal of open honest reactions between free individuals may yet turn out to be a step in the wrong direction.[34]

Notes

1. See C. Bennett, "Public Opinion and Democratic Control of Sentencing Policy" in J. Ryberg and J. V. Roberts (eds.), *Popular Punishment: On the Normative Significance of Public Opinion* (Oxford: Oxford University Press): 146–162; and "What Is the Core Normative Argument For Greater Democracy in Criminal Justice?" *The Good Society* 23, no. 1 (2014): 41–54.

2. D. Garland, *The Culture of Control: Crime and Social Order in Contemporary Society* (Oxford: Oxford University Press, 2001). For a different reading of the same phenomenon, which cautiously emphasizes its emancipatory potential, see I. Loader, "Fall of the Platonic Guardians": Liberalism, Criminology and Political Responses to Crime in England and Wales," *British Journal of Criminology* 46, no. 4 (2006): 561–586. For a much earlier but still important contribution that again sees both potential danger but also promise in "popular" control of criminal justice policy—depending on whether it is carried out in the name of "right-wing" or genuinely popular, socialist criminology—see I. Taylor, *Law and Order: Arguments for Socialism* (London: Macmillan, 1981).

3. Garland, *Culture*, 13.

4. On the question of how we should understand "the public" see Liz Turner, "Penal Populism, Deliberative Methods and the Production of 'Public Opinion' on Crime and Punishment" *The Good Society* 23, no. 1 (2014): 87–102; and this volume.

5. See, e.g., M. Hough and J. V. Roberts, *Attitudes to Punishment: Findings from the 1996 British Crime Survey* (London: Home Office, 1998).

6. For figures concerning state-by-state imprisonment rates in the US, see *The Sentencing Project* (www.sentencingproject.org/the-facts#map). On prison conditions, see, e.g., R. Lippke, "Against Supermax," *Journal of Applied Philosophy* 21, no. 2 (2004): 109–124. On the right to vote, see for instance, M. Mauer, "Voting Behind Bars: An Argument for Voting by Prisoners" *Howard Law Journal* 54, no. 3 (2011): 549–566; N. Demleitner, "Continuing Payment on One's Debt to Society: the German Model of Criminal Disenfranchisement as an Alternative," *Minnesota Law Review* 84, no. 4

(2000): 753–804. For a careful examination of the evidence surrounding policies like three strikes, see L. Kazemian, "Assessing the Impact of a Recidivist Sentencing Premium" in J. Roberts and A. von Hirsch (eds.), *Previous Convictions at Sentencing: Theoretical and Applied Approaches* (Oxford: Hart, 2010): 227–250. On criminal record restrictions, see Z. Hoskins, "Ex-Offender Restrictions," *Journal of Applied Philosophy* 31, no. 1 (2014): 33–48.

7. For a good analysis, see P. Pettit, "Is Criminal Justice Politically Feasible?" *Buffalo Criminal Law Review* 5, no. 2 (2002),: 427–450; and "Depoliticizing Democracy," *Ratio Juris* 17, no. 1 (2004), 52–65.

8. N. Lacey, *The Prisoner's Dilemma: Political Economy and Punishment in Contemporary Democracies* (Cambridge: Cambridge University Press, 2008): 191–192.

9. For this suggestion, see also Pettit, "Is Criminal Justice Politically Feasible?" and F. E. Zimring, G. Hawkins, and S. Kamin, *Punishment and Democracy: Three Strikes And You're Out in California* (New York: Oxford University Press, 2001). For a related proposal, see also L. Sherman, "Evidence and Liberty: the Promise of Evidential Criminology," *Criminology and Criminal Justice* 9, no. 1 (2009): 5–28. For discussion of Zimring et al., see D. Greenberg, "Striking Out in Democracy," *Punishment and Society* 4, no. 2 (2002): 237–252; and of Sherman, see I. Loader, "Is it NICE? The Appeal, Limits and Promise of Translating a Health Innovation into Criminal Justice," *Current Legal Problems* 63, no. 1 (2010): 72–91.

10. Lacey, *Dilemma*: 19.

11. An example would be the UK health policy setting body, the National Institute for Clinical Excellence (NICE). The NICE case introduces complexities in part because it has mixed "expert" and "lay" membership, and deserves consideration in a further chapter. For some discussion, see Loader, "Is it NICE?"; A. Weale, "Democratic Values, Public Consultation and Health Priorities" in A. Oliver (ed.), *Equity in Health and Health Care* (London; The Nuffield Trust, 2004): 41–51; and "What Is so Good about Citizens' Involvement in Healthcare?" in E. Andersson, J. Tritter and R. Wilson (eds.), *Health Democracy: The Future of Involvement in Health and Social Care* (London: Involve and NHS National Centre for Involvement, 2007): 37–43; and Annabelle Lever, "Democracy, Deliberation and Public Service Reform: the Case of NICE" in S. Griffiths, H. Kippin and G. Stoker (eds.), *The Public Services: A New Reform Agenda* (London: Bloomsbury, 2010): 91–106.

12. A. W. Dzur, *Punishment, Participatory Democracy and the Jury* (Oxford: Oxford University Press, 2014). References in parentheses in the main text are to this work. See also Dzur, "The Myth of Penal Populism: Democracy, Citizen Participation, and American Hyperincarceration" *Journal of Speculative Philosophy* 24, 4 (2010): 354–379. The spirit of Dzur's arguments can be traced back to Nils Christie, "Conflicts as Property," *British Journal of Criminology* 17, no. 1 (1977): 1–15.

13. Dzur, *Punishment*, 33.

14. Dzur, *Punishment*, 31–32.

15. Dzur, *Punishment*, 33.

16. Though see Dzur, *Punishment*, 48–51, for some discussion.

17. D. Held, *Models of Democracy* 2nd ed. (Cambridge: Polity Press, 1996).

18. For this claim, see R. Arneson, "Democracy is Not Intrinsically Just" in K. Dowding, R. E. Goodin and C. Pateman (eds.), *Justice and Democracy: Essays for Brian Barry* (Cambridge: Cambridge University Press, 2004): 40–58.

19. L. Davis, "The Cost of Realism: Contemporary Restatements of Democracy," *Western Political Quarterly* 17, no. 1 (1964): 37–46; quoted in C. Pateman, *Participation and Democratic Theory* (Cambridge: Cambridge University Press, 1970): 21.

20. Though see J. P. McCormick, *Machiavellian Democracy* (Cambridge: Cambridge Univesity Press, 2011): 91–92: "election is a magistrate selection method that directly and indirectly favors the wealthy and keeps political offices from being distributed widely among citizens of all socioeconomic backgrounds." I am grateful to Ian Loader for this reference.

21. J. Waldron, "A Rights-Based Critique of Constitutional Rights," *Oxford Journal of Legal Studies* 13, no. 1 (1993): 18–51; "Participation: the Right of Rights," *Proceedings of the Aristotelian Society* 98 (1998): 307–337; "The Core of the Case Against Judicial Review," *Yale Law Journal* 115, no. 6 (2006): 1346–1406. For some critical discussion, see C. Fabre, "The Dignity of Rights," *Oxford Journal of Legal Studies* 20, no. 2 (2000): 271–282; A. Kavanagh, "Participation and Judicial Review: A Reply to Jeremy Waldron" *Law and Philosophy* 22, no. 5 (2003): 451–486; and Arneson, "Democracy is Not Intrinsically Just."

22. The names I have given to the theses in this section are generally my own, but I have taken this one from Dzur—see his Ch. 4.

23. For some discussion, see J. Kleinig and J. Levine (eds.), *Jury Ethics: Jury Conduct and Jury Dynamics* (Boulder, CO: Paradigm Publishers, 2006).

24. Studies on the effectiveness of restorative justice often report lower recidivism rates and greater victim satisfaction. These measures can perhaps serve as a proxy for evidence that citizens take their responsibilities in such forums seriously and discharge them competently. For a recent study, see J. Shapland, G. Robinson, and A. Sorsby, *Restorative Justice in Practice: Evaluating What Works for Victims and Offenders* (Abingdon: Routledge, 2011).

25. Lord McCluskey, *Law, Justice and Democracy* (London: Sweet and Maxwell, 1987): 70; quoted in G. Johnstone, "Penal Policy Making: Elitist, Populist or Participatory?" *Punishment and Society* 2, no. 2 (2000): 161–180.

26. Though one way to go here would be to consider arguments regarding the Condorcet Jury Theorem: for a nice recent discussion, see A. Poama, "Whither Equality? Securing the Lay Citizens' Place Inside the Criminal Justice System," *Swiss Political Science Review* 19, no. 4 (2013): 472–491.

27. For an interesting recent contribution, see D. Sciulli, "Democracy, Professions and Societal Constitutionalism" in K. T. Leicht and J. C. Jenkins (eds.), *Handbook of Politics: State and Society in Global Perspective* (Leiden: Springer, 2010): 81–109.

28. This thesis and the next comprise what I have previously called the "Common Ownership thesis." See my "Core Normative Argument." For this rhetorical reason it seemed acceptable to sacrifice strict gender-neutrality and talk of the "rule of men."

29. For something like this theme, see C. Taylor, *The Ethics of Authenticity* (Cambridge, MA: Harvard University Press, 1992).

30. Something like this argument is put forward in R. Dworkin, "Political Judges and the Rule of Law," *Proceedings of the British Academy* 64 (1978). Of course, Dworkin defends the institution of law and has in mind a different conception of the rule of law to the one attacked by the Rule of Men thesis, albeit that it is adjudicated largely by judges rather than juries. For criticism of the Dworkin approach—and by extension, even more

so, of the Rule of Men thesis—see T. Campbell, *The Legal Theory of Ethical Positivism* (Farnham: Ashgate, 1996).

31. For a classic formulation of this view, see F. H. Bradley, "My Station and Its Duties" in *Ethical Studies*, 2nd edition (Oxford: Clarendon Press, 1927).

32. M. Feeley and J. Simon, "The New Penology: Notes on the Emerging Strategy of Corrections and its Implications," *Criminology* 30, no. 4 (1992): 449–474.

33. Feeley and Simon, "Penology": 454.

34. This chapter has been presented to workshops in Oxford and Sheffield, to the Association for Social and Political Philosophy Annual conference in Amsterdam, June 2015, and to the Society for Applied Philosophy Annual conference in Edinburgh, July 2015. I am grateful, where relevant, to the organisers of these meetings; and to audiences in each of these places for helpful comments and discussion. In particular I would like to thank Antony Bottoms, Tim Chapman, Albert Dzur, Roger Hood, Gerry Johnstone, Ian Loader, Annabelle Lever, Piero Moraro, Andrei Poama, Julian Roberts, Jennifer Sloan, Joanna Shapland, and Bill Wringe.

CHAPTER 7 | Punitive Restoration

Giving the Public a Say on Sentencing

THOM BROOKS

Introduction

Mass incarceration is at near pandemic proportions. Over half the world's nine million prisoners are either in the United States, Russia, or China. The United States leads the world in mass imprisonment with 737 in 10,000 incarcerated. England and Wales imprisons 148 in 10,000 and Scotland 134 in 10,000, but still these British figures are historically high.[1] These alarming statistics contribute to evidence of poor public confidence in how sentencing is handled by the criminal justice system with most finding the courts too lenient.[2] This is because these high prison rates appear to do little to dispel concerns that sentencing practices remain too lenient and ineffective, only exacerbated by correspondingly high recidivism rates.

This chapter considers this problem about public confidence and sentencing from a distinctive angle: if public confidence in sentencing is so poor, then why not include the public more in sentencing decision-making? Greater public inclusion in determining sentences might help improve public confidence in sentencing decisions more generally.[3] There have been other measures attracting popular support that give the public a voice in the criminal justice system, such as the jury trial and the use of victim impact statements.[4] But should we go further?

There are several reasons for why decisions about incarceration are not made by the public. The most common concerns are that the public would exercise its judgment poorly choosing counterproductive punishments of greater severity made worse through inconsistent sentences. Imprisonment is a serious infringement of a person's liberties and should be determined by a professional judge as an important safeguard, or so it has been argued.[5] Taking the public's voice more seriously compounds one problem on top of another in a tragedy of errors. But does it?

This chapter defends a different approach to sentencing. Restorative justice is best understood as a big tent encompassing several related approaches rather than a single approach to managing criminal justice outside the more strict confines of the formal courtroom. These approaches will be shown to have the key to unlocking the problems associated with permitting the public to have a voice on outcomes. Restorative justice can secure the necessary safeguards for offenders with the promise of improving crime reduction efforts at lower costs.

It could be argued that restorative justice is the wrong place to look for defending an approach to sentencing. This is because imprisonment and other forms of hard treatment are not normally a part of restorative contracts. In fact, proponents of restorative justice sometimes self-identify as "abolitionists" insofar as they support greatly restricting, if not abolishing, the use of prisons.[6] Some even speak of abolishing "the prison paradigm" through promoting restorative justice.[7] So to speak of a restorative approach to sentencing policy might seem like a betrayal of what restorative justice is fundamentally about.

Restorative justice is about a kind of restoration, if nothing else. What is restored is a matter of controversy, but the approach's outcomes receive their justification, in part, according to how well they enable a restoration to take place. Mass incarceration may often make offenders' situations much worse. But my point is that hard treatment, including the use of prisons, need not do so and there is evidence that they can support restoration under certain conditions. A restorative justice that is open to using a wider variety of outcomes, including punitive measures, I call and defend as "punitive restoration." One part of my discussion argues that punitive restoration provides a more plausible view of restorative justice with a greater variety of applicability to more cases. Those looking for a way to better embed restorative justice in the criminal justice system should look to punitive restoration, where citizens come together and determine sentences in a deliberative setting.

A second part of my discussion focuses on punitive restoration's justification. I argue for a principle of stakeholding: those with a stake should have a say in outcomes. Stakeholding is an idea embedded in the restorative justice literature, but rarely developed in any philosophical depth. Stakeholding helps us answer important questions about membership in the restorative process and highlight important linkages between stakeholding and civic membership in the criminal justice system. In conclusion, stakeholding is a crucial element to punitive restoration by providing a civic justification for the practice and its membership.

The chapter begins examining the diversity of approaches falling under the restorative justice tent and their conceptual and practical limits. The following section presents punitive restoration as a more coherent view of restorative justice and why it should be preferred. The chapter then considers the importance of stakeholding for this account and how it provides a crucial civic justification for restorative practices and the membership on restorative forums.

Restorative Justice and Its Limits

I will argue that restorative justice is a promising first step toward including the public in sentencing decisions. We should begin by clarifying what is restorative justice and why it does not currently normally extend to sentencing decisions. This section provides this crucial background.

"Restorative justice" is not one thing, but many and refers to a wide range of approaches rather than any single practice.[8] There are significant differences about how these approaches are understood and applied.[9] For example, restorative justice is applied in schools,[10] prison interventions,[11] and South Africa's Truth and Reconciliation Commission.[12] This diversity and disagreement about what restorative justice is about can make it difficult to discuss without a sharp focus.[13] One person's understanding of restorative justice can be very different in form and content from another's. It might appear that restorative justice is in the eye of its many beholders, but this is untrue and our discussion will be focused on a particular use of restorative justice in order to avoid the problems that the diversity of restorative approaches can create.

My discussion focuses narrowly on the uses of restorative justice approaches as *an alternative* to traditional sentencing practices. I understand traditional practices to be sentencing decisions determined in a formal courtroom process, like Magistrates' Court or the Crown Court in England and Wales. Restorative justice is an alternative to these practices because it is an informal process outside the courtroom. Typically, restorative justice adopts one of two forms in this specific context: victim–offender mediation or restorative conferencing.[14] Instead of proceeding to a courtroom trial, restorative justice is an option that permits relevant persons to conduct a meeting outside of the formal trial process to determine penal outcomes.

The wide diversity of restorative approaches should not mask the golden thread, or "conceptual umbrella," that unites most restorative approaches. This is their focus on bringing closure to a conflict through informal, but not unstructured, deliberation with the aim of enabling understanding and healing.[15] T. F. Marshall's classic working definition of restorative approaches is that "restorative justice is a process whereby all parties with a stake in a particular offence come together to resolve collectively how to deal with the aftermath of the offence and its implications for the future."[16] We shall come to his use of stakes and stakeholding later, but Marshall's focus on restorative justice as a *process* illuminates a distinctive difference with traditional sentencing. Judges and magistrates determine sentencing outcomes from their courtroom benches following a set of formal procedures, such as the use of sentencing guidelines.

The use of restorative justice for determining an offender's punishment works differently. There is no judge or magistrate to conduct proceedings. Instead, there is a trained facilitator who conducts meetings more informally than in any courtroom setting. Normally, the offender is required to admit before a restorative meeting can take place. Offenders are permitted a legal representative, but they are not usually requested to be present and offenders are expected to engage directed with others. A key element of restorative justice is that there is dialogue between the victim, offender, and others.

Both mediation and conferences begins by the facilitator clarifying the parameters and purposes of the meeting with guidance available from the Restorative Justice Council.[17] The victim is then provided an opportunity to speak next to address the offender and explain the impact of the offender's crime on her. Restorative conferences next permit any members of the victim's support network, such as friends and family present, as well as select members of the local community to discuss how the offender's crime impacted on them. The offender speaks last and expected to account for his crimes, typically including an apology to the victim. These meetings conclude by participants confirming a restorative contract that the offender is asked to agree. If the offender does not or if he fails to honor its terms in full, then the next step can include a transfer to having the alleged offense considered in the courtroom where potential outcomes can be more punitive.[18] But the contractual terms exclude hard treatment and, if terms are honored in full, the offender will not have a criminal record.

Restorative approaches are more than a process: they aim to provide real benefits in terms of their outcomes. The first is that mediation and conferences lead to "restorative contracts" agreed by all parties, including offenders, in about every restorative meeting: studies have found contracts agreed in up to 98 percent of cases.[19] Restorative outcomes are not imposed from above by a judge or magistrate like in courtroom sentencing, but agreed between all parties after deliberation.

The second benefit is the contracts agreed improve the reduction of reoffending by offenders. These contracts can better target the specific needs of offenders because of the greater flexibility of the more informal process of restorative meetings. Standard outcomes include requirements that offenders attend treatment to overcome their substance abuse or problems with anger management, training is provided to improve employ-ability and general life skills, some compensation to the victim is agreed, and there is often some element of community sentencing included. This improved targeting of offender needs has been found to contribute to up to 25 percent less reoffending than alternatives.[20]

Restorative approaches are found to improve significantly problems associated with victim displacement. Nils Christie argues:

> The victim is a particularly heavy loser in this situation. Not only has he suffered, lost materially or become hurt, physically or otherwise. And not only does the state take the compensation. But above all he has lost participation in his own case. It is the [state] that comes into the spotlight, not the victim. It is the [state] that describes the losses, not the victim.[21]

Restorative justice approaches address these problems in a potentially fruitful way. Victims report high satisfaction with restorative approaches, especially participation in restorative conferencing—and this is true for all participants, including offenders.[22] While victims regularly report feelings of alienation for their cases heard in courtrooms, restorative meetings outside the courts provide a more informal and less intimidating context where victims are encouraged to vocalize their experience of crime and its personal effects in an attempt to find closure in a safe and constructive environment. Likewise, offenders are encouraged to engage through apology and dialogue which can assist them finding closure, too. Victims gain some insight into crimes committed against them and offenders benefit from greater knowledge about the consequences of their actions.

Finally, restorative approaches are much less expensive than traditional sentencing. One study found restorative approaches saved £9 for every £1 spent.[23] Not all might agree that significant savings are a sufficient justification for the use of restorative justice. However, the high rate of agreeing restorative contracts, the lower recidivism rates and the higher satisfaction of all participants along with major cost savings are a potent combination that speak to the positive potential of restorative justice as a more attractive model of punishment. In particular, specific additional benefits were found with the use of restorative conferences over victim mediation: conferences were more likely to lead to higher participant satisfaction. This may speak to the less confrontational and informal setting of the conference than the victim–offender meeting.

Restorative justice has much promise, but also several limits that also merit close scrutiny. We have already noted the fact of the diversity of restorative approaches. Perhaps what most approaches hold in common is what they are not: they are not conducted in courtrooms, do not follow the same formal procedures used in traditional criminal justice practices, do not exclude victims from participation, and so on. The problem of the fact of these diverse restorative practices is it raises difficulties for any discussion of restorative justice as a single entity. This diversity extends to the forms restorative justice approaches can take from mediation to conferencing and beyond, but also to differences in dynamics for restorative meetings. Restorative justice approaches best achieve their desired benefits such as improved targeting of offender needs through their more informal structure, but it is precisely this informality that leaves some part of the success of any restorative meeting to the specific dynamics from the particular participants involved. While facilitators are trained to minimize such differences, they can and do work.[24]

A second obstacle is the limited application of restorative justice approaches. Generally, they are restricted to less serious offenses by youths and only rarely used in situations where the offender is an adult.[25] Restorative justice approaches may be considered an incomplete view of punishment because they are limited to a relatively modest set of offenders and crimes.[26] It is not an approach considered for use in many or indeed most criminal cases.

The reason for limited applicability may be a third, related obstacle of limited confidence that may prevent restorative justice approaches being considered for more serious crimes. There is a concern the public may view these approaches as some kind of soft option for more serious offenses. The problem for restorative justice approaches is that, even if they proved more effective at reducing reoffending, they might prove politically unpalatable. There are several recent illustrations of criminal justice policies receiving popular support while undermining crime reduction efforts. One such example is California's so-called three-strikes-and-you're-out law requiring offenders convicted of a third eligible criminal offense face a minimum of twenty-five years imprisonment.[27] Studies confirm this law has led to a negligible deterrent effect of no more than 2 percent alongside an explosion in the prison population and its associated costs.[28] Populist proposals like three-strikes-and-you're-out indicate the public's willingness to support more punitive penal policies mistakenly believing they will lead to improved crime reduction.[29] Public support for greater punitiveness is counterproductive to why it is supported: more punitiveness has not delivered less offending. So the worry about popular support is that restorative justice's benefits are counterintuitive to the public's generally held beliefs about what kinds of punishment might be most effective and justified.

The problems of limited application and limited confidence are connected to a fourth obstacle, namely, that restorative alternatives to traditional sentencing are constrained by their limited available options. The restorative justice approaches considered here like restorative conferences do not include so-called hard treatment options like imprisonment, nor suspended sentences as a part of their available options for a restorative contract. Indeed, some claim restorative justice approaches do not offer us a view about punishment because hard treatment is not an option for contracts agreed at restorative meetings.[30]

Not all proponents of restorative justice would agree about how these problems should be addressed. For example, the exclusion of hard treatment as an option for restorative contracts is justified on the grounds that it is counterproductive to reducing reoffending. If the aim of restorative justice is to resolve conflicts between those with a stake in them, the concern is that some alternative *both* to the formal courtroom *and* to the use of hard treatment is the way forward in order to better promote healing and "restoration." If restorative justice is limited—as it is—to only some cases and not others, then the way forward is to deliver the same process in these new areas. We require more of the same, not something different. Or so it could be argued.

Restorative justice proponents make such claims based on well-founded concerns about the problems that imprisonment can impose on reducing reoffending. Too often imprisonment is not the start of an individual's longstanding problems, but a confirmation of them and where bad situations can often become much worse. Consider the common risk factors for reoffending, such as economic insecurity, employment insecurity, financial insecurity, and housing insecurity, to name only a few.[31] These can often become exacerbated through even brief time spent in prison.

Some research suggests the prison may even be "criminogenic" because it may contribute to a greater likelihood an imprisoned offender reoffends on release.[32]

But the fact that hard treatment can be and often is counterproductive to reducing crime does not entail that it must always be true. The problem is not that prisons are used at all, but the ways in which they are used and should be improved. Perhaps most proponents of restorative justice celebrate its promise as an alternative to prisons where hard treatment is not on offer. This is often held to be a compelling feature of this broadly abolitionist approach. The use of restorative approaches might not apply to every case, but at least can help curtail the use of prison to ensure it is a last resort.

The reason for limiting options for restorative approaches to exclude the use of prison is connected to a final obstacle concerning the lack of clarity these approaches offer about what is "restored" through a specific restorative approach. Strictly speaking, restorative justice approaches reject the use of prison because it is held imprisonment is a barrier to "restoration."[33] This is a contestable empirical claim that mistakes how we find many prisons with how prisons should be found while raising new questions about what is meant by restoration.

Restorative justice approaches claim they enable a restoration of the damaged relationship between an offender and the wider community. This raises several questions unique to restorative justice, such as which community, and who are the relevant members? Many, following Andrew Ashworth, argue that this claim "remains shrouded in mystery."[34] He says:

> If the broad aim is to restore the "communities affected by the crime," as well as the victim and the victim's family, this will usually mean a geographical community; but where an offence targets a victim because of race, religion, sexual orientation, etc., that will point to a different community that needs to be restored.[35]

There are two concerns here. The first is the problem of identifying the appropriate community to be restored and the second is the problem of selecting persons from that community to participate in a restorative meeting. The first problem of identifying the appropriate community affected by a crime is significant because restorative justice requires a restoration of members within that community. Yet we each identify with multiple and sometimes overlapping communities rendering it unclear how we should choose between them. These communities are rarely static and our identities are not created in a vacuum suggesting that even if we could identify the community, this may be of limited practical benefit for the purposes of achieving restorative justice.[36]

A further problem concerns the general idea of restoration. Restorative justice aims at a restoration of an offender with the wider community. The claim is that there is a wrong to be made right and an injustice requiring closure between affected persons. If this is the case, then it is unclear how important a criminal offense is to justify a restorative approach. This is because restoration may bring benefits where no crime has taken place. One clear example is the case of restorative approaches used in schools for children to resolve conflicts and promote healing. If this is our goal, then crimes can be incidental to whether restoration is required.

Restorative justice approaches bring several potential benefits, including higher victim satisfaction, more effective crime reduction, and at lower costs. These benefits are not without their own costs. Restorative justice approaches are difficult to pinpoint and offer broad comparisons given their diversity; they have limited applicability, they suffer from limited public confidence, they operate with limited options by excluding prison, and they are subject to a serious problem concerning what is restored and by which community.[37]

Restorative justice approaches may be worth defending, but we require a new approach to yield the potential benefits while avoiding these obstacles. Otherwise, restorative justice approaches might remain an underutilized resource at the margins of mainstream criminal justice policy. This situation might change if there is a new formulation of restorative justice that could address these challenges.

Punitive Restoration: Bringing the Public Back In

This section presents and defends a particular approach to achieving restorative justice in a novel way: the idea of *punitive restoration*.[38] Punitive restoration offers a distinctive view about restorative justice. It is a single practice taking the form of a conference setting where the victim, the offender, their support networks, and some local community members are represented. Punitive restoration is *restorative* insofar as it aims to achieve the restoration of rights infringed or threatened by criminal offenses. This is accomplished through recognition of the crime as a public wrong leading to a contractual arrangement agreed by stakeholders. Punitive restoration is punitive because it extends the available options for a restorative contract to achieve restoration, and this may include forms of hard treatment, such as drug and alcohol treatment in custody, suspended sentences, or brief imprisonment. These claims will now be defended.

Restorative justice approaches lack clarity about what is to be restored and how it should be achieved. Its claim to bring restoration to a community may be criticized because restorative approaches do not all insist on the community's involvement, and the overwhelming majority of restorative meetings are victim–offender mediations where the community is excluded.

Punitive restoration operates with a more specific understanding about restoration. The model of punitive restoration is a conference meeting, not unlike restorative conferencing. This is justified on grounds of an important principle of stakeholding: *that those who have a stake in penal outcomes should have a say in decisions about them.*[39] Stakeholding has direct relevance for sentencing policy.[40] Stakeholders are those individuals with a stake in penal outcomes. These persons include victims, if any, their support networks and the local community of stakeholders. Each marks himself or herself out as a potential stakeholder in virtue of his or her relative stake.

This view of restoration endorses the primary working definition from Marshall noted earlier that is used by most proponents of restorative justice restated here: "Restorative justice is a process whereby all parties *with a stake* in a particular offense come together *to resolve collectively* how to deal with the aftermath of the offense and its implications for the future."[41] Restorative justice has often been understood as a process bringing "stakeholders" together.[42] Its distinctive form as punitive restoration better guarantees this understanding by promoting the conference meeting and not victim–offender mediation.

Relevant stakeholders become more easily identifiable as persons immediately involved or connected with a criminal offense. This does not require *all* such persons to participate, but rather that opportunities exist for persons beyond the victim and offender to take part. Similarly, there must be opportunities for members of the general public to take part. This working idea of a conference setting is without any specific recommendation on capping the number of persons included although feasible may render groups of ten or more impractical. The key idea is that if restoration is worth achieving, then it should not be a private affair between only the victim and offender: crimes are public wrongs that affect all members of the community, not least the support networks of victims and offenders.[43] These individuals have a stake in the outcome that should not be silenced.

Restorative conferencing demonstrates this model is achievable and successful: participant satisfaction is higher in this setting than in mediation.[44]

We should take the idea of stakeholding as central to restorative justice approaches more seriously and ensure that any restoration of offenders with their community is enabled through including the community—as this is too often not the case. It is the normative importance of stakeholding that those with a stake in outcomes should have a say about them that drives inclusion in restorative conferences. Opportunities for public participation are key because of stakeholding's normative force—and the use of conferencing better facilitates the major successes of restorative justice than victim–offender mediation at achieving less reoffending and higher participant satisfaction. We can achieve the goods of restoration best through including stakeholders and this favors the conferencing model of punitive restoration.

So one benefit of punitive restoration is its specifying the restorative process. Restoration is aimed at stakeholders through a conference setting. Furthermore, we should recall that our focus is on alternatives to sentencing: punitive restoration is conceived an alternative to the formal procedures of the criminal trial and sentencing guidelines. Punitive restoration can then overcome the obstacle of the diversity of restorative approaches. This is because our speaking of punitive restoration is linked with a particular informal use of restorative justice as an alternative to the trial and sentencing. We can then better compare the dynamics and outcomes from punitive restoration given the more specified content.

Another benefit is that punitive restoration can better address the issue of community than alternative restorative approaches. This is because punitive restoration endorses the principle of stakeholding where those who have a stake should have a say. There is no need to engage in the more difficult task of discerning which type of community is most relevant for restoration, but rather focus on identifying the primary stakeholders and engage them. Some stakeholders are more easily identifiable than others. Victims and offenders clearly have a stake in outcomes. Their families and close friends may also have a stake as the support networks for victims and offenders. The public members of their local community have a stake as well, but there is no need to include all. One reason is that requiring everyone in the community to have a say on every case of criminal conduct would be unworkable and impractical. We need not require every individual in the community to participate in a restorative conference for the community's voice to be heard. A working model in restorative practice is to allow the public to voluntarily participate in conferencing as a representative of the public—and a model that appears to work well.[45] So the criticism that restorative justice has trouble identifying participants is not a problem for my stakeholder.

Note that orthodox restorative justice approaches standardly require the participation of victims and offenders. An additional benefit of punitive restoration over these approaches is only punitive restoration can address situations of so-called victimless crimes or where a victim is either unable or unwilling to participate. Those offenses most often considered victimless, such as possession of illegal drugs, might normally be unavailable to a restorative approach and the potential benefits it can offer. While there may be no specific victim, there will be stakeholders if only some members of the local community that will have a stake in how criminal offenses—irrespective of their seriousness—are managed. So unlike other forms of restorative justice like victim–offender mediation, an account of restorative justice based on stakeholding does not require that there be identifiable victims that can participate for punitive restoration to take place.[46]

The principle of stakeholding informing punitive restoration better helps us identify persons to participate in conference meetings and expand their applicability to a wider range of offenses. Not all persons we might name as stakeholders may wish to participate. But this is in line with the principle of stakeholding. Those who have a stake should have a say, but it is up to stakeholders to speak. Individuals may not choose whether they have a stake, but they can choose what they wish to do with it. It is important that opportunities exist for individuals to become educated and receive information about the restorative process and participation in it, but participation should remain voluntarily. Elections are a legitimate procedure for choosing political leaders even if not everyone with a vote cast it. Likewise, stakeholding remains legitimate even if not all stakeholders wish to take part.

The remaining obstacles for restorative justice approaches concern their limited applicability to less serious offenses, the limited confidence the public may have in restorative approaches because they may be viewed as too soft an option and their limited available options by excluding any use of hard treatment. Punitive restoration takes these obstacles together. It enables *wider* applicability through *increasing* its options. Punitive restoration does not assume that restoration must never require the use of hard treatment. While incarceration may often make successful crime reduction efforts more difficult, it is also clear that prisons can and should be transformed to improve their disappointing results.[47]

For example, restorative contracts regularly include an obligation on offenders to participate in programs designed to develop their employability and life skills as well as undertake treatment for any drug and alcohol abuse.[48] There is no reason to accept these activities could never be delivered successfully within a prison or other secure facility. Perhaps hard treatment should be used sparingly: this is still not grounds for avoiding custodial sentences *tout court*. It is realistically possible that prisons may prove the best environment for some offenders in specific cases.[49] Prisons might also be reorganized so that prison officers could become Personal Support Officers if provided suitable training: these persons have most frequent contact with imprisoned offenders and this relationship could be harnessed to produce an improved system of pastoral support.[50]

Prisons can and should be transformed so incarceration does not undermine offender rehabilitation. Short-term imprisonment is associated with high rates of reoffending. This is a significant problem because most offenders receive short-term sentences of less than 12 months and about 60 percent will reoffend within weeks of their release.[51] Most offenders receiving short-term imprisonment do not receive any rehabilitative treatment. This is a major contributing factor to the likelihood these offenders will reoffend when released from prison. This problem may be overcome through providing effective treatment. Brief intensive interventions have been employed to address problems associated with drug and offenders were found to benefit from "significant gains in knowledge, attitudes and psychosocial functioning."[52] These sessions were corrections-based treatment of moderate (thirty outpatient group sessions three days per week) or high intensity (six-month residential treatment) has been found to yield cost savings of 1.8 to 5.7 the cost of their implementation.[53] These policies suggest prisons can and should be reformed to better support offender rehabilitation and improve postrelease crime reduction efforts without sacrificing cost-effectiveness. Prisons must better accommodate restoration. But my point is that restoration and hard treatment need not always be at cross-purposes. Instead, hard treatment may be a useful option for enabling restoration in some cases, such as through intensive treatment.[54]

These reforms have important relevance for punitive restoration. This is because individuals guilty of more serious, even violent, crimes may require more punitive outcomes than currently available to restorative justice approaches. For example, these approaches reject all uses of hard treatment including the imposition or its threat in contracts agreed at restorative meetings. If these contracts are not agreed or satisfied in full, the offender may have his case transferred for consideration by a magistrate where hard treatment can become a possible outcome.

Punitive restoration might permit the inclusion of a suspended sentence for noncompliance of a contract within the contractual agreement. This option would extend the flexibility of punitive restoration to more varieties of offense-types and offenders bypassing the need for a trial in cases of noncompliance and further reducing potential sentencing costs. Nor should this be problematic: offenders receiving a suspended sentence in a punitive restoration conference meeting would retain access to legal representation throughout, must confirm any guilt without coercion and agree all terms presented to him or her at the conclusion of this meeting *for committing offenses where the alternative—through the traditional formal procedures of the courtroom—would include options that are at least as punitive*. Note that one major difference is that only with punitive restoration would the *possibility* of hard treatment be an issue that must be agreed by the offender prior to its use.

Let us consider two further instances where punitive restoration might justify some form of hard treatment. One is the idea of prison as a form of cooling off. Recall that imprisonment is often not the beginning of an offender's socioeconomic and legal difficulties, but rather their confirmation after an extended escalation. Imprisonment is characteristically *disruptive*. A consequence is that this can end already fragile support networks and render an individual's road to sustainable prosperity tenuous. This is a significant problem for most offenders, but not all. Perhaps for only a small, yet important minority the disruption from strongly negative support networks or difficult personal circumstances can provide an opportunity for offenders to take a break where they might become open to personal transformation possible only through a prison-like environment.

A second form of hard treatment that punitive restoration might incorporate is the idea of *less* time in prison with *more* intensity. This addresses on the fact most offenders serve short-term sentences without receiving any rehabilitative treatment. These treatments are costly and so prison wardens normally reserve expensive rehabilitative programs for offenders serving more than one year in prison: it is claimed this permits sufficient time for these programs to be effective.[55] However, these programs are rarely intensive and—as already noted above—such high-intensity programs have been found to be effective at reducing drug and alcohol abuse, for example.[56] More such programs would increase costs, but these might be accounted for by reducing the overall time spent in prison made possible by intensive rehabilitation programs: the savings from the reduced time spent in prison overall could contribute to the increased costs of ensuring all inmates have access to the appropriate intensive rehabilitative programs. Further savings might accrue through less reoffending on release if the programs are successful. A recent study on the length of time spent in prison and employment prospects found that offender prospects worsened only for sentences in excess of six months. So using prison for shorter, more intensive periods for rehabilitative purposes may yield additional benefits for acquiring employment on release.[57]

Punitive restoration might be objected to on the grounds that hard treatment, even for a few days, is a major curtailment of individual liberty that requires special safeguards only the formal procedures of the courtroom could satisfy. The problem with this objection is that only a relatively few cases are brought to trial.[58] These cases are never heard in court, and so victims and others affected by a crime are not permitted opportunities to gain a better understanding of why crimes occurred or receive an apology from their offenders. It is hardly surprising to recall the widespread dissatisfaction many victims have with the traditional sentencing model. Punitive restoration is a concrete approach that can overcome this problem by providing greater opportunities for restorative meetings where victims express much higher satisfaction.

Punitive restoration might also be objected to for a lack of any stated purpose beyond its endorsing the principle of stakeholding: this may help identify relevant participants, but which penal purpose should inform their sentencing outcomes? Punitive restoration is more than an improvement over alternative approaches to restorative justice, but an illustration of a compelling perspective on penal purposes in practice. Punishment is often justified in reference to a justifying aim or purpose, such as retribution, deterrence or rehabilitation. Philosophers disagree about which among these is most preferable despite general agreement that hybrid combinations of two or more purposes often suffer from inconsistency.[59] This is illustrated well by section 142 of the Criminal Justice Act 2003, which states that punishment must satisfy at least one of five penal purposes. This claim is restated in more recent sentencing guidelines. However, there has been no attempt to claim how two or more such purposes can be brought together in a coherent, unified account. This "penal pluralism" may be legally possible, but its practicality remains questionable.[60]

Punitive restoration is one form that a *unified theory of punishment* might take. This is because it is able to bring together multiple penal purposes within a coherent, unified framework.[61] For example, desert is satisfied because offenders must admit guilt without coercion prior to participation in a conference meeting. The penal goals of crime reduction, including the protection of the public, and enabling offender rehabilitation are achieved through targeting stakeholder needs arising from the meeting. The satisfaction of these goals is confirmed through the high satisfaction all participants report, which suggests a general unanimity that the appropriate set of contractual stipulations have been agreed by all and the improvements in reducing reoffending suggest success in crime reduction and treatment consistent with deterrence and rehabilitation.[62] The argument here is not that any such unified theory is best or preferable to alternative theories. Instead, it is claimed punitive restoration is an example of how multiple penal principles might be addressed within a coherent, unified account.[63]

Conclusion: Letting the Public Have a Say

Mass incarceration is at historic highs and public confidence in sentencing is at historic lows. Current prison policies are not making the public feel any safer and its beneficial effects on reducing reoffending are minimal. Restorative justice offers a promising alternative. It shows how public confidence might be improved while reducing reoffending at lower costs. But this is not to say it does not require important reforms. A 2015 public opinion polls by Ipsos-Mori found that the public was more aware about restorative justice than only a couple years ago and was positive about restorative justice, but also clear concerns that outcomes may be too soft and ineffective.[64]

This chapter has argued that restorative justice can become more deeply embedded in the criminal justice system—and used much more widely across more types of offenses and offenders—if its range of options were expanded to include more punitive outcomes. Hard treatment can often be counterproductive, but it need not always be so. There is evidence that well-targeted intensive drug and alcohol treatment can improve crime reduction at lower costs. Hard treatment can be made to work. This does not only benefit offenders who may no longer come into contact again with the criminal justice system, but benefits victims and the wider community by taking their views as stakeholders seriously and providing a forum whereby their voices might be heard.

Punitive restoration is a model for how restorative justice can be transformed from a process for a few can be extended to the many—and potentially yield the promising benefits of restorative justice to far more cases.

Part of this story is better ensuring prison is a last resort and where it is used ensuring that prisons are reformed to better address risk factors. Perhaps the key to reducing the increasing use of counterproductive imprisonment and low public confidence is to bring the public in, provide the public a voice on penal outcomes within the informal structure of restorative justice, and ensure that any use of hard treatment is more focused and, in a word, restorative.[65]

Notes

1. See BBC, "World Prison Populations," http://news.bbc.co.uk/1/shared/spl/hi/uk/06/prisons/html/nn2page1.stm.

2. See Mike Hough, Ben Bradford, Jonathan Jackson, and Julian Roberts, *Attitudes to Sentencing and Trust in Justice: Exploring Trends from the Crime Survey for England and Wales* (London: Home Office, 2013), 2 and Julian V. Roberts, "Public Opinion and Sentencing Policy," in Sue Rex and Michael Tonry (eds.), *Reform and Punishment: The Future of Sentencing* (London: Routledge, 2011), 26. These same studies find public attitudes become more lenient the more that they learn about individual cases.

3. See D. Smith, *Confidence in the Criminal Justice System: What Lies Beneath?* (London: Ministry of Justice, 2007).

4. For example, see Thom Brooks, "The Right to Trial by Jury," *Journal of Applied Philosophy* 21 (2)(2004): 197–212 and Paul G. Cassell, "In Defense of Victim Impact Statements," *Ohio State Journal of Criminal Law* 6 2009): 611–648.

5. See House of Commons Justice Select Committee, "Democratic and Judicial Voices," in *Sentencing Guidelines and Parliament: Building a Bridge,* www.publications.parliament.uk/pa/cm200809/cmselect/cmjust/715/71506.htm.

6. See Barbara Hudson, "Restorative Justice: The Challenge of Sexual and Racial Violence," *Journal of Law and Society* 25 (2)(1998): 237–256; Theo Gavrielides, "Restorative Justice—the Perplexing Concept: Conceptual Fault-lines and Power Battles within the Restorative Justice Movement," *Criminology and Criminal Justice* 8 (2) (2008): 165–183; and Vincenzo Ruggiero, "An Abolitionist View of Restorative Justice," *International Journal of Law, Crime and Justice* 39 (2)(2009): 100–110.

7. See Judy C. Tsui, "Breaking Free of the Prison Paradigm: Integrating Restorative Justice Techniques into Chicago's Juvenile Justice System," *Journal of Criminal Law and Criminology* 104 (3)(2014): 635–666.

8. See John Braithwaite, *Restorative Justice and Responsive Regulation* (Oxford: Oxford University Press, 2002) and Thom Brooks, *Punishment* (London: Routledge, 2012), 64–85.

9. Gerry Johnstone and Daniel W. Van Ness, "The Meaning of Restorative Justice," in Gerry Johnstone and Daniel W. Van Ness (eds.), *Handbook of Restorative Justice* (London: Routledge, 2007), 5.

10. See Brenda Morrison, "Schools and Restorative Justice," in Gerry Johnstone and Daniel W. Van Ness (eds.), *Handbook of Restorative Justice* (London: Routledge, 2007), 325.

11. See Jennifer Brown, Sarah Miller, and Sara Northey, *What Works in Therapeutic Prisons: Evaluating Psychological Change in Dovegate Therapeutic* Community (Basingstoke: Palgrave Macmillan, 2014) and Kimmett Edgar and Tim Newell, *Restorative Justice in Prisons: A Guide to Making It* Happen (Winchester: Waterside Press, 2006).

12. See Jennifer J. Llewellyn and Robert Howse, "Institutions for Restorative Justice: The South African Truth and Reconciliation Commission," *University of Toronto Law Journal* 49 (3)(1999): 355–388.

13. See Joanna Shapland, Gwen Robinson, and Angela Sorsby, *Restorative Justice in Practice: Evaluating What Works for Victims and Offenders* (London: Routlegde, 2011), 4 ("The restorative justice agenda . . . encompasses a very broad range of practices and approaches, such that a definitive definition has proven elusive"). See also Chris Cunneen and Carolyn Hoyle, *Debating Restorative Justice* (London: Hart, 2010).

14. The focus is on restorative approaches that serve as an alternative to traditional sentencing in England and Wales, such as victim–offender mediation and restorative conferencing. This specification is important. There is a need to provide a more definitive and less contested model of restorative practices. The focus on one—admittedly significant— part of restorative practices is intended to help identify this new model, in part, by its distinctive form of application for England and Wales. This new model, punitive restoration, is discussed in this context, but it is not suggested that it cannot have a wider applicability to other jurisdictions.

15. Shapland, Robinson, and Sorsby, *Restorative Justice in Practice*, 4.

16. T. F. Marshall, *Restorative Justice: An Overview*, Home Office Occasional Paper (London: Home Office, 1999).

17. See Restorative Justice Council, "Best Practice," https://www.restorativejustice. org.uk/sites/default/files/resources/files/Best%20practice%20guidance%20for%20re- storative%20practice%202011.pdf (2011).

18. Offenders admitting guilt to a criminal offense for the purposes of engaging in victim–offender mediation or restorative conferencing and who either do not agree a restorative contract or fail to honor its terms in full need *not* admit guilt for this offense if the case is transferred to either a magistrates' court or the Crown Court. This would appear to undermine the sincerity of the earlier admittance and it might be preferable to end this anomaly given that any admittance of guilt remains free of coercion and legal representation for offenders continues to be available, although this policy suggestion is not considered further here.

19. See Joanna Shapland, Anne Atkinson, Helen Atkinson, Becca Chapman, E. Colledge, James Dignan, Marie Howes, Jennifer Johnstone, Gwen Robinson, and Angela Sorsby, *Restorative Justice in Practice: The Second Report from the Evaluation of Three Schemes* (Sheffield: Centre for Criminological Research, University of Sheffield, 2006) and Joanna Shapland, Anne Atkinson, Helen Atkinson, Becca Chapman, James Dignan, Marie Howes, Jennifer Johnstone, Gwen Robinson, and Angela Sorsby, *Restorative Justice: The Views of Victims and Offenders* (London: Ministry of Justice, 2007), 27.

20. See Joanna Shapland, Anne Atkinson, Helen Atkinson, James Dignan, Lucy Edwards, Jeremy Hibbert, Marie Howes, Jennifer Johnstone, Gwen Robinson, and Angela Sorsby, *Does Restorative Justice Affect Reconviction? The Fourth Report from the Evaluation of Three Schemes* (London: Ministry of Justice, 2008) and Restorative Justice

Council, *What Does the Ministry of Justice RJ Research Tell Us?* (London: Restorative Justice Council, 2011).

21. Nils Christie, "Conflicts as Property," in Andrew von Hirsch and Andrew Ashworth (eds.), *Principled Sentencing: Readings on Theory and Policy* (London: Hart, 1998), 314.

22. See Shapland et al., *Restorative Justice*, 25–26.

23. See Shapland et al., *Restorative Justice in Practice: The Second Report* and Restorative Justice Council, *What Does the Ministry of Justice RJ Research Tell Us?* (London: Restorative Justice Council, 2011).

24. See Declan Roche, *Accountability in Restorative Justice* (Oxford: Clarendon, 2003).

25. See Brooks, *Punishment*, 173–188 and James Dignan, "Juvenile Justice, Criminal Courts and Restorative Justice," in Gerry Johnstone and Daniel W. Van Ness (eds.), *Handbook of Restorative Justice* (London: Routledge, 2007), 269.

26. See Brooks, *Punishment*, 67–68.

27. See Francis T. Cullen, Bonnie S. Fischer, and Brandon K. Applegate, "Public Opinion about Punishment and Corrections," *Crime and Justice* 27 (1)(2000): 1–79 and Franklin E. Zemring, Gordon Hawkins and Sam Kamin, *Punishment and Democracy: Three Strikes and You're Out in California* (Oxford: Oxford University Press, 2001).

28. See Steven N. Durlauf and Daniel S. Nagin, "Imprisonment and Crime: Can Both Be Reduced?" *Criminology and Public Policy* 10 (1)(2011): 28 and *Brown v. Plata*, 563 US (2011).

29. See Monica Williams, "Beyond the Retributive Public: Governance and Public Opinion on Penal Policy," *Journal of Crime and Justice* 35 (1)(2011): 93–113.

30. See Andrew Ashworth, "Sentencing" in Mike Maguire, Rod Morgan and Robert Reiner (eds.), *The Oxford Handbook of Criminology* (Oxford: Oxford University Press, 1994), 822.

31. See Brooks, *Punishment*, 179–187.

32. See Durlauf and Nagin, "Imprisonment and Crime," 14, 21–23. See also Richard L. Lippke, *Rethinking Imprisonment* (Oxford: Oxford University Press, 2007) and Michael Tonry, "Less Imprisonment is No Doubt a Good Thing: More Policing is Not," *Criminology and Public Policy* 10 (1)(2011): 138, 140–141.

33. See John Braithwaite, *Restorative Justice and Responsible Regulation* (Oxford: Oxford University Press, 2002).

34. Andrew Ashworth, *Sentencing and Criminal Justice, 5th ed.* 94 (Cambridge: Cambridge University Press, 2010). See John Braithwaite, "Setting Standards for Restorative Justice," *British Journal of Criminology* 42 (3)(2002): 563–577.

35. Andrew Ashworth, "Responsibilities, Rights and Restorative Justice," *British Journal of Criminology* 42 (3)(2002): 583.

36. See Bhikhu Parekh, *A New Politics of Identity: Political Principles for an Interdependent World* (Basingstoke: Palgrave Macmillan, 2008), 1, 21–26.

37. There is a further concern that there is a gap between the rhetoric of restorative justice approaches and their practical achievements that will not be considered here. See Kathleen Daly, "Mind the Gap: Restorative Justice in Theory and Practice," in Andrew von Hirsch, Julian V. Roberts, Anthony Bottoms, Kent Roach, and Mara Schiff

(eds.), *Restorative Justice and Criminal Justice: Competing or Reconcilable Paradigms?* (Oxford: Hart, 2003), 219.

38. See Brooks, *Punishment*, 123, 132, 136, 142–143, 147–148 and Thom Brooks, "Stakeholder Sentencing," in Jesper Ryberg and Julian Roberts (eds.), *Popular Punishment: On the Normative Significance of Public Opinion for Penal Theory* (Oxford: Oxford University Press, 2014), 183–203.

39. See Thom Brooks, "The Stakeholder Society and the Politics of Hope," *Renewal* 23 (1—2)(2015): 44–54 and Thom Brooks, "Justice as Stakeholding," in Jay Drydyk and Krushil Watene (eds.), *Theorising Justice: New Directions and Future Insights* (Lanham, MD: Rowan & Littlefield, 2016), forthcoming.

40. My defense of restorative conferences and not victim–offender mediation is partly because conferencing alone recognizes that stakeholders are more than victims and offenders, but it is also partly because conferencing has been found to be more effective at reducing reoffending and achieving higher participant satisfaction. So my proposal for a form of conferencing would itself mark a significant departure from standard practice, but it has the potential to yield greater benefits. See Shapland and Robinson, *Restorative Justice in Practice*, 98–100.

41. Marshall, *Restorative Justice*.

42. See Braithwaite, *Restorative Justice and Responsive Regulation*, 11, 50, 55.

43. One study found that restorative conferences often include friends and family of the victim and of the offender, respectively, in 73 percent and 78 percent of cases examined. Parents were far more likely to attend restorative conferences (50 percent of offenders and 23 percent of victims) than partners (3 percent of offenders and 5 percent of victims). Shapland et al., *Restorative Justice*, 20.

44. See Shapland and Robinson, *Restorative Justice in Practice*, 98–100.

45. See Lawrence C. Sherman and Heather Strang, *Restorative Justice: The Evidence* (London: Smith Institute, 2007).

46. My point is that a process like victim–offender mediation presupposes that there are victims and that they will participate. But not all crimes have victims, or have identifiable victims, and not all victims may want to take part. Restorative practices can still take place within the stakeholder framework of punitive restoration because what we require are stakeholders—and they may or may not be victims.

47. See Alison Liebling, *Prisons and Their Moral Performance: A Study of Values, Quality and Prison Life* (Oxford: Clarendon, 2006).

48. See Brooks, *Punishment*, 66–67, 73–75. On prison-based programs designed to improve tackling drug and alcohol abuse, see Graham J. Towl, "Drug-Misuse Intervention Work," in Graham J. Towl (ed.), *Psychological Research in Prisons* (Oxford: Blackwell, 2006).

49. See Deanna M. Perez and Wesley G. Jennings, "Treatment Behind Bars: The Effectiveness of Prison-Based Therapy for Sex Offenders," *Journal of Crime and Justice* 35 (3)(2012): 435–450.

50. See Jenny Chapman and Jacqui Smith, "Cutting Crime and Building Confidence," in Robert Philpott (ed.), *The Purple Book: A Progressive Future for Labour* (London: Biteback, 2011), 215, 228.

51. See Ministry of Justice website, http://open.justice.gov.uk/home/.

52. See George W. Joe, Kevin Knight, D. Dwayne Simpson, Patrick M. Flynn, Janis T. Morey, Norma G. Bartholomew, Michele Staton Tindall, William M. Burdon,

Elizabeth A. Hall, Steve S. Martin, and Daniel J. O'Connell, "An Evaluation of Six Brief Interventions That Target Drug-Related Problems in Correctional Populations," *Journal of Offender Rehabilitation* 51 (1—2)(2012): 9–33.

53. See M. Daly, C. T. Love, D. S. Shepard, C. B. Peterson, K. L. White, and F. B. Hall, "Cost-Effectiveness of Connecticut's In-Prison Substance Abuse Treatment," *Journal of Offender Rehabilitation* 39 (3)(2004): 69–92.

54. While we differ on other points, I agree with Lucia Zedner that reparation is reconcilable with retribution. I also agree that there is a danger that attempting to accommodate reparation to more punitive measures puts at risk its rehabilitative potential. This is why any punitive measure is only permitted if it contributes to restoration. This offers an important threshold acceptable measures must pass. See Lucia Zedner, "Reparation and Retribution: Are They Reconcilable?" *Modern Law Review* 57 (2) (1994): 228–250.

55. See Brooks, *Punishment*, 142–143.

56. See Joe et al., "An Evaluation of Six Brief Interventions That Target Drug-Related Problems in Correctional Populations," and Daly et al., "Cost-Effectiveness of Connecticut's In-Prison Substance Abuse Treatment."

57. See Anke Ramakers, Robert Apel, Paul Nieuwbeerta, Anja Dirkzwager, and Johan van Wilsem, "Imprisonment Length and Post-Prison Employment Prospects," *Criminology* 52 (3)(2014): 399–427. See also Christopher Uggen, Mike Vuolo, Sarah Lageson, Ebony Ruhland, and Hilary K. Whitham, "The Edge of Stigma: An Experimental Audit of the Effects of Low-Level Criminal Records on Employment," *Criminology* 52 (4)(2014): 627–654.

58. See Andrew Ashworth and Mike Redmayne, *The Criminal Process,* 3rd ed. (Oxford: Oxford University Press, 2005), 6–7.

59. See Brooks, *Punishment*, 89–100.

60. On penal pluralism, see Thom Brooks, "On F. H. Bradley's Some Remarks on Punishment," *Ethics* 125 (1)(2014): 223–225.

61. A unified theory of punishment may be constructed in different ways. The construction favored here is to view crime as a harm to individual rights and punishment as "a response" to crime with the purpose of protecting and maintaining individual rights. This model rejects the view that penalties and hard treatment have different justificatory foundations, but rather they share a common justificatory source: the protection and maintenance of rights. The model of a unified theory can then better address the fact that penal outcomes are often multidimensional and include both financial and punitive elements. See Brooks, *Punishment*, 123–148 for a defense of the unified theory of punishment.

62. If satisfied, these conditions may be consistent with the idea of "empirical desert." See Paul H. Robinson, "Competing Conceptions of Modern Desert: Vengeful, Deontological, and Empirical," *Cambridge Law Journal* 67 (1)(2008): 145–175.

63. See Thom Brooks, "Punishment: Political, Not Moral," *New Criminal Law Review* 14 (3)(2011): 427–438 and Thom Brooks, "Hegel and the Unified Theory of Punishment," in Thom Brooks (ed.), *Hegel's Philosophy of Right* (Oxford: Blackwell, 2012), 103–123.

64. See Restorative Justice Council, "New Polling Demonstrates Overwhelming Support for Restorative Justice," July 15, 2015, http://restorativejustice.org.uk/news/new-polling-demonstrates-overwhelming-support-restorative-justice.

65. Earlier drafts were presented at the All Souls Criminology Seminar at the University of Oxford and the Political Theory Seminar at Sciences Po—Paris. I am very grateful to audience members on both occasions for their terrific discussion and several others, including Nick Bowes, Sadiq Khan, Rick Lippke, Ian Loader, Andrei Poama, Harvey Redgrave, Julian Roberts, Angela Smith, Astrid von Busekist, Nicola Wake, and Lucia Zedner. I am grateful once more to Ian and also to Albert Dzur and Richard Sparks for their extremely useful written feedback in developing this chapter. I also owe a very special debt of thanks to Bhikhu Parekh, whose insights and friendship is a source of great inspiration here and elsewhere.

CHAPTER 8 | # After Penal Populism
| *Punishment, Democracy, and Utopian Method*

LYNNE COPSON

Introduction

As the late twentieth and early twenty-first centuries have borne witness to certain increasingly punitive responses to crime in a number of advanced liberal countries, reflected in the apparent crisis of mass incarceration in the United States and its echoes and sequels elsewhere,[1] concerns about the influence of penal populism on criminal justice policy have come to play a pivotal role in discussions of how we might realize more effective and just policy responses. While recognizing that these trends have not unfolded identically across different contexts,[2] within these discussions a tension is drawn between those who advocate insulating questions of crime and justice from the vagaries of an ill-informed and punitive public (or, if not the public themselves, public discourse surrounding responses to crime), instead committing them to the safety of "expert" decision-making, beyond the sway of public opinion and political electioneering; and those seeking to engage these publics in such questions in an active and meaningful way. At its heart, this tension raises important questions regarding the relationship between policymaking (perhaps most acutely in a criminal justice and penal context, but certainly not limited to this), liberalism and democracy, and, ultimately, the polarizing question of whether the issue is one of *too much* public engagement in the development of public policy or *not enough*.[3]

Animating these opposing perspectives on the contemporary problem of democracy in policymaking which I term "insulation" and "reinvigoration," lies an increasing polarization between, on the one hand, liberal concerns to preserve criminal justice policymaking from becoming a tool of oppression and domination, and, on the other, a normative project of social democratic change.[4] We are also faced with an implicit question of how these apparently opposing, and certainly divergent, tendencies might be reconciled.

Against this backdrop, this chapter examines debates regarding the most effective way to respond to the problem of penal populism. It argues that much of the apparent problem of penal populism and contemporary responses to it lies in the failure of those interested in criminal justice and penal reform to connect their particular agendas to the broader concerns and lives of lay members of the public. Specifically, I argue that the contemporary production of criminological knowledge forms part of the apparent problem insofar as the current organization and production of knowledge arguably *creates* or reifies the problem of "populist punitiveness" itself.[5] Consequently, I advocate the need new forms of producing and utilizing criminological knowledge as a means of creating "spaces of hope" through which more meaningful policy alternatives,[6] and more engaged publics, can be imagined and developed. In so doing, I offer the example of the recent Scottish Independence Referendum as an implicit realization of such a space, suggesting that amid a sense of a shifting mood in response to the apparent crisis of mass incarceration, such an opportunity for challenging penal populism might be on the horizon. While not a specifically criminological example, it nevertheless demonstrates the need for more holistic and integrated conceptualizations of social problems, which seek to tie particular interests and issues to a broader project of social change. Indeed, this is the very point of the example, for it challenges the insulationist tendency within some areas of academic criminology to sever issues of crime and justice from their location in a broader politics and normative questions as to what type of society we believe is both desirable and achievable. Finally, I propose a solution to identifying strategies for implementing change in the form of a "method of utopia" as a means of taking advantage of such "spaces of hope" when they arise.[7] Advanced as a means of reconnecting abstract political theory with a practical commitment to institutional design, this method offers a point of access into more systematic thinking about crime and its solution.[8] Moving beyond, for example, concentrating on the existing criminal justice and penal system and narrow debates over ameliorating mass incarceration and advocating piecemeal reforms, it locates such issues in more holistic accounts of social change. It is also envisaged as a means of reengaging a disenfranchised public with questions about crime and justice insofar as it has been described as "an active device in reflexive and collective deliberations about possible and desirable futures."[9]

In arguing thus, it is maintained that while the issues concerning democracy, liberalism, and political legitimacy may be brought to the fore and rendered particularly acute by the contemporary crisis of mass incarceration and concerns about penal populism, they ultimately reflect much wider questions concerning the development of public policy in contemporary society. Therefore, this chapter is not intended as a commentary on mass incarceration or possible routes to the development of alternatives to prison per se. Rather, it uses this context as a lens through which broader concerns about how to build a more socially just society can be meaningfully discussed and articulated, focusing specifically on the ways in which the relationship between expert knowledge and public policy might be more effectively democratized.

Finally, by way of introduction, it is important to qualify the term "utopia" as it is employed in this chapter. As a frequently contested concept, the particular use of utopia as a method is distinguished from other uses. Without wishing to become entangled in the problems of definition, for the purposes of this chapter, there are two (related) definitions of "utopia" on which I intend to draw: an analytical definition and a descriptive one.

At the analytical level, in the absence of a clear or agreed definition of "utopia," Ruth Levitas has identified the idea of desire as a key unifying theme underpinning competing definitions. Accordingly, she advances a broad definition of utopia as "the expression of the desire for a better way of being."[10] At the descriptive level, a general definition of utopia is adopted whereby "utopia" is commonly used to identify and refer to an outline of an ideal or perfectly organized society, which is currently nonexistent and considered desirable. These two are related insofar as (as will be demonstrated), the application of Levitas's "utopian methodology" to different theories of crime and justice policymaking, provides the means of translating the abstract analysis of such "expressions of desire for a better way of being" into a more holistic reimagining of an ideal society that is currently nonexistent and considered desirable.[11]

It has been suggested that utopias present "a determinate type of *praxis*" in their presentation of alternative societies.[12] By bringing into relief the alternative (and often competing) visions of the good society implicit within different theories of, and responses to, crime and justice, the utopian method invites critical evaluation on both the desirability and practicability of such proposed measures. It enjoins us to consider the type of society we want to live in, and how best this might be realized as well as what "kind" of people we think we are or could be. These are ultimately political, normative questions about the world, requiring us to move beyond the disjointed and "value-neutral" modes of engagement currently dominant within academia.[13]

Thus, the utopian method offers a possible means for returning questions of crime and justice from the insulated realm of academic expertise and institutional particularism, to normative public deliberation and debate and social universalism. By teasing out a holistic account of the good society from the particularities of expert discourse on crime and justice, this method is anticipated as a more productive means for effecting social improvement and subjecting both contemporary society and its concomitant social theories and political programs to public engagement, dialogue, and deliberation. The need that this approach discloses is for experts to make clearer the relevance of specialist forms of expertise to the lives of the public, thereby helping create an informed, engaged, public involved in devising more imaginative responses to crime.

Pathways Out of Mass Incarceration: Insulation or Reinvigoration?

The starting point for my analysis is the growing concern among academics and so-called experts over the danger of penal populism in the contemporary climate. The trend toward mass incarceration in contemporary Anglophone countries arguably reflects the apotheosis of such populism. It has often been presented as a key site for articulating concerns about the dangers of holding criminal justice policy hostage to political interests and the need for new ways of thinking about, and responding to, crime and justice.

Defined by Simon as "the tremendous changes in the scale of incarceration that began in the late 1970s and became visible to readers of imprisonment charts by the middle of the 1980s,"[14] the problem of mass incarceration has gained increasing traction as a locus of critique over the past thirty years. Criticisms regarding the effectiveness, legitimacy and harmfulness of mass imprisonment are well-documented and do not bear repetition here.[15] However, as the voices of such criticism have gained increasing attention and political traction, we are arguably now witnessing a *watershed moment* in its development whereby the prospect of continuing along such punitive lines appears increasingly untenable.[16]

Consequently, we have begun to witness both concern regarding the relationship of criminal justice and penal policymaking to professional expertise and public opinion, and growing interest in the role of democratic theory in developing contemporary responses to mass incarceration, in order to stem the tide of "populist punitiveness" and offer new, and more effective, alternatives for responding to crime and justice.

In response to this opportunity, commentators have noted two opposing tendencies in reaction to concerns over the relationship between public opinion and professional expertise in relation to this issue: what shall be termed here *"insulationism"* and *"reinvigorationism."*[17]

As appeals to populist sentiments stand accused of diluting the authority of criminal justice expertise and interfering with the shaping of its research and policy agenda, one response has been to problematise an apparent excess of democracy in criminal justice policymaking.[18] The charge here is that there is a fundamental problem with criminological expertise and professional decision-making being held hostage to the tyranny of a public opinion that is taken to be ill-informed and unduly laden with emotion. I use the term *"insulationism"* to describe those who call for the decontamination of issues of criminal justice policymaking from public political discourse, locating them instead within independent, professional, regulatory bodies formed of criminal justice experts.[19] The claim is that such professional bodies will serve to *insulate* criminal justice policy responses from the exigencies of an emotionally aroused and vengeful public bent on punishment (or, at least, the construction and deployment of criminal justice policies in such ways that presume such public sentiment around the issues).[20]

On the other hand, it has been argued that the assumption of an automatic punitiveness among the general public is overstated.[21] Rather than indicating "too much democracy" creating a populist response to crime, it is claimed there is a crisis of civic engagement in contemporary society and a sense of "too little democracy."[22] In a climate of increasing insecurity and declining civic participation, apparent populist punitiveness arguably reflects the alienation of the public from meaningful engagement in policymaking processes and, in turn, from a sense of public responsibility for these processes. Instead of removing issues of crime and justice policy from the realm of popular opinion, it is argued, the aim should be to move beyond the tokenism of political elites. Reinvigorated normative public debate around issues of crime and justice coupled with reinvesting the public with a sense of civic responsibility for crime and justice, it is anticipated, will not only loosen the grip of "populist punitiveness," but will also serve as the handmaiden to more creative, democratically imagined (and thereby legitimate) responses to crime and justice.[23]

Central to understanding the reinvigorationist approach is recognizing this as not so much a strategy intended to come to a majoritarian conclusion about penal policy, but one designed to foster dialogue and discussion in more meaningful ways for developing more effective, while also legitimate, responses to issues of crime and justice. As such, it taps into broader concerns within political theory that challenge both the uneasiness toward democracy found within liberalism, but also the fundamental individualist premises upon which it is predicated. For example, as Young argues:

> Liberal political theory represents individuals as occupying private and separate spaces, as propelled only by their own private desires. This is a consumer-oriented conception of human nature, in which social and political relations can be understood only as goods instrumental to the achievement of individual desires, and not as intrinsic goods. This atomistic conception generates a political theory that presumes conflict and competition as characteristic modes of interaction.[24]

A variety of commentators have similarly challenged the premises that Young identifies, pointing toward the effects that these have on promoting an "instrumentalist" and "privatized" approach to politics.[25] Moreover, they have also highlighted concerns that echo those noted above, about the way in which the knowledges we produce (in this case liberal political theory) *construct* publics in particular ways through the values they embody, despite formal appeals value neutrality.[26] For example, Walzer argues that "the liberal ideology of separatism cannot take personhood and bondedness away from us. What it does take away is the *sense* of our personhood and bondedness, and this deprivation is then reflected in liberal politics."[27]

The tension that the divergent projects of insulationism and reinvigorationism reflect is not peculiar to the field of criminal justice, but speaks to broader antagonisms animating the production of knowledge directed toward effecting social change and a more general problem regarding our understanding of, and response to, social problems.

Insulationism, Liberalism, and Illiberalism

Throughout the second half of the twentieth century, especially in the aftermath of the disasters wrought by the social experiments of Nazism and Soviet Communism, the need to balance liberalism and the protection of individual freedoms with the pursuit of utopia or "the good society,"[28] has haunted Western thought.[29] Indeed, the imposition of various visions of utopia in the last century has arguably realized the adage that one person's paradise is another's hell only too well.

As hopes for wholesale social reform have given way to what are now considered brutalizing regimes, thinkers such as Hayek, Popper, and Gray have led the way in championing the liberal cause for the protection of individual liberty against the dangers of unbridled progressivist tendencies.[30]

This is further reflected in a divergence in orientation to the means of effecting social change. More conservative, liberal approaches arguably tend toward small-scale, piecemeal reform within the existing regime, while more radical, social reformist perspectives seek more holistic social change. While for the former position, the danger of the latter is the imposition of a vision of the good which infringes on the rights, liberties, and protections to which all are entitled in civilized, humane, and liberal society; for the latter, the danger of the former is a tendency to prop up a system which may, itself, be unjust.

Walzer has argued:

> The standard liberal argument for neutrality is an induction from social fragmentation. Since dissociated individuals will never agree on the good life, the state must allow them to live as they think best, subject only to John Stuart Mill's harm principle, without endorsing or sponsoring any particular understanding of what "best" means. But there is a problem here: The more dissociated individuals are, the stronger the state is likely to be, since it will be the only or the most important social union. And then membership in the state, the only good that is shared by all individuals, may well come to seem the good that is "best."[31]

Here, Walzer sums up the basis for the insulationist approach, both in terms of its animating impulse (namely, to curtail the imposition of particular visions of the good life upon individuals), but also in terms of its implicit danger, that of its own capacity for dysfunction. In seeking to prevent the tyranny of the masses, the danger is that this can, all too easily, be substituted for another form of tyranny: in the case of criminal justice policy as articulated by proponents of insulationism, tyranny of an expert and professional criminal justice elite. Thus, this strategy may in turn also raise questions of the legitimacy of any policies so devised. Indeed, as even the fiercest defenders of liberalism have highlighted, within a liberal polity, some degree of democratic engagement and accountability are essential means for diluting potential excesses of power and holding social institutions in check.[32]

Insofar as the criminal law has historically been conceived as an "index of social solidarity,"[33] reflecting the common morality and presenting a declaration of the shared obligations and restrictions on individuals within a given society,[34] the so-called "insulationist approach to penal policy",[35] which advocates the restriction of penal affairs to professional expertise, seems normatively untenable. Thus Dzur has argued that

> an insulated approach to criminal justice policy seems particularly inapt given the central normative place of the public in defining the very meaning of a criminal act. What separates a criminal from a civil offense, . . . is the fact that the public is also thought to have a stake. . . . Additionally, prominent in American political thought is a robust argument for the transparency of the criminal law grounded by the fundamental injustice of ordinary citizens being held accountable to rules that they did not authorize, cannot check, and may not understand. If at the core of criminal codes is a normative foundation that is inherently public, it is inappropriate to exclude the public from meaningful participation in criminal justice policymaking.[36]

Therefore, as Turner has highlighted, concerns about crime and the appropriate responses to it, are ultimately not technical issues, but rather, are fundamentally questions of values, such that "neither politically nor normatively is there any good reason why criminologists' opinions should count more than anyone else's."[37]

There is also a more fundamental concern as to the role of insulationism in potentially reifying penal populism or "populist punitiveness" itself and the implications of this for criminal justice policymaking. This concerns the question of whether the "populist punitiveness" from which the insulationist approach seeks to protect criminal justice policy formation is based on a mythical account of public opinion, as well as questioning the role of the construction of academic knowledge in creating this account.

As Dzur has noted,

to advocate exclusion and deference as the public's role in criminal justice
... is to say that the public ... is careless regarding the lives of others and
needs restraints, expert guidance to dampen down normally poor impulse
control. But this assumption of carelessness is too broad, and risks being a
self-fulfilling prophecy.[38]

Key questions raised by an interrogation of the insulationist perspective
include consideration of the extent to which this position reifies the presumption of penal populism in the first place, as well as that of who the
assumed public from which it is seeking to guard criminal justice policy
is? Is the population necessarily as punitive as this position supposes, and
how does our own knowledge and research in this field shape this public
and its attitudes in the first place?

For example, Hough and Roberts have found that what might appear to
be punitiveness among the lay public might actually reflect a propensity
to "systematically under-estimate the severity of sentencing patterns,"[39]
and, hence, ignorance over typical penalties awarded rather than a desire
to mete out harsher penalties per se. However, they also suggest that while
research has typically focussed on public attitudes regarding criminal
justice policymaking, few have explored public knowledge of the issues
involved and "fewer still have explored public opinion as a function of
public knowledge."[40] By contrast, these authors have found that current
approaches toward gauging public attitudes regarding criminal justice and
penal policy are typically flawed and, despite perceptions of lenient sentencing, members of the public still tend to award more lenient sentences
than typical sentencing practice.

In this way, the production of knowledge arguably plays a role in the
construction of human subjectivity and penal populism itself and the insulationist approach might serve to reify such constructions by lending
them durable institutional form. This is reflected, for example by Turner's
account of how measurement of social phenomena (such as attitudes to
crime and justice policies) can constitute "the public" and their attitudes
in particular ways.[41]

Accepting the validity of these data, one might question the logic of
further insulating penal decision-making from the apparently punitive
public rather than trying to better engage them in such practices. This
seems particularly problematic given that evidence suggests that when
publics feel engaged and are informed about criminal justice policy
and decision-making they are more likely to moderate "previously held
punitive views."[42] Concurrently, however, it also points to the need for

alternative processes and forms of knowledge in constructing alternative public attitudes and perceptions regarding both crime and its appropriate policy responses.

The Antidote to Insulationism

It is against this backdrop and the perceived implications of the insulationist project that reinvigorationist calls for more (and better) democratic participation in public policymaking are situated. The danger becomes that through the implicit normativity it presupposes, the strategy of insulationism becomes the instigator of penal populism rather than the solution to it.

From the reinvigorationist perspective, what is sought are new ways of constructing crime and justice problems and solutions, to reinject normativity into our responses to crime. By moving away from established ways of viewing the public, the aim is to alter the contemporary terrain of knowledge production and consumption in order that we can enable the emergence of more informed and democratically engaged publics. If, then, the problem is in the construction and circulation of knowledge, it seems possible that therein might also lie the solution. How then then might we build this more democratically responsive mode of knowing and talking about questions of crime and punishment in practice?

As Dzur has pointed out, all too often while lip-service may be paid to the inclusion of the public in criminal justice processes via superficially participatory forms of justice (such as those reflected within some restorative justice processes), core normative issues and decisions which lie at the heart of criminal justice policies and responses remain insulated from genuine public democratic debate and dialogue.[43] In response, Dzur highlights the need for the active construction and creation of places of public participation in which people can explore these issues in a deliberative, participatory manner.[44] The danger is that, without such spaces, public consultation falls into tokenistic legitimation of the liberal elites, thereby leaving political decision-making the hostage of expertise, while also reifying the very conditions of egoistic individualism upon which the insulationist strategy is based in the first place.

One such route toward opening up more progressive and constructive spaces for public deliberation and debate has been identified by Albert Dzur in his specific call for a reimagining and reinvigoration of the role of the jury in criminal justice processes.[45] The problem with most current approaches to public inclusion in penal policymaking is precisely the detachment of criminal justice processes and decision-making from the realms of public debate. For example, Dzur argues that while trial by jury is conventionally heralded as "a cornerstone of democracy,"[46] in reality the bureaucratic processes of the criminal trial relegate public participation to the formal role of passive spectatorship rather than meaningful participation in the construction of justice.[47] This, in turn, is facilitated by increasing individualism and a declining sense of community within contemporary society.[48] The danger becomes that the jury serves as purely a symbolic form of legitimation for what is, ultimately, expert-decision-making.

Consequently, where public engagement within the criminal justice system is still demanded, participation is typically "more appendage than antidote" to the formal, bureaucratized, professionalized criminal justice system.[49] The key argument for proponents of the reinvigorationist perspective, therefore, is that it is the alienation of criminal justice decision-making from public democratic deliberation that results in the apparent punitiveness of contemporary society. Therefore, the antidote is not to eschew public engagement but to reawaken it:

> Lay participation in criminal justice is needed because it brings otherwise attenuated people into contact with suffering human beings, draws attention to the ways laws and policies and institutional structures prolong that suffering, and makes possible – though does not guarantee – greater awareness among participants of their own responsibility for laws and policies and structures that treat people humanely.[50]

In this way, a reimagining and redesign of the jury into a site of load-bearing civic responsibility is proposed by Dzur. By allowing active participation of jury members in trial proceedings; resisting increased removal of questions of criminal and penal policy from public deliberation; and connecting decisions of guilt and innocence with issues of appropriate penalty, it is anticipated, the jury can be "rediscovered" as a progressive site of civic engagement and resistance to penal punitiveness and mass incarceration in the name of popular democracy.

The Need for Spaces of Hope in (and Beyond) Criminal Justice

Assuming the necessity of more, rather than less, democratic public participation as the means by which we might move beyond punitiveness and mass incarceration, the danger is that so long as this focus remains solely on the criminal justice system and penal policy, this strategy continually risks ultimate recapitulation of the criminal justice system.

Indeed, critical Marxist geographer David Harvey has argued that "the re-making and re-imagining of 'community' will work in progressive directions only if it is connected *en route* to a more generalized radical insurgent politics."[51] The problem, he argues, is that, political movements are typically located at the level of a particular issue, debate or group and struggle to "transcend particularities, and arrive at some conception of a universal alternative to that social system which is the source of their difficulties."[52]

The particular claim for more public deliberation and active democratic engagement in issues of crime and justice perhaps reflects a more general concern regarding the need for what Harvey has termed "spaces of hope" in response to declining belief in the possibilities of any radical alternatives to the contemporary social order.[53] Highlighting the way in which contemporary politics in general serves to disconnect particular issues from more universal principles, Harvey argues that social concerns become segmented into particular interest groups, issues, and so on that exist as disjointed silos. This, he suggests, ultimately results in problems of capacity to effect social change and difficulties in terms of changing scale from particular concerns to universal issues and vice versa. On the other hand, however, lies the danger of abstract universal theorizing with no clear means of practical translation. While this is arguably a tendency borne out across social science research, in no small part reflective of the contemporary context of knowledge production, it seems to be brought into relief particularly starkly by criminology and the historical battle lines that have been drawn between "administrative or governmental" and "critical or emancipatory" criminologies.[54] Underpinning such divisions (though recognizing that few theorists totally identify with either end of what is, ultimately, a spectrum) lies a tension between a commitment to effecting real-world social change, and belief about the best means by which it can be achieved: small-scale reform from inside the existing system or wholesale radical change from without. On the one hand, the danger is of lapsing into particularism and reforms concerned with "tinkering at the edges" but leaving the general structure of society and its institutions (and by extension its organizing assumptions and principles), untouched. On the other, is the risk of offering an abstract critique of society, without any concrete means of institutional realization or agenda for reform.

Mapping on to such divisions, Harvey also points to the way in which visions of the good society either tend toward a focus on a static vision of that good society, without any clear means of the way in which it might be implemented, or focus on the *process* of creating change, without any clear sense of direction or goal. Moreover, attempts to implement social change also risk accusations of authoritarianism or the privileging of particular issues (neglecting the situated production of knowledge) if any attempt is made to implement them.

In response, Harvey identifies "spaces of hope" in which the prospects and possibilities for alternatives to existing institutions and responses can be explored. Such spaces, he argues, must be rooted in the spatiotemporal realities of the contemporary social order, while also able to look beyond them. The question, of course, arises as to how and where such spaces of challenge and intervention can be generated. As Harvey notes: "We cannot engage in endless problematization and never-ending conversations ... without translation, collective forms of action become impossible. All potential for an alternative politics disappears."[55]

Instead, he identifies a need for what he calls "dialectical utopianism" and the need for "mediating institutions" that can serve to connect the particular to the universal and vice versa.[56] Central to this is a need for political and intellectual humility among those working on particular interests, to look beyond them, and seek to translate their particular concerns or problems into meaningful dialogue with those who might be animated by other interests or concerns.

In this context, the criminal justice system can be considered a "mediating institution," serving to "translate" the underlying abstract universal organizing principles of society into particular applications. However, such mediating institutions can themselves become sites of power and reification of the dominant discourse of society and must tread carefully to ensure recognition and successful negotiation of the dialectic between particular institutional reform and more wholesale social change.[57] For example, while growing recognition of the limitations of conventional criminal justice processes for addressing offending and realizing "justice" (however defined) have resulted in increasing uses of restorative justice responses, these have typically been accommodated *within* conventional criminal justice apparatus, rather than developed as genuine *alternatives* to it.[58]

The danger is that attempts by philosophers, political theorists, and criminologists to challenge contemporary ways of thinking, talking and responding to crime and justice beyond "populist punitiveness" and mass incarceration that focus solely at the redemocratization of the criminal justice and penal decision-making processes in isolation, arguably neglect the way in which the production of their own knowledge is a socially situated, political, and normative exercise. Too often responses to apparent populism by experts either seek to exclude publics all together (as reflected in the insulationist strategy) or only seek to present the issues or debates in ways that are meaningful to those working in those fields.

Accordingly, it may only be by reconnecting the problems of penal populism and declining civic engagement to a broader, more holistic examination of society that we can avoid simply extending and reifying existing conceptions and responses to crime. Otherwise, potential spaces for realizing progressive alternatives can all too easily end up buttressing and legitimizing the existing social system and the values it promotes, unless clearly tied to a more universal politics of social change. Thus, the danger of current responses to apparent penal populism which advocate the reengagement of a disenfranchised public as a means of opening up a space in which alternatives to mass incarceration might be imagined, is that they risk isolating issues of crime and justice as particular expressions of more abstract principles, from their broader location in a holistic social order.

The converse danger, of course, is that by demanding an all-or-nothing commitment to wholesale social reform, we stagnate under abstract universalism without a particular strategy for realizing social change within the contemporary spatiotemporal order.

Consequently, in considering how contemporary democratic theory might try to think beyond mass incarceration and ask how the normative complexity of criminal justice might be addressed, so too must those working in this arena recognize and reflect on how they might also think beyond crime and justice if they are to realize more genuinely democratic alternatives.

Building Spaces of Hope

In advocating the need for the development and articulation of spaces of hope, questions inevitably turn to the practical building and institution of these spaces. While advancing the need to engage in collective political struggles that move in scale from the local to the global and back again, the question, in practical terms, becomes the translation of particularities into a universal agenda.

The temptation might be to announce an impasse between these two camps and continue the problematization of translating normative theorizing into practical change, or critique attempts to effect social change for the absence of normative theorizing regarding the bigger picture. However, while one can reject the imposition of a blueprint of social democratic organization as the route to more holistic, engaged, and democratic responses to social problems, one can, at least, suggest means of opening dialogue that might foster such means of communication and dialogue currently in operation in nascent form within our own lived social reality. The next stage now is, surely, to build these in practice.

Here I invoke an example from my own recent experience which, I think, perhaps indicates the way in which we are seeing more democratic forms of politics and the nascent creation of "spaces of hope," with particular agendas tied more overtly and explicitly to a vision of "the good society."

On September 18, 2014, Scotland held a referendum to decide whether it wanted to become an independent nation, separate from the rest of the United Kingdom. This was a significant moment, played out in the media and analyzed considerably since. What was notable about this event, from the point of view of this observer, was the way in which discussion and debate about specific policies, such as taxation, education, welfare, defense, healthcare, and nationalism,[59] were translated from particular issues into a broader debate about the type of society people envisaged as possible and desirable. As one journalist in the *Scotsman*, Peter Jones, put it: "Groups backing No and Yes sprang up all over the place, some marshalled by common interests and occupation, many more drawn together by ties of community."[60] Thus there was a clear translation from particular interests to broader, unapologetically normative discussions about the type of society people wanted to live in and thought possible. As then Scottish Cabinet Secretary for Education and Lifelong Learning, Michael Russell said to the Utopian Studies Society in July 2013, describing the referendum:

It is a debate which starts with the question about what *kind* of Scotland we want to live in.

And that is a real utopian project.

In the spirit of Owen,[61] it is a *practical* utopianism – one that is wide in its ambition and scope.

In this sense, every single Scot is a negotiator of independence.

The question that will be asked of every Scot in 14 months' time won't simply require a "yes" or "no" answer.

And, it won't merely ask them to side up with one or other political party.

Rather, it will require them to envision a better Scotland—a Scotland that *will* exist—and to think how, by working with their fellow citizens, they could work toward making that vision real.[62]

Further, it is interesting to note that despite formally voting to maintain the status quo (in terms of preserving the same formal relationship between Scotland and the rest of the United Kingdom prior to the independence referendum), as Paterson has noted: "If Scotland was not sovereign unless independent, then its capacity to set the agenda since it voted has been quite remarkably autonomous."[63]

While admittedly this is simply one account from one particular observer and the legacy of the referendum still remains unclear, it does demonstrate one way in which we might carve out "spaces of hope" insofar as particular issues were tied to larger questions about the structure of society and its implications for creating new forms of meaningful public engagement (and, by extension, an engaged public with a record 84.6 percent turnout).[64] For example, during this period topics that featured in debates ranged from concerns about nuclear arms, education, healthcare, jobs, the economy, identity, and the future for today's youth. Concerns or hopes articulated around a particular aspect (such as the renewal of the Trident nuclear missile system or the continuation of free higher education in Scotland) were raised as part of a larger discussion of what was possible and desirable for society, as well as whether this was better achieved within the United Kingdom or as part of an independent Scotland. In this way, one saw a constant shifting in registers: from particular policy concerns to a broader question about how to organise society; and from big questions about the norms and values animating Scottish society and how the structural organization of society (in this case, a different relationship with the rest of the United Kingdom), might (or might not) also allow us to better realize these in the way we address particular policy problems. There was, then, a constant connection of individual interests to broader questions of the social organization of society. In this way, different and often disparate particular areas policy or interest could be recognized as interconnected with bigger, bolder, "utopian" questions about what type of society the people of Scotland want to live in and why. This suggests that when debates and issues are made meaningful and accessible to the public, the public will engage with them. It also suggests the need for new ways to connect particular policies and debates, or interests, hopes, and fears to broader normative questions about the type of society we want to live in and why, in which all citizens have a stake.

The Method of Utopia as a Means to Holistic Reimagining of Society

Part of the problem of the contemporary disenfranchisement of the public from criminal justice decision-making is perhaps the failure to recognize that the concerns of the general public are not necessarily aligned to those of criminal justice professionals. Most people are not immediately connected to issues of crime and justice either as victims or offenders, and, as noted above, the operations of the criminal justice system further serve to present issues in a way that is foreign to and detached from the realities of many lay people's daily lives. Accordingly, if those working in the fields of criminal justice wish to engage the public in debates and decisions of criminal justice and penal policy, so too must they engage in the issues about which the public *are* concerned. This means demonstrating the connections between these questions and the broader social order that immediately affects that public in their daily lives.

What is needed, then, is a means by which we can reconnect such particular debates concerning crime, control, and justice to broader, universal concerns and thereby make them relevant and accessible to the general public from whom they have become alienated. Here, it is suggested that the development of a "utopian method" as a form of "speculative sociology" may prove a useful candidate.[65]

Levitas offers the idea of utopia as a method for considering the values implicit within social theories and political programs, and their implications, both for the institutional organization of society and for the type of people necessitated by such a society.[66] Identifying three aspects: *archaeology, architecture*, and *ontology*, the utopian method is thus advanced as "a means of exposing these normative assumptions and constructions of society to critique and critical comparison."[67]

Taking as a starting point this idea that all social theories and political programs can be seen as containing an implicit, if repressed, vision of the good society, together these three aspects of archaeology, architecture, and ontology offer a means of representing holistic accounts of the good society implicit within contemporary social theories. Shifting away from a focus within these programs on piecemeal reform, the utopian method encourages an expanded evaluation of their implications, requiring "judgment, not simply about the attractiveness of such abstract values as freedom, justice, inclusion, equality, but about how these might actually be played out in institutional form."[68]

Taking "insulationist" approaches to criminal justice policymaking, premised upon liberal concerns to protect policies from populist punitiveness, the application of the utopian method in archaeological mode reveals a fundamental premise (notwithstanding the various species of liberalism that exist) that the "good" or "desirable" society is that in which individual autonomy and choice regarding one's individual pursuit of the good is protected so far as is compatible with guaranteeing that same right or capacity for each individual.

These assumptions, in turn, feed into the institutional implications or *architecture* of the insulationist approach to criminal justice policy. Within its commitment to liberalism, one can identify the inspiration of an institutional structure that protects individuals from assaults to these rights via the exercise of power. This arguably also reflects a particular normative view of how the good (or at least the best attainable) society ought to be constituted which, in turn, implies a notion (albeit a quite general one), of how society might be institutionally constructed to realize this end. For example, Shklar suggests that in terms of maximizing individual liberty, "limited government and the control of unequally divided political power constitute the minimal condition without which freedom is unimaginable in any politically organized society."[69] Essential to this is the rule of law as a protection from the arbitrary use of punishment by governments, bolstered by the "division and subdivision of political power."[70]

Finally, in terms of the third aspect identified within Levitas's method, that of *ontology*, it is here that one can also find a particular ontological position concerning the construction of selves and human subjectivity and this is reflected in the insulationist concerns. The liberal position presupposes the existence of individual selves who may differ in their identification and pursuit of the good. The requirement that each person's individual pursuit of the good be respected and preserved as far as compatible with that of all others, reflects a priority of the individual and the role of the state as consisting in solving a Hobbesian coordination problem, where the interests of some threaten to impinge those of others. The ontological implications of this position, therefore, reflect a liberal individualism that consists in the individual with his/her interests existing prior to and distinct from the group's.[71]

Thus, despite an overt rejection of any attempt to impose upon others a normative vision of the good life not of their own design, an implicit (albeit nascent) vision of the good society can nevertheless be extrapolated from the values fundamental to the liberalism of fear that arguably dominates contemporary expert responses to contemporary social phenomena. However, without explicit normative commitment to social reform, and commitment to specialized forms of knowledge, the result typically becomes a tendency toward piecemeal reforms *within* the existing system rather than radical, wholesale challenges to the status quo. However, this itself reflects a normative position insofar as through the denial of normative, wholesale, theorizing, the implication is that the current organization of society is the best we can hope for.

Absent from the liberal commitment to the rejection of utopia, therefore, is an awareness of the way in which this system may itself impose a vision of the good (that may or may not be shared by all). It also presupposes liberalism as the only route to democratic and humane decision-making. Both of these assumptions are, moreover, arguably reified by the insulationist approach and challenged by the strategy of reinvigoration in response to concerns over contemporary penal populism. Therefore, it is also important to reflect on the liberal assumptions informing the insulationist response to penal populism regarding the nature of the human subjectivity and the role such approaches play in constructing both the public and penal populism, embedded as they are in the contemporary processes and strategies of knowledge production noted above.

Although space precludes a more detailed elaboration, the brief application of this method to the liberal insulationist approach also demonstrates how apparently particular concerns about crime and justice policymaking encode a bigger set of assumptions about how society can and should be organized. A commitment to the preservation of individual liberty as a central premise of the underpinning of criminal justice policymaking, as part of a bigger (albeit implicit) vision of the good society, arguably also implies a similar approach to other policymaking arenas (such as housing policy, education policy, welfare policy, etc.). Taken together, more holistically, the possibility and desirability of institutions designed on such principles might be examined. So too could the compatibility of different policies pertaining to different spheres of public life (such as housing, welfare, education, criminal justice), be considered. This is particularly important given the current segmented approach to policymaking, which may potentially allow policies in different areas to be developed on fundamentally different assumptions and principles, regarding what is both desirable and achievable for the good society.

Conclusion

Following the analysis undertaken in this chapter, it seems clear that what is fundamentally required in this context is more systematic thinking about questions of crime and justice that is also allied to practical means for fostering dialogue and discussion between different factions, interest groups, and forms of knowledge. There are a number of registers at which this could fruitfully take place. Firstly, insofar as expert discourse, as evidenced above, shapes our understanding of social problems and the responses of the public to social problems, there is a need to find conceptual tools that allow us to act as *"democratic under-labourers"* and translate our superficially "technical" discussions into normative debates in which publics are necessarily invested.[72] The utopian method as identified by Levitas is offered as one potential means for doing this.

At the same time, however, one must be wary of trying to impose a particular space of hope, artificially and externally, lest it become ideological or tokenistic. That said, given that we are witnessing what has been described as a *watershed moment* in terms of increasing questioning of contemporary trends in penal sanctions and mass incarceration, both by experts and others the present is perhaps more promising in this regard than the recent past. Situated within a broader context of public engagement with and questioning of established orders and practices of powers (as evidenced through, for example, the Scottish Independence Referendum, but also other local and global social movements such as the Occupy protests and, more recently, the #BlackLivesMatter movement in the United States), which have often seen local concerns connected with broader social injustices and issues, we may just be witnessing the potential opening of such "spaces of hope" on the horizon.

Thus, to conclude, it is the central argument of this chapter that criminal justice experts can and should seek to address and involve people in matters of policymaking by rendering them relatable to their lives if it wishes to have a genuinely informed and engaged public, equipped to resist the populist temptation.[73] Rather than lament the failure of publics to resist the lure of vengeance, as empirical evidence has demonstrated, it is incumbent upon criminal justice experts to engage those publics in meaningful ways, and to approach their subject with both "political humility" and normative clarity.[74] Admittedly, this is not easy given the current climate of knowledge production and the tendency toward specialization and the suppression of normativity. The utopian method is offered here as a suggestion for changing how we understand, produce, and present our knowledge, in ways that may render them more meaningful and accessible to lay publics.

Notes

1. See Jonathan Simon, *Mass Incarceration on Trial* (New York: The New Press, 2014); Loïc Wacquant, *Prisons of Poverty* (Minneapolis: University of Minnesota Press, 2009); David Garland, *The Culture of Control: Crime and Social Order in Contemporary Society* (Oxford: Oxford University Press, 2001). I am grateful to the editors for their helpful comments on earlier drafts of this chapter.

2. For example, the phenomenon of mass incarceration is typically considered a distinctly US phenomenon. See David Garland, "Introduction: The Meaning of Mass Imprisonment," in D. Garland (ed.) *Mass Imprisonment: Social Causes and Consequences* (Thousand Oaks, CA: Sage, 2001), pp. 1–3. ; Garland, *The Culture of Control: Crime and Social Order in Contemporary Society* (Oxford: Oxford University Press, 2001), 135.

3. Albert Dzur, *Punishment, Participatory Democracy, and the Jury* (Oxford: Oxford University Press, 2012), Chapter 2.

4. See Ian Loader and Richard Sparks, *Public Criminology?* (New York: Routledge, 2011).

5. The term "populist punitiveness" is coined by Anthony Bottoms. See Bottoms "The Philosophy and Politics of Punishment and Sentencing," in C. Clarkson and R. Morgan (eds.), *The Politics of Sentencing Reform* (Oxford: Clarendon Press, 1995), 40. See also John Pratt, *Penal Populism* (New York: Routledge, 2007).

6. The term "spaces of hope" is taken from David Harvey. See Harvey, *Spaces of Hope* (Edinburgh: Edinburgh University Press, 2000).

7. This method has been devised and developed by Ruth Levitas. See Levitas, *Utopia as Method: The Imaginary Reconstitution of Society* (Basingstoke: Palgrave Macmillan, 2013); Levitas, "Being in Utopia," *The Hedgehog Review* vol. 10 (no. 1) (2008): 19–30; Levitas, "The Imaginary Reconstitution of Society: Utopia as Method," in T. Moylan and R. Baccolini (eds.), *Utopia Method Vision: The Use Value of Social Dreaming* (Bern: Peter Lang, 2007), pp.47–68; Levitas, "Looking for the Blue: The Necessity of Utopia," *Journal of Political Ideologies* vol. 12 (no. 3)(2007): 289–306; Levitas, "The Imaginary Reconstitution of Society or Why Sociologists and Others Should Take Utopia More Seriously," Inaugural Lecture, University of Bristol, October 24, 2005, www.bris.ac.uk/spais/files/inaugural.pdf; Levitas, "Against Work: A Utopian Incursion into Social Policy," *Critical Social Policy*, vol. 21 (no. 4) (2001): 449–465.

8. See also Lynne Copson, "Towards a Utopian Criminology," in M. Malloch and B. Munro (eds.), *Crime, Critique and Utopia* (Basingstoke: Palgrave Macmillan, 2013), pp. 114–135.

9. Ruth Levitas, "Back to the Future: Wells, Sociology, Utopia and Method," *The Sociological Review* vol.58 (no. 4) (2010): 530–547, at 530.

10. Levitas, *The Concept of Utopia* (London: Phillip Allen, 1990), 8.

11. Ibid.

12. Frederic Jameson, "Of Islands and Trenches: Naturalization and the Production of Utopian Discourse," *Diacritics*, vol. 7 (no. 2) (1977): 2–21 at 6. See also Peter Young, "The Importance of Utopias in Criminological Thinking," *British Journal of Criminology* vol. 32 (no. 4) (1992): 423–437.

13. Copson, "Towards a Utopian Criminology," 131.

14. Simon, *Mass Incarceration on Trial*, 3.

15. See, for example, Simon, *Mass Incarceration on Trial.*

16. See Ian Loader and Richard Sparks, "Beyond Mass Incarceration?," *The Good Society* vol. 23 (no. 1) (2014): 114–120, at 115; David Green, "Penal Populism and the Folly of 'Doing Good by Stealth'," *The Good Society* vol. 23 (no. 1) (2014): 73–86, at 82.

17. See Dzur, *Punishment, Participatory Democracy, and the Jury*; Loader and Sparks, *Public Criminology?*; and Green, "Penal Populism and the Folly of 'Doing Good By Stealth'."

18. This has been highlighted by Dzur in his *Punishment, Participatory Democracy, and the Jury*; 22–24.

19. For examples, see Philip Pettit, "Depoliticizing Democracy," *Ratio Juris* vol.17 (no. 1) (2004): 52–65; Franklin Zimring, Gordon Hawkins, and Sam Kamin, *Punishment and Democracy: Three Strikes and You're Out in California* (Oxford: Oxford University Press, 2001); Franklin Zimring, "Populism, Democratic Government, and the Decline of Expert Authority: Some Reflections on Three Strikes in California," *Pacific Law Journal* vol. 28 (no. 1) (1996): 243–256. See also Dzur, *Punishment, Participatory Democracy, and the Jury*, 27–30 for a discussion of this approach.

20. See Dzur, *Punishment, Participatory Demcoracy, and the Jury*, 27–30. See also Albert Dzur, "Participatory Democracy and Criminal Justice," *Criminal Law and Philosophy* vol. 6 (no. 2) (2012): 115–129.

21. See Elizabeth Turner, "Beyond 'Facts' and 'Values': Rethinking Some Recent Debates about the Public Role of Criminology," *British Journal of Criminology* vol. 53 (no.1) (2013): 149–166; Roger Matthews, "The Myth of Punitiveness," *Theoretical Criminology* vol. 9 (no. 2) (2005): 175–201; Mike Hough and Julian Roberts, "Sentencing Trends in Britain: Public Knowledge and Public Opinion," *Punishment & Society* vol. 1 (no. 1) (1999): 11–26.

22. Dzur, *Punishment, Participatory Democracy, and the Jury*, 32–36.

23. See Dzur, *Punishment, Participatory Democracy, and the Jury*; Dzur, "Participatory Democracy and Criminal Justice." See also Green, "Penal Populism and the Folly of 'Doing Good By Stealth' "; Liz Turner, "Penal Populism, Deliberative Methods, and the Production of 'Public Opinion' on Crime and Punishment," *The Good Society* vol. 23 (no. 1) (2014): 87–102; and Ian Loader, "Fall of the 'Platonic Guardians': Liberalism, Criminology and Political Responses to Crime in England and Wales," *British Journal of Criminology* vol. 46 (no. 4) (2006): 561–586.

24. Iris Young, *Justice and the Politics of Difference* (Princeton, NJ: Princeton University Press, 1990), 228.

25. Ibid.; For examples of commentators who have challenged the individualism upon which liberalism is premised, see Brooke Ackerley, "Is Liberalism the Only Way Toward Democracy?: Confucianism and Democracy," *Political Theory* vol. 33 (no. 4) (2005): 547–576; and Michael Walzer, "The Communitarian Critique of Liberalism," *Political Theory* vol. 18 (no. 1) (1990): 6–23.

26. See Michael Sandel, *Liberalism and the Limits of Justice* (Cambridge: Cambridge University Press, 1982), 11.

27. Walzer, "The Communitarian Critique of Liberalism," 10.

28. Lawrence Douglas, Austin Sarat, and Martha Umphrey, "Law and the Utopian Imagination: An Introduction," in A. Sarat, L. Douglas, and M. Umphrey (eds.), *Law and the Utopian Imagination* (Redwood City, CA: Stanford University Press, 2013), pp. 1–22.

29. See, for example, Ruth Levitas, "Dystopian Times? The Impact of Death of Progress on Utopian Thinking," *Theory, Culture & Society* vol. 1 (no. 1) (1981): 53–64; Judith Shklar, "The Liberalism of Fear," in N. Rosenblum (ed.), *Liberalism and the Moral Life* (Cambridge, MA: Harvard University Press, 1989), pp. 21–38; and my own "Towards a Utopian Criminology."

30. See Friedrich Hayek, *The Road to Serfdom* (Chicago: University of Chicago Press, 1944); Karl Popper, "Utopia and Violence," *World Affairs* vol.149 (no. 1) (1986): 3–9; John Gray, *Black Mass: Apocalyptic Religion and the Death of Utopia* (London: Penguin Books, 2008).

31. Walzer, "The Communitarian Critique of Liberalism," 16–17.

32. For example, Shklar argues: "Without enough equality of power to protect and assert one's rights, freedom is but a hope. Without the institutions of representative democracy and an accessible, fair, and independent judiciary open to appeals, and in the absence of a multiplicity of politically active groups, liberalism is in jeopardy. . . . It is therefore fair to say that liberalism is monogamously, faithfully, and permanently married to democracy—but it is a marriage of convenience," "The Liberalism of Fear," 37.

33. Robert Reiner, "Crime, Law and Deviance: the Durkheim Legacy," in S. Fenton (ed.), *Durkheim and Modern Sociology* (Cambridge: Cambridge University Press, 1984), pp. 175-201, at 177.

34. See Emile Durkheim, "Crime and Social Health," Translated and reprinted as "Durkheim's Reply to Tarde," in S. Lukes and A. Scull (eds.), *Durkheim and the Law* (Oxford: Martin Roberston, 1983 [1895]), pp. 92–101); and Emile Durkheim, *The Division of Labor in Society* (New York: The Free Press of Glencoe, 1964 [1893]).

35. Dzur, "Participatory Democracy and Criminal Justice," 118.

36. Dzur, *Punishment, Participatory Democracy, and the Jury*, 31–32.

37. M. Tonry and D. Green (2003), at 492–493 in Turner, "Beyond 'Facts' and 'Values': Rethinking Some Recent Debates about the Public Role of Criminology," 154–155.

38. Dzur, *Punishment, Participatory Democracy, and the Jury*, 32.

39. Hough and Roberts, "Sentencing Trends in Britain: Public Knowledge and Public Opinion," 11.

40. Hough and Roberts, "Sentencing Trends in Britain: Public Knowledge and Public Opinion," 13.

41. See Turner, "Penal Populism, Deliberative Methods, and the Production of 'Public Opinion' on Crime and Punishment."

42. Green, "Penal Populism and the Folly of 'Doing Good By Stealth'," 82.

43. Dzur, "Participatory Democracy and Criminal Justice"; Albert Dzur, "The Myth of Penal Populism: Democracy, Citizen Participation, and American Hyperincarceration," *Journal of Speculative Philosophy* (New Series) vol. 24 (no. 4) (2010): 354–379.

44. Dzur, *Punishment, Participatory Democracy, and the Jury*.

45. Ibid.

46. Dzur, *Punishment, Participatory Democracy, and the Jury*, 6.

47. Dzur, *Punishment, Participatory Democracy, and the Jury*.

48. Dzur, *Punishment, Participatory Democracy, and the Jury*, 32.

49. Dzur, *Punishment, Participatory Democracy, and the Jury*, 19.

50. Dzur, *Punishment, Participatory Democracy, and the Jury*, 14.

51. Harvey, *Spaces of Hope*, 240.

52. Harvey, *Spaces of Hope*, 241.

53. Harvey, *Spaces of Hope*.

54. Loader and Sparks, *Public Criminology?*, 72.

55. Harvey, *Spaces of Hope*, 245.

56. Harvey, *Spaces of Hope*, 35-36 and *passim*

57. Harvey, *Spaces of Hope*, 241–243.

58. See Tony Marshall, "The Evolution of Restorative Justice in Britain," *European Journal of Criminal Policy and Research* vol. 4 (no. 4) (1996): 21–43; Barbara Hudson, *Understanding Justice: An Introduction to Ideas, Perspectives and Controversies in Modern Penal Theory*, 2nd ed. (Buckingham: Open University Press, 2003), Chapter 5.

59. See, for example, Julie Gilbert, "Independence Referendum: Grassroots Campaigners Explain Why they are Voting Yes or No," *Daily Record*, September 18, 2014, www.dailyrecord.co.uk/news/local-news/independence-referendum-grassroots-campaigners-explain-4280302; Cabinet Secretary for Education and Lifelong Learning, "Speech to the Utopian Studies Society," New Lanark, July 3, 2013, http://news.scotland.gov.uk/Speeches-Briefings/Speech-to-the-Utopian-Studies-Society-24c.aspx.

60. Jones, "Referendum Shows the Power of the People," *The Scotsman*, September 22, 2014, http://www.scotsman.com/news/opinion/peter-jones-referendum-shows-the-power-of-people-1-3549512. See also Lindsay Paterson, "Utopian Pragmatism: Scotland's Choice," *Scottish Affairs* vol. 24 (no. 1) (2015): 22–46.

61. Robert Owen, industrialist and so-called utopian socialist. Owen sought the practical institution of the good society attempted at New Lanark. By emphasizing education, training, and the fostering of charity and goodwill among people, and eradicating the exploitation of one group by another upon which capitalism was based, Owen anticipated that "society may be formed as to exist without crime, without poverty, with health greatly improved, with little, if any misery, and with intelligence and happiness increased a hundredfold." See Robert Owen, *An Address to the Inhabitants of New Lanark* (London: The Informal Education Archives, January 1, 1816), www.infed.org/archives/e-texts/owen_new_lanark.htm. For more on Owen's designation as a utopian socialist, see Friedrich Engels, *Socialism: Utopian and Scientific* (London: Bookmarks, 1993 [1880]); and Karl Marx and Friedrichs Engels, *The Communist Manifesto* (Oxford: Oxford University Press, 1992 [1888]).

62. Cabinet Secretary for Education and Lifelong Learning, "Speech to the Utopian Studies Society."

63. Paterson, "Utopian Pragmatism: Scotland's Choice," 23.

64. The Electoral Commission, *Scottish Independence Referendum: Report on the Referendum Held on 18 September 2014*, December 2014, www.electoralcommission.org.uk/__data/assets/pdf_file/0010/179812/Scottish-independence-referendum-report.pdf, 1.

65. Levitas, *Utopia as Method*, xiv and *passim*; See also "Being in Utopia"; "The Imaginary Reconstitution of Society: Utopia as Method"; "Looking for the Blue"; "The Imaginary Reconstitution of Society or Why Sociologists and Others Should Take Utopia More Seriously,"; and "Against Work."

66. For a more detailed discussion of this method and also to trace its development, see Levitas, *Utopia as Method*; "Being in Utopia"; "The Imaginary Reconstitution of

Society: Utopia as Method"; "Looking for the Blue"; "The Imaginary Reconstitution of Society or Why Sociologists and Others Should Take Utopia More Seriously"; and "Against Work."

67. Copson, "Towards a Utopian Criminology," 130. See also Copson, "Towards a Utopian Criminology," 125–131 for a more detailed discussion of this method.

68. Levitas, "The Imaginary Reconstitution of Society: Utopia as Method," 57; See also Copson, "Towards a Utopian Criminology," 129.

69. Shklar, "The Liberalism of Fear," 28.

70. Shklar, "The Liberalism of Fear," 30.

71. See Walzer, "The Communitarian Critique of Liberalism"; Young, *Justice and the Politics of Difference*; Sandel, *Liberalism and the Limits of Justice*.

72. Loader and Sparks, *Public Criminology?*, Chapter 5.

73. See Loïc Wacquant, "From 'Public Criminology' to the Reflexive Sociology of Criminological Production and Consumption: A Review of *Public Criminology?* by Ian Loader and Richard Sparks (London: Routledge, 2010)," *British Journal of Criminology*, vol. 51 (no. 2) (2011): 538–548; Loïc Wacquant, "Ordering Insecurity: Social Polarization and the Punitive Upsurge," *Radical Philosophy Review*, vol. 11 (no. 1) (2008): 9–27; Hans Boutellier, *The Safety Utopia: Contemporary Discontent and Desire as to Crime and Punishment* (Dordrecht: Kluwer Academic Publishers, 2004).

74. Loader and Sparks, *Public Criminology?*, 132.

CHAPTER 9 | Liberty, Justice, and All

The Folly of Doing Good by Stealth

DAVID A. GREEN

Introduction

Americans are at present witnessing an unprecedented confluence of events and ideationally seismic shifts in the realm of crime and punishment.[1] The subsequent churn promises, at least, to disturb the status quo in fundamental ways and on a scale not seen since the 1970s. These factors tear and pull at the fabric of established orthodoxies, sometimes in opposing directions, but the overall combined effect is all the more disruptive and potentially transformative for it.

The first of these mutually reinforcing events is the mystifying yet undeniably real decline in the prevalence of street crime since the early 1990s. For now, at least, crime remains low on the list of citizens' most troubling priorities, providing politicians and policymakers a layer of protection from the mass-mediated public scrutiny that for two decades ensured this particularly delicate policy arena remained highly politicized. At both the state and federal levels, where penological pessimism and the harshest possible rhetoric were once so conspicuous, a flurry of discursive and legislative change continues apace at the time of writing, riding a new wave of "penal optimism" about crime control and recidivism reduction.[2] Prominent conservatives have demonstrated the most dramatic shifts in this regard, lobbying for decarcerative reforms guided by a reconstructed typification of a redeemable and needful offender who remains, as Kansas Republican Sam Brownback put it, "a beautiful, unique soul, a child of a living God, regardless of whether they [sic] are in prison or not."[3]

The second catalytic event is the 2008 collapse of the financial markets and the lingering effects the subsequent recession continues to have on both criminal justice and correctional budgets at the federal and state levels, and on the public confidence previously enjoyed by unfettered market capitalism. The subsequent proliferation of cost-saving "humonetarianism" discourse in criminal-justice debates has called the American experiment with mass incarceration into question on fiscal grounds, among others.[4] Moreover, the Occupy Wall Street protests of 2011 helped inject the issues of income and social inequality into the mainstream where phrases like "the one percent" are now well established, resonant, and widely understood. The growing gap between the richest and poorest Americans and descriptions from economists that we are in the midst of a "new Gilded Age" have helped to make inequality a key issue in the 2016 election campaigns.[5] It likely accounts for the surprising durability at the time of writing of the candidacies of Bernie Sanders and Donald Trump, each of whom speaks for a constituency exercised in very different ways by inequality and its insecurities. It remains to be seen whether the issue can survive the din of Republican anti-immigration jeremiads, which have only proliferated and intensified since the recent terrorist attacks in Paris, Brussels, and Orlando.

At the same time, critics continue to attack mass incarceration and its various feeder attitudes, policies, and practices on both moral and instrumental grounds. Perhaps the most prominent and well-known among them is Michelle Alexander, whose bestselling book *The New Jim Crow* has done more than any other recent work to indict the drug war, and the "racial indifference" underpinning it, as an abuse of state power, devastating to entire, primarily black communities that are already deeply disadvantaged. Meanwhile, widespread public outrage in the wake of a series of high-profile cases of brutality, arrogance, and overreach by an increasingly militarized police force has raised to prominence concerns about police legitimacy that have been elevated further by movements like Black Lives Matter.[6] Added to this volatile mixture is the critique, especially from the libertarian right, of overzealous, unaccountable prosecutors and the "overcriminalization" of behaviors lacking the usual requirements of criminal intent and moral blameworthiness.[7]

In isolation each of these recent developments might seem mild in its long-term impact, insufficient to alter all that much the terms of public debate. Together, however, they can be read more portentously as evidence of a shifting and uncertain set of social and political conditions that pose new and potentially consequential challenges for democratic legitimacy. They question, contest, even oppose a range of conventional wisdoms, habits of mind, and patterns of action. Combined they also open a window of opportunity to make good on the promises of liberal democracy, to reconsider and redesign "institutions of just ordering" by expanding opportunities for citizens to participate meaningfully in their own governance and in debates about how and why they are policed, prosecuted, sentenced, and punished.[8]

My analysis to follow is based on one empirical claim and two normative suppositions. The claim is that what I shall call the "penal-populist calculus" is predicated in part on a perception by elected officials that their legitimacy in the eyes of their publics is waning and endangered. Late-modern state governance is such that governments are seen to be less effectual than previously in regulating a range of insecurities, both objective and subjective, as markets expand and borders erode.[9] In the face of these challenges, the criminal-justice and penal-policy realms are sites where the power of state sovereignty can be most forcefully reasserted.[10] Penality becomes the means by which a state may demonstrate delivery of a core function, ostensibly to preserve what Richard Nixon called "the first civil right": "to be free from domestic violence."[11] This sociopolitical context tended to increase the salience of crime and punishment, ensuring it remained a high-profile priority for policymakers. This exposure in turn has tended to increase incentives to engage in penal populism, that is, the cynical but expedient politicization of crime and the fears that attend it.

The two normative suppositions invoke both faces of liberal democracy. The first supposition holds that democratic procedures convey legitimacy to policy outcomes. It further contends—especially in this era of mass incarceration—that the philosophical rationales and utilitarian justifications for crime-control and penal policies ought to be drawn out in the open, into the public sphere, where the citizens subject to them can consider their pros and cons and struggle to make the often-confounding trade-offs that choosing among them involves. This is more democratically defensible than treating citizens as a "bewildered herd" of passive dupes and hysterical hotheads.[12]

The second supposition takes seriously and places its emphasis on the liberal component of liberal democracy. The values embedded in liberalism as a political doctrine, particularly in Rawls's conception of "justice as fairness,"[13] ensure that all "reasonable" citizens participate in their own governance, as "free and equal persons" who accept "fair terms or cooperation" guided by principles of reciprocity and mutuality. Although this participation can occur, for instance, via direct democracy or through the delegation of decision-making to elected representatives, models of deliberative democracy appear the most fruitful means to realize the promises of liberalism. The reasons why are to follow.

This chapter, therefore, makes the liberal case that the expansion of opportunities for greater public deliberation could foster a body of better-informed public knowledge about criminal and penal justice than currently exists. This deliberative activity could, moreover, build legitimacy for criminal-justice and penal policies in new, more defensible ways, by undercutting the very calculus of penal populism and, even more importantly, by producing policy outcomes that maximize the potential for all citizens to experience the liberty and justice promised to Americans in their Pledge of Allegiance and to citizens of many other countries in their democratic constitutions.

The analysis unfolds in the following way. The first part of the chapter is primarily diagnostic and descriptive of aspects of the Anglo-Saxon penal climate. The first section attempts to clarify the increasingly murky concept of "penal populism." It delimits its meaning, describes the "penal-populist calculus," and sets the contextual groundwork for what follows. The next section presents a typological model of penal policy-making strategies and examples of each, including what Drakeford and Vanstone have called "doing good by stealth."[14] This refers to the tendency, especially of progressives, to advocate for less-than-tough penal policies but only in secret, behind a smokescreen of contradictorily harsh and punitive rhetoric. The strategy is pursued once progressives cede this policy ground to those whose views are more in tune with penal-populist rhetoric. Part I ends by surveying the cases for and against this strategy.

The chapter's second part is more prescriptive and offers a framework for a more deliberative, and therefore more democratically defensible, mode of politics. Its first section draws on principles embedded in the political philosophy of liberalism and methods of deliberative democracy to trace the outlines of an alternative strategy. It is one which aims to ameliorate the unjust and injurious effects of penal populism by robbing it of its allure, in part by achieving the latent goal it serves—bolstering waning state legitimacy—more adaptively, directly, and defensibly, without simply "acting out" repressively in response to crime and criminality.[15]

Penal Populism and the Folly of Doing Good By Stealth

Penal Populism and the Penal-Populist Calculus

The morally and financially costly effects of penal populism abound in the criminological literature, but the concept itself has lost its focus and some of its explanatory power. Roberts et al. provide the clearest characterization:

> *Penal populists allow the electoral advantage of a policy to take precedence over its penal effectiveness.* In short, penal populism consists of the

pursuit ... and promotion of policies which are electorally attractive, but *unfair, ineffective, or at odds with a true reading of public opinion* [emphasis added].[16]

This definition usefully disentangles the *tactic* of penal populism from the myriad late-modern conditions—the *context*—that make the tactic seem useful and necessary. The tactic of penal populism is a response to a constellation of political problems and incentive structures in a context; it cannot be both cause and consequence. Defined this way, then, penal populism does not metaphorically "set down roots" in a culture like an invasive weed, as might, for instance, the unsettling anxieties associated with the "ontological insecurity" of living amid the "precariousness" of late modernity.[17] The latter forces condition sensibilities and social interactions. Penal populism does not. Instead, it is a political tactic attractive to politicians because of its putative utility in winning votes by tapping the broader public insecurities inherent to late modernity, signaling public reassurance, and reestablishing state legitimacy through tough postures and policies.

Moreover, the penal-populist calculus is a decision-making process conditioned by all the insecurities, pressures, and disembedding social effects of late modernity causally implicated in the rise of mass incarceration and the culture of control.[18] Central among these is the perception that nation-states, however mighty their crime-control apparatus, have lost the capacity to guarantee order and effectively address public insecurities because their sovereign power of command has been hollowed out by uncontrollable social, economic, and technological change. The calculus determines when the tactic of penal populism seems useful or necessary to employ, informed by what a policymaker or government hopes to achieve—consciously (e.g., reelection) and latently (e.g., greater state legitimacy)—by engaging in penal populism, and how useful a demonstration of punitive will is assessed to be. This distinction further distinguishes the political-discursive tactic of penal populism from the goals it serves.

Yet even with this distilled definition, the potential confusion of analytical concepts remains. Garland makes a convincing case that penal populism could just as easily encapsulate leniency as punitiveness, provided it were derived from, or had some resonance among, "the people."[19] In this formulation penal populism as a concept—*contra* Roberts et al., among others—is lexically neutral; it can accommodate a range of modifiers to distinguish a number of possible varieties, including, for instance, progressive, repressive, pessimistic, optimistic, punitive, or redemptive penal populism. Its neutrality leaves that which is populist open to change and to interpretation. Penal populism is frequently, though problematically,[20] used interchangeably with the term "populist punitiveness,"[21] which refers expressly to a particular strain of punitive populism and does, terminologically, just "what it says on the tin." However, the potentially nimbler notion of penal populism allows for Garland's conceptual expansion in response to changes in penal attitudes and sensibilities—of the sort, for instance, that Americans appear now to be experiencing, which are indicative of a disillusionment with the merely punitive.[22]

That said, two points of clarification are necessary. First, the version of penal populism invoked in this chapter remains consistent with the traditional one most established in the literature, referring to a political tactic associated with harsh rhetoric and punitive outcomes. Second, just as important to this discussion is the guiding notion that cynical opportunism, electoral expediency, and political pusillanimity drive penal populism, regardless of whether its outcomes in rhetoric and policy are evaluated as punitive or not. In short, penal populists lack political courage and pander instead. Without this key element penal populism is bled of meaning and analytical utility, at least for the purposes of the present discussion.

A Typology of Penal Policymaking Strategies

Until recently, a certain conventional wisdom governed the decision-making of Anglo-Saxon politicians on both sides of the Atlantic. Its establishment was complete once the parties of the Left recognized the electoral utility of a punitive posture in response to the perceived threats criminality posed. With a combination of tough-on-crime, moralizing rhetoric and a harsher, though schizoid, set of crime-control and penal policies, Tony Blair's Labour Party beat out the Conservatives in the 1990s to become the party most trusted on law and order in Britain.[23] Labour's strategy was based on the bedrock assumption that the electorate's intuitions favored the hardy and sure condemnation of wrongdoing. Pronouncements and policies consistent with those intuitions were likely to resonate well. Labour had famously promised to be "tough on crime, tough on the causes of crime." The slogan indicted the Conservatives for failing while in office to be anything more than tough in the face of rising crime. It is also illustrative of the political context at time when the optics were such that exploitably soft measures to target the root causes had to be offset by clear displays of toughness. Astute observers at the time noticed Labour's predicament:

The problem remains ... for a Party which was prepared to embrace a competitive law and order agenda, of pursuing reform without becoming vulnerable to a new outbreak of popular punitiveness. As a result, Labour's struggle is to find a way of reducing the prison population, without appearing to do so—or of *doing good by stealth*. This is in itself complicated by other policy trends within the same administration which are likely to add to prison numbers [emphasis added].[24]

Few progressive or conservative politicians publicly challenged the wisdom of assuming a tough-on-crime posture. Instead it became a default setting in a range of jurisdictions, at least since the Willie Horton affair helped defeat Michael Dukakis in 1988.[25] It became a defining and successful tactic in the subsequent elections of Clinton's New Democrats in 1992 and Blair's New Labour Party in 1997. The notion of what Drakeford and Vanstone have called "doing good by stealth"—the quiet pursuit of sound and sensible policy behind a smokescreen of harsh and condemnatory rhetoric—distils the received wisdom in a period when crime was highly politicized, when it seemed that the only way for governments to achieve fair and effective penal outcomes was either to sell selected policies as harsh or, if that was impossible, to avoid selling them at all.

The pressures applied by the penal-populist calculus are better appreciated when viewed within the conceptual model provided in Figure 9.1,

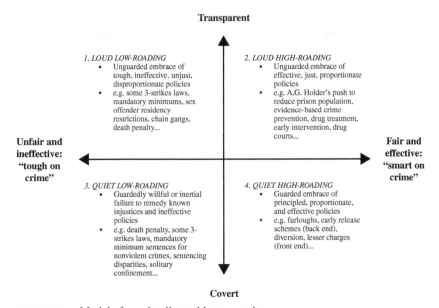

FIGURE 9.1 Model of penal policymaking strategies

which arranges four sets of penal policymaking strategies along the two axes of a compass. The vertical axis depicts a continuum running from the transparent or "loud" support of policy in the north to covert or "quiet" policymaking in the south. The horizontal axis runs from unjust and ineffective policies in the west to principled, just and effective policies in the east.[26]

The typology's remaining terminology plays on the expression that the high road is taken by the morally righteous, and the low road by the morally depraved. This is surely an exaggeration of the meanings I intend to convey, but it nonetheless captures the essence of the distinction. Put less melodramatically, "high-roading" denotes defensible actions, those consistent with moral principles of justice, with empirical evidence, and so on. "Low-roading" captures indefensible actions that defy these criteria.

Four strategies are discerned in the typology. The first is "loud low-roading," in the northwest quadrant, where tough-sounding but ineffective or unjust policies are found. The second quadrant denotes the much rarer practice of "loud high-roading" and includes the transparent, open pursuit of just and effective policies. The third is "quiet low-roading," which includes both the willful and the inertial failure to remedy or repeal unjust and ineffective policies. Finally, the fourth strategy of "quiet high-roading," in the southeast, includes those just and effective policies guardedly pursued because of fear of public opprobrium. Quadrants 1, 3, and 4 represent strategies that are contingent and dependent upon the penal-populist calculus, as each is directly conditioned by a fear of the public's disapproval of those principled, just, and effective policies that policymakers perceive to lack a sufficiently punitive bite to survive public scrutiny.

The following examples of each strategy are drawn from the Anglophone countries. They are intended to be illustrative, not comprehensive.

Loud Low-Roading

Loud low-roading is most readily associated with penal populism, as it yields high-profile initiatives proposed to serve the political goals of public reassurance and electoral expediency rather than the penological aims of more justice or less crime. They are also those associated with "stealth" strategies, as they are often symbolic policies that do less than they promise, lacking the retributive or consequentialist bite to match the punitive bark. Not all loud low-roading yields stealthy policies. Some policies, like California's three-strikes laws, for example—even more so before their recent reform[27]—do just what they promise and are in practice just as harsh as the rhetoric used to sell them. While such policies can be troublesome, as they often violate principles of both justice and utility, they are not stealthy. This chapter's analysis is concerned most with the stealthy varieties of loud low-roading.

For example, the Clinton administration's push for federal three-strikes legislation was intended to be an operationally toothless but symbolically powerful gesture.[28] Similarly, Senator Alfonse D'Amato conceded that his "unenforceable" changes to mandatory-minimum sentencing laws in 1991 would have little effect: "But," he said, "it does bring about a sense that we are serious."[29] Doob and Webster provide five examples of stealthy loud low-loading, all drawn from a range of penal-policy changes in Canada in the 1990s and early 2000s involving parole eligibility and juvenile transfers.[30] All were meant to sound tough, but none, they argue, changed practice appreciably. Other examples include the "willful and subterranean" circumvention of mandatory-minimum penalties by judges, prosecutors, and defense attorneys that does much to nullify the rhetorical harshness of the law's letter.[31] All of these high-profile policies accomplish much less than they promise, and that this was the case was no secret to their champions.

Loud High-Roading

Examples of loud high-roading were, until recently, much harder to come by. The forthright political advocacy of policies and penological aims that are not first filtered through the penal-populist calculus might still be rare, but they are increasing. One striking example is Attorney General Eric Holder's public and full-throated condemnation of mandatory-minimum penalties and the " 'truth-in-sentencing' mindset" that has led to "longer-than-necessary prison terms" and "over-incarceration," which, he argued,

> crushes opportunity. We know it prevents people, and entire communities, from getting on the right track ... The United States will never be able to prosecute or incarcerate its way to becoming a safer nation ... [The] astonishing rise in incarceration—and the escalating costs it has imposed on our country, in terms both economic and human—have not measurably benefited our society.[32]

Loud high-roading in public speeches like this indicates the extent to which the American penal climate has changed since the days when loud low-roading was a routine default.

Quiet Low-Roading

In the penal-populist calculus, the strategy of quiet low-roading has been another default condition. It is represented in the quiet, willful retention—or in the less willful, inertial acceptance—of existing injustice and ineffectiveness. Quiet low-roading is responsible, for instance, for sentencing disparities; disproportionate penalties; prison overcrowding; inadequate rehabilitative and reentry services; the well-documented, unjust outcomes of mandatory-minimum sentences; and so on. In short, quiet low-roading helps account for the unexamined reliance on the punitive and the harsh, even in the face of overwhelming evidence that more effective, more defensible, and more just alternatives exist. The penal-populist calculus holds that the accumulation of such injustices alienates few politically powerful constituencies, so the political costs of inaction are low.

Quiet High-Roading

Cases of quiet high-roading—part of the dyad that enables "doing good by stealth"—are difficult to identify because the opacity of their implementation and results is often intended. Under the cover provided by loud low-roading's bluster, policymakers pursue more measured aims more measuredly. The Blair-era Labour Party often neglected publicly to champion promising crime policies and programs, choosing instead to highlight their toughest-appearing initiatives.[33] Blair believed that the public would "only listen to people who show understanding of their plight as potential victims," and that Labour had to combat the perception that the party was soft on crime by remaining "in touch with gut British instincts."[34] A leaked memo from 2000 written by Blair encapsulates and lays bare the penal-populist calculus and the perceived necessity for loud low-roading:

> On crime, we need to highlight the tough measures ... The Met Police are putting in place measures to deal with it [street crime]; but, as ever, we are lacking a tough public message along with the strategy. We should think now of an initiative, e.g., locking up street muggers. Something tough with immediate bite which sends a message through the system ... This should be done soon and I, personally, should be associated with it.[35]

However, at the time, community-service orders, Youth Offending Teams, and the National Reassurance Policing Programme were proving successful, but few of the public were likely to know much about them. These initiatives were pursued discreetly, apparently because the government deemed them to be hostages to fortune—"soft" options that, if exposed by the opposition party or the hostile press, would prove politically costly, especially if not coupled with the clamor of loud low-roading.[36]

Doing Good By Stealth?

Drakeford and Vanstone's description of the Labour Party's problem in the 1990s is one in which loud high-roading is out of the question, the inertial effects of quiet low-roading persist, and a combination of loud low-roading and quiet high-roading provide the best political strategy to bring about any kind of meaningful and progressive penal-policy reforms. This policy goal—though recognized by New Labour as a social good—can only be achieved, when considered through the penal-populist calculus, by stealth.

The very existence of eye-catching, tough-sounding laws that do less than they promise generates certain benefits and harms. Quietly pursued progressive reforms do the same. I outline the potential benefits of stealth first. There are at least three.

First, loud low-roading strategies may send signals of reassurance to a rationally ignorant public. Hamilton argues that it is "irrational to be politically informed" about complex policy matters because of the "low returns" one citizen can expect from the effort.[37] Schudson similarly describes the uninformed but "monitorial citizen," one who scans and monitors important issues on the horizon, and who will take greater interest and act when necessary, but only then.[38] The rational ignorance of the monitorial citizen suggests that loud low-roading policies and pronouncements might offer reassurance to a public audience who is barely paying attention, serving a function similar to that of a news headline or bumper-sticker slogan. This construction of the public asserts that to expect more reflective and engaged policy discussion would be asking too much of a largely ignorant and uninterested citizenry, increasingly more so now that media coverage has fragmented and news consumers and outlets are siloed within niche markets.[39] It suggests as well that doing good by stealth is strategically preferable to the alternatives.

Second, through loud low-roading, stealth strategies have the benefit of serving useful psychological and social functions. Humans often respond in prerational, unconscious ways to perceptions of threats and to uncertainty. A range of phenomena from a broad assemblage of experimental, social-psychology research offers some justification for stealthy penal-policy strategies. These various theories and the mechanisms they trace together suggest that punitive impulses on the individual level function to reestablish equilibrium in the face of unsettling stimuli.[40] For instance, the findings of "terror management theory" suggest that one's primordial instincts kick in to defend one's worldview in the face the existential threat posed by a reminder of one's mortality.[41] These subconscious defenses typically manifest in the punitive derogation of out-group members, often in defiance of rational considerations. Viewed through this lens, loud low-roading might allow for the purge of emotion and for the satisfaction that comes from neutralizing normative threats to one's worldview. Because these symbolic policies do little in practice, the financial and human costs of this emotional off-gassing are minimal.

Third, a Durkheimian perspective offers a similar argument in defense of loud low-roading.[42] Tyler and Boeckmann demonstrated that punitive attitudes toward criminal offenders are deeply rooted, reflecting perceptions of normative threat and broader, sociotropic concerns about the moral health of the collective.[43] Punitive condemnation serves, then, both a micro-level function of maintaining and buttressing moral boundaries in the face of perceived threats—particularly for those with authoritarian dispositions who experience those threats most acutely[44]—as well as a macro-level function of building social solidarity in an increasingly fragmented society.

Doing Ill By Stealth?

The preceding perspectives provide a few latent, potentially salubrious effects of punitive invective and policy, but the harms of stealth outweigh them. Stealth's "loose coupling" of policy symbols, on the one hand, and operational realities and outcomes, on the other, is deeply flawed for at least five reasons.[45] First, loud low-roading strategies inflate public expectations beyond what can be delivered. Quiet high-roading and loud low-roading discursively reaffirm toughness as the most appropriate priority, implying that more punishment will yield a safer society. Stealth tactics also threaten further to undermine the public's trust and confidence if quiet high-roading is exposed or if loud low-roading policies are revealed to do less than promised.

Second, the dissembling nature of stealth tactics is hard to defend on democratic grounds. The contradictory strategies of loud low-roading and quiet high-roading should be suspect in liberal democracies, for reasons explored more fully below, especially when public confidence in the criminal justice system is low and the legitimacy of politicians is in decline. Stealth policymaking and the penal-populist calculus reflect what Dzur describes as "thin populism,"[46] which pays mere lip service to public concerns and, in so doing, sows the seeds of even greater citizen dissatisfaction. Publics are not engaged as citizens but treated instead as consumer audiences to whom policies are either openly sold for their toughness or censored for public consumption because they lack punitive selling points. As Dzur warns,

> In the long term, failure to engage the public is risky because sealing off the criminal justice process does nothing to educate, share responsibility, or build the trust that experts and professionals require to do their work. Public opinion is left to simmer, only to lash out as soon as the experts get something wrong.[47]

Third, rhetoric matters. Its accumulation provides citizens with "ideational resources"[48]—vocabulary, concepts, and narratives—that become their "tools to think with" when assessing the philosophical grounds, wisdom, and utility of proposed or existing policy.[49] By merely reaffirming toughness as a solution, leaders fail to engage citizens in conversations about the complicated trade-offs sentencers and policymakers face. This increases the incentives for penal populism by legitimating the penal-populist calculus and reifying the erroneous notion that publics can only have confidence in a penal regime that prioritizes toughness over justice and good sense.

Fourth, a well-established literature demonstrates that the simple notion of a monolithically punitive public is a myth.[50] Research on public deliberation suggests publics have greater capacity to make informed and just decisions than the penal-populist calculus suggests. In fact, when publics are informed and engaged in making difficult criminal-justice decisions, many formerly punitive views shift to become more considered and moderate.[51] For instance, juries are capable of making important, difficult distinctions and decisions, many of which contradict what simple surveys tell us about punitive publics.[52] While nearly everyone wants offenders to be punished for their crimes, most also believe that rehabilitation is important and that offenders should make amends for what they have done to victims.[53]

Finally, the changing penal climate suggests, tentatively, that doing good by stealth may no longer be necessary.[54] The predicament that once faced the Labour Party in Britain appears to have been resolved. A recent Conservative Justice Secretary publicly sought a "rehabilitation revolution" while openly trying to reduce the prison population. Former Attorney General Eric Holder's public condemnation of mass incarceration in the United States came late in the wake of accumulating evidence that a political shift has been underway for some time. It can be seen in President

George W. Bush's unexpected advocacy for addressing the needs of released prisoners through the Second Chance Act 2007, which he himself catalyzed. More recently, Right on Crime, a coalition of high-profile, stalwart conservatives, have made additional progress in opening a more nuanced dialogue about penal-policy reform that relies much less on tough rhetoric and harsh policy. Even the American Legislative Exchange Council (ALEC)—associated in the 1990s with truth-in-sentencing, mandatory-minimum, and stand-your-ground laws—has become a "loud" advocate for penal reform, calling for a reassessment of the tough-on-crime ethos at the center of the penal-populist calculus.

The Decline of Penal Populism?

Now more than any other time in at least a generation, the thinking that says high-roading must go on quietly, and that low-roading strategies must go on at all, does not survive scrutiny. Three problems lie at the heart of penal populism and help drive it: the erroneous belief in a monolithically punitive public; a mass-scale lack of public knowledge, both about the lived realities of crime and punishment and about what the evidence and guiding principles suggest can and ought to be done about it; and legitimacy deficits, made evident in the general erosion of public confidence government's ability to do things well and in the more specific and growing rise of popular resistance to state methods of policing and punishment. Each of these problems is better addressed directly, inclusively, and transparently.

A window of opportunity has opened to consider—more publicly and deliberately—the complex trade-offs that animate decisions about crime control and punishment. The expansion of meaningful public involvement in governance has been shown to increase government legitimacy, social capital, civic participation, and trust.[55] Elected officials ought to grasp the wisdom of sponsoring a new mode of politics more consistent with liberal principles that expands opportunities for greater democratic participation. Citizens, in turn, ought to grasp these opportunities to contribute more meaningfully to government decision-making, to improve policy outcomes, and to increase social justice.

Framing a New Practical Ideal

In the first part of this chapter I diagnosed the problem of penal populism by describing the incentive structures that especially governed American and English penal policy decision-making since the early 1990s, at least until recently. In what follows I make a case to expand and extend democratic participation in ways that elevate the principles of liberalism as a political philosophy and that centralize the role of pubic deliberation in the formulation of crime-control and penal policy. The normative and practical arguments behind this "practical ideal" draw heavily on the principles and practices of deliberative democracy, those which are best able to make good on liberalism's promises.[56] Were this expansion of public participation to occur within the parameters of the democratic framework outlined below, it is arguably less likely that penal and criminal-justice policies, practices, and outcomes would be as ineffective, unfair, and morally offensive as they remain.

Some scholars believe the fruits of just and effective criminal-justice policy can only grow in soil insulated from the heat of public scrutiny, where the often-dirty business of policymaking is reprofessionalized.[57] This position shares with the penal-populist calculus the assumption that popular sentiments always or at least predominantly press in a punitive direction. Other scholars rightly call instead for greater democratization of penal policy and punishment. Dzur, for instance, calls for a "thick" populism that—unlike the thin, uninformed, easily exploitable variety expressed by the exercised hothead, which relies on the plebiscite and demands no citizen responsibility beyond the indication of a preference—employs citizens in "load-bearing participation" that is informed by a broad range of information and opinion and that "holds the agent responsible for a collective outcome."[58] Load-bearing participation, in turn, builds trust and legitimacy transparently and sustainably. By "thickening" the quality of citizen involvement in justice decision-making, the tactic of penal populism loses its appeal. Publics are treated as citizens rather than as the passive consumer audiences whose aggregate but uniformed preferences are so readily manufactured by polls and so easily manipulated by anyone powerful enough to command an audience.

Liberalism and Democracy

Critics raise valid concerns that expanding democracy in ways that deliberative democrats advocate might be used to legitimize unjust policies, further marginalize excluded groups, and undermine those individual liberties that remain—ostensibly if not always in practice—the fundamental political values in advanced democracies like the United States and United

Kingdom. To be sure, democratic procedures have historically produced a litany of illiberal and unjust policies. Majority sentiment has been used to justify Jim Crow segregation and lynching, to deny equal rights to a long list of marginalized groups, and to perpetuate systems of capital punishment with demonstrably inequitable outcomes for poor, especially minority, citizens.[59]

Yet this tension between liberalism and democracy is not irreconcilable. Rawls's political conception of "justice as fairness" includes a distinction between the rational and the reasonable that clarifies the tension and points the way toward a resolution.[60] According to Rawls, citizens will hold views and support policies that are both rational and reasonable but not all rational views will be reasonable. Rational views are those that are self-servingly beneficial to one citizen or faction; it may be perfectly rational for one faction situated in a "superior bargaining position" to oppress and subjugate another by excluding them from participating in the democratic system.[61] However, to do so is unreasonable and unjust because a truly liberal democracy embodies the values of equality, reciprocity, and mutual respect (see Ramsay, this volume). For example, an individual or faction might justify Jim Crow segregation and other examples of institutionalized injustice on rational grounds. However, if rational views violate the principle of mutual respect governing a just political system in a free society committed to liberal values, they are rejected as unreasonable.

Rawls's conception of the reasonable means that limits must be placed on the exercise of democratic power so that the values of individual liberty and mutual respect are upheld. By creating space for reasonable claims and arguments, and by disallowing those that are merely rational, Rawls's liberalism imposes boundaries around the democratic field to facilitate justice as fairness. This ensures some protection from what John Adams and James Madison called the tyranny of the majority because, unlike the ethically neutral goals of majoritarian democracy, liberalism has

> only one overriding aim: to secure the political conditions that are necessary for the exercise of personal freedom. Every adult should be able to make as many effective decisions without fear or favor about as many aspects of her or his life as is compatible with the like freedom of every adult.[62]

Deliberative democracy, too, elevates principles of equality and mutual respect, and "these substantive values in turn act as external constraints on the content of possible outcomes of majority decisions."[63] This is also what constitutional democracies do by setting limits on the use of power and by establishing a set of constitutional protections, like the Bill of Rights.[64] It is only by limiting the scope of democracy that the liberalism which animates and legitimizes it can be preserved.

The Liberalism of Fear and Deliberative Democracy

The emphasis on the liberalism in liberal democracy should help alleviate the concern that thick populism and greater load-bearing participation in a more deliberative democracy would produce illiberal and unjust policy outcomes. In fact, the opposite seems more likely. The sober version of liberalism Shklar favors is a "liberalism of fear," which contrasts with those more "realistically utopian" versions of liberalism that elevate natural rights (Locke) or human development (Mill).[65] Shklar is clear-eyed about the historical tendency of concentrated power to produce and perpetrate cruelty. The liberalism of fear is premised on "a duty to establish protective public agencies and the right to demand that they provide us with opportunities to make claims against each and all."[66] The liberalism of fear aims to disperse power because "some agents of government will behave lawlessly and brutally in small or big ways most of the time."[67] Rowan calls for a "radical democracy," the priority of which is to secure, for the weakest among us, "freedom from the abuse of power and intimidation of the defenseless."[68] His version of democracy is radical because it is focused on those groups typically excluded or underrepresented in currently lopsided policy debates, whose views a truly inclusive and liberal system would incorporate as a matter of course.

The liberalism of fear has been invoked to validate greater "penal moderation,"[69] because the former's priority is the prevention of cruelty and fear, both of which are characteristic of relations between the weakest and the most powerful players in the performance of criminal justice, particularly so in an era marked by mass incarceration. Moreover, "what is to be feared is every extralegal, secret, and unauthorized act by public agents or their deputies"[70]—all those acts that violate the liberal principles of publicity, deliberation, and fairness. This means that policymaking strategies that attempt to do *anything* by stealth, whether the effects are good or ill, violate liberalism's values.

Like Rawls, Shklar does not prescribe a mode of politics through which policy itself should be deliberated or morally evaluated. However, the liberalism of fear's dispersion of power and inclusivity suggests deliberative democracy is best suited to deliver on liberalism's ideals and enable the most just outcomes for three reasons.

The first draws on what Rawls calls "the fact of reasonable pluralism." Even when citizens set aside differences in their *rational* interests, some of which may be unreasonable and unjust, there still remain "profound and irreconcilable differences in citizens' *reasonable* comprehensive religious and philosophical conceptions of the world, and in their views of the moral and aesthetic values to be sought in human life."[71] This fact of reasonable pluralism means that moral consensus is nearly always impossible to achieve in public-policy debates. The best a liberal and just political system can achieve is to accommodate the widest possible range of reasonable views in ways that demonstrate its commitment to individual liberty and to the unfettered, free exchange of ideas. Deliberative democracy shares just these aims. It can better accommodate the fact of reasonable pluralism than other models of democracy can, and in doing so, it comes closest to ensuring some measure of "liberty and justice for all."

Second, deliberative democracy is the best means of achieving liberal goals because it does not prescribe criteria for legitimate decision-making beyond the principles of "reciprocity, publicity, and accountability [which] are the chief standards regulating the conditions of deliberation."[72] The reciprocity of "mutual reason giving" is a prerequisite of just outcomes because binding policies must be justified to the citizens governed by them. This sets deliberative democracy apart from majoritarian models that create fertile conditions for the perpetuation of injustice—whether through loud low-roading's blusterous activity or through quiet low-roading's failure to act. Deliberative democracy more readily affords citizens the opportunity to challenge and oppose policies they find unjust and unreasonable, in ways that majoritarian conceptions of democracy do not.

Third, in Rawls's terminology, deliberative democracy creates the conditions to distinguish the reasonable from the rational, to evaluate the empirical and moral validity of claims made in the public sphere. Under the incentive structures embedded in majoritarian procedures, which is the prevailing method of determining popular will in aggregative democracies,[73] the fact of *reasonable* pluralism has been subjugated by the fact of *rational* pluralism. Majoritarianism—abetted by a mass-media culture of consumer-driven news and infotainment—violates liberal principles by legitimating both the *rational* and the *unreasonable*, granting them equal weight and significance. It substitutes "the principle of majority rule for principles of utility, liberty, fair opportunity, or a community's conception of the good life as the moral foundation for justifying decisions, and it does so prior to any actual political decision-making."[74]

Recall that penal populism's currency is, in Rawlsian terms, the rational but unreasonable claim. Deliberative democracy's emphasis is on evaluating the quality and reasonableness of claims, and the evidence marshaled to support them, in an ongoing deliberative process of mutual reason giving. Such a process helps ensure that policy outcomes are soundly justified and legitimized by reasonable claims, not merely rational ones.

A Framework for Institutions of Just Ordering

The chapter's introduction outlined the confluence of various contextual factors—including historically low crime rates, the recession, growing popular resistance to excessive policing, and bipartisan disillusionment with mass incarceration—that suggest that the timing is such that mutual agreement could arguably cohere around a new practical ideal, a new mode of liberal politics that creates the conditions by which all citizens can expect an equal measure of liberty and justice. Loader and Sparks provide one useful starting point by offering three constituent principles intended to inform and sustain what they call "institutions of just ordering."[75]

The first principle is well aligned with the liberalism of fear and ensures fundamental human-rights protections to preserve the liberty and safety of the individual. This principle is especially resonant now in the context of recent public outrage about police misuse of deadly force and the unfettered discretion of unaccountable prosecutors. The principle provides some level of "damage control" at a time when overcriminalization, the collateral consequences of imprisonment and the war on drugs, racial disparities in sentencing, and the moral and financial costs of mass incarceration occupy policymakers' agendas.[76]

The second principle of just ordering involves social solidarity and the depth of popular consent for how and why citizens in a just society are policed, prosecuted, and punished. In New York City in 2014, the police came under withering fire after a grand jury failed to indict an officer caught on camera killing an unarmed black man with an illegal chokehold. Offended by what he perceived as the mayor's failure to support his officers, the leader of the New York City Police Department's patrolmen's union said, without irony, that in defiant protest, officers should avoid making arrests "unless absolutely necessary." That arrests are ever made when they are not absolutely necessary indicates the degree of ignorance about or callousness toward the myriad stigmatizing, degrading, and disruptive effects that intrusions by justice institutions have on human lives. The second principle of just ordering, thus, recognizes

> a basic social fact about police and penal institutions—namely, that they confer and withhold dignity in ways that make them powerful mediators of status identity and belonging ... The acts and omissions of these institutions ... send authoritative signals about empathy, recognition and respect, and stand as powerful markers of people's membership of a political community, and their place within its hierarchies.[77]

By elevating the recognition of the human consequences of individuals' contact with criminal-justice institutions, Loader and Sparks provide a much-needed governing rationale for moderation and parsimony in the deployment of police and penal power.

To that end, the third element of just ordering concerns itself with the creation of "institutions whose ordering priorities and practices are meaningfully shaped by, and minimally credible to, all those who are affected by them."[78] Deliberative democracy provides the means for such institutions to ensure the delivery of justice for all, and to enhance both democratic accountability and legitimacy, providing all citizens equal access to the policymaking process.

What's to Be Done?

Given the number of potentially upheaving conditions they now face, elected representatives, especially in the United States, ought to be deeply concerned about these issues of consent and legitimacy, particularly given that Congress's approval ratings are at all-time low. Low crime rates and high levels of reform optimism suggest now is the time for a reorientation of priorities, from a preoccupation with the elimination of "social bads" to a focus on the generation of social goods.[79]

The groundwork for this new politics can be laid by pursuing reform along three avenues. First, smaller scale models of public deliberation like Deliberative Polls, citizen juries, and the like would be useful to produce and then clarify more informed "public judgments" about the most pressing issues citizens face.[80] Methods like these move publics beyond the realm of mere opinion and the thin populism it encourages. By institutionalizing expanded opportunities for meaningful public deliberation, governments would also help restore public confidence in the political process and reestablish its legitimacy. The latent goals of penal populism are thereby achieved without engaging in it.

Second, reforms to justice systems must reflect in—letter and in spirit—the fundamental values of liberalism and deliberative democracy. Greater lay participation in justice decision-making could be fostered, for instance, by expanding the practice of restorative justice—whose liberal aim is "to institutionalize [the] *restoration of dignity* for offenders"[81]—and by granting sentencing power to juries. Borrowing Tocqueville's metaphor, Dzur views "jury trials as a circulatory system to purge ... the distrust that can grow when professional and official domains are outside the people."[82] Though six American states currently allow for lay participation in felony sentencing, more research is needed to determine whether jury sentencing generates outcomes deemed to be just, increases public confidence in the courts, or enhances the criminal justice system's public legitimacy.

Third, the elevation of liberal principles through deliberative democracy requires much larger-scale innovations in the ways that citizens meaningfully contribute to the formulation of public policy more generally. For example, community-justice programs increase collective efficacy and improve policy outcomes locally by enlisting lay participants to inform the way their communities are policed and the methods used to reduce crime and improve lives.[83] Similar models could be used to enable meaningful lay participation in policy decision-making in other similarly impactful policy realms, like education, healthcare, or environmental policy. Leib goes much further to propose the establishment of a fourth, popular branch of government to enshrine a role for public deliberation in a truly deliberative democracy.[84] Both models share liberalism's contention that citizens ought to, and can, exercise greater control over how the institutions set up to serve and protect them prioritize and perform their functions.

Conclusion

Penal populism, tough-on-crime posturing, and doing either good or ill by stealth are all products of majoritarian preoccupations. The thin populism of the penal-populist calculus is cynically concerned with the assessment, management, and manipulation of popular consent in support of policies and outcomes that are too often unjust and ineffective. From citizens it demands nothing and allows little—even from those who are most engaged in the political process—beyond one-off indications of preference for a candidate or an initiative at the ballot box or to a pollster.

Truly liberal democracies can and must do better by elevating liberal values and establishing institutions of just ordering through the procedures of deliberative democracy. This is not to suggest that any liberal democracy is always or ever good at delivering on its commitments to liberty and mutual respect for all. The United States has historically and repeatedly fallen far and exceptionally short of these rhetorical aspirations. Yet the principles of liberalism and the tools of deliberative democracy form the bedrock for a mode of politics though which to strive for a public-policy agenda and set of policy outcomes much more aligned with those liberal values espoused, however erroneously, as exceptionally American.

Notes

1. I am grateful to all three volume editors for their helpful comments.

2. David A. Green, "Penal Optimism and Second Chances: The Legacies of American Protestantism and the Prospects for Penal Reform," *Punishment & Society* 15, no. 2 (2013): 123–146; and David A. Green, "US Penal-Reform Catalysts, Drivers, and Prospects," *Punishment & Society* 17, no. 3 (2015): 271–298.

3. US Senate Joint Economic Committee, Hearing, *Mass Incarceration in the United States: At What Cost?* October 4, 2007.

4. Hadar Aviram, "Humonetarianism: The New Correctional Discourse of Scarcity," *Hastings Race & Poverty Law Journal* 7, no. 1 (2010):1–52; Marie Gottschalk, "Cell Blocks and Red Ink: Mass Incarceration, the Great Recession and Penal Reform," *Daedalus* 139, no. 3 (2010): 62–73; and Elizabeth K. Brown, "Foreclosing on Incarceration? State Correctional Policy Enactments and the Great Recession," *Criminal Justice Policy Review* 24, no. 3 (2013): 317–337; Green, "US Penal-Reform."

5. Paul Krugman, "Why We're in a New Guilded Age," *New York Review of Books*, May 8, 2014, www.nybooks.com/articles/archives/2014/may/08/thomas-piketty-new-gilded-age/.

6. Radley Balko, *Rise of the Warrior Cop: The Militarization of America's Police Forces* (New York: Public Affairs, 2014); see President's Task Force on 21st Century Policing, *Final Report of the President's Task Force on 21st Century Policing* (Washington, DC: Office of Community Oriented Policing Services, 2015).

7. In *Overcriminalization: The Limits of the Criminal Law* (New York: Oxford University Press, 2008) Doug Husak lays out a theory of criminalization in response to the massive accumulation of American criminal law, and the excessive and unjust punishments violators suffer. For examples of acts, see The Heritage Foundation. n.d., "Overcriminalization," www.heritage.org/issues/legal/overcriminalization.

8. Ian Loader and Richard Sparks, "Beyond Lamentation: Towards a Democratic Egalitarian Politics of Crime and Justice," in Tim Newburn and Jill Peay (eds.), *Policing: Politics, Culture and Control* (Oxford: Hart Publishing, 2012), 11–41.

9. David Garland, "The Limits of the Sovereign State: Strategies of Crime Control in Contemporary Society," *The British Journal of Criminology* 36, no. 4 (1996): 445–471; Garland, *The Culture of Control: Crime and Social Order in Contemporary Society* (Oxford: Clarendon Press, 2001); Jock Young, *The Exclusive Society: Social Exclusion,*

Crime and Difference in Late Modernity (London: Sage, 1999); and Young, *The Vertigo of Late Modernity* (London: Sage, 2007).

10. Jonathan Simon, *Governing through Crime: How the War on Crime Transformed American Democracy and Created a Culture of Fear* (New York: Oxford University Press, 2007).

11. Quoted in Naomi Murakawa, *The First Civil Right: How Liberals Built Prison America* (New York: Oxford University Press, 2014), 1.

12. Walter Lippman, *The Phantom Public* (New Brunswick, NJ: Transaction, 2011 [1930]), 145.

13. John Rawls, *Justice as Fairness: A Restatement* (Cambridge, MA: Belknap Press, 2001), 6.

14. Mark Drakeford and Maurice Vanstone, "Social Exclusion and the Politics of Criminal Justice: A Tale of Two Administrations," *Howard Journal of Criminal Justice* 39, no. 4 (2000): 369–381.

15. Garland, *Culture of Control.*

16. Julian V. Roberts, Loretta J. Stalans, David Indermaur, and Michael Hough, *Penal Populism and Public Opinion: Lessons from Five Countries* (New York: Oxford University Press, 2003), 5.

17. John Pratt, *Penal Populism* (London: Routledge, 2007), 6; Anthony Giddens, *The Consequences of Modernity* (Cambridge: Polity, 1990); Young, *Exclusive Society.*

18. Young, *Exclusive Society*; Zygmunt Bauman, *Postmodernity and Its Discontents* (Oxford: Polity, 1997); Garland, *Culture of Control*; and Giddens, *Consequences of Modernity.*

19. David Garland, "What Is Penal Populism? Politics, the Public and Penological Expertise," in Alison Liebling, Joanna Shapland, and Justice Tankebe (eds.), *Crime, Justice, and Social Order: Essays in Honour of A. E. Bottoms* (Oxford: Oxford University Press, forthcoming).

20. See David A. Green, *When Children Kill Children: Penal Populism and Political Culture* (Oxford: Oxford University Press, 2008), 20–21.

21. Anthony E. Bottoms, "The Philosophy and Politics of Punishment and Sentencing," in C.M.V. Clarkson and Rod Morgan (eds.), *The Politics of Sentencing Reform* (Oxford: Oxford University Press, 1995), 17–49.

22. Green, "Penal Optimism."

23. David Downes and Rod Morgan, "Dumping the 'Hostages to Fortune'? The Politics of Law and Order in Post-War Britain," in Mike Maguire, Rod Morgan, and Rob Reiner (eds.), *The Oxford Handbook of Criminology* (Oxford: Oxford University Press, 1997), 87–134.

24. Mark Drakeford and Maurice Vanstone, "Social Exclusion and the Politics of Criminal Justice: A Tale of Two Administrations," *Howard Journal of Criminal Justice* 39, no. 4 (2000): 369–381 at 377.

25. David C. Anderson, *Crime and the Politics of Hysteria: How the Willie Horton Story Changed American Justice* (New York: Times Books, 1995).

26. This model is certainly imperfect. Of course, some policies can be just but ineffective or effective but unjust. It also entangles, as policymakers do, often-incompatible consequentialist and retributivist aims. The model is intended to be conceptual, offering ideal types to frame thinking along particular axes for a particular analytical purpose.

27. See Proposition 36, a ballot initiative passed by a wide majority in 2012 that, among other things, limits to violent and serious offenses the felonies that trigger the third-strike sentence of twenty-five-years-to-life in prison.

28. Trevor Jones and Tim Newburn, "Three Strikes and You're Out: Exploring Symbol and Substance in American and British Crime Control Policies," *The British Journal of Criminology* 46, no. 5 (2006): 781–802.

29 Quoted in Michael Tonry, "Determinants of Penal Policies," *Crime and Justice: A Review of Research* 36 (2007): 1–48.

30 Anthony N. Doob and Cheryl Marie Webster, "Countering Punitiveness: Understanding Stability in Canada's Imprisonment Rate," *Law & Society Review* 40, no. 2 (2006): 325–368.

31 Michael Tonry, "The Mostly Unintended Consequences of Mandatory Minimum Penalties: Two Centuries of Consistent Findings," *Crime and Justice: A Review of Research* 38 (2009): 65–114, at 110.

32 Eric H. Holder, "Prepared Remarks of Attorney General Eric H. Holder, Jr.: Shifting Law Enforcement Goals to Reduce Mass Incarceration," The Brennan Center for Justice, New York University, September 23, 2014, www.brennancenter.org/analysis/keynote-address-shifting-law-enforcement-goals-to-reduce-mass-incarceration.

33 Polly Toynbee, "Why Blair Won't Admit That Prison Doesn't Work," *Guardian*, March 10, 2004.

34 Paul Richards, ed. *Tony Blair: In His Own Words* (London: Politico's Publishing, 2004), 56 and 200.

35 Quoted in ibid., 201.

36 Downes and Morgan, "Dumping the 'Hostages to Fortune'?"

37 James T. Hamilton, *All the News That's Fit to Sell: How the Market Transforms Information into News* (Princeton, NJ: Princeton University Press, 2004).

38 Michael Schudson, *The Good Citizen: A History of American Public Life* (New York: Free Press, 1998).

39 Farhad Manjoo, *True Enough: Learning to Live in a Post-Fact Society* (Hoboken, NJ: Wiley, 2008).

40 Marc J. Hetherington and Jonathan Daniel Weiler, *Authoritarianism and Polarization in American Politics* (New York: Cambridge University Press, 2009); Karen Stenner, *The Authoritarian Dynamic* (New York: Cambridge University Press, 2005); John T. Jost, Jack Glaser, Arie W. Kruglanski, and Frank J. Sulloway, "Political Conservatism as Motivated Social Cognition," *Psychological Bulletin* 129, no. 3 (2003): 339–375; and Jonathan Haidt, *The Righteous Mind: Why Good People Are Divided by Politics and Religion* (New York: Vintage, 2012).

41 Jeff Greenberg, Tom Pyszczynski, Sheldon Solomon, Abram Rosenblatt, Mitchell Veeder, Shari Kirkland, and Deborah Lyon, "Evidence for Terror Management Theory II: The Effects of Mortality Salience on Reactions to Those Who Threaten or Bolster the Cultural Worldview," *Journal of Personality and Social Psychology* 58, no. 2 (1990): 308–318; and Fenna van Marle and Shadd Maruna, "'Ontological Insecurity' and 'Terror Management': Linking Two Free-Floating Anxieties," *Punishment & Society* 12, no. 1 (2010): 7–26.

42 Emile Durkheim, *The Division of Labor in Society* (New York: The Free Press, 1893/1933).

43 Tom R. Tyler and Robert J. Boeckmann, "Three Strikes and You Are Out, But Why? The Psychology of Public Support for Punishing Rule Breakers," *Law & Society Review* 31, no. 2 (1997): 237–265.

44 Stenner, *Authoritarian Dynamic*.

45 Franklin E. Zimring, Gordon Hawkins, and Sam Kamin, *Punishment and Democracy: Three Strikes and You're Out in California* (New York: Oxford University Press, 2001).

46 Albert W. Dzur, *Punishment, Participatory Democracy, and the Jury* (New York: Oxford University Press, 2012).

47 Ibid., 30.

48 Seymour Martin Lipset and Richard B. Dobson, "The Intellectual as Critic and Rebel: With Special Reference to the United States and the Soviet Union," *Daedalus* 101, no. 3 (1972): 137–198; and Theodore Sasson, *Crime Talk: How Citizens Construct a Social Problem* (New York: Aldine de Gruyter, 1995).

49 See David A. Green, "Feeding Wolves: Punitiveness and Culture," *European Journal on Criminology* 6, no. 6 (2009): 517–536.

50 Francis T. Cullen, Bonnie S. Fisher, and Brandon K. Applegate, "Public Opinion About Punishment and Corrections," *Crime and Justice: A Review of Research* 27 (2000):1–79; and Julian V. Roberts and Loretta J. Stalans, *Public Opinion, Crime, and Criminal Justice* (Boulder, CO: Westview Press, 1997).

51 James S. Fishkin, *The Voice of the People: Public Opinion and Democracy* (New Haven, CT: Yale University Press, 1995); and Albert W. Dzur, "The Myth of Penal Populism: Democracy, Citizen Participation, and American Hyperincarceration," *Journal of Speculative Philosophy* 24, no. 4 (2010): 354–379.

52 Julian V. Roberts, "Determining Parole Eligibility Dates for Life Prisoners," *Punishment & Society* 4, no. 1 (2002): 103–113, at 109.

53 Cullen et al., "Public Opinion."

54 Green, "US Penal-Reform."

55 Kerstin Jacobsson, "Discursive Will Formation and the Question of Legitimacy in European Politics," *Scandinavian Political Studies* 20, no. 1 (1997): 69–90.

56 James Bohman, "The Coming Age of Deliberative Democracy," *Journal of Political Philosophy* 6, no. 4 (1998): 400–425, at 422.

57 Nicola Lacey, *The Prisoners' Dilemma: Political Economy and Punishment in Contemporary Democracies, The Hamlyn Lectures 2007* (Cambridge: Cambridge University Press, 2008); and Zimring et al., *Punishment and Democracy*.

58 Dzur, *Punishment*, 163.

59 David Garland, *Peculiar Institution: America's Death Penalty in an Age of Abolition* (Cambridge, MA: Belnap Press, 2012).

60 In *Justice as Fairness: A Restatement* (Cambridge, MA: Belknap Press, 2001), John Rawls places limits on his standard. The conception of justice as fairness provides the framework for a political system and is not intended as a set of standards by which the nature of policies themselves can be judged as either just or unjust.

61 Rawls, *Justice as Fairness*, 7.

62 Judith N. Shklar, "The Liberalism of Fear," in Nancy L. Rosenblum (ed.), *Liberalism and the Moral Life* (Cambridge, MA: Harvard University Press, 1993), 21–38, at 21.

63 Bohman, "The Coming Age," 404.

64 In "Democracy and Punishment: A Radical View," *Theoretical Criminology* 16, no. 1 (2012): 43–62, Mike Rowan reminds us that the Bill of Rights was itself the producet of an "elitist and undemocratic" process.

65 Rawls, *Justice as Fairness*, 4.

66 Shklar, "Liberalism of Fear," 26.

67 Ibid., 28.

68 Rowan, "Democracy and Punishment"; Shklar, "Liberalism of Fear."

69 Ian Loader, "For Penal Moderation: Notes Towards a Public Philosophy of Punishment," *Theoretical Criminology* 14, no. 3 (2010): 349–367.

70 Shklar, "Liberalism of Fear," 30.

71 Rawls, *Justice as Fairness*, 3, emphasis added.

72 Amy Gutmann and Dennis Thompson, *Why Deliberative Democracy?* (Princeton, NJ: Princeton University Press, 2004), 133.

73 Ibid., 14.

74 Ibid., 130.

75 Loader and Sparks, "Beyond Lamentation."

76 Shklar, "Liberalism of Fear," 27.

77 Loader and Sparks, "Beyond Lamentation," 30–31.

78 Ibid., 31.

79 Ibid.

80 Daniel Yankelovich *Coming to Public Judgment: Making Democracy Work in a Complex World* (Syracuse, NY: Syracuse University Press, 1991); David A. Green, "Public Opinion Versus Public Judgment About Crime: Correcting the 'Comedy of Errors,'" *The British Journal of Criminology* 46, no. 1 (2006): 131–154.

81 John Braithwaite, "Restorative Justice and a Better Future," in Eugene McLaughlin and Gordon Hughes (eds.), *Restorative Justice: Critical Issues* (London: Sage, 2003), 54–66, at 57, emphasis in the original.

82 Dzur, *Punishment*, 67–68.

83 Adam Crawford and Todd R. Clear, "Community Justice: Transforming Communities through Restorative Justice?" in Eugene McLaughlin and Gordon Hughes (eds.), *Restorative Justice: Critical Issues* (London: Sage, 2003), 215–229.

84 Ethan J. Leib, *Deliberative Democracy in America: A Proposal for a Popular Branch of Government* (University Park: Pennsylvania State University Press, 2004).

CHAPTER 10 | Mass Incarceration and Public
Opinion on Crime and Justice:
*From Democratic Theory to Method
and Reality*

ELIZABETH R. TURNER

Public opinion does not exist ... in the form which some people, whose
existence depends on this illusion, would have us believe.[1]

Introduction

This chapter considers the extent to which rethinking "public opinion"
can provide support for challenging penal excess and mass incarceration.
I assume from the outset that challenging these trends in penal policy is
desirable and seek to explore a remedy which has received growing attention in recent years: expanding opportunities for the public to engage
in deliberation about the policies which they think should be adopted in
response to crime, and favoring the opinions captured via deliberative processes over those captured using more conventional surveys. This chapter
considers why this shift is considered desirable and the barriers that must
be surmounted if it is to occur.

The chapter is structured as follows. First I explain why the role of
public opinion in bringing about mass incarceration requires exploration
and, in particular, why we should attend to the different ways in which
public opinion is conceptualized and operationalized. Second, I identify
the influence of democratic theory on the work of those who are concerned with undoing the punitive trend, focusing on the apparent benefits
of making greater use of more deliberative practices in consultation and

research. Third, I consider the distinction between deliberation as practice, and as research method. Fourth, I consider the prospects for a "deliberative turn" in criminal justice politics, identifying perceptions of legitimacy as a barrier to increased uptake of deliberative methods. Fifth, I explore a way in which this barrier might be not so much surmounted but, perhaps more realistically, vandalized such that a movement in favor of demolishing the barrier can begin to gain momentum. This, I conclude, is necessary in order to realize the full democratic potential of deliberative practices in consultation and research.

My core argument draws on a range of theoretical resources, but in particular the science and technology studies (STS) literature and specifically the ideas elaborated by John Law.[2] I argue that critics of greater use of deliberation as a method for understanding public opinion premise their arguments on the idea that deliberative methods produce knowledge about an artificially created reality, and that this is a misleading accusation because *all* forms of knowledge production must "craft" the objects they purport to represent, enacting reality as they do so.[3] I suggest that if deliberative approaches to public opinion are to dislodge aggregative approaches from their current position of dominance, and thus disincentivize what Green has termed the "penal populism calculus," then their proponents must try to make space for a "politics of the real."[4] This chapter, therefore, is an attempt to begin to develop a novel and innovative perspective on contemporary penal politics by emphasizing the role played by researchers of public opinion, including academic researchers, in enacting and reenacting extant democratic realities.[5]

Mass Incarceration, Penal Populism, and Problems with Public Opinion

Leading the world in its use of imprisonment, the United States effectively defines the phenomenon which has been termed "mass incarceration." Yet US mass incarceration is perhaps only the most dramatic illustration of a more widespread trend in some countries toward the increased use of both imprisonment and other restrictive and intrusive penal sanctions against those individuals identified as the most suitable targets for regulation through criminalization.[6] Whether or not this ought properly to be described as a "punitive turn" is a matter of dispute, with some pointing to the diverse and contradictory nature of developments,[7] or to an alternate "strategic formulation in the penal field" that has "neither a punitive nor a rehabilitative logic."[8] The ultimate rationale behind mass incarceration (if such a thing exists at all) is not clear-cut, then, and may reflect a combination of several different more or less explicit objectives.[9]

Criminologists concerned about the increasingly punitive treatment of offenders often ground their resistance to this trend in the claimed ineffectiveness of increasing the severity of sanctions.[10] The claim that policy has shifted in a punitive (and therefore, it is implied, ineffective) direction usually rests upon a linked claim that criminologists, as the "experts" on what is effective in dealing with crime, have suffered a loss of status in the criminal justice policymaking process.[11] Criminologists, then, are said to have suffered a loss of status that is all too evident in "government policies [which] fly directly in the face of research evidence, and would seem to almost wilfully ignore expert opinion."[12]

A frequently cited explanation for the alleged shift in policymaker attention away from experts and research evidence is the increasing attention being paid to the expectations, preferences, and assessments of ordinary members of the public. This trend is said to reflect an increase in the extent to which criminal justice has become an arena for political conflict.[13] Some have interpreted the apparently increasing significance of public opinion as indicative of a growing and, at times, potentially positive sensitivity to public preferences on the part of politicians. However, others suggest that what politicians have been doing is not *responding* to the views of the public, but rather *exploiting* them by engaging in what has been termed "penal populism."[14]

The adequacy and utility of the idea of penal populism has been disputed.[15] Yet while there is likely some truth in the suggestion that the currency of penal populism has been overinflated, this does not mean that we should neglect the importance of public opinion for understanding the development of penal policy and practice. There is ample evidence that over the last four decades political debates about crime and justice have become more prominent and electorally significant in many countries and that, correspondingly, politicians have at least appeared to be paying more attention to various representations of public opinion. Politicians in many societies are now, perhaps more than ever before, keen to ensure that they command the support of the public when it comes to their ability to deal with crime, and in some places at some times this has had a direct impact not just on rhetoric, but also on the policies which have been adopted.

There are, of course, always going to be complex historical, political, cultural, and economic factors underpinning public sensibilities toward crime, as well as the way in which matters of crime and punishment are talked about, in a given society at a given time. Seen against the backdrop of this complexity, the idea of penal populism can seem to be rather a blunt tool for analysis. Nonetheless, accounts and examples of penal populism in action point us toward the importance of analyzing the texts, devices, and political dynamics which texture the relationship between the public, politicians, and penal experts, and the way in which these help to shape policies and practices. These texts, mechanisms, and dynamics include ways of (and representations of ways of) *getting at* public opinion, as well as the representations themselves (which is to say the putative "content" of that opinion).

So, how have researchers tended to get at public opinion on crime and criminal justice? Most frequently, investigations focus on generating quantitative data about the proportion of the population who express confidence in, or satisfaction with, the criminal justice system or some part of that system (e.g., the police, judges), or who think that that system should be doing something differently (e.g., sending more people to prison, getting tough with offenders).[16] Data in this form has been the product of both the kind of opinion polls conducted by commercial polling organizations (which feature frequently in the news media) as well as more substantial, sophisticated, and methodologically robust attitude surveys conducted by government departments or academic researchers. While there are certainly some significant differences between these different kinds of research, they do share the following characteristics: (1) they are based on the *aggregation* of individual views; (2) they are usually (especially in terms of their "headline" questions) focussed on *general* (e.g., the criminal justice system, or "sentencing" or "the police") rather than specific matters (e.g., police or judicial conduct in specific cases); (3) they are premised on a conception of the public as *atomized* individuals who hold (and are entitled to hold) in isolation from others their own personal opinions or attitudes; and (4) they (only) permit their participants to express their opinions in the *passive*, noninteractive way that is typical of the survey method. I refer to knowledge about public opinion that is produced in this way as Aggregative General Atomized Passive (or AGAP for short).[17]

Knowledge produced through the AGAP approach has dominated political understandings of public opinion about crime and criminal justice over the last thirty years, despite a number of identified problems with the approach. Research from the United Kingdom and Canada established that most members of the public were not aware of key facts about crime and criminal justice (e.g., crime rates and trends, prison populations and conditions, typical sentencing for key offenses).[18] Noting this, researchers developed some alternative, more specific methods for eliciting public assessments of sentencing. In one often cited study survey respondents were provided either with the kind of information about specific cases and defendants that had been available to the court, or with the media coverage of the case. Perhaps unsurprisingly, those respondents who received the more detailed information available to the courts evaluated the sentences passed more favorably.[19]

The lesson it was suggested policymakers should draw from the findings on poor levels of public knowledge, and from studies examining differences in sentencing preferences based on providing different levels of information, was that they "should not interpret the public's apparent desire for harsher penalties at face value."[20] General measures of public opinion about criminal justice were thus described as capturing "false shadows" rather than "true substances," their alleged methodological shortcomings meaning that they "overstated" public appetites for the imposition of harsher punishments.[21] Indeed, general questions were described by the UK Home Office's own researchers as "insufficiently precise to answer whether sentencing is in line with public opinion,"[22] and policymakers were enjoined to treat findings about general public opinion with caution.[23] During the 1980s, many researchers examining different facets of public opinion about crime, criminal justice, and sentencing regarded the public's general ignorance as undermining the value of AGAP approaches to research in this area. As Hough and Moxon observed: "Questions designed to find out whether offenders are generally thought to get their just deserts can only be sensibly asked if people hold accurate beliefs about current practice."[24]

In response, some argue that the public ought to be educated about crime and criminal justice so that their opinions (as captured via AGAP-style questions) are more meaningful. But adopting this approach indicates a subtle shift in the way in which AGAP measures of public opinion are regarded. So, when Hough and Roberts suggest that "public dissatisfaction [with the UK criminal justice system] stems from public ignorance of the system,"[25] they imply (however unintentionally) that rather than being a reason for policymakers to treat general measures of dissatisfaction with care, poor public knowledge should instead be treated as a *causal factor* in public dissatisfaction with sentencing (and thus with unfavorable opinions of the criminal justice system as a whole).

Following the lead of Hough and Roberts, UK Home Office researchers subsequently argued that there was "increasing awareness of the importance of educating the public about crime and criminal justice."[26] There then followed a number of studies that used experimental methods to assess the effectiveness of educational materials at improving (i.e., making more favorable) public assessments of the criminal justice system.[27] In this way, the origins of the inadequacies previously identified with AGAP measures of public opinion were relocated. Instead of lying in the approach to measurement itself, the inadequacies were now found to be in the people subjected to (and by) the approach to measurement. In other words, the problem with AGAP approaches was not created by the researchers who designed them, but by the people upon whom they did their research.

An alternative perspective on the problems with AGAP methods has been articulated by those who have set out proposals to introduce more opportunities for public deliberation about criminal justice issues. These proposals seek to combat the tendency for traditional survey-based methods for gauging public opinion to capture "shallow, unconsidered" responses.[28] These proposals draw inspiration from the body of democratic theory that has been described as representing a "deliberative turn."[29] This body of work is first and foremost a normative theoretical project which, very broadly, reflects the conviction that a vibrant civic culture of informed public dialogue and debate is vital to the health and proper functioning of authentically democratic societies.[30] Deliberative democratic theories have informed a range of experiments in institutional design and practical application, from small-scale "citizens' juries" to much larger "deliberative poll" events involving representative samples of the population.[31] Characteristically, these processes involve a group of lay people receiving some form of input on the facts of the matter for discussion from relevant experts in the field, and the engagement by all participants in organized dialogue with one another.

From Theory to Practice: Claimed Benefits of a Deliberative Turn

Engaging in an appropriately calibrated deliberative process is claimed to help bring about, and make available for somehow *getting at*, what Yankelovich calls "public *judgment*," which is "the state of highly developed public opinion that exists once people have engaged an issue, considered it from all sides, understood the choices it leads to, and accepted the full consequences of the choices they make."[32] The overarching purpose of deploying a deliberative approach appears to be that of assisting participants in moving from expressions of what has been termed "mere opinion" toward more "refined" opinions about the matter at hand.[33] In effect, these events and processes attempt to reengineer the phenomenon we have come to know as public opinion in order to provide more "defensible" assessments of what members of the public want the criminal justice system to do.[34] Rather than deflecting blame from researchers, proponents of deliberative approaches see getting at public opinion as a collaborative undertaking: both researchers and those who they research must take some responsibility for producing defensible representations of public opinion.

The enhanced defensibility of public opinion as captured through the deliberative process is often attributed to the space which deliberation creates for citizens to become informed and to engage in rational dialogue. Defensibility, then, is associated with making citizens more *expert-like*, taming their supposedly irrational and vengeful tendencies by creating space for the release of "bees in bonnets."[35] Deliberative forums may, it is suggested, provide a means to "redirect" the intense emotions ignited by crime by "bringing the emotionally laced experience and demands of citizens in from the shadows . . . opening them up to the scrutiny of public, communicative reason."[36] In other words, the deliberative forum can act as a disciplining influence on raw emotion, by tutoring participants to move beyond the expression of opinions based on fear or anger. However, others have suggested that engagement in deliberation may not merely "cool down" emotions, but may also utilize the "heat" that they generate for good: deliberation does not merely inform participants but also, by engaging them in deliberation with fellow citizens, makes them more aware of the views and life experiences of groups with whom they may not usually come into contact, operating as a "circulatory system keeping them alive to social reality."[37] This may mean that citizens who participate in deliberation will not only be more informed about expert opinion, but also, potentially, more interested in and, perhaps, more concerned about and sympathetic toward their fellow citizens.

More radical accounts of democratic theory in particular emphasise the affective and transformative aspects of deliberative engagement. A robust democracy must have space for much more than the institutionalization of carefully controlled deliberative spaces for expert-like discourse that can simply reproduce and legitimise existing inequalities and injustices.[38] Healthy democracies must also accommodate the kind of successful "activist communities" that highlight, expose and challenge unfairness by calling on people to "face up" to injustice.[39] In other words, being a citizen in an *authentically* democratic society comes with responsibilities, as well as rights, and methods for getting at public opinion should be calibrated so as to bring these responsibilities to the fore, rather than erasing them (as AGAP approaches tend to do). So participants should come to deliberative processes not only with a view to becoming more informed, but also with a disposition which is ready to respect the political equality of fellow participants, and to listen to their perspectives with an open mind, and a willingness to change—what Young calls "deliberative uptake." According to this view, then, the whole purpose of the democratic deliberative process is "the transformation of private, self-regarding desire into public appeals to justice."[40] This will take place when participants are required to justify their perspectives and preferences through appeal not to self-interest—actually a form of coercion—but rather to justice or fairness.[41]

Engaging in respectful, nonself-interested dialogue about important social issues, then, requires participants to think in a public-spirited way, and may therefore help to induce a more permanent shift toward public-spirited thinking in participants. It is not merely that deliberative approaches facilitate the production of more *informed* opinions. It is also that by placing certain requirements and responsibilities on participants—to face up to injustice, to respect others, to be willing to change their mind—deliberative approaches are conducive to the development of a more selfless kind of political thinking. This is because when citizens engage in public-spirited, open-minded dialogue with others, about matters which affect their lives, they must acknowledge both their links to, and their responsibility for, those others.[42]

It is, perhaps, this strand of more radical deliberative theory—stressing the affective, transformative, and justice-oriented elements of deliberation—that gives proponents of deliberation a particular sense of hope that through deliberative approaches, harsh, punitive penal policy, and mass incarceration can be effectively challenged.[43] It is the hope and expectation that deliberation will induce a change not just of mind, but also of heart, that seems to underpin at least some of the enthusiasm for deliberative approaches among those who wish to see an end to mass incarceration. Yet while the normative theoretical case for deliberation's value to democracy is rather compelling, and the hopeful accounts of its likely positive effects are seductive, it is necessary for the purposes of this chapter also to consider available evidence on what actually happens when people deliberate about crime and punishment.

Fortunately, the available evidence is promising. A weekend-long deliberative poll conducted in the United Kingdom indicates that engagement in deliberation can moderate punitive preferences, at least in the short term,[44] while a comparative study of the background political cultures of US states with different rates of incarceration argues that higher levels of public participation in political and criminal justice institutions can nurture more moderate, "less coercive" approaches to penality.[45] A further study highlights the relationship between the background political and media conditions and criminal justice approaches and outcomes in two apparently quite similar cases of children killing other children.[46] The indications are clearly there, at both the macro level examined by comparative studies, and the micro level of specific deliberative events, that deliberative processes and political cultures tend to support more moderate, less punitive approaches to criminal justice. However, recognizing the value of deliberative approaches is one thing; working out how to make their use more common, influential, and embedded in societies where they are currently rather marginal, is quite another.

Is Deliberation a Practice or a Method?

It is prudent at this point to examine what distinction (if any) can be made between deliberation as process or *practice* and deliberation as *method*, and to consider which of these is most immediately relevant when it comes to challenging punitive penal policy and mass incarceration. The term "deliberative methods" has been applied to various approaches to opinion research that attempt to operationalize aspects of deliberative theory by, as a minimum, emphasizing the active engagement of research participants in a process of exploring and deliberating together upon the facts of the matters on which their opinion is sought.[47] The distinction between deliberation as practice and deliberation as method may rest upon the reasons (explicit and implicit) why the deliberative process is convened. It may also rest (relatedly) on the status accorded to its outcome or end product (if such product results). However, the distinction may also hinge upon what counts as "method": what are its characteristics, and do deliberative processes have them?

First, let's consider whether we can distinguish between deliberation as practice and deliberation as method on the basis of the reasons for deliberating and the status of outcomes. A deliberative process can be convened in order to support citizens in making a decision about what is to be done. The most familiar contemporary example is the use of a jury to decide whether an offender is to be found guilty of a crime (and, more rarely, on their sentence). In this case the outcome of the deliberative process is a decision, and its status is legally binding (although potentially subject to appeal). Citizen involvement in the deliberative process is therefore "load-bearing."[48] More recently, some countries have (usually at the regional or local level) introduced elements of deliberation to public decision-making processes on more general policy issues; however, these have tended to be closely controlled and deliberation is used here in a limited sense as a prelude to a vote open to people who did not necessarily take part in the deliberation.[49] At most the outcome of the deliberation might shape the choices that are subsequently available for citizens to vote on. Much more commonly a deliberative process might be used to allow citizens to be involved or participate in decision-making without allowing them to actually make the final decision for themselves, in which case the eventual status of the deliberation's outcome can be unclear, and the way it is used may be more or less obscure. In effect, these various forms of public involvement or participation (so-called) are largely confined to citizens being "consulted,"[50] in which case the outcome of any deliberative process would merely have the status of a statement about what "the public" believes ought to happen (in other words, the end product is knowledge).

The term "deliberative practice" can encompass a range of things, from the activities of load-bearing, decision-making forums like juries, to the use of deliberation as a consultation method where deliberation is regarded as a way to *get at* public judgment (understood as a more "refined" version of "mere opinion"). In the latter case the outcome of both deliberation as consultation and deliberation as method would appear to be the same: the production of knowledge about what the public believes. However, some social scientists will bridle at this suggestion that *any* attempt to produce knowledge should be regarded as a method. As Law notes, "method talk," at least in its hegemonic form, places "rules" and "rigour" centre stage: what can count as a method is thus bounded by a set of assumptions about reality (implicitly singular, preexisting, and independent) and the best way to apprehend it.[51] In particular, the idea of method requires the active engagement of the researchers in analysis, interpretation, and representation. When, as in deliberative processes of consultation, participants are supposed to be empowered to reach a conclusion by themselves, the hegemonic idea of method unravels: "The aim is . . . not to document or analyse what citizens say but to create a process through which these concerns can be expressed or made visible to others."[52] The role of the researcher thus becomes very unclear, placing social science in a potentially perilous position as it loses its capacity to claim any special expertise about the public.[53]

So, the idea of using deliberative practices as a *method* for producing knowledge appears somewhat problematic for established conceptions of the nature of method and the role of the researcher. But if we are interested in how to make deliberation more common, influential, and embedded, we need to consider the status (and possible alternate statuses) of the outcomes (knowledge?) it produces. Because deliberative processes—be they load-bearing, consultative, or simply knowledge-producing—are always used in particular historical, political, and cultural contexts. And for all that the proponents of increased deliberation may make strong moral and practical arguments for such a shift, it is the wider social and political context that plays a big part in shaping the extent to which deliberative processes are seen as legitimate in their different capacities, which is to say as decision-making, decision-shaping, or knowledge-producing. In the next part of this chapter I explore one of the key barriers to gaining legitimacy which deliberation faces in particular in respect of its knowledge-producing role.

Legitimate Knowledge-Production: Science or Politics?

Bourdieu famously argued that "public opinion does not exist ... in the form which some people, whose existence depends on this illusion, would have us believe."[54] Bourdieu's critique of public opinion focused on the failure by researchers working in this area to develop adequate methods for capturing public opinion as it *really* is. He argued that it was necessary to distinguish between "mobilized opinion" and "inclinations," and that the latter should not be considered to have attained "the status of opinion." For Bourdieu, the measurements provided by opinion polls were "artefacts," capturing opinions from people "in a situation which is not the real situation in which opinions are formed."[55] The crux of his argument was that

> the opinion survey treats public opinion like the simple sum of individual opinions, gathered in an isolated situation where the individual furtively expresses an isolated opinion. In real situations, opinions are forces and relations of opinions are conflicts of forces. Taking a position on any particular problem means choosing between real groups.[56]

Like the distinction between "false shadows" and "true substances" made by Doob and Roberts,[57] then, Bourdieu's critique relies on reality as a key reference point: the problem with the kinds of general measures of public opinion that he critiques is that they fail to *capture* "reality," and instead *produce* something false or artefactual.

Now this seems a reasonable criticism (although it turns out, as I discuss further, that the situation is more complex than Bourdieu allows), but it does not necessarily help us advance the cause of deliberative approaches. This is because, as Bourdieu himself later explored,[58] widespread use of opinion polling has made us accustomed to the idea that public opinion simply *is*:[59] that it exists prior to the moment when it is captured, and that it can be captured using something like the general opinion poll mechanism. What Bourdieu called the "petit-bourgeois pretension" that individuals carry with them at all times "personal opinions" on a vast range of issues—personal opinions to which they feel entitled, and which, when aggregated with other personal opinions make up public opinion—is therefore generally regarded not as artifice, or social construction, but as fact. This is the social and political context into which advocates of deliberative practices are attempting to insert, and assert the legitimacy of, an alternative way of *getting at* public opinion.

This is where the importance of recognizing the instability of the distinction between deliberation as *practice* and deliberation as *method* comes in useful. Because the dominant position that the AGAP conception of public opinion holds in the current social and political context simply reinforces the conviction that there *are* "methods" through which public opinion "as it is" (i.e., its *reality*) can be accurately "mirrored."[60] This, in turn, allows critics of the use of deliberative practice as method to suggest that what such processes access and represent is something interesting, valuable even, but that it is not "real," in contrast to the "real" opinions elicited through traditional AGAP-style surveys. For example, Hough and Park suggest that a deliberative poll is a "useful adjunct" to "the standard representative poll," and Walker and Hough suggest that deliberative methods that provide survey respondents with specific sentencing scenarios are useful only in so far as they enable researchers "to assess the 'mechanics' of opinion formation."[61] The stark truth, according to this perspective, is that research which involves providing participants with more information or input than they would access in their normal daily routine is "to put them in a position in which they will not find themselves in *real life*."[62] And if alternate methods are thus cast as accessing some kind of *unreal life*, then, their legitimacy as knowledge-producing mechanisms is clearly undermined.

Rather than resisting this characterization of their findings as "artificial" or "unreal," advocates of deliberative methods appear to accept it by, for example, describing the deliberative polls as providing a "glimpse of a *hypothetical* public."[63] This phraseology confirms the view that what deliberative approaches represent has been entirely created by the research mechanism, so that the findings emerging from this method are, and must be "produced."[64] So, as deliberative poll advocate James Fishkin indicates, the suggestion is that researchers using deliberative methods attempt to "model what the public *would* think, had it a better opportunity to consider the questions at issue."[65] The clear implication is that citizens *cannot* "achieve public judgment unassisted."[66] Indeed, citizens are said to require the "treatment" which the deliberative process provides so that their "raw" and "debilitated" "actual" opinion can become "refined" and "deliberative" "counterfactual" opinion.[67] According to these descriptions, the deliberative poll provides a true representation of a normatively ideal reality which *does not exist outside of the research context.*

The situation confronting us, then, is as follows. Bourdieu's classic critique of public opinion suggests that inadequate opinion poll methods suggest findings that are mere artefacts, as opposed to representations of real situations. Doob and Roberts suggest that general opinion questions capture only false shadows of the true substances (which are, presumably, "really" there).[68] Meanwhile Walker and Hough and Hough and Park suggest that both survey questions that provide specific case details *and* studies that engage members of the public in deliberation can only ever capture opinions which have been *produced* by the particular approach to research, and therefore cannot capture "real life."[69] Even proponents of deliberative approaches appear to accept that they capture and represent something that does not and cannot "really" exist unless the public is provided with some assistance by the researchers.

The problem here is that while each of these perspectives seems to take as a basic point of reference the idea that there is a reality of public opinion that preexists and is independent from the mechanisms applied to capture and represent it, each of them also appears to be premised on slightly different understandings of what counts as "real." There is a tension between the general ontological presumption that reality exists, and the specific presumptions made about its characteristics. The notion of the "hypothetical public" that has come to be associated with deliberative approaches lends additional credence to the idea that public opinion ("raw," "debilitated," "actual") *exists*, it is *real*, it can be *measured* and its "mechanics" can be understood. This encourages us to think about the difference between traditional, AGAP surveys of public opinion and deliberative processes as one of existence versus aspiration, of real versus unreal, of objective versus subjective, of science versus politics, of legitimate knowledge-producing mechanism versus illegitimate knowledge-producing mechanism.

The chances of being able to nurture a more deliberative approach to opinion research under these conditions begin to look rather uncertain. For if deliberative approaches should be viewed as premised on "normative" rather than "scientific" aspirations,[70] then why should we treat their "findings" as knowledge at all? Why should we not go along with Hough and Park, who argue that "whatever the *desirability* of having a well-informed and thoughtful public, deliberative polls are irrelevant as politicians need to take account of the reality of public opinion"[71]? One response to this suggestion is to point out that it is defeatist: there *is*, as noted above, evidence that politics *can* be carried on in a different, more deliberative fashion; citizens can be successfully involved, in a range of different ways, in both load-bearing decision-making scenarios and in deliberative approaches to consultation and research. There is also evidence that jurisdictions which do more deliberation often have a more moderate kind of penal politics that does tend to result in less punitive outcomes for offenders. But this line of argument misses the point.

The key barrier to deliberative approaches being perceived as legitimate is not a lack of awareness of the positive impact they can have; rather it is the accusation that the findings they produce offer knowledge about something which is not "real," whereas AGAP approaches can, if properly designed, capture the reality of public opinion (a reality which populist politicians do so crave to understand). Thus far, proponents of deliberative methods have not found a way to effectively challenge the damage that this accusation does to their cause. Indeed, as noted above, they often admit to the accusation by emphasizing the "hypothetical" or "produced" nature of the phenomenon they capture. Surmounting this barrier is necessary (in order for deliberation to gain greater legitimacy), but it requires a change of tack. Proponents of deliberative methods must undermine the very idea that a single reality of public opinion exists prior to and independently of the mechanisms used to represent it. They must politicize the "real."

From Method to Reality: Politicizing the Real

In using a quotation from Bourdieu to start off this chapter I probably signaled that this piece may contain a fairly orthodox critique of public opinion research. However, in the final part of the chapter I extend this critique by drawing on the science and technology studies (STS) literature, specifically the ideas elaborated in John Law's *After Method: Mess in Social Science Research* (2004). But first I want to revisit some of Bourdieu's claims about the impact of opinion surveys. Bourdieu argued that individuals in the age of the opinion survey, being repeatedly exposed to representations of public opinion, develop what he called the "opinionated habitus," a set of dispositions which are compatible with dominant ways of knowing about public opinion and which form part of the structure of our democratic architecture.[72] As such, the very fact that AGAP-style questions about public opinion are repeatedly asked, and their results repeatedly reported has "deeper cognitive effects on how people remember, envision, and think about public opinion and the public that has opinions."[73]

Developing a more Foucauldian perspective on what opinion research does, Osborne and Rose have argued that "people *learn* to have opinions; they become 'opinioned' ... people come to 'fit' the demands of the research; they become, so to speak, persons that are by nature 'researchable' from that perspective."[74] It is not, then, merely that people are altered (in unpredictable ways) by their experiences of being the objects of research, and reading about such research carried out on others (which is a somewhat obvious point). It is rather that the research *produces* subjects and objects; it calls upon individuals to constitute themselves as subjects in certain ways, and it fashions them into research objects by categorizing and ordering their subjectivities (those "things," like emotions, cognitions, preferences, evaluations which we consider to be the "stuff" of the subjective). In this way, social scientific research produces "reality effects" whereby "the version of the world that could be produced under [their] description ... become[s] true."[75]

Drawing upon this notion of "reality effects" we might consider, then, that AGAP-style research and analysis on public opinion, *no less than deliberative methods*, creates the public whose views it purports to represent. It creates the public by presenting individual respondents with narrow channels of opportunity for expressing their opinions and by making them accustomed to these methods as the most appropriate way for their views to be captured. Indeed, drawing on the work of John Law, we can take this suggestion further, arguing that research methods *must* "perform" or "enact" reality.[76] In the case of research on public opinion, surveys perform the theory of the subject upon which they are premised (e.g., the notion of the citizen as individualized consumer), and the aggregative approach to public opinion *"enacts a very particular version of the collective ... it performs it as a countable population."*[77]

Further to this, we should remember that opinion research is rarely (if ever) *only* research (or method), but that it also transmits (or attempts to transmit) information to politicians about the preferences of their public (by acting as what Dryzek terms a "transmission mechanism"[78]). As such opinion research (whether AGAP-style and survey-based, or deliberative) is always also a political practice, providing support for particular kinds of democratic principles: "Democratic principles come alive (are 'lived') through the medium of formal decisional mechanisms or *devices* which are designed to activate them and come to be justified in terms of them."[79] So, AGAP-style research on public opinion enacts a particular democratic reality: producing knowledge that is congruent with the existing "voting-centric" institutions of liberal democracy.[80] Thus, those social scientists who embrace this project do more than merely provide a "workable empirical rendering" of reality;[81] they "enact" a reality which is compatible with the institutions and practices of the dominant political regime and with Euro-American ontological assumptions (which is to say, a reality which is "out there," singular, definite, independent from and preexisting of the methods used to capture it.)[82] Their method (aggregative, general) both reproduces and reinforces the atomized, passive-style of political engagement required of citizens when they vote in elections. The method turns out to be conveniently congruent with and nourishing for prevailing ontological and political forces in contemporary society.

As AGAP-style research on public opinion repeatedly seeks out, orders, categorizes, and represents "reality" in certain ways, its purveyors are also engaged in *containing* the possibilities of reality. This is not simply because they close off or crowd out other possible *interpretations* of an (implicitly) preexisting reality,[83] but rather because they conceal (and deny) the fact that their methods are in fact enacting a particular kind of democratic reality, and that other realities are, or at least may be, possible. This denial is achieved by implying that the "rules" of method are imposed upon researchers by a preexisting, independent, singular reality.[84] Under cover of this "ontological illusion,"[85] AGAP approaches to researching public opinion are all the time enacting and strengthening a particular form of "democratic" project, and are therefore (albeit presumably unintentionally) stifling attempts to articulate and realize a different kind of democratic reality, such as that different reality articulated by proponents of deliberative approaches to democracy. As Law has argued, "to try to shoehorn non-coherent realities into singularity by insisting on direct representation and Othering whatever does not fit is . . . to (try to) enact a particular version of ontological politics."[86]

Once we explicitly recognize and acknowledge that research works in such a way as to enact reality, a space is opened up for "a politics of the real ... in which we might try to strengthen some realities while weakening others."[87] This idea that we can politicize the real opens up a new (and exciting) space within which social scientists and democratic theorists might collaborate to consider the way in which social science, in providing knowledge for democracy (such as knowledge of public opinion) contributes to the promotion of ideas about what democracy is and what it might be. It is within this space that we can start to think about the conditions under which deliberative theories, and the methods they have inspired, might help to unravel those forces which have brought about mass incarceration in the United States and an unnecessarily punitive approach to criminal justice in a number of other jurisdictions.

In short, if deliberative methods are to displace the dominant AGAP approach to researching public opinion on matters of crime and criminal justice and help to undo mass incarceration, then we are going to need "a politics of the real." We are going to need it because it allows us to be more assertive in challenging those who promulgate data produced through the AGAP survey-based method. Proponents of AGAP approaches should be required to acknowledge the contingent ontological and political premises upon which their method is based, as well as the ontological and political consequences it enacts and reenacts. In order to begin to dislodge the demand for the product (AGAP knowledge about public opinion) it will be necessary to directly challenge the supposed "unique selling point" ("mirror-like access to reality") promoted by those who supply it.

This approach is compatible with the normative counsel of C. Wright Mills, who argued that social scientists should seek "to combat all those forces which are destroying genuine publics and creating a mass society ... to help build and to strengthen self-cultivating publics."[88] And this expansive, open-ended project, rather than the more limited notion of better publicizing research evidence or educating citizens, could provide a more ambitious and democratic orientation for the vague and disputed notion of public criminology. The task of beginning to unpick and facilitate debate about the relationship between research methods and (democratic) realities would, perhaps, be a worthy project for Loader and Sparks's "democratic underlabourer" working in the mode of the knowledge "diplomat" shuttling between different camps to facilitate critical self-reflection by requiring them to account for how they construct the knowledge to which they lay claim.[89]

Conclusion

Advocates of deliberative democracy and of the approaches to consultation and research which they have inspired see AGAP approaches to capturing public opinion as assuming and assembling an impoverished public sphere, devoid of the lively conversation, exchange, and deliberation which, they have suggested, help to make a democratic way of life possible. Instead, impressions of public opinion are formed from the aggregated, unreflective, and narrowly channelled private preferences which people are permitted to express in response to the AGAP-style survey. Such preferences are treated not as temporary manifestations of opposing sentiments that may necessitate further reflection and willingness to compromise. Rather, they are regarded as sacrosanct objects that individuals may legitimately possess, express, and, where they are significant in number, expect to be taken into account. This is detrimental to the cultivation of responsible democratic citizenship, and has, as discussed above, contributed toward the punitive turn.

Deliberative practices, on the other hand (for decision-making, decision-shaping and knowledge-producing), appear highly likely (although by no means guaranteed) to promote shifts in political orientations that could unravel those forces which have combined to underpin the drift toward mass incarceration. They will do this by making much greater and more meaningful demands upon participants than the mere requirement that they express an instantaneous evaluation or preference that may (quite legitimately) simply reflect their own self-interest. Perhaps just as importantly, deliberative engagements will offer their participants an opportunity to reflect upon the different ways in which democracy is and can be enacted, and the different ways in which the responsibilities of democratic citizenship can be understood. However, deliberative practices must overcome a significant challenge if they are to be used more frequently in research and consultation. This challenge is the often-repeated idea that deliberative practices produce and make available for capture something "unreal" (or, if you prefer, "hypothetical") while AGAP survey-based methods capture reality. On this basis, it is argued that deliberative practices are interesting experiments but will *never* replace the conventional survey. This idea forms a barrier to progress in promoting a more deliberative approach to penal politics.

The ideas that I have elaborated in this chapter are an attempt to start to vandalize this barrier. I invoke the idea of vandalism because I am highly aware that dismantling the barrier entirely is not in my—or indeed any one individual researcher's—gift. None of us alone can take the barrier down, or indeed persuade politicians to give the proponents of deliberative approaches a leg up so that they can climb over it. But one option currently available to us (I would hesitate to claim that it is the only option) is to find ways to deface or vandalize the barrier to such an extent that we can eventually agree to pull it down. This chapter is a first attempt, but there is much more work to be done. Indeed, as noted earlier, future work might explore how political and social theorists can work together to consider the relationship between research methods and the enacting and reenacting of different democratic realities, potentially unpicking and rebundling the components parts of research methods and political practices in novel, unexpected ways. The argument offered here may appear to endorse a strongly *anti*realist perspective in all respects. But I would rather suggest that it advocates for the value of a flexible and optimistic attitude toward the "real" and its possibilities, in particular when it comes to assembling and representing publics in a manner which inevitably presses upon and interferes with our sense of what is politically possible.

But now I return to the specific matter of deliberation as method. This chapter has been underpinned by a belief which deserves and needs to be made more explicit: that the greatest value in so-called deliberative *methods* is not (as their proponents sometimes seem to suggest) that they have the capacity to access a deeper, more "real," or considered "truth" about public opinion. Rather, their key strength is that they *enact the reality* that makes that "truth" (if indeed that is the best word) possible. In so doing, they operate with a much fuller account of the potential and appropriate role of research subjects as political agents, and they recognize that any and all claims to "know" about what citizens think, or want, are also political acts. Deliberative methods therefore offer both a more democratically appealing vision of the social scientific method *and* a more democratically responsible approach to its ontological productivity. And it is the latter point that, to my mind at least, makes it a matter of democratic urgency to move beyond the idea of the "hypothetical public" and acknowledge how deeply implicated social scientific activity is in the production and maintenance of democratic realities.

Notes

1. Pierre Bourdieu, "Public Opinion Does Not Exist," in A. Mattelart and S. Siegelaub (eds.), *Communication and Class Struggle* (New York: International General, 1977), 129.

2. John Law, *After Method: Mess in Social Science Research* (London: Routledge, 2004); John Law, "Seeing like a Survey," *Cultural Sociology* 3, no. 2 (2009): 239–256.

3. Law, *After Method*, 54.

4. David Green, "Penal Populism and the Folly of 'Doing Good by Stealth,'" *The Good Society* 23, no. 1 (2014): 73–86.

5. Cf. Law, *After Method*, 54; Law, "Seeing like a Survey."

6. See David Garland, "The Limits of the Sovereign State: Strategies of Crime Control in Contemporary Society," *British Journal of Criminology* 36, no. 4 (1996): 445–471; Pat O'Malley, "Volatile and Contradictory Punishment," *Theoretical Criminology* 3, no. 2 (1999): 175–196; Mick Ryan, "Penal Policy Making Towards the Millenium: Elites and Populists; New Labour and the New Criminology," *International Journal of the Sociology of Law* 27, no. 1 (1999): 1–22; David Garland, "The Culture of High Crime Societies: Some Preconditions of Recent 'Law and Order' Policies," *British Journal of Criminology* 40, no. 2 (2000): 347–375; Simon Hallsworth, "Rethinking the Punitive Turn: Economies of Excess and the Criminology of the Other," *Punishment and Society* 2, no. 2 (2000): 145–160; Nikolas Rose, "Government and Control," *British Journal of Criminology* 40, no. 2 (2000): 321–339; Arie Freiberg, "Affective Versus Effective Justice: Instrumentalism and Emotionalism in Criminal Justice," *Punishment and Society* 3, no. 2 (2001): 265–278; David Garland, *The Culture of Control* (Chicago: University of Chicago Press, 2001); Julian V. Roberts, Loretta, J. Stalans, David Indermaur and Mike Hough, *Penal Populism and Public Opinion: Lessons from Five Countries* (Oxford: Oxford University Press, 2003); Neil Hutton, "Beyond Populist Punitiveness?" *Punishment and Society*, 7, no. 3 (2005): 243–258; Loïc Wacquant, *Prisons of Poverty* (Minneapolis: University of Minnesota Press, 2009); Ian Loader, "Playing with Fire? Democracy and the Emotions of Crime and Punishment," in S. Karstedt, I. Loader, and H. Strang (eds.), *Emotions, Crime and Justice* (Oxford: Hart, 2011): 347–362.

7. For example, it has been suggested that the descriptor "punitive" may be being used as shorthand for *any* "increase in the range and intensity of formal interventions." Roger Matthews, "The Myth of Punitiveness," *Theoretical Criminology* 9, no. 2 (2005): 179. See also: O'Malley, "Volatile and contradictory punishment"; Garland, "The Limits of the Sovereign State"; Jock Young and Roger Matthews, "New Labour, Crime Control and Social Exclusion," in Jock Young and Roger Matthews (eds.), *The New Politics of Crime and Punishment* (Cullompton: Willan, 2003): 1–32; Michael Tonry, *Thinking about Crime: Sense and Sensibility in American Penal Culture* (Oxford: Oxford University Press, 2004); Tim Newburn and Robert Reiner, "Crime and Penal Policy," in Anthony Seldon (ed.), *Blair's Britain 1997–2007* (Cambridge: Cambridge University Press, 2007): 318–340.

8. Malcolm Feeley and Jonathan Simon, "The New Penology: Notes on the Emerging Strategy of Corrections and Its Implications," *Criminology* 30, no. 4 (1992): 449; O'Malley, "Volatile and contradictory punishment" 177.

9. Explaining both the existence and the extent of the trend toward the increasing use of imprisonment (and other punitive sanctions) is a complex business and few (if any) attempts to date have managed to deal comprehensively with all relevant factors, or to account for divergences in the use of imprisonment within and between nations which appear to have comparable background conditions. See Vanessa Barker's *The Politics of Mass Imprisonment: How the Democratic Process Shapes the Way America*

Punishes Offenders (New York: Oxford University Press, 2009) and Michael Tonry's "Explanations of American Punishment Policies: A National History," *Punishment and Society* 11, no. 3 (2009): 377–394 for further discussion of this issue.

10. For example see Garland, "The Limits of the Sovereign State"; Hallsworth, "Rethinking the Punitive Turn"; Rose, "Government and Control"; Roberts et al., *Penal Populism and Public Opinion*; Jock Young, "Winning the Fight Against Crime? New Labour, Populism and Lost Opportunities," in Jock Young and Roger Matthews (eds.), *The New Politics of Crime and Punishment* (Cullompton: Willan, 2003): 33–47.

11. For example see David Brereton, "Does Criminology Matter? Crime, Politics and the Policy Process," *Current Issues in Criminal Justice* 8, no. 1 (1996): 82–88; Roberts et al., *Penal Populism and Public Opinion*; Tonry, *Thinking about Crime*; Ian Loader, "Fall of the 'Platonic Guardians': Liberalism, Criminology and Political Responses to Crime in England and Wales," *British Journal of Criminology* 46, no. 4 (2006): 561–586.

12. Young, "Winning the Fight against Crime?," 36.

13. See David Downes and Rod Morgan, "Dumping the 'Hostages to Fortune'? The Politics of Law and Order in Post-War Britain," in Mike Maguire, Rod Morgan, and Robert Reiner (eds.), *The Oxford Handbook of Criminology*, 2nd ed. (Oxford: Oxford University Press, 1997); John Pratt, *Penal Populism* (Abingdon: Routledge, 2007); Peter K. Enns "The Public's Increasing Punitiveness and Its Influence on Mass Incarceration in the United States," *American Journal of Political Science* 58, no. 4 (2014): 857–872.

14. One of the most widely cited accounts of the factors shaping penal policy is the 1995 essay by Anthony Bottoms, in which he coined the term "populist punitiveness," a term which is "intended to convey the notion of politicians tapping into, and using for their own purposes, what they believe to be the public's generally punitive stance" Anthony Bottoms, "The Philosophy and Politics of Punishment and Sentencing," in Chris Clarkson and Rod Morgan (eds.), *The Politics of Sentencing Reform* (Oxford: Oxford University Press, 1995); in their *Penal Populism and Public Opinion*, Roberts et al. adapted this term to describe a political approach which "involves the exploitation of misinformed opinion in the pursuit of electoral advantage."

15. For example see Matthews, "The Myth of Punitiveness," and Michael Tonry, "Explanations of American Punishment Policies: A National History," *Punishment and Society* 11, no. 3 (2009): 377–394.

16. For example, a review of the UK literature on "public confidence in the criminal justice system" found that purely quantitative studies dramatically outnumbered qualitative studies. See Liz Turner, Elaine Campbell, Andy Dale, and Ruth Graham, *Creating a Knowledge-Base of Public Confidence in the Criminal Justice System: Report 2: Literature Review* (Newcastle upon Tyne: Newcastle University, 2007), http://criminaljusticeresearch.ncl.ac.uk/index_files/All_Reports/2_LiteratureReview.pdf.

17. In an earlier publication I abbreviated this to Aggregated, General, Individualized, Passive (AGIP). See: Liz Turner, "Penal Populism, Deliberative Methods, and the Production of 'Public Opinion' on Crime and Punishment," *The Good Society* 23, no. 1 (2014): 87–102

18. See Simon Shaw, *The People's Justice: A Major Poll of Public Attitudes on Crime and Punishment* (London: Prison Reform Trust, 1982); Anthony Doob and Julian V. Roberts, "Social Psychology, Social Attitudes, and Attitudes Towards Sentencing," *Canadian Journal of Behavioural Science* 16, no. 4 (1984): 269–280; Anthony Doob

and Julian V. Roberts, "Public Punitiveness and Public Knowledge of the Facts: Some Canadian Surveys," in Nigel Walker and Mike Hough (eds.), *Public Attitudes to Sentencing: Surveys from Five Countries* (Aldershot: Gower, 1988); Mike Hough and David Moxon, "Dealing with Offenders: Popular Opinion and the Views of Victims—Findings from the British Crime Survey," *The Howard Journal* 24, no. 3 (1985): 160–175; Julian V. Roberts and Anthony Doob, "Sentencing and Public Opinion: Taking False Shadows for True Substances," *Osgoode Hall Law Journal* 27, no. 3 (1989): 491–503.

19. Doob and Roberts, "Social Psychology, Social Attitudes, and Attitudes Towards Sentencing."

20. Ibid., 277.

21. Roberts and Doob, "Sentencing and Public Opinion," 515.

22. Hough and Moxon, "Dealing with Offenders," 162.

23. In Mike Hough and Pat Mayhew, *Taking Account of Crime: Key Findings from the Second British Crime Survey* (London: Home Office, 1985), 43.

24. Hough and Moxon, "Dealing with Offenders," 162.

25. Mike Hough and Julian V. Roberts, *Attitudes to Punishment: Findings from the British Crime Survey* (London: Home Office, 1998), 27.

26. Joanna Mattinson and Catriona Mirrlees-Black, *Attitudes to Crime and Criminal Justice: Findings from the 1998 British Crime Survey* (London: Home Office, 2000), 2.

27. See Becca Chapman, Catriona Mirrlees-Black, and Claire Brawn, *Improving Public Attitudes to the Criminal Justice System: The Impact of Information* (London: Home Office, 2002); Heather Salisbury, *Public Attitudes to the Criminal Justice System: The Impact of Providing Information to British Crime Survey Respondents* (London: Home Office, 2004); Lawrence Singer and Susanne Cooper, *Inform, Persuade and Remind: An Evaluation of a Project to Improve Public Confidence in the Criminal Justice System* (London: Ministry of Justice, 2008).

28. See David A. Green, "Public opinion versus public judgment about crime: Correcting the 'Comedy of Errors,'" *British Journal of Criminology* 46, no. 1 (2006): 131–154. Green draw in particulars on the work of James Fishkin, *The Voice of the People: Public Opinion and Democracy* (New Haven, CT: Yale University Press, 1995). In a subsequent work (*When the People Speak: Deliberative Democracy and Public Consultation* [Oxford: Oxford University Press, 2009]) Fishkin has written about the intention to improve on what he calls "raw" and "debilitated" opinion by replacing (or at least supplementing) AGAP surveys with mechanisms which require participants to engage with "facts" and participate in deliberation with fellow citizens.

29. John Dryzek, *Deliberative Democracy and Beyond: Liberals, Critics, Contestations* (Oxford: Oxford University Press), 1.

30. Proponents of deliberative theory have been (at least partly) prompted to pursue this theoretical direction by indications that such a culture of public deliberation and debate has been increasingly undermined. See Jurgen Habermas, *The Structural Transformation of the Public Sphere* (Cambridge, MA: MIT Press, 1989).

31. For example, see Greg Munno and Tina Nabatchi, "Public Deliberation and Co-Production in the Political and Electoral Arena: A Citizens' Jury Approach," *Journal of Public Deliberation* 10, no. 2 (2014): 1–29; see also Robert Luskin, James Fishkin, and Roger Jowell, "Considered Opinions: Deliberative Polling in Britain" *British Journal of Political Science* 32, no. 3 (2002): 455–487

32. Daniel Yankelovich, *Coming to Public Judgment: Making Democracy Work in a Complex World* (Syracuse, NY: Syracuse University Press, 1991), cited in Green, "Public Opinion versus Public Judgment About Crime."

33. Albert W Dzur and Rekha Mirchandani, "Punishment and Democracy: The Role of Public Deliberation," *Punishment and Society* 9, no. 1 (2007): 151–175; cf. Fishkin, *When the People Speak.*

34. See David Green, *When Children Kill Children: Penal Populism and Political Culture* (Oxford: Oxford University Press, 2008), 242.

35. Yankelovich, *Coming to Public Judgment*, cited in Green, "Public Opinion versus Public Judgment."

36. Loader "Playing with Fire?," 356.

37. Albert Dzur, *Punishment, Participatory Democracy and the Jury* (Oxford: Oxford University Press, 2012), 54.

38. See Iris Marion Young, *Inclusion and Democracy* (Oxford: Oxford University Press, 2000).

39. See Mike Rowan, "Democracy and Punishment: A Radical View," *Theoretical Criminology* 16, no. 1 (2012): 43–62.

40. Young, *Inclusion and Democracy*, 25 and 51.

41. Dryzek, *Deliberative Democracy and Beyond.*

42. Dzur, *Punishment, Participatory Democracy and the Jury*, 162.

43. For example, this certainly seems to underpin the claims made by Bell, who argues that a form of "public criminology" which embraces "genuine *public* participation" in the form of deliberative engagement, has the potential to create an "exit strategy" from punitiveness. This "genuine democratization" imagines, will involve prisoners themselves in dialogue in order to foster "solidarity" and ensure that the public are "intimately acquainted with the prison and those who are confined within its walls." See Emma Bell, "There Is an Alternative: Challenging the Logic of Neoliberal Penality," *Theoretical Criminology* 18,no. 4 (2014): 489–505.

44. Robert Luskin, James Fishkin, and Roger Jowell, "Considered Opinions: Deliberative Polling in Britain," *British Journal of Political Science* 32, no. 3 (2002): 455–487.

45. See Vanessa Barker, *The Politics of Mass Imprisonment: How the Democratic Process Shapes the Way America Punishes Offenders* (New York: Oxford University Press, 2009).

46. Green, *When Children Kill Children.*

47. Robert Evans and Inna Kotchetcova, "Qualitative Research and Deliberative Methods: Promise or Peril?" *Qualitative Research* 9, no. 5 (2009), 627.

48. Cf. Dzur, *Punishment, Participatory Democracy and the Jury.*

49. For example, the idea of "participatory budgeting," made famous by its use in the Brazilian city of Porto Alegre, has been applied in some local authority areas in England in order to help local people decide how to use small portions of available public funds. See Department for Communities and Local Government, *Communities in the Driving Seat: A Study of Participatory Budgeting in England* (London: Department of Communities and Local Government, 2011).

50. Arnstein's ladder-based typology of citizen participation remains a go-to source for examining the extent to which citizens are *really* empowered by political activities

purporting to "involve" them. See Sherry Arnstein, "A Ladder of Citizen Participation," *Journal of the America Institute of Planners* 35, no. 4 (1969): 216–224.

51. See Law, *After Method*.

52. Evans and Kotchetkova, "Qualitative Research and Deliberative Methods," 626.

53. Ibid, 640–641.

54. Bourdieu, "*Public Opinion Does Not Exist*," 129.

55. Ibid., 128.

56. Ibid., 128.

57. Doob and Roberts, "*Social Psychology, Social Attitudes, and Attitudes Towards Sentencing*."

58. See Pierre Bourdieu, *Distinction: A Social Critique of the Judgement of Taste* (Cambridge, MA: Harvard University Press, 1984).

59. Beniger observes that "public opinion" has come to be understood as having the following characteristics: (1) being the aggregate or sum of the views of *individuals* who are all treated as equally well-informed and able to produce an opinion; (2) being potentially unconscious but able to be both measured and manipulated; (3) being held apart from actual political discourse and positions; and (4) being entirely independent of the uses to which it might be put. See James R. Beniger, "The Impact of Polling on Public Opinion: Reconciling Foucault, Habermas and Bourdieu," *International Journal of Public Opinion Research* 4, no. 3 (1992): 217.

60. Cf. Fishkin, *When the People Speak*, 17.

61. Mike Hough and Alison Park, "How Malleable Are Attitudes to Crime and Punishment? Findings from a British Deliberative Poll," in Julian V. Roberts and Mike Hough (eds.), *Changing Attitudes to Punishment: Public Opinion, Crime and Justice* (Cullompton: Willan, 2002), 182; Nigel Walker and Mike Hough, *Public Attitudes to Sentencing: Surveys from Five Countries* (Aldershot: Gower, 1988), 14.

62. Walker and Hough, *Public Attitudes to Sentencing*, 220, emphasis added.

63. Luskin et al., "Considered Opinions," 458, emphasis added.

64. Loader, "Playing with Fire?," 357.

65. Fishkin, *The Voice of the People*, 162, emphasis added.

66. Green, "Public Opinion versus Public Judgment About Crime," 145.

67. Fishkin, *When the People Speak*.

68. Doob and Roberts, "Social Psychology, Social Attitudes and Attitudes Towards Sentencing."

69. Hough and Park, "How Malleable Are Public Attitudes to Crime and Punishment?"; Walker and Hough, *Public Attitudes to Sentencing*.

70. Cf. Hough and Park, "How Malleable Are Public Attitudes to Crime and Punishment?"

71. Ibid., 166.

72. Bourdieu, *Distinction*.

73. Beniger, "The Impact of Polling on Public Opinion," 217.

74. Tim Osborne and Nikolas Rose, "Do the Social Sciences Create Phenomena: The Case of Public Opinion Research," *British Journal of Sociology* 50, no. 3 (1999): 392.

75. Ibid., 382.

76. Law, "Seeing like a Survey."

77. Ibid., 248, *emphasis in original*.

78. Dryzek, *Deliberative Democracy and Beyond*, 51.

79. Michael Saward, "Enacting Democracy," *Political Studies* 51, no. 1 (2003), 166, emphasis added.

80. Cf. Dzur and Mirchandani, "Punishment and Democracy."

81. Vincent Price and Peter Neijens, "Opinion Quality in Public Opinion Research," *International Journal of Public Opinion Research* 9, no. 4 (1997), 336.

82. Cf. Law, *After Method*.

83. See Zygmunt Bauman and Timothy May, *Thinking Sociologically* (Oxford: Blackwell, 2000), 176.

84. Law, *After Method*, 5.

85. Cf. Rom Harré, "When the Knower Is Also the Known," in Tim May and Malcolm Williams (eds.), *Knowing the Social World* (Buckingham: Open University Press, 1998), 38.

86. Law, *After Method*, 93.

87. Law, "Seeing like a Survey," 243.

88. C. Wright Mills, *The Sociological Imagination* (Oxford: Oxford University Press, 2000), 186.

89. Ian Loader and Richard Sparks, *Public Criminology?* (London: Routledge, 2010); cf. Bruno Latour, *War of the Worlds: What about Peace?* (Chicago: Prickly Paradigm Press, 2002). For a fuller discussion of this see Elizabeth Turner, "Beyond 'Facts' and 'Values': Rethinking Some Recent Debates about the Public Role of Criminology," *British Journal of Criminology* 53, no. 1 (2013): 149–166.

CHAPTER 11 | A Trade-Off Between Safety and Democracy?

An Empirical Investigation of Prison Violence and Inmate Self-Governance

AMY E. LERMAN AND VESLA MAE WEAVER

Introduction

Much attention has been given in recent years to the phenomenal growth of America's criminal justice system and in particular to the rise of mass incarceration. Scholars, pundits, and activists have noted with alarm that the imprisoned population has reached historic levels, with one in a hundred of the nation's adults behind bars as the first decade of the new century drew to a close.[1] This extraordinarily high rate of incarceration represents a stark contrast with other developed democracies, but also a dramatic break with our nation's own history.

While the burgeoning size of the nation's correctional system is noteworthy, equally remarkable are the many significant changes that took place behind the nation's prison walls. At the same time that prison populations were growing, the culture of incarceration and ideologies of punishment were undergoing dramatic revisions. The rehabilitation ideal that had briefly dominated American corrections was retrenched in favor of a punitive ethos, as a "just deserts" rhetoric about the purpose of incarceration began to take hold in both state and federal politics.[2] And the rise of a "new penology" increasingly focused attention on the quantitative management of risk, with new and sophisticated tools emerging to monitor and assess inmates during and after incarceration.[3]

These changes have received considerable discussion in recent scholarship. What has received much less attention is that at the same time these changes were taking place, a short-lived experiment with democracy in prison was also coming to an end. In a series of decisions beginning in the 1970s and continuing to the present, American courts began to restrict the democratic freedoms of prison inmates.[4] One notable example is that the courts began to allow prison personnel to ban inmate unions, councils, and other organizations from their institutions. Culminating in the Supreme Court case of *Jones v. North Carolina*, the courts have established precedent that essentially places the "legitimate penological objectives" of the institution before the constitutional right to freedom of association. In *Jones*, the Court concluded that "the fact of confinement and the needs of the penal institution impose limitations on constitutional rights, including those derived from the first amendment."[5] Indeed, in many cases, warding off prison violence was the primary justification for allowing prison authorities to limit a range of freedoms, including the rights of inmates to associate with others, to govern themselves through advisory councils and unions, to access certain types of information, and even to publish prison newspapers.[6] In their decisions, the court gave wide latitude to prison staff to determine when rights needed to be curtailed, on the assumption that they had specialized knowledge about the internal life of prisons and that prison officials were uniquely positioned to make decisions about how to reduce violence within their institutions.

The courts were not alone in legitimizing the idea that prison authorities should have the ability to ban inmate association under the violence/disorder rationale. Instead, a variety of notable voices began to argue that the activism of inmates, or other collectivist activities of inmates that brought them together in common cause, posed a potential threat to institutional safety. John DiIulio, in his account of governing models in California, Texas, and Michigan prisons in *Governing Prisons*, argued that "reliance on inmates to control other inmates is a recipe for compromising security and violating laws" and that prisons where inmate governance was allowed had higher levels of disorder and vice.[7]

In this chapter, we assess the idea of a trade-off between safety and democracy in the modern American prison by examining one important case: inmate advisory councils in the state of California (IACs, or inmate advisory councils). Our first task is empirical: to discern whether there is support for the idea that greater participation in inmate councils is associated with higher rates of inmate violence. Using data from three sources, we find little evidence to support the notion that more active inmate advisory councils are associated with a greater prevalence of violence. Rather, even when we account for risk factors, prison conditions, and other types of prison organizations, we find a significant and *negative* association between higher participation in inmate self-governance and the incidence of violence. In fact, we find some evidence that the presence of advisory councils might actually offset the prevalence of gang violence within the prison.

Our findings do not confirm a causal relationship; our evidence relies only the limited data available to us, which present just a descriptive snapshot of prisons in one state, at one point in time. In addition, an important caveat is that we cannot account for selection; specifically, it may be that the prisons at which authorities enable or encourage greater participation in IACs are precisely those where administrators have less concern about violence to begin with or are those that are engaged in other proactive responses to ensure the safety of inmates. We discuss this possibility further after presenting our results. However, we believe that our findings can be taken to suggest that the basic justification for limiting inmate associations (and other democratic rights and processes in the prison system)—that it necessarily increases violence—may rest on shaky empirical ground.

Our larger ambition is to begin the work of theorizing the democratic deficits of prisons today and to suggest to scholars of the carceral state that procedural justice and legitimacy should be considered within the prison environment. Elsewhere, we have documented the antidemocratic features of the modern American criminal justice system.[8] American criminal justice institutions over the past half-century have steadily embraced policies and practices that stand in stark contrast to our basic democratic norms and values. Citizens who encounter police, pass through the nation's court system, and are held in the country's prisons and jails are for at least some period of time denied a host of fundamental rights to speech and association; their access to information is restricted; they are made subject to state authority with limited avenues to demand accountability or responsiveness.

We would not argue that some restrictions are not wholly necessary for the purpose of maintaining order and security. There is perhaps an inevitable tension in crime control institutions between the democratic values of a free and open citizenship and the practical needs of a system for deterring and punishing law-breaking. In a democracy, however, there should be a very high bar for limiting citizens' most fundamental constitutions rights. While the evidence we offer here is preliminary, we find little evidence to support the need for restricting rights in the case of inmate governance through prison councils.

A Brief History of Inmate Advisory Councils

One of the primary ways that incarcerated citizens might participate politically, express their opinions, protest treatment within the institutions that hold them, and petition the government is through inmate political associations and prison unions, particularly given the broad and encompassing restrictions on inmate voting, access to the media, and censorship of their writing.[9] In particular, inmate councils and other self-governance organizations provide inmates with a formal vehicle through which their collective needs and concerns can be identified, discussed, and communicated to the institution. In theory, prison inmate councils are formally recognized associations, comprised of elected representatives of the inmate population that are tasked with regularly bringing concerns on behalf of the inmate population to the prison authorities. In practice, council organizations vary in structure, function, and power, but most operate as a representative body with a formal constitution and an executive leadership that consults inmates on a wide range of issues, deliberates, and communicates the needs of prison inmates vis-à-vis the institution, meeting regularly with staff and prison managers. Rather than making decisions or issuing directives to the prison authorities, they serve as advisory bodies meant only to convey the perspectives of inmates on issues that affect the prison institution and make recommendations.[10] Inmate councils serve a two-way function of both presenting inmate grievances to the administration as well as communicating to the inmates the messages, point of view, and directives of the prison administration.[11]

Inmate political organizations (and research on these associations) flourished during the 1960s and 1970s.[12] While poor prison conditions were often the primary target, reformers and activists during this period also envisioned a more democratic and responsive institution, and proposed inmate participation in governance through elected inmate councils. "Traditional prison management is based on an authoritarian regime with a rigid hierarchy," observed one scholar during the 1970s, where "inmates occupy the lowest level on the hierarchy."[13] Proposals for inmate government aimed to change this structure, seeing a need to draw inmates into the decision-making process of the institution, and giving them an avenue to take responsibility for and shape the prison environment. By involving inmates in proactive and productive behaviors and giving them a formal channel to express their collective interests and concerns, the democratic prison was imagined to produce more responsible citizenship; inmates would learn democracy by practicing it firsthand and by seeing it function.

The idea was not new; mutual aid leagues and inmate councils developed in the early twentieth century in the United States, organized by reformers such as Thomas Mott Osborne and Rev. E. M. Wells, who envisioned inmates as able to effectively self-govern. Several brief experiments in inmate self-government and prison democracy during this earlier era involved inmates meting out discipline, formulating education programs, and managing inmate labor. Osborne developed inmate councils at Sing Sing prison and the Naval prison in Portsmouth, NH, based on the Mutual Welfare League at Auburn where a representative body of elected inmates had the power to decide institutional rules and to guide outcomes in response to inmate grievances of major offenses against inmates. The warden of a Norfolk, Massachusetts prison, Howard Gill, became convinced of the inmate participation idea after the building of a prison wall fell behind schedule and required the enlisting of inmates to work alongside engineers to finish construction. Gill introduced inmate participation in governance in the 1920s to create "a prison community that would be as close to normal community as possible" and developed an advisory council that had staff representation.[14] Ultimately, both Osborne's and Gill's experiments in inmate organization and participation were shut down, mostly due to external political factors.

But the idea reemerged after prison disturbances during the 1960s made the logic of the authoritarian prison regime increasingly untenable.[15] With no system for getting grievances across, prisons historically were places of frequent unrest, rampant violence, and revolution. As one scholar notes in discussing the nation's most infamous prison rebellion and violent repression, "Attica brought into stark relief the contradictions that existed between the use of imprisonment with its closed, often brutal and controlling hierarchical system and democratic ideals like egalitarianism, liberty and transparency that supposedly informed American government."[16] Prison reformers believed that inmate councils and other forms of participatory prison management could reduce tensions by providing nonviolent avenues for expressing claims and resolving conflicts. Democratic voice within the prison was seen by some as a way to ward off other, more violent forms of demand-making. Inmate self-government emerged at the Washington State Penitentiary in Walla Walla, Washington after inmate strikes in the 1960s in response to hair regulations. The warden formed an inmate advisory council to deal with minor grievances but the council held little decision-making power. The threat of disorder and violence was an immediate rationale for the inmate council: to "co-opt the radical and neutralize the violent potential of traditional politics."[17] After racial turmoil erupted in the prison, a Resident Government Council (RGC) was formed in 1971 with a constitution and eleven members elected by the inmates directly. The RGC seemed to have power; they could veto decisions of the prison superintendent, and they were able to implement a plan for inmate council members to participate in committees that classified prisoners. The experiment marked the "break up of an undifferentiated prisonized mass and its transformation into a pluralistic multiethnic political culture."[18] The RGC ultimately began to dissolve after a 1974 incident in which the Walla Walla inmates took hostages at a prison hospital.

An even more striking case of prison democracy occurred at Walpole prison in Massachusetts, one of the most violent institutions in the nation and where prison conditions were wretched: "Many cell blocks were ankle-deep in trash and corridor walls were stained by feces and urine."[19] A strike began in March of 1973, but this time it was not by the inmates but the correctional staff themselves, who handed the keys to the entire institution to a civilian observer while the whole staff called in sick. Over the ensuing weeks and months, the prisoners themselves managed life inside with just a "skeleton crew of officers and trainees from other institutions" to oversee them. Scholars who have written about Walpole based on detailed notes from the civilian observers found extraordinary organization among the prisoners to maintain order and reduce violence, and establish solidarity and negotiate conflict, with activities including the formation of deliberative assemblies and voting.[20]

Yet despite anecdotal evidence that inmate councils could improve prisons, encourage good citizens, and lead to greater self-esteem among inmates, they largely either failed to take hold or declined in practice over time.[21] Inmate representation was not always welcomed by prison authorities, who sometimes responded to these expansions in inmate power with actions to undermine their efficacy. For example, the April 1952 uprising in the New Jersey State Prison led to the creation of an inmate council, which could present inmate grievances to the prison administration; however, when the council's grievances were not addressed, the council staged a sit-down strike for several days, leading prison officials to transfer the council's chairman and others on the council to other institutions.[22]

More importantly, the experiment in inmate councils stalled owing largely to the precarious legal footing of the right of inmates to freedom of association, including but also beyond advisory councils. As early as 1974, in the case of *Paka v. Manson*, a federal district court upheld a prison ban on the formation of inmate unions, holding that inmates did not have a constitutional right to form such an organization, even when the union would serve primarily as a grievance mechanism rather than to organize labor. Inmates had begun forming the union organization primarily to communicate inmate complaints to staff and develop proposals for better prison operations, when several leaders of the organization were transferred to other prisons or put in isolation. Prison officials also began intercepting the union's mail.[23] Reviewing the case, the court concluded that alternative grievance mechanisms existed, including an ombudsman. More importantly, however, the court accepted prison officials' claim that the state's interest in maintaining security was more compelling than the abridgment of the inmates' right to associate, even if the alternative means did not allow for as much inmate participation in the grievance process.[24] In essence, the court ruled that prison officials had the authority to impose first amendment restrictions if they believed that the union represented a threat to prison order, however defined.

The Supreme Court went even further in *Jones v. North Carolina Prisoner Union* (1977). *Jones* concerned a prison union that had formed in North Carolina, had operated peacefully for several months, and had acquired a membership of two thousand inmates across forty institutions before it was banned from meeting and soliciting new members by prison authorities. The union's purpose was to improve working conditions in North Carolina correctional facilities. Again in this case, the prison administration argued that inmate unions threatened to disrupt the security of the institution. In deciding the case, the court formally acknowledged that the right to associate can be "curtailed whenever the institution's officials, in the exercise of their informed discretion, reasonably conclude that such associations ... possess the likelihood of disruption to prison order or stability, or otherwise interfere with the legitimate penological objectives of the prison environment."[25] Thus the mere potential for disruption, as articulated by the staff, would constitute enough of a legitimate government interest to abridge the constitutional rights of inmates. In addition, unlike the previous federal court decision, the Supreme Court in *Jones* held that the prison was not a "public forum" where the democratic voices of individual citizens need necessarily be protected and expressed.[26]

This decision pushed the prison further from the principles of democracy by collapsing the ability of confined citizens to organize and associate. At the same time, it showed the nation that "there are segments of our society which, due to a seemingly justified need for stricter governmental supervision, will not enjoy as broad first amendment protections as the rest of society."[27] In their dissent, Justices Thurgood Marshall and

William Brennan were accurate in their prediction of what would happen to inmates' rights in the wake of the decision, arguing that inmates' rights would be quickly eroded in the name of prison security.[28] As one scholar noted: "If the courts were suggesting that inmates' constitutional freedoms could be limited by prison administrators' pervasive fears about the security of their institutions, then even before the Supreme Court's opinion in *Jones*, one could have predicted that prison unions had a questionable future. After all, if the courts refused to analyze the positive capabilities of a carefully structured prison organization, and only considered the alleged security threat which unions may pose, then the first amendment rights of inmates would lose out to the 'governmental interest' every time."[29] While some lower courts continued to protect the rights of inmates to organize and associate,[30] *Jones* essentially "sounded the death knell" for prison unions across the country.

The Prison Council Today

Despite their substantial decline, inmates at some prison facilities in the United States still enjoy access to and representation in prison councils. While we do not have comprehensive and reliable data on the prevalence of such councils in the nation's correctional facilities, a 2004 survey found that approximately 6.5 percent of inmates in state prisons and 6.2 percent of inmates in federal prisons report belonging to an inmate assistance group or council.[31] To compare, slightly over 30 percent reported involvement with a religious group, 4 percent reported belonging to a racial or ethnic group, and 9 percent reported involvement with other inmate self-help or assistance groups.

Even less is known about whether and how prison inmate advisory councils shape the prison environment. The studies that do exist—many conducted decades ago and some in European countries—suggest that by giving inmates a platform for democratic expression, councils (or unions) could produce positive outcomes: they could improve communication and yield better relations between prison authorities and their wards, provide a source of legitimacy that incentivizes inmates to comply with prison rules, reduce the us/them division and resentment between staff and inmates, mitigate inmates' hostility toward the system, lead to a more relaxed community atmosphere, heighten trust between different groups of inmates, and cultivate responsibility among inmates to help produce rehabilitative outcomes.[32]

This is not to say that council governance is not fraught with issues. Studies outline a range of important concerns regarding how councils might function in practice; existing studies identify examples of prison staff using the council process to coerce inmates, inmate representatives using the council toward self-serving ends, or the development of councils as a token way to subvert attention from broader issues of prison conditions. Moreover, some councils enjoy little buy-in from inmates, who see them as nothing more than a symbolic group with little power and not an effective avenue of inmate expression.[33] In many California prisons, which are required to have IACs, wardens and prison staff maintain a high degree of control over how these organizations function, with strong oversight of their activities, elections, distribution of meeting minutes, eligibility of inmates to represent the council, and constitution. For this reason, some inmates have charged that the IAC is a "dog and pony show" that carries no real power or initiates very little change among prison staff.[34] In one scathing article, a prisoner contends that if an IAC representative gets too powerful, he is removed and that when a council attempts substantive change or takes meaningful action on larger issues, the prison administration will quickly oust the entire leadership; as a result, holding an IAC leadership position is not respected or considered honorable by inmates.[35]

One of the only systematic studies of several prison councils, conducted in the United Kingdom, found that rather than actually changing policy (though they could sometimes influence policy direction on less contentious issues), councils "functioned as a kind of focus group ... to inform prisoners of matters or to canvass prisoners' views on matters upon which they chose to invite feedback."[36] Rather than directly changing prison policy or directly adjudicating complaints from inmates, these organizations played an agenda-setting role. But most ideas of how inmate councils may matter for the prison environment or for inmate attitudes and behaviors have yet to be examined; for instance, we know of no empirical assessment of the effects of councils on prison culture and order, inmates' perceptions of institutional legitimacy and trust in authority, inmates' sense of political empowerment and self-efficacy, or the relationship between inmate advisory councils and membership in other informal groups, including gangs.

The limited extant scholarship therefore leaves us with little understanding of how prison councils operate in the modern prison and little systematic evidence of even the most important outcomes of prison councils. Our intention here is to take a first step toward understanding the most basic issue: the relationship of prison councils (or their absence) to the development of factional groups, namely gangs, and to the prevalence of violence within the institution. This is of particular importance given the centrality of the supposed connection between councils and prison order to key court decisions that allowed prisons to curtail inmate organizations.

There are several reasons why we might expect prison councils to be associated with lower levels of gang activity and fewer violent disruptions in the prison environment. First and most basically, prison councils might serve as an outlet of frustration for a group of highly disempowered individuals in an environment where they otherwise command little control over their daily lives and where alternative mechanisms for the formal recognition of grievances are generally weak.[37] In theory, the presence of inmate advisory councils could help move institutions that are structured around hierarchy and dependence toward a model where agency, dialogue, and exchange have at least some small role, providing a potential escape valve for inmate frustration, alienation, and resentment. As one correctional officer noted, "although it is not a decision-making body, it does allow the prisoners to feed through their concerns. It gives them a voice."[38]

By giving the inmate population formal channels through which their collective voice could be heard, and by giving institutional authorities an opportunity to be regularly responsive to inmates, prison councils may diminish the prevalence of more aggressive, violent forms of expression, resistance, and claims-making. Though writing of labor unions, one scholar noted that inmate bargaining power provides a "realistic alternative to litigation or insurrection" and led to a decline in militancy.[39] In fact, as we have already noted, the violence-reduction potential of inmate associations was often cited as a key rationale by reformers during the height of the movement toward a more participatory prison; inmate unions and councils were believed to lessen the incidence of violent confrontation between inmates and with staff by replacing violent contestation with collective bargaining and offering inmates a way to resolve conflicts peacefully. "By providing a formal and legitimate mechanism for the communication of grievances," one scholar argues, "the inmate is given a feeling that he has a vested interest in the maintenance of order."[40] By changing how inmates orient themselves toward prison staff and also toward one another, the presence of advisory councils may indirectly bear on the overall level of violence within the institution.

Second, and related to this notion, inmate participatory mechanisms like councils may not only be an outlet of frustration that dampens violent outbreaks, it may be an *outlet of democratic expression* that cultivates democratic habits above more disorderly expressions. In practice, prisons strip inmates of democratic voice.[41] In contrast, inmate councils—in theory and perhaps also in practice—can promote democratic habits, skills, and sensibilities. Through participation, inmate participatory groups promote "the interdependence of union members and the responsibility they have to one another and to the larger community to which they belong."[42] Scholars have extolled the democratic benefits of other inmate governance groups, like unions, where inmates not only have a place to communicate grievances, but also learn compromise, cooperation, bargaining, and civic engagement.[43] For example, one officer in a study of UK prisons noted that "the level of violence has reduced because we discuss frankly the effect on the population that violence has."[44]

More broadly, by participating in a democratic group, taking on civic roles, and witnessing the positive outcomes of their collective efforts, inmates may develop a sense that they are endowed with the responsibilities of good citizenship. "Participation in formal bargaining can encourage a sense of responsibility, dignity, and self-respect."[45] Through the council process, individual prisoners experience a variety of phenomena that might lead them toward more pro-social (and less violent) behaviors and attitudes: they may witness the pursuit of collective ends and objectives through democratic debate, inspiring solidarity and collective action; they may gain a sense that their own interests, as well as the collective interests of the group, are being represented and recognized; they may gain a sense of control over their fate, which may lead to a diminution in anomie and alienation; they may gain a sense of positive identity that encourages them to take on pro-social roles and see themselves as members of a community; they may gain a sense of belonging in the public sphere. Again, these psychological changes may mitigate the propensity for prison misconduct and violence.

At the same time, because inmate councils are premised on deliberation and bottom-up engagement, instead of top-down authority, they may have the capacity to bring people together in an inclusive dialogue. In turn, by promoting inmate–staff dialogue and rituals of deliberation and cooperation, a more trusting environment may emerge, one where the first recourse is discussion, not threatening or turning to physical remedies. "Collective bargaining between inmates and administrators," notes one scholar, "can effectively correct institutional problems and avert disorder."[46]

Inmate councils may also increase the legitimacy of the institution in the eyes of its wards. If the institution is responsive to the council rather than treating it as purely symbolic, inmates may come to feel a sense that using democratic channels to pursue their interests (as opposed to other tactics, including violence) can be a successful way to accomplish their goals. Moreover, research on procedural justice shows that regardless of the outcome, people who feel they have been treated fairly by institutions come to regard those institutions as legitimate sources of authority. In this way, perceptions of legitimacy promote law-abiding behavior. This, in turn, may serve to mitigate violence; when people believe in the legitimacy of an authority, even when they disagree with an outcome of a decision made by that authority, they are more likely to follow the rules. The inmate advisory council, within a prison that is by definition authoritarian, may heighten the legitimacy of the institution in the eyes of inmates by providing for a more participatory process for the resolution of grievances and disputes. It may likewise inspire more positive attitudes toward prison authorities, who come to be seen as willing to listen and consider the needs of inmates.

Third, and consistent with earlier research on prison organizations, councils may provide a viable alternative to prison gangs, which flourish where formal structures for community governance are too weak to ensure the maintenance of order. Gresham Sykes's famous study, *The Society of Captives*, developed the idea that informal systems tend to form in prison environments when formal systems are unresponsive to prisoner needs. Where prison institutions lack a mechanism of self-governance, and where officers' control and authority are seen as weak or illegitimate, inmates may turn to prison gangs as a system of "forced reciprocity" between inmates and staff.[47] As prison scholar David Skarbek argues, "Prison gangs end up providing governance in a brutal but effective way ... they impose responsibility on everyone ... prisons run more smoothly because of them."[48] While this may be true, certainly inmate councils provide a far more preferable means of establishing structure, norms, and rules, constituting an "identifiable social system that provides mechanisms that help alleviate the pains of imprisonment."[49]

Finally, inmate councils could lead to actual outcomes, such as improved prison conditions, that benefit inmates and better their relations with other inmates and staff (but see DiIulio's account in *Governing Prisons*). There is little evidence, however, to either support or refute the claim that advisory councils are successful in making substantial changes in prison operations. One news account describes an advisory council in California developing an "honor yard" and an inmate council in Maryland that successfully advocated for and ultimately established a career center. As one inmate argues, the advisory council "helps ensure that there is a proper system for putting issues across, so it is not ad hoc. It is a voice you can use to get results. It is good that we have a council otherwise a lot of things would get pushed aside."[50]

Data

Each prison facility in the state of California is required to have an Inmate Advisory Council (IAC) that is tasked to "advise and communicate with the warden and other staff those matters of common interest and concern to the inmate general population."[51] While levels of participation vary by facility, as we discuss later, the structure and function of IACs are mandated by policy. Most importantly, IACs must be constituted by regular elections where each inmate has an equal vote, and IACs operate under a council-designed constitution and bylaws. In some cases, IACs are structured so as to be representative of each racial/ethnic group or designated housing unit. Representatives are elected by the inmate population or subgroups of inmates, who in turn elect their leadership (chairman, vice chairman, secretary, treasurer, sergeant at arms) for a term of one year. The prison facility must provide the IAC with space to assemble and any supplies that are needed to communicate their activities and decisions with the inmate population. Council meetings are recorded in minutes and after being approved by the warden, meeting minutes are distributed. IACs at one facility can "correspond and exchange copies of meeting agenda and minutes with councils at other department facilities."[52] After deciding on an agenda that is submitted to prison authorities, wardens or their designees are required to meet with the council at least once every month and "shall provide the council with a timely written response which shall indicate what action ... was taken, the reasons for the action and, when applicable, the manner and appropriate time of implementing the action."[53]

We rely on two primary sources of data to explore the relationship between participation in advisory councils in California prisons and the prevalence of violence at the institutional level: the California Correctional Officer Survey (CCOS) and COMPSTAT reports from the California Department of Corrections and Rehabilitation (CDCR). The CCOS is a survey conducted in 2006, which was distributed by mail to all active correctional officers in California's thirty-three adult state prisons in that year.[54] The survey yielded 5,775 completed questionnaires, for a response rate of 33 percent. The final sample was roughly representative of the total population on key demographics, and although response rates varied somewhat across institutions, no prisons had to be dropped from the sample due to a lack of respondents.

The CCOS asked officers a wide range of questions concerning the prison facility where they work. These data provide our key indicators of the proportion of inmates in councils and the proportion of inmates in gangs, as well as our outcomes of interest: frequency of gang-related violence and frequency of inmate violence in the prison. In addition, we use three measures of prison conditions as control variables in our multivariate analyses: assessments of dirt and litter, assessments of rodents and insects, and overall assessments of prison conditions. As our analysis is conducted at the level of the institution, we aggregate officers' responses by prison.

The COMPSTAT Branch of CDCR compiles data for the Division of Adult Institutions, which are available as thirteen-month statistical reports. These reports capture an array of metrics at the institution level. From these data, we employ a series of measures that serve as controls in our multivariate analyses. First, we use both security level (percentage of inmates at Level 1, Level II, Level III, and Level IV) and overcrowding as proxies for the relative risk of violence at the institution. In addition, we use a variety of measures to control for participation in informal organizations (inmate leisure groups, Alcoholics Anonymous, Narcotics Anonymous, and veterans groups) and also in other formal groups and programs (academic programs, vocational programs, work assignments, and substance abuse programs).

Our third data source provides evidence from a national sample. The Bureau of Justice Statistics (BJS) regularly conducts surveys of inmates across a broad swath of the nation's state and federal prison facilities. In one, the *Survey of Inmates in State and Federal Correctional Facilities, 1997*, inmates were asked several questions (omitted from later surveys) that allow us to explore the relationship between inmate safety and participation in inmate councils at the level of the individual.[55] In this 1997 survey, a large sample of 14,285 state inmates and 4,041 federal inmates completed interviews of about an hour in length; under strict confidentiality procedures, they were asked for information about their sentence length, the type and characteristics of their criminal offenses, criminal histories and prior incarcerations, socioeconomic status, substance abuse, and participation in prison services and programs. The data include information on the type of prison facility (male, female, coed, confinement, or community-based), level of security, and type of housing unit. In addition to a sample of forty federal facilities, the sample consisted of inmates in each of the nation's thirteen largest male state prisons, seventeen largest female prisons, and a sample of 223 male and 47 female prisons selected from the remaining facilities with a probability proportional to the size of the facility.

IACs, Gangs, and Prison Violence in California

According to correctional officers, participation in IACs varies widely across California's adult prison institutions. While on average about 30 percent of inmates are estimated to be involved with their IAC in some way, average estimated participation ranges from a low of 18 percent at one prison to a high of 36 percent at another. There is even greater diversity across prisons in the percentage of inmates estimated by correctional officers to be involved with gangs. According to officer estimates, about 75 percent of inmates are involved in some way in gangs or gang activity, but this ranges from a low of 42 percent at one prison, to a high of more than double that (87 percent) at another prison. Similarly, officers estimate an average of eleven different gangs operating in their prison, with estimates ranging from eight at one prison to twenty at another.

As shown in Figure 11.1, levels of participation in both gangs and IACs are higher in higher security prisons. Compared to 24 percent of inmates in Level I facilities who participate in the IAC in some capacity, IACs experience roughly 31 percent participation in Level IV facilities. Like IACs, participation in gangs increases in higher security levels; gangs range from 67 percent participation in Level I facilities, to 71 percent in Level II, 73 percent in Level III, and 81 percent in Level IV. Variation in gang and IAC membership across security levels, however, is likely endogenous to a wide variety of other attributes of the institution and the individuals assigned to them that will affect the propensity of individuals to join these groups. Security levels dictate a great deal of prison life, from the security infrastructure, to the correctional orientation of custody staff, to the range of offenses and propensity for violence of the inmate population. To account for these differences, it is therefore useful to examine how participation in IACs and gangs vary *within* the subset of prisons at a particular security level.

A preliminary examination of prison institutions conducted separately by each security level shows a negative relationship between the percentages of inmates participating in IACs and gangs. For instance, Figure 11.2 graphs the relationship between the two for Level II facilities (defined as institutions where the majority of inmates are classified

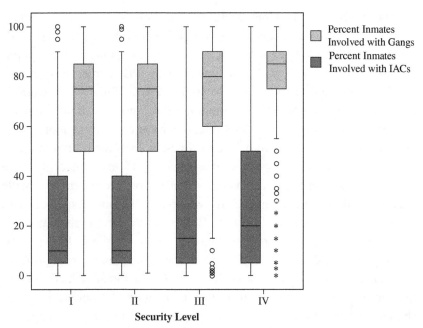

FIGURE 11.1 Mean and Range of Participation in IACs and Gangs, By Prison Security Level

Data are estimates provided by correctional officers assigned to each security level. N=288 for Level I; 786 for Level II, 1374 for Level III; and 1571 for Level IV

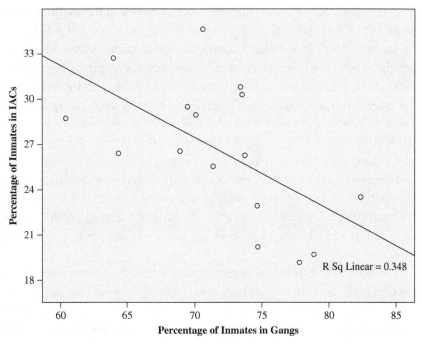

FIGURE 11.2 Percentage of IAC and Gang Participation for Level II Prisons

at this security level). Comparing distributions of age, race, primary commitment offense, and county of commitment for each Level II facility in the California system reveals reasonably comparable prison populations.[56] The average age of inmates varies little across institutions, ranging from 32.4 years at CCC to 36.8 at CMC. Equally consistent is the distribution of controlling commitment offenses: while those institutions also housing higher classifications have on average more property crimes, the proportion of drug crimes in each institution is about 20 to 30 percent and property crimes between 15 to 25 percent.[57] The racial composition of inmates varies slightly more around the statewide average of about 33 percent each for whites, blacks, and Hispanics, with the percentage of whites lowest at CVSP (21.87) and highest at CCC (41.6). This is in part due to the geographic areas from which each institution primarily draws.[58] Despite these similarities, there are significant differences in the associational life of different Level II facilities. As the figure shows, prisons with higher percentages of people in gangs (based on correctional officer perceptions) have lower percentages of people involved in IACs (again, based on perceptions). The correlation between the two is -.59, and the relationship appears roughly linear.

A Tradeoff Between Safety and Democracy?

The survey of correctional officers also provides a more qualitative assessment of IAC activity. Activities by both gangs and IACs are seen by many officers as a direct response to issues in the prison, including problems between inmates and staff or problems with prison conditions. Not surprisingly, however, this is much more so the case for IACs than for gangs. When asked how frequently activity by each group is motivated by problems between inmates and staff, or problems with prison conditions, about 27 percent of officers say this is true of gangs often, very often, or all the time. Another 30 percent believe this to be true now and then, and 44 percent say this is true only rarely, very rarely, or never. By contrast, fully 58 percent believe that these sorts of issues motivate IAC activities often, very often, or all the time; 27 percent say this is true now and then; and only 14 percent say this is the case only rarely, very rarely, or never.

There are also differences in perceptions of how each organization contributes to the maintenance of prison security. While gangs are rarely seen by correctional officers as playing a positive role in the prison, this is not the case with IACs. About 29 percent of California officers believe that some types of IAC activity at the prison where they work makes the prison less safe, and another 34 percent feel that it has no effect. However, more than a third (38 percent) believe that the IAC actually makes their prison safer. By comparison, only 4 percent of officers believe that gang-related activity, in response to inmate problems with staff or prison conditions, makes the prison safer; 22 percent believe it to have no effect, and a full 74 percent feel that this makes the prison less safe.

Figure 11.3 shows the relationship between officer perceptions of the proportion of inmates in IACs relative to the proportion of inmates in gangs, and both general prison violence (Figure 11.3a) and gang violence, specifically (Figure 11.3b). As the figures show, the higher the estimated proportion of participation in IACs relative to gangs at a given institution, the lower the estimated rate of each type of violence. Specifically, the ratio of inmate participation in IACs relative to gangs is negatively correlated with gang violence at −.40, and negatively correlated with general prison violence at −.35.

As we have already described, however, prison institutions differ along a variety of dimensions—security level in particular—that are likely to be correlated with both participation in IACs and gangs and also with prison violence. We address this in a series of multiple regressions, in which we control for various categories of confounders. Each is measured at the level of the prison institution. We first employ four measures that help control for the risk of violence. These include the estimated number of different gangs at that institution (CCOS), the percentage of inmates classified at each security level, as dummy variables for Level I, II, and II (COMPSTAT), and overcrowding, measured as the proportion of housed inmates relative to the number of inmates for which an institution was designed (COMPSTAT). Our second set of variables helps to account for other types of inmate associations within the prison. These measures include levels of engagement by inmates in ILTAGs (COMPSTAT), Alcoholics Anonymous (COMPSTAT), Narcotics Anonymous (COMPSTAT), and veterans groups (COMPSTAT). Third, we include measures of formal program participation, such as academic programs (COMPSTAT), vocational programs (COMPSTAT), work assignments (COMPSTAT), and formal substance abuse treatment programs (COMPSTAT). Our last set of control variables captures basic measures of prison conditions: the extent to which dirt and litter are perceived as a problem (CCOS), the extent to which rodents and insects are a problem (CCOS), and a general subjective evaluation of the prison's physical condition (CCOS).

(a)

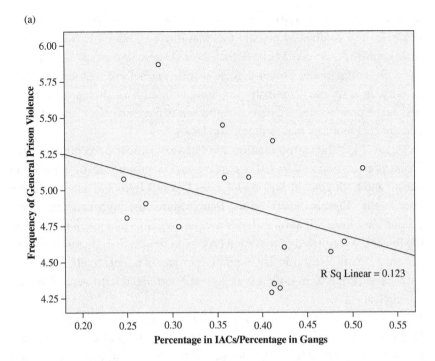

(b)

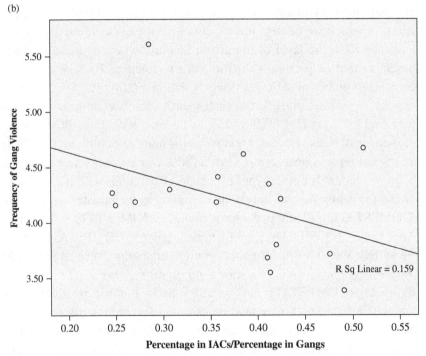

FIGURE 11.3 Violence and Proportional Participation in IACs and Gangs

11.3a. General Prison Violence

11.3b. Gang Violence

TABLE 11.1 Modeling the Relationship between IAC Participation (and IAC/Gang Participation) and Prison Violence

	WITHOUT CONTROLS	WITH CONTROLS FOR RISK OF VIOLENCE	WITH ALL CONTROLS
Specification 1			
IV: Proportion in IACs			
General violence	.01 (.006)#	−.011 (.004)*	−.009 (.007)
Gang-related violence	.026 (.020)	−.039 (.014)**	−.033 (.020)#
Specification 2			
IV: Proportion in IACs/Proportion in Gangs			
General violence	−.20 (.22)	−.13 (.28)***	−1.26 (.57)#
Gang-related violence	−3.01 (.57)***	−4.23 (.95)***	−3.5 (1.38)*

In multiple regressions (shown in Table 11.1), we estimate the relationships between our key independent variable—the estimated percentage of inmates involved in IACs, and also the percentage involved in IACs relative to the percent in gangs—and measures of both general prison violence and gang violence, specifically. We first estimate the simple bivariate relationships (shown in column I), then introduce controls for risk of violence (column II) and the full set of controls (column III). The results are generally confirmatory of our previous analyses. Greater participation in IACs, particularly in relation to the proportion of inmates estimated to be gang involved, is associated with decreased levels of both general and gang-related violence.

Individual Level Data on Inmate Councils and Safety

In these basic models, there appears to be a negative relationship between inmate councils in California and the incidence of prison violence, both gang and non-gang related. While not confirmatory, this should at least call into question the idea that participatory avenues for inmates diminish the security of the prison by increasing violence or gang activity. However, we might be concerned that officers' evaluations, which are the source of the data we have just described, may not be an accurate portrayal of inmate behavior, either in terms of IAC participation rates or real rates of violence. We might also be concerned that an analysis at the level of the institution does not accurately capture the individual-level behaviors at the root of our inquiry: inmate participation in IACs, and inmate's engagement in violence. We therefore turn to our other source of data, the Bureau of Justice Statistics inmate survey, which reports perceptions of violence and council participation from inmates themselves, and which is available at the level of the individual prisoner.

Our main outcomes of interest come from questions unique to this year of the survey. First, inmates were asked "how safe do you feel from being hit, punched, or assaulted by other inmates?" and given a choice of five response categories (safe, somewhat safe, neither safe nor unsafe, somewhat unsafe, unsafe). Slightly over half of inmates (54 percent) felt safe from physical assault, 20 percent felt somewhat safe, 8 percent felt neutral, 8 percent felt somewhat unsafe, and 11 percent reported feeling unsafe. Inmates were also asked about their participation in fights and the actual incidence of violence against them: "Since your admission, have you been in any fights or been hit or punched?" Of the total sample, about 22 percent of inmates reported that they had been in a fight or been assaulted. Unfortunately, and in contrast to the California data, the inmate survey did not seek to measure gang involvement or the frequency of gang activity at the facility.

In addition, inmates were asked about their involvement with various organizations and programs within the prison. Our main explanatory variable is whether the inmate was involved in one type of group in particular: inmate assistance groups (which include worker unions, advisory councils, inmate liaison groups, and prisoner counseling groups). Among the inmates in the sample, 8.2 percent reported participating in such a group, a proportion that did not significantly vary by security level or facility type. To compare, participation in other groups ranged from a high of one-third in bible clubs and one-third in groups like Alcoholics Anonymous to 15 percent in groups like Jaycees and Toastmasters, to a low of 5 percent in ethnic/racial groups like the NAACP.

In the analysis that follows and consistent with our institutional analysis from California presented above, we include a variety of controls that reflect differences in an individual's risk of violence, as well as differences at the level of the facility where prisoners are housed. Although the BJS data do not include information about prison conditions and quality (i.e., overcrowding), we control for other factors related to the prison experience: housing type (dorm, individual cell, etc.); type of housed population (general population, administrative segregation, protective, etc.); number of people housed where you sleep; facility type (community based or confinement); state or federal prison; gender of prison; security level; and region. We also control for inmate characteristics and risk of violence: participation in other programs and groups (job training, work assignments, educational, religious groups and activities, life skills classes, substance abuse groups, ethnic/racial organizations, outside community activities, and arts and crafts); individual demographics (age, race, gender); offense category (violent, drug, property, public order); criminal history, prior incarceration and prior arrests; criminal justice status (sentenced, awaiting trial, etc.); and whether the individual was ever armed when committing crimes.[59]

At the bivariate level, there does not appear to be a tradeoff between perceptions of physical security and inmate participation in councils, but neither is council participation related to diminished perceptions of threats to physical safety (see Table 11.2). Approximately 72 percent of inmates in councils felt safe or somewhat safe from physical assault compared to 74 percent of inmates who did not report participating in councils. The difference was not statistically significant or substantively meaningful. Explorations of these associations by security level or facility type did not reveal a difference in this general pattern. Introducing controls for features of the prison environment and risk of violence did not change this relationship. There does appear to be a positive relationship between participation in inmate assistance groups and being in physical altercations since admission to prison at the bivariate level. However, once controls for facility type and background characteristics of the inmate are introduced, there is no longer a statistically meaningful relationship.

TABLE 11.2 Modeling the Relationship between Participation in Inmate Assistance Groups and Subjective Perceptions of Safety and Violence

OUTCOME OF INTEREST	WITHOUT CONTROLS	WITH CONTROLS FOR RISK OF VIOLENCE	WITH ALL CONTROLS
Subjective Perception of Security From Violence ("Feel Safe")	.033 (.059)	.022 (.061)	−.092 (.066)
Been in a Fight, Hit, Punched in Prison	.470*** (.066)	.432*** (.073)	.117 (.084)
N	17,307	17,026	17,026

Discussion

In this chapter, we have examined the question of whether participation in prison self-governance organizations is associated with higher rates of violence. Using three data sources, and at two levels of analysis, we find little evidence of a positive correlation. At the individual level, we find no statistically significant association between how safe inmates feel or whether they have been involved in physical confrontations and participation in inmate councils, worker groups (unions), liaison, or prisoner counseling groups. At the institution level, we actually find a *negative* relationship between officer perceptions of the proportion of inmates participating in inmate self-governance organizations and levels of both general violence and gang-related violence specifically. This relationship remains unchanged when a variety of controls are introduced. These findings are important, as the idea that allowing inmate advisory councils might jeopardize the safety and security of the institution has been used as a legal and theoretical justification for banning these types of organizations; the argument in *Jones v. North Carolina* and in other cases has frequently been that limiting association is necessary to secure safety and order within the prison. In our admittedly preliminary assessment, we find no compelling empirical evidence to support this claim. In fact, where a relationship does appear, it seems to point to a potentially positive role of IACs; as the proportion of inmates participating in advisory councils increases, prison violence appears to be less of a concern.

It might still be true that safety and self-governance are legitimately in conflict at some institutions and that these instances are not represented in these data. Most obviously, we might not see an association because inmates are not given the opportunity to participate in associations at particular prison institutions. In California, advisory councils are mandated by policy. However, prison administrators still maintain discretion to disband councils if they are seen as promoting or contributing to violence: "The membership of representatives or the activities of the entire council may be suspended when the warden determines that the representative or council presents a threat to facility security or the safety of persons, or that the representative's or council's actions are counterproductive to the best interest and welfare of the general inmate population."[60] Councils therefore might be banned in locations where they have been previously co-opted by gangs or used as locations for violent activity. At these places, we would not be able to see what happens if participation increases, because inmates do not have the opportunity to take part in (absent or limited) organizations.

The analysis we have presented here is therefore just a first cut at an important set of questions, and begs nearly as many questions as it answers. First and foremost, we recognize a number of ways that the data employed here are imperfectly suited to our task. The CCOS data provide the only comprehensive measure we know of that specifically assesses levels of IAC participation across all of California's adult prisons. However, this measure is taken from a survey and so represents the subjective assessment of prison personnel. We would prefer a more objective measure, such as IAC meeting attendance, proportion of inmates casting votes in IAC elections, or other indicators taken from administrative records. Unfortunately, no such data are available. The individual data we employ here are likewise from surveys, and so are likewise potentially subject to biases, misreporting, and subjectivity.

We also have little information in our data about the character of participation in governance councils, or the quality of the councils themselves. It is not hard to imagine that participation can mean a range of things—from running for or holding office to regularly participating in IAC activities to little more than casting the occasional ballot when new leadership is elected—that have different consequences for how the council operates within the prison. Similarly, as we have already mentioned, some advisory councils might be well organized, respected, and impartial arbiters that play an important role within the prison; others may be weak, co-opted by gangs or by staff, and be generally dismissed by the prison administration rather than taken seriously as a part of how decisions are made. Understanding the nuances of how these organizations work would be a necessary precursor to a more robust analysis of their effects on violence and other outcomes.

And finally, the question of causality is key here, and unfortunately outside the scope of this chapter. Our data provide us with the ability to paint a broad picture of the descriptive relationship between IAC participation and violence. Despite having modeled this relationship with a host of controls, we cannot rule out the possibility of a confounding variable that both decreases violence and increases IAC participation. Similarly, we are certainly not able to untangle any direction of causality; to the extent that we see a significant correlation, we do not know whether more IAC participation leads to lower violence, or lower violence enables greater participation in IACs.

In light of this, our most pressing implication is a call for a renewed interest in the role that inmate self-governance organizations, as well as related associations like inmate unions, can and do play in the operation of American prisons. While the literature of the 1960s and 1970s provides more optimism than evidence on the wide range of effects that such organizations could have, we argue that there are compelling reasons to believe that self-governance organizations might indeed have the capacity to shape individual and institutional outcomes in important ways. In addition, Americans have long held that self-governance is a fundamental aspect of American citizenship that should be fiercely protected from unnecessary restriction. As de Tocqueville observed, local government is critical because individual participation in self-governance molds democratic citizens and safeguards democracy. The same, we would suggest, might well hold true for those in the nation's prisons.

More broadly, we would argue that the internal management and culture of prison institutions has been too long neglected as a topic of serious inquiry. As the United States neared the end of the first decade of the new century, fully one in every hundred American adults was behind bars. For racial minorities and the poor, the proportions in prison and jail are significantly higher. Thus, prisons and other criminal justice institutions have become a primary point of contact between citizens and the state, and a key part of the infrastructure of our nation's governance and democracy. Understanding the complex inner worlds of correctional institutions, and the role that prisons play in shaping violence and a host of other individual and social outcomes, remains a critical topic of inquiry.

Notes

1. Pew Center on the States, *One in 100: Behind Bars in America* (Washington, DC: The Pew Charitable Trust, 2008).

2. Amy Lerman, *The Modern Prison Paradox* (Cambridge: Cambridge University Press, 2014).

3. Malcolm M. Feeley and Jonathan Simon. The New Penology: Notes on the Emerging Strategy and Its Implications, *Criminology* 30, no. 339 (1992): 449-474

4. Amy Lerman and Vesla Weaver, *Arresting Citizenship: The Democratic Consequences of American Crime Control* (Chicago: University of Chicago Press, 2014).

5. *Jones v. North Carolina Prisoners' Union*, 433 US 119 (1977).

6. Lerman and Weaver, *Arresting Citizenship*.

7. John J. DiIulio, *Governing Prisons* (New York: Simon and Schuster, 1990), 237.

8. Lerman and Weaver, *Arresting Citizenship*.

9. Ibid.

10. Enver Solomon and Kimmett Edgar, *Having Their Say: The Work of Prisoner Councils* (London: Prison Reform Trust, 2004).

11. J. E. Baker, "Inmate Self-Government," *Journal of Criminal Law, Criminology, and Police Science* 55, no. 1 (1964): 39–47.

12. Elmer H. Johnson, "Potential of Inmate Self-Government," *Criminology* 15, no. 2 (1977): 165–178; Charles Stastny and Gabrielle Tyrnauer, *Who Rules the Joint?: The Changing Political Culture of Maximum-Security Prisons in America* (Lanthan, MD: Lexington Books, 1982).

13. Seth Allan Bloomberg, "Participatory Management: Toward a Science of Correctional Management," *Criminology* 15, no. 2 (1977): 149–163, 151.

14. Stastny and Tyrnauer, *Who Rules the Joint?*, 54.

15. Burt Useem and Peter Kimball, *States of Siege: U.S. Prison Riots, 1971–1986* (Oxford: Oxford University Press, 1991).

16. Susan Blankenship, "Revisiting the Democratic Promise of Prisoners' Labor Unions," *Studies in Law, Politics and Society* 37 (2005), 241-269.

17. Stastny and Tyrnauer, *Who Rules the Joint?*, 154.

18. Ibid., 93.

19. Christopher D. Berk, "On Prison Democracy: The Politics of Participation in a Maximum Security Prison." Accepted for publication at *Critical Inquiry*.

20. Ibid.

21. James L. Regens and William Hobson, "Inmate Self-Government and Attitude Change: An Assessment of Participation Effects," *Evaluation Quarterly* 2, no. 3 (1978): 455-479.

22. Gresham M. Sykes, *The Society of Captives: A Study of a Maximum Security Prison* (Princeton, NJ: Princeton University Press, 2007).

23. Bradley B. Falkoff, "Prisoner Representative Organizations, Prison Reform, and Jones V. North Carolina Prisoners' Labor Union," *Journal of Criminal Law and Criminology* 70, no. 1 (1979): 42–56.

24. Sidney Zonn, "Inmate Unions: An Appraisal of Prisoner Rights and Labor Implications," *University of Miami Law Review* 32 (1977): 613-635.

25. Quoted in Regina Montoya and Paul Coggins, "Future of Prisoners' Unions: Jones v. North Carolina Prisoners' Labor Union," *Harvard Civil Rights – Civil Liberties Law Review* 13 no. 3 (1978):799-826. (1978): 801.

26. Zonn, "Inmate Unions," 629.

27. Ibid, 627.

28. They argued that "prisoners eventually would be stripped of all constitutional rights, and would retain only those privileges that prison officials, in their 'informed discretion,' designed to recognize. The sole constitutional constraint on prison officials would be a requirement that they act rationally." Quoted in Zonn, "Inmate Unions," 629.

29. Falkoff, "Prisoner Representative Organizations," 47.

30. One case held that prisons had to allow legal communication from lawyers on union-related matters. Another upheld an inmate's right to wear a union pin. See Michael Mushlin, *Rights of Prisoners, St. Paul, MN: Thomson West* (Thomson West, 2002).

31. United States Department of Justice, Bureau of Justice Statistics, *Survey of Inmates in State and Federal Correctional Facilities, 2004*, ICPSR04572-v1 (Ann Arbor: Inter-University Consortium for Political and Social Research [distributor], 2007-02-28), http://doi.org/10.3886/ICPSR04572.v1

32. Enver Solomon, "Criminals or Citizens? Prisoner Councils and Rehabilitation," *Criminal Justice Matters* 56, no. 1 (2004): 24–25; Tom Murton, "Shared Decision Making as a Treatment Technique in Prison Management," *Offender Rehabilitation* 1,

no. 1 (1976): 17–31; Thomas P. Wilson, "Patterns of Management and Adaptations to Organizational Roles: A Study of Prison Inmates," *American Journal of Sociology* 74, no. 2 (1968): 146–157; Hans Toch, "Inmate Involvement in Prison Governance," *Federal Probation* 59, no. 2 (1995): 34. While journalistic, one account reveals many benefits: Alice Fishburn, "The Inmates Who May Hold the Key to the Prisons Dilemma" *The Times* (London), National Edition, 66–67 July 2, 2010. http://www.thetimes.co.uk/tto/law/article2583373.ece

33. Baker, "Inmate Self-Government"; Paul R. Comeau, "Labor Unions for Prison Inmates: An Analysis of a Recent Proposal for the Organization of Inmate Labor," *Buffalo Law Revier.* 21 (1971): 963-986.

34. Tom Watson, "Part 2: Alternative Methods and Problems, Bringing Complaints Through the Mens' Advisory Council," in Prison Appeals System, www.oocities.org/three_strikes_legal/prison_appeals.htm.

35. Ibid.

36. Solomon and Edgar, *Having Their Say*, 15.

37. Lerman and Weaver, *Arresting Citizenship*.

38. Solomon, "Criminals or Citizens?," 26.

39. Comeau, "Labor Unions," 985.

40. Luis Jorge DeGraffe, "Prisoners' Unions: A Potential Contribution to the Rehabilitation of the Incarcerated," *New England Journal on Criminal and Civil Confinement* 16, no. 2 (1990): 234.

41. Lerman and Weaver, *Arresting Citizenship*.

42. Blankenship, "Democratic Promise of Prisoners' Labor Unions," 261.

43. Ibid.

44. Solomon, "Criminals or Citizens?," 25.

45. DeGraffe, "Prisoners' Unions," 228.

46. Comeau, "Labor Unions," 976.

47. Sacha Darke, "Inmate Governance in Brazilian Prisons," *Howard Journal of Criminal Justice* 52, no. 3 (2013): 272–284.

48. Graeme Wood, "How Gangs Took Over Prison Councils," *The Atlantic*, October 2014.

49. David B. Kalinich and Stan Stojkovic, "Contraband The Basis for Legitimate Power in a Prison Social System," *Criminal Justice and Behavior* 12, no. 4 (1985): 435–451.

50. Solomon, "Criminals or Citizens?," 25.

51. California Department of Corrections and Rehabilitation, "California Code of Regulations: Title 15, Crime Prevention and Corrections" Subchapter 3: Inmate Councils, Committees, and Activity Groups, http://www.cdcr.ca.gov/regulations/adult_operations/docs/Title15-2015.pdf.

52. Ibid.

53. Ibid.

54. Lerman, *Modern Prison Paradox*.

55. US Dept. of Justice, Bureau of Justice Statistics, and US Dept. of Justice, Federal Bureau of Prisons. *Survey of Inmates in State and Federal Correctional Facilities, 1997*. Compiled by US Dept. of Commerce, Bureau of the Census. ICPSR ed. (Ann Arbor: Inter-University Consortium for Political and Social Research [producer and distributor], 2000).

56. There are eleven institutions in the state of California that admit male inmates with a Level II security classification. These include Avenal State Prison (ASP), California Correctional Center (CCC), California Correctional Institution (CCI), California Men's Colony (CMC), CA Rehabilitation Center (CRC), San Quentin State Prison (SQ), Folsom State Prison (FOL), CA Substance Abuse Treatment Facility (SATF), Chuckawalla Valley State Prison (CVSP), Sierra Conservation Center (SCC), and California State Prison, Solano (CSP-SOL).

57. Exceptions to this are CRC, where the drug rehabilitation program accepts a large number of inmates committed on short sentences for drug crimes, and SCC, which houses a higher percentage of property crime offenders deemed eligible for training in firefighting. In both cases, however, these populations are housed separately.

58. County of commitment varies between the populations of each prison, as the state attempts to place inmates as close to their county of residence as possible. For example, San Quentin, located in the northern part of the state near the San Francisco Bay, reports 72.8 percent of its inmates committed from that part of the state. Nearby CCC and Solano report 56 percent and 75.3 percent respectively from the Bay Area and North and Central areas combined. Conversely, Southern California prisons predominantly house Southern California inmates, at levels of 89 percent, 76.5 percent, and 77.6 percent for CCI, CMC, and CRC respectively.

59. Due to missingness on this last item, we run models both with and without it. Substantive results do not change.

60. California Department of Corrections and Rehabilitation, Subchapter 3 Inmate Activities.

CHAPTER 12 | Violent Crime, Constitutional
Frameworks, and Mass Publics

LISA L. MILLER

Introduction

Violent crime is what public policy scholars refer to as a "valence" issue.[1]
Whereas one can be for or against the criminalization of other activities,
such as illicit drugs or pornographic movies, there is only one side of the
violent crime issue: *everyone is against it.* To be sure, there is plenty of
disagreement about the causes of, and appropriate mechanisms for ameliorating, violence; but no interest groups, social movements, political parties,
or popular initiatives openly advocate decriminalizing aggravated assault,
robbery, or rape, let alone murder. As Stuart Scheingold noted thirty years
ago, movies, television, and novels frequently draw on our collective fears
of such events—murder of children, rape of a loved one, armed robbery or
brutal assault of a friend—and then offer us satisfying retributive consequences for the guilty parties.[2]

   This reality about violent crime as a social and political issue has led to
three core assumptions at the intersection of democratic political institutions and crime: first, that the fear-realm of the brain will almost always
trump the more rational, frontal lobe, leading to rash policymaking;
second, that lawmakers will find crime a valuable electoral political com-
modity; and third, that the public, writ large, will serve as a hanging judge,
brooking little by way of excuses from offenders about the circumstances
that led them to their criminal ways.

   What follows from these foundations is that democratic systems that
provide for mechanisms through which the public can readily influence
policymaking on crime and punishment—for example, referenda, local

election of mayors and prosecutors, many elections, and many venues for political participation—are likely to produce more punitive policy outcomes than those where elected officials and criminal justice experts are more insulated from public pressure. The United States, in this formulation, is the veritable poster child for excessive democratic influence.[3]

In this chapter I reconsider this assessment, and argue that while institutional design vis-à-vis constitutional structures is a crucial aspect of the politics of crime and punishment in democratic systems, the concept of democratic accountability on crime issues, as well as the assumptions about mass publics and crime, are deeply undertheorized. As a result, the presence of many elections and venues for political engagement are conflated with democratic accountability, and punitive policy output is taken as evidence of a punitive electorate. These conclusions, I argue, are rooted in an overreliance on the US case and a fundamental misunderstanding about the nature of American politics and policy.

In contrast to conventional wisdom, I propose that the United States suffers from a *democratic deficit*, in broad terms, and a particularly deep deficit with respect to violence and punishment, stemming from precisely the institutional arrangements that scholars typically equate with heightened political participation and accountability. This counterintuitive claim is rooted in a definition of democratic accountability that requires real government capacity to respond to social risks, and few opportunities for vetoing the preferences of mass publics. Thus, I turn traditional understandings on their head and argue that American constitutional arrangements *inhibit* the accountability of lawmakers to mass publics on a wide range of social risks, including crime. This then leads to ad hoc, fragmented social policymaking that contributes to high levels of violence and reduces trust in the capacity of the state to respond to risk of violence in any way other than through high levels of punishment. By contrast, constitutional systems that *facilitate* accountability to public demand are likely to have less crime and less punishment.

I begin by defining two core concepts: democratic accountability and security from violence. In the first concept, I argue for a definition of democratic accountability that includes, at a minimum, the *capacity* of governing parties or coalitions to implement their preferred policies, and the citizenry to know *whom* to hold accountable for policy outcomes. On the concept of security from violence, I highlight the political significance of serious crime. I then compare the United States and the United Kingdom on these dimensions, paying particular attention to fundamental constitutional arrangements, including unitary versus federal arrangements, parliamentary versus presidential systems, the role of political parties, and the place of the judiciary.

I contrast these two countries because, on the one hand, both have common-law legal structures, two-party systems, and share a wide range of social, cultural, linguistic, and economic values and institutions. Moreover, they are frequently conceptually linked in the literature by a number of prominent scholars, including David Garland and Nicola Lacey.[4] However, the two countries diverge on several key constitutional structures: notably, the United Kingdom is a (largely) unitary, Parliamentary system, with little intervention by courts into lawmaking, while the United States is a federal, presidential (separation of powers) system with state-wide referenda and extensive judicial review. Moreover, though both countries experienced increases in imprisonment in the latter half of the twentieth century, rates of imprisonment and rates of violence are dramatically higher in the United States than in the United Kingdom. The *lowest* homicide rate in the United States in the postwar period (4.6 per 100,000 in the early 1950s), for example, was nearly two and a half times higher than the *highest* rate in England and Wales (1.9 per 100,000 in the early 2000s). Peak homicide rates in the United States are three or four times the highest rates in Britain. Imprisonment rates display similarly dramatic disparities. In 2000, the US imprisonment rate of nearly 700 per 100,000 dwarfs that of England and Wales (124) and Scotland (116).

Democratic Accountability and Security from Violence as a Public Good

In the area of crime and punishment, as noted above, democratic accountability is largely seen as dangerous.[5] The term "accountability," however, is rarely defined, let alone understood as a continuum that would allow us to discern lower or higher versions of it. Here I propose several crucial criteria for democratic systems if we are to deem them highly accountable to the public. I do not suggest that these are the only features of democratic accountability (certainly free and fair elections are fundamental), but, rather, I focus on institutional dimensions that facilitate or hinder the capacity of the electorate retain *meaningful power* to turn out governments that are unable or unwilling to attend to the needs, and fulfill the interests, of the large groups of people who elected them.[6] Where institutional obstacles exist to such outcomes, democratic accountability is diminished.

At a minimum, two features of political institutions that originate in constitutional structures are essential for democratic systems to advance public goods. First, issues of pressing public need must be addressed in political venues with the capacity to respond to those needs. The severing of political capacity—both in fiscal and logistical terms—from electoral liability renders democratic accountability more difficult. Such arrangements run the risk of providing the *illusion* of accountability without the ensuing *capabilities* to offer change, causing voters to suffer from jurisdictional confusion, and hampering their ability to know whom to hold accountable. I have elsewhere referred to this as equating political responsiveness with political accountability.[7] The two are not one and the same.

To be sure, this type of electoral liability—the coupling of responsiveness with the institutional capacity to make policy change—is precisely what worries those who advocate insulating criminal justice decision-making from the public. My point here is that a definition of democratic accountability that is defined by the exposure of lawmakers to the demands of the electorate must also take account of whether the elected officials are actually situated to make a broad range of policy changes once they are in government. Where concerns about social risks—employment, health, education, and violence, for example—are politically salient and contribute to election outcomes, fiscal capacity must match this agenda to make democratic accountability real.[8]

Second, elected government must be able to enact the social policy proposals it has proffered, once elected. That is, the public must have confidence that, if elected, the promised policies and reforms can readily be passed into law and implemented. Where majority-elected governments or plurality coalitions can be stymied by multiple obstructions and veto points, democratic accountability is diminished because mass publics cannot translate their preferences into actual policy.

Multiple veto points in the political process, for example, can allow elites, whose need for public goods is less acute, to block efforts by the majority to redistribute benefits and burdens in ways that spread benefits across a wider range of the population.[9] Veto points may also allow extreme views to block more centrist ones that address the needs of mass majorities, and sectarian cleavages can be exacerbated where comprehensive social policy benefits can be conferred on some populations and not others. I will say more about this later, but for now, I simply wish to highlight the general problem of institutional obstacles to implementing majority or plurality preference as a contraindication of democratic accountability.

In brief, in order for the collective needs of the citizenry, writ large, to be met, there must be mechanisms through which those needs can be named and shaped into political preferences. Moreover, the political capacity of institutions must allow governing parties to produce the policies they promised the electorate, and fiscal capacity and electoral accountability must be closely aligned. To the extent that these features are severely constrained, democratic accountability is as well.

Security from Violence

The other concept of central importance that requires some discussion here is security from violence.[10] Understanding how constitutional arrangements shape the political dynamics of crime and punishment requires situating both in the larger context of the role of the state in ameliorating (or exacerbating) social risks. Security from violence is a foundational role of the state, a core value, and state obligation. Ian Loader and Neil Walker have provided a particularly compelling account of this crucial state function with respect to the police and the role law enforcement plays in modern governance.[11]

The focus on imprisonment and other repressive practices in criminological scholarship has obscured the fact that insulating members of the body politic from random acts of violence is a first-order political problem. Taken together, security from street violence *and* from state violence form the core expectations of the modern state. This is a substantially different understanding of the intersection of crime and politics from those who view them as so deeply intertwined as to be largely indistinguishable. In that view crime is a political framework available for myriad ends, rather than an objective social condition that legitimately worries the body politic.[12] I do not preclude such understandings here, but I wish to draw attention to the real problem of serious violence and the collective interest of the polity in securing protection from it.

To do so, I begin from the premise that security from violent crime is a social good, much like low unemployment, protection from communicable disease, and access to basic healthcare. While all democracies, particularly those with less regulated market economies, have disparities in the degree to which these goods are distributed across racial, ethnic, and sectarian cleavages, in the aggregate they are markers of the health and well-being of a polity. Indeed, democracies vary in the extent to which state provision of such goods is more or less equal across the population. In some cases, as I argue below, discreet populations within a polity are routinely exposed to substantially more risk than others. Situating violent crime in this context allows us to think more systematically about the relationship between institutional structure and the capacity of the state to insulate the body politic from serious social and material risk.

Contrasting the United Kingdom and the United States

US Exceptionalism in Violence and Punishment

Though often linked, the United States and Britain are quite different with respect to crime, criminal justice and political institutions. As Table 12.1 illustrates, the United States is an outlier on lethal violence and by large margins. At their lowest rates in the postwar period, homicide was *seven times* as common in the United States as in England and Wales and Scotland. Peak rates exhibit a narrowing of this gap, but still the difference was four to fivefold. In fact, the peak rates throughout Britain were lower than the lowest rates in the United States. This is also reflected in the life risk data, which calculates the likelihood of being murdered if the homicide rate were to remain stagnant at the peak rate for an average lifespan. An astonishing one in 133 Americans could expect to be murdered, had homicide rates remained at 10.2 per 100,00, as they were in 1980.

It is also important to note that although the annual homicide rate peaked in 1980 in the United States, the three-year moving average for homicide in 1980 was 9.6 and in 1993, it was 9.5. Peak rates are often cited as an illustration of how crime and imprisonment are unrelated after 1980, but this overlooks the persistently high rates of violence in the United States and the second peak of serious violence in the 1990s. It is not until the turn of the twenty-first century that the drop in homicide appears to be a real and sustained phenomenon.

TABLE 12.1 Homicide Differences, England and Wales, Scotland, United States*

	ENGLAND AND WALES	SCOTLAND	UNITED STATES
Homicide rate in 1960	0.62	0.66	4.7
Homicide rate at peak	1.9 (2003)	2.8 (1980)	10.2 (1980)
Difference with US at peak	+437%	+264%	—
Lifetime risk at peak	670	480	130

Of course, race and class stratification means that some populations are more insulated from this risk than others. Minority populations and the poor are consistently more likely to be victims of murder than whites and the well-off in both the United Kingdom and the United States.[13] It would be a mistake, however, to see murder as an issue that primarily concerns racial minorities in the United States. While rates are highly disproportionate, whites in the United States, especially males, are also murdered at much higher rates than those in the United Kingdom At the peak of white homicide in 1980, nearly eleven white males per 100,000 were murdered, compared to less than two per 100,000 around the peak of homicides in England and Wales in the early 2000s.[14] Moreover, between 1965 and 1985, the rate of homicide for white males in the United States increased to a greater extent than other race/gender combinations. Thus, homicide in the United States is a much more pronounced and prevalent social condition than in the United Kingdom, *across* demographic groups.

As shown in Table 12.2, the United States also has much harsher sanctions compared to the United Kingdom. Mandatory life sentences, as well as life sentences without parole (LWOP), apply only to murder in both England and Wales and Scotland, but in the United States, a much wider array of serious crimes are subject to such sanctions. In at least thirty-seven states,

TABLE 12.2 Criminal Justice Differences, England and Wales, Scotland, United States[*]

	ENGLAND AND WALES	SCOTLAND	UNITED STATES
Incarceration rate 2008–9	153	120	753
Scope of mandatory life sentence	Murder only	Murder only	Murder, drug kingpins, habitual offenders
Mandatory life sentences for juveniles	No	No	Yes
Average prison term served under mandatory life sentence	16	13	Variable, but some states at least 25 years
Scope of life without parole sentence ("whole life")	Murder only	Murder only	Murder, drugs, sexual assault, aggravated assault
Death penalty	No (abolished 1965)	No (abolished 1965)	Yes—43 people executed across nine states in 2012

[*] *Note:* International Centre for Prison Statistics (www.prisonstudies.org), Scottish Police Services (www.sps.gov.uk), Bureau of Justice Statistics (www.bjs.gov).

LWOP sentences are available for crimes such as burglary, car jacking, kidnapping, and robbery. In addition, while LWOP is mandatory for murder in some states, it is also mandatory for habitual offenders in some states.[15] Both mandatory and LWOP sentences can also be applied to offenders who were juveniles at the time of their offense. Such sentencing practices increased in the last few decades in the United States at the same time that the United Kingdom was eliminating mandatory life sentences for crimes other than homicide. And, of course, the death penalty is the extreme outlier with respect to sanctions for criminal conduct. The United States is alone, among rich democracies, in continuing to use this ultimate penalty.

Constitutional Systems Compared

There are also important constitutional differences across these countries, listed in Table 12.3. Notably, the United States has many more legislative venues through a combination of federalism, decentralization, separation of powers, coequal chambers of the legislature, and judicial supremacy, than the United Kingdom. Though federalism and decentralization are often conflated, they are distinct institutional arrangements that have different effects on political processes. At their most basic level, federations are governmental structures characterized by (at least) two loci of political authority, each with constitutionally prescribed bargaining power in relation to one another.[16] Devolution of specific and delineated authority to subnational governments, as in the creation of the Scottish Parliament in 1999, can generate more or less negotiation, bargaining, and tension between units, depending on how clearly authority is delineated in the devolving legislation.

TABLE 12.3 Institutional Differences, United States and United Kingdom

	UNITED STATES	UNITED KINGDOM
Organization of powers	Presidential	Parliamentary
Federalism/unitary	Hyperfederalism	Unitary/Quasi-federal (Scotland)
Strength of parties	Weak	Moderate
Legislative chambers	Two—coequal	Two—House of Commons supreme
Public initiated policy	Referenda provisions	Rare referenda
Judiciary	Judicial supremacy	Some judicial review
Voter turnout	62.77% (high—1960)	77.7% (high—1992)
(high and lo, 1960-2010)	49.0% (low—1996)	59.4% (low—2001)

Note: Voter Turnout from UK Election Statistics: 1918–2004 House of Commons Library 28 July 2004; Voter Turnout from U.S., Presidency Project, University of California Santa Barbara.

Decentralization, by contrast, largely refers to the delegation of authority from the central government to subordinate units. Such practices often provide some degree of local control or local autonomy in policy implementation in ways that allow local authorities to tailor central policy formulations to local interests. The basic contours of social policy, however, are determined at the level of centralized authority, and such policies can be recentralized without negotiating constitutional rules. The distinction is important because in federalism, jurisdictional control is a result of negotiation and bargaining whereas with decentralization, the central government decides major policy but implementation occurs "downstream" at lower levels of government.

Taking a closer look at each constitutional structure will help to illuminate the extent to which each system facilitates or hinders democratic accountability.

United Kingdom

The United Kingdom is a combination of both decentralization and federalism, though the latter in only a limited sense. The long history of Scotland as a distinct people and culture, as well as the fact that some policy areas—namely law and education—have always been separated from Westminster, means that devolution has not, to date, generated the kind of jurisdictional uncertainty or fluidity that characterizes the United States and to a lesser degree, Canada.[17] Though there is some evidence that Scotland follows England and Wales on certain public safety policy and programs, particularly recent emphases on situational crime prevention, it is also clear that the Scottish tradition of linking crime prevention with social justice, egalitarianism and the challenges of urban inequality are a separate and distinctive tradition.[18] The Police and Crime Commissioners (PCC) in England, by contrast, are a kind of decentralization where criminal statutes and policing policy remain centralized, but the PCCs provide opportunities for local implementation to be responsive to local communities and needs.

In practice, England, Wales, and Northern Ireland, function largely as a unitary, Parliamentary system, and Scotland forms a kind of partial federalism. Notwithstanding potential changes such as substantial devolution to Wales and Northern Ireland, the supremacy of the British Parliament over the vast majority of laws is an important political institutional context and contrasts sharply with the United States.

With respect to legislative chambers, the British Parliament does have a second chamber in the House of Lords, though it is all but impossible for the Lords to override actions of the House of Commons, particularly where there is broad popular support for the party in control of the Commons. Traditionally, the House of Lords served the function of judicial review, though its power today is largely limited to slowing down the legislative process with respect to legislation to which it objects. The ability of the House of Lords to reject Acts passed by Parliament is all but nil.

The creation of the UK Supreme Court in 2009 (Constitutional Reform Act of 2005), however, introduces some new dimensions into the British constitutional system. In addition to assuming the judicial functions that had been exercised by the House of Lords, the Supreme Court can also make declarations of incompatibility, consistent with the Human Rights Act of 1998 and the European Court of Human Rights. Notably, however, the Supreme Court does not have authority to directly overturn acts passed by Parliament.

United States

By contrast, the United States is a complex combination of federalism, separation of powers, decentralization, local control, as well as judicial supremacy. The national government increased its jurisdictional reach considerably in the decades after the Second World War, sometimes enacting and implementing policy on its own and other times devolving policy implementation to the states, with wide latitude on standards and practices (c.f., civil rights, environmental regulation, workplace protection). State governments, meanwhile, have maintained constitutional authority to enact legislation in a wide range of areas entirely on their own, such as education, crime, insurance regulation, consumer protection, and healthcare, so long as they do not run afoul of a few, specific national rules, and they are often offered incentives by the federal government—in the way of support for core projects such as roads, for example—for adopting federal law.[19] A long history of constitutional federalism recognizes these state powers and the more conservative justices of the Supreme Court have reiterated that national lawmakers may not extinguish state power altogether or render it superfluous.[20] Moreover, many local municipal governments in the United States are also empowered through statute or state constitutions to enact public policy in their interest on issues such as education, minimum wage, housing, and policing.[21]

While many of the major jurisdictional battles over policy are long settled, the simple fact that constitutional and statutory powers reside in many different places at once generates a complexity and "thickness"—that is, a high level of institutional density and jurisdictional disarray—which stands in contrast to the more unified and centralized Parliamentary system in Britain.

Adding to the jurisdictional complexity in the United States is separation of powers in two ways: the two chambers of the US Congress (House of Representatives and the Senate, elected separately and coequal in lawmaking); and separation of powers between Congress and the president. All members of the House of Representative, along with one-third of the Senate, stand for reelection every two years and every other cycle includes the general election for president. Alongside elections for national office, state gubernatorial elections are on the ballot for a portion of the states. On odd years after presidential elections, two states, New Jersey and Virginia, hold elections for governor.

On top of this plethora of electoral opportunities and legislative spaces, twenty-six states also have some form of referenda, thirty-eight states have judicial elections for at least some of their judgeships, forty-seven states elect chief prosecutors (all but Alaska, Connecticut, and New Jersey), and many of the over 19,000 municipalities in the country elect the chief prosecutor (district attorneys).

The federal court system is yet another venue, albeit a distant one. The tendency of American political conflicts to work their way into the legal system is as at least as old as Tocqueville's prescient observations in *Democracy in America*, and current research suggests that the use of law as a means to solve political conflict remains an important feature of American politics.[22] The Supreme Court of the United States not only has substantially more power the that of the United Kingdom—including the power to declare acts of legislatures and executives unconstitutional, rendering them void—but, due to the ambiguity and fluidity of the jurisdictional authority of Congress, hears many cases involving some of the most contentious and important social policy issues in the country, serving as a kind of über-decision-making body of judges.

The Limits of Fragmentation and Checks and Balances

Taken together on a prima facie basis—local, state, and national legislative venues, separation of powers, referenda—there would appear to be more than enough political spaces for the American public to hold its lawmakers accountable for their actions or inactions. Multiple venues seem to require a high degree of responsiveness to public demand of the moment, and separation of powers, federalism, and referenda all provide additional opportunities for public involvement with lawmakers. In contrast to the largely unified and centralized British system, the United States appears as a kind of hyperdemocratized system with a high potential for political accountability.

With respect to crime, for example, specific local, state, and national elections could create many political spaces for the public to oust lawmakers if they are insufficiently punitive, for lawmakers to display their "tough on crime" credentials frequently, and for referenda to force legislators to act on whatever horrific crime consumes the public imagination in the moment.[23] In addition, elections of mayors (who generally appoint police chiefs) and local prosecutors provide an even more intimate venue for public pressure at the level where crime is felt most acutely. State judicial elections offer additional opportunities for political responsiveness to public punitiveness on crime.[24]

The institutional density and fragmentation of American politics, however, provides for fewer *demos-enhancing* opportunities than this arms-length view suggests. There is some evidence that federal systems, in general, produce obstacles to the production of public goods because there are more veto opportunities for those that pay the concentrated costs of such goods to block efforts to impose them. Indeed, federal systems are associated with lower social welfare spending (though it is not entirely clear that the two are causally related).[25]

But the United States is much more than a federal system (or, as some argue, not a federal system at all).[26] It is a complex labyrinth of policymaking venues, divided institutions, multiple elections, prospect of referenda, and judicial supremacy, and each of these features can have *counterdemocratic* consequences in practice, not to mention in combination. Though the system appears highly responsive to mass publics, with lawmakers exceptionally accountable to them, when we drill down to a more concrete understanding of accountability, particularly in terms of responding to democratic majorities' preferences on protections from social risk, the US system looks quite different. I offer three illustrations to highlight the challenges to democratic accountability in the United States and suggest that these limitations impose obstacles to the provision of public goods—such as security from violence—which decrease trust and legitimacy in the political system and increase the likelihood of punitive outcomes.

Veto Points and Constraint on Accountability

Often overlooked in the assessment of the American political system as highly democratized is the fact that institutional density provides not only opportunities for participating, but also opportunities for hindering. An important example is the ever-present potential for divided government at the national level, which provides opportunities for political minorities to veto the policies of the majority party, making it difficult for the party winning the White House to enact its preferred legislation.[27] Examples abound. An examination of 184 major executive proposals to Congress within the first two years of the executive's election, since 1948, reveals that only 63 percent became law (116).[28] Among the failures were major social goods provisions on which the presidential candidates had campaigned, such as federal aid to education (Truman, Kennedy), middle income housing support (Truman), increases in corporate, gift, and estate taxes (Truman), national health reform (Eisenhower, Truman, Nixon, Clinton), child care programs, economic stimulus, lobbying reform, and a minimum wage hike (Clinton).

Furthermore, even with unified government—the same party controlling all three venues—the Senate is a vastly disproportionate wild card. Though the House of Representatives is elected proportionally, each state has two senators, resulting in an imbalance of representation as much as seventy-one to one. California, home to nearly 12 percent of the population (roughly 38 million), has the same number of senators as Wyoming, with approximately *two-tenths of one percent* of the population (just under 600,000). Thus, it is possible for a fraction of the population, through the Senate, to block the ability of the senators representing the majority to pass popular—even highly popular—legislation.

A recent example is the failure of bill that would have required background checks for gun sales. Public opinion polls showed the public overwhelmingly in favor of background checks in the wake of the horrific mass murder of twenty children and six teachers at the Sandy Hook Elementary School in Sandy Hook, Connecticut (91 percent supported mandatory criminal background checks for all gun sales; Gallup Poll, January 19–20, 2013).[29] Nonetheless, the bill failed to pass the Senate, despite a vote of 54 in favor and 46 against. Though the filibuster rule has garnered much attention for the failure of the bill to pass, it is also the case that 54 votes in favor of the background checks represented not just a majority vote in this body, but a full *62 percent of the population.*[30] In fact, the senators from

the twenty-one states where *both* senators voted in favor of the bill represented 50 percent of the American population (50.2 percent).[31]

A similar bill failed to pass during the Clinton administration in 1999
for a different reason, but one that also highlights the inherent veto points
in American politics. After a mass shooting in 1999 that killed twelve students and one teacher at Columbine High School in a suburb of Denver,
Colorado, President Clinton and Senate Democrats proposed a comprehensive gun control bill that would have required background checks at
gun shows, child safety locks for new handguns, and a ban on the impor-
tation of large-capacity ammunition clips.

The most contentious part of the bill involved mandatory background checks for gun purchases at certain gun shows and it was included only after Vice President Al Gore broke a 50–50 deadlock in
the Senate and cast his vote in favor of the amendment. The full bill,
attached to a tough juvenile crime package, then passed the Senate but
the leadership of the House of Representatives, by then in the control of Republicans, separated the background checks from the rest of
the juvenile crime bill. The mandatory background checks bill that the
House put forward for a vote on June 18, 1999, dramatically narrowed
the types of events in which buyers would be subject to the checks
and included in the requirement that guns be sold with safety devices.
Both gun control advocates and opponents found the bill unaccept-
able and the bill failed to pass the House, with 197 Democrats and 82
Republicans voting against the bill.[32]

In both cases, large majorities of the public supported most, if not all,
of the gun control provisions. The inability of the US Senate to pass a
bill supported by more than 90 percent of the American public not only
reveals the highly undemocratic nature of the Senate, but also the pitfalls of multilevel, overlapping governance. Because states can pass gun
control legislation, the pressure for change shifted, again, to the states
and the Senators who voted down the bill faced few serious political
repercussions for having done so. *Some* gun control bills will get passed
at the state level (as happened in Colorado), but the larger issue of the
free availability of firearms goes unaddressed. More people will go to
jail for longer for committing crimes with guns but the pervasiveness
of guns, their ease of access, even for those with criminal records and
serious mental health backgrounds, remains unresolved.[33] The inability
of the national government to pass comprehensive legislation that could
reduce the illegal transfer of guns throughout the United States, again

and again, must surely demobilize the electorate or, at the least, demoralize it.

And there are still more veto possibilities, even when legislation does pass through Congress. The federal courts can narrow or outright block such policies, making it difficult for the national government to enforce equitability among the states. After passage of the Gun Free Schools Zones Act in 1990, for example, the Supreme Court determined it to be unconstitutional because its constitutional foundation—the commerce clause of Article I., Section 8—was insufficiently broad to encompass such legislation.[34]

Such uses of the court have more been aimed at narrowing or reversing comprehensive social policies. A recent example is the Patient Protection and Affordable Care Act, colloquially known as Obamacare (2010), which, among other features, offered states incentives to expand their Medicaid programs—programs that provide health insurance to the poor. Rather than leap at the opportunity to equalize fiscal resources and expand access to healthcare to the worst off, seventeen states opted to reject the expansion and their decisions were validated by the Supreme Court in 2012 in *National Federation of Independent Businesses v. Sebelius*.[35] Of the fourteen states that currently have not expanded their Medicaid programs, it is worth noting that eight are states whose congressional delegations also voted against the Civil Rights Act in 1964[36]—another piece of national legislation, it should be noted, that was challenged in court as unconstitutional.[37]

Meanwhile, decades of litigation and legal arguments urging federal courts to disrupt the steady march of increasing punishment over the past forty years have failed to reduce arrest and imprisonment, nor have they controlled serious violence or other risks. On the contrary, federal courts have been largely deferential to legislatures on criminal punishments, increases in mandatory minimum sentences, and other punitive policies, some of which have widened racial disparities in the justice system.[38] In *McKlesky v. Kemp, U.S. v. Johnson* and *U.S. v. Armstrong*, defendants sought relief based on racially disproportionate prosecutions or sentences, but federal courts have been unwilling to second-guess legislatures or executive actors in this area. Moreover, in racial profiling claims, when law enforcement agencies have been able to provide nonracial reasons for stopping citizens, federal courts have usually upheld the police practice and declined to inquire into the thinking behind officers' actions or evidence of systematic bias on the part of police departments.[39]

Thus, while the federal courts provide venues for limiting or blocking broad social policymaking at the center (Congress), they have largely rubber-stamped the muscular prison state. Space limitations do not allow for extensive elaboration on this point, but one of the reasons for the incongruity here is that the US constitutional system has long recognized states as retaining jurisdictionally independent powers over which the national government has only limited control. Thus state and local policing, prosecutions, and imprisonment are areas of policymaking and action that the federal courts are reluctant to second-guess, absent some exceptionally clear evidence of state violations of the Constitution or federal law.

Some of the same arguments about state jurisdiction and powers are made with respect to other social issues. The primary mechanisms for congressional policymaking on major social issues has been the power granted to that body under Article I, Section 8 of the Constitution, which allows for Congress to regulate "commerce . . . among the states." Opponents of national policy to address poverty, discrimination, inequality, healthcare disparities, unemployment, and other social risks have often made legal claims that Congress has overstepped its constitutional authority under the Commerce clause in passing such legislation. While rarely successful in the post-World War II era, a few victories, along with the ability of such litigation to fracture fragile coalitions within government, have stymied the success of such policies.[40]

The institutional density of American politics, then, while seemingly open and porous to majoritarian pressures, actually facilitates veto of many social policies by political minorities, particularly those seeking to block redistribution.

Many Venues, Less Accountability?

For the reasons laid out above, as well as others I discuss here, the many avenues for participation in the fragmented American system should not be equated with political accountability. Even where political venues are responsive to majorities and difficult to challenge, mere opportunity for participation tells us little about who participates, or whether such participation is associated with any real power. Neither do we know whether the various venues for political engagement have any real capacity to respond to public demand.

Sharp differences in the political and fiscal capacities of the varying legislative venues in American politics, such as national, state, and local governments, have important implications for social policy. Many core social goods, including public safety, but also education, public transportation, housing, many social services, and even healthcare—social goods, it should be noted, that are often linked to crime reduction—are largely the political and fiscal responsibility of state and local governments. Neither level of government, however, can borrow money at the levels and rates of the national government, nor can they run deficits, manipulate monetary policy, or punish corporate entities for moving their business from one state or locality to another. Thus, the capacity of states and localities to keep pace with growing cost or shifting needs with respect to these social issues is limited. Though national politics has its own set of constraints, the US government rivals few in its ability to borrow and spend as it chooses.

States and localities are not only excluded from such borrowing; they also face the problem of luring businesses that can enrich the public coffers through taxation and employment opportunities away from neighboring states, and thus have incentives to limit spending on public goods and to provide tax breaks and other incentives for private enterprise. The political capital and fiscal resources spent on such activities, with little benefit to the public, is nicely illustrated in the long-standing "tax incentive arms race" that Kansas City, Missouri, and Kansas City, Kansas engaged in as they spent years trying to maintain or lure businesses from one state to the other. Because of their geographic proximity (the two cities are roughly three miles apart), movement of corporations such as AMC Entertainment have little impact on jobs in the region but cities offer substantial tax incentives in order to lure businesses across the border anyway. Kansas, for example, reportedly offered AMC entertainment a ten-year tax rebate worth more than 40 million dollars. One wonders what value such a move has for Kansas.[41]

This feature of the American federal system is often analyzed from the perspective of economic efficiency by focusing on whether reliance on state or local governments for social goods provisions ultimately produces locally relevant goods more efficiently than the central government. Indeed, a copious literature in fiscal federalism has sought to identify the optimal balance between levels of government for maximum fiscal efficiency, and there is general agreement that at a most basic level, the central government should have responsibility for macro-economic policy and redistribution, while the provision of public services should be at the lowest level of government with jurisdictional responsibility over a particular set of interests and needs.[42]

At first blush, the American system would seem to fit this framework well. But such an approach assumes an equitable distribution of necessary resources across these lower governmental levels, a kind of "topping up" from the central government for areas that are in greater need and unable to provide basic social goods at a threshold, uniform level. But such funding is sporadic, ad hoc, and rarely sufficient, leaving states and localities to resolve major social problems with inadequate resources.[43] Much of what local municipalities can do in response to crime, for example, is confined to police and prosecution. While the local electorate typically controls local school boards, such entities face enormous funding challenges since school budgets are tied to local property taxes and raising property taxes is usually a one-way ticket to electoral defeat.

A contemporary example is the city of Philadelphia, the nation's fifth-largest city, whose school district has been in deep financial distress for more than a decade with very few options for resolving the budget deficit of several hundred million dollars, beyond shrinking staff and operating costs.[44] The Department of Education has provided grants, but such funding is usually targeted to specific goals (as opposed to operating funds) and is only temporary.[45] There is simply no institutional mechanism for confronting such a problem. Nor can cities comprehensively or effectively confront poverty or healthcare or create low-skilled employment opportunities. It is, therefore, difficult to have genuine political accountability for public safety when crime prevention is largely cut off from other social policy initiatives and criminal justice agencies have the most robust resources and voice.

A recent study provides a vivid example.[46] Policing and prosecutions are locally controlled and increasing their harshness is a relatively low-cost option for local taxpayers since the cost of prisons and jails is spread across the entire state population. That is, while homeowners pay substantial local taxes in the form of property taxation, the increase in such taxes required to make substantial overhaul to core conditions that generate crime—such as education or employment opportunity—would be both acute and immediate for homeowners. By contrast, the state level spreads the costs of imprisonment across a wide population, making increases in law enforcement and imprisonment spending less likely to be on the forefront of voters' minds and to have far less of an impact on any given homeowners budget. Moreover, states have enormous budgets and broad political mandates, relative to municipalities, and thus are able to move money around to cover new expenses—such as prison construction—whereas municipality budgets and political mandates are narrower. Thus, the cost of increasing punishment is not fully imposed on the voters who choose such policy options. By contrast, improving schools, job training, employment opportunities, and the like come from city budgets, imposing additional taxes on property owners and substantially reducing their attractiveness to voters.

As Paul Peterson cogently noted in his 1981 book *City Limits*, local municipalities in the United States are highly constrained with respect to redistributive policymaking. Local elected officials find themselves largely trying to appease the tax base, primarily businesses and the more affluent residents of the city, lest those elements of the city depart for suburban communities (with their incorporated and wholly separate tax structure and governance) or other states entirely. In the more than thirty years since Peterson revealed these severe limitations on city capacity, we can see a similar set of constraints on state governments confronting social policy problems of the twenty-first century. Healthcare, environmental issues, energy, and crime—particularly gun violence—are issues over which states theoretically have jurisdictional control, but such issues are so deeply national in scope—both in terms of the limits on fiscal resources of states described above, as well as the negative externalities that result from state-by-state decision-making—that ameliorating those problems is extremely difficult in the absence of centralized policymaking.[47]

In both cases, even where voters may prefer a more comprehensive crime reduction strategy, there are structural incentives against making such choices since the costs of punitiveness are passed up the federalism ladder (as in the case of local prosecutions and state prisons, but also with respect to federal financial support for state prison construction), whereas the costs of more inclusionary or social welfare based approaches will be felt acutely by increases in state or local taxes.

Of course, cities in the United States can and do produce a myriad of public goods, but this is more a function of economies of scale and the concentration of talent than it is of the fiscal and political capacity of urban municipalities. Indeed, inequalities in income, wealth, education, and risk of violence vary enormously *within* cities. A recent analysis of PCCs in the UK concerned the possibility of losing the concept of the *police* to a more vague and perhaps less accountable notion of *policing*. The discussion here suggests we should also be concerned with equating police with crime reduction, because community safety requires the marshaling of far more collective resources than simply the state's apparatus for monopolizing the use of force.[48]

Finally, with respect to many venues, referenda deserve some attention. They are ubiquitous in the United States (thirty states have some form of referenda or initiative), and often serve as the archetype hyperdemocratized American state. Referenda, however, are simply an up or down vote on a predetermined policy proposal. The now famous three-strikes-and-you're-out provisions that passed by referenda in California in 1994, for example, was just such a referendum where all of the important decisions and points of contention had been decided before the public was faced with voting on it. The public was simply provided with a choice to increase sentences in the wake of decades of rising violence in the state (vote in favor of the referendum), or retain the status quo (vote against it or do not vote at all).[49]

If we approach this from the framework of security from violence as a core state function, the increase in violent crime in California prior to the referendum is an important and usually overlooked part of the referendum story. As illustrated in Figure 12.1, the homicide rate in California rose 255 percent between 1960 and its peak, 13.5 per 100,000, in 1981 (based on the moving average). The rate dropped slightly and leveled off during the mid-1980s but hovered near 11.1 homicides per 100,000, more than two and a half times the rate during the mid-1960s (4.3) and still higher than the 1970s (9.6). A rapid increase began again in 1989 and culminated in a second peak of 12.8 per 100,000 in 1993, virtually indistinguishable from the previous peak. Violent crime follows a similar trajectory (the two are correlated at 0.90) but the second wave begins earlier, in 1985, and goes well beyond the previous peak in 1982, culminating in an extremely high violent crime rate of 1095.8 per 100,000. In fact, in terms of peak homicide rates, California had the tenth highest homicide rate in

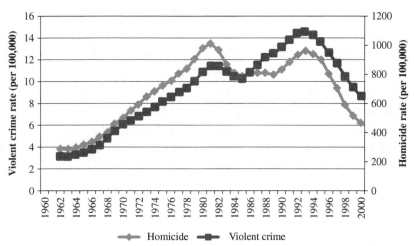

FIGURE 12.1 Homicide and Violent Crime Rates, Per 100,000, in California, 1960–2000

the country (tied with New York) and was one of only four states in the top eleven that was outside the South (California, Alaska, Nevada, and New York). California was also one of only five states with violent crime rates that went above 1,000 per 100,000 residents during the crime wave (with Florida, New York, Nevada, and Maryland).

Given this backdrop, voters were asked, in November 1994, to simply vote yes or no on Proposition 186, which strengthened a three-strikes law passed by the California legislature earlier that year. The ballot summary was:

Increased sentences: repeat offenders

- Increases sentences for defendants convicted of any felony who have prior convictions for violent or serious felonies such as rape, robbery, or burglary.
- Convicted felons with one such prior conviction would receive twice the normal sentence for the new offense. Convicted felons with two or more such prior convictions would receive a life sentence with a minimum term three times the normal sentence or twenty-five years, whichever is greater.
- Includes as prior convictions certain felonies committed by juveniles sixteen years of age or older.
- Reduces sentence reduction credit which may be earned by these convicted felons.

The referendum passed overwhelmingly. We could read this development as evidence of an open democratic system responding to an unyielding and mercurial public, and certainly analyses of the origins of the three-strikes law provide some evidence for this. Stopping there, however, brushes aside three decades of rising and high violence and neglects the lack of *alternatives* from which the public might choose. Added to this is the decline of venues where the public might be called upon to reflect on crime and criminal justice concerns, as evidenced by the decline of jury trials in the twentieth century. The plethora of venues for participation in the highly fragmented American system is less democratic in practice than it would appear if we simply add up the places for democratic interaction or the structure of the formal law.[50]

The Siren Call of Local Control

Finally, the many venues of American politics have a third, counterdemocratic consequence for the political dynamics of crime and punishment: the localization of a collective problem. Much is made of "local needs" and "local interests" in both the United States and the United Kingdom, with respect to crime and policing. But if security from violence is a collective good, emphasis on local responsiveness and accountability obscures the *shared interest* of a democratic public in being secure from random violence and other forms of social disorder that have both individual and collateral consequences. In other words, if a crucial promise of the state is to secure the citizenry from violence, as well as excessive use of state force, a robust political narrative at the level of national discourse and policymaking may be important in ensuring that the state makes good on those promises across communities.

Consider, for example, the social welfare of the unemployed or the poor educational outcomes among many inner-city students. Both unemployment and failure to complete high school are associated with a higher likelihood of involvement in crime and subsequent imprisonment. While it is true that there is substantial geographic and demographic variation in the extent to which different populations are exposed to such risks, without a robust national norm of state action to provide at least some measure of security against them, there is the danger of local interests becoming a mechanism for providing less than adequate protection for those at greatest risk. A related concern is the pluralization and fragmentation of policing types that have proliferated in recent decades, including private policing, supranational policing, and localized, voluntary surveillance of neighborhoods. Without tethering such policings to the common good, we risk highly specialized police services that further exacerbate extant inequalities in security from violence and community safety writ large.[51]

The US case reveals how the emphasis on local needs in a highly fragmented system can obscure the shared interest in protection from violence *and* from state use of force. The American political and legal discourses are replete with claims about how valuable the American federal system is for "increasing opportunities for citizen involvement ... making government more responsive" and, more commonly, "assur[ing] a decentralized government that will be more sensitive to the diverse needs of a heterogenous society."[52] With respect to policing, in addition to the numerous national law enforcement organizations (e.g., the Federal Bureau of Investigation, Drug Enforcement Agency, and Bureau of Alcohol, Tobacco, and Firearms), there are over 18,000 state and local law enforcement agencies, more than two-thirds of which are local police departments, all of which work largely independently of one another, and are accountable to locally elected mayors and municipal legislatures. County sheriffs and state law enforcement agencies are accountable to a different but overlapping set of publics.[53]

Moreover, the community-policing wave that swept the country in the 1990s generated further independence as local councils and community organizations were established to further force police departments to respond to local needs. Phrases like "local innovation," "local control," and "community justice" are bandied about freely, with little explanation about what issues might best be addressed locally and why, or how collective goods with respect to policing are improved upon through local autonomy. The emphasis on local needs that is facilitated by the many venues of the US political system, then, obscures the *shared interest in security*, dividing urban, suburban, rural, and small town collective action and resources, and putting localities in competition for state resources and states in competition for national resources.

It is not that locally derived programs have no security value. But I wish to distinguish local *implementation* of social goods provisions from national decision-making about the *quality and quantity of such goods*. Certainly in the United States, some of the criminal justice programs that developed in highly localized contexts were quite successful, such as the Ten Points/Operation Ceasefire Project in Boston, which is sometimes credited with reducing murder among young people in the 1990s.[54] But there is nothing incompatible about such programs with more centralized policymaking on public safety. In fact, pushing problems of security from violence, and the social goods associated with lower criminogenic conditions, down to local authorities in the United States moves the venue for providing a collective good to the level of government with the least capacity to do so, as noted earlier.

Given this, it is not clear what added *democratic accountability* value is provided by developing and implementing independent strategies on collective problems through piecemeal efforts—state by state or, even worse, locality by locality—that come with localization. The drug, gang, and gun violence problems facing Boston in the 1990s, for example, were almost identical to those facing other urban areas at that time. And yet the fragmentation of the US political system meant that such programs took years to reach into other communities, if they arrived there at all, because local law enforcement, governing bodies, and a wholly different set of political actors were required to pay the start-up costs to adopt similar policies (though *some* policy learning clearly transfers from one jurisdiction to the next). Furthermore, as the plethora of daily deaths from gun violence in cities like New Orleans, Chicago, and Washington, DC illustrate, this localized attention, if it has had reductive effects at all, has left many US communities extremely dangerous and exposes all Americans to random acts of murder at a rate three-, four-, and fivefold as frequently as in other rich democracies.[55]

Not unrelated is the growth of situational crime prevention in the United Kingdom that seeks to narrow the concept of public safety to simply management of high-crime areas. On the UK government webpage about the Police and Crime Commissioners, for example, the site makes much of the ability of PCCs to help people focus police activities on local problems. "They [PCCs] will ensure the police focus on the crimes that matter most to you."[56] Much of the justification for the PCC is about "giving local people a direct voice in policing."[57] Given the regional variation in exposure to serious violence that I just described, it is indeed tempting to localize problems of crime and violence, to assume that unique, local contexts require unique, local responses. While the root causes of crime and disorder are often well beyond the control of individuals or communities, we certainly experience the risk of violence and victimization (or lack thereof) in a very local way.[58]

This emphasis on local needs, however, risks untethering security from violence from the broader vision of social welfare that is more readily offered by central governments with fiscal capacity and broad legislative mandates. As one black political activist in London told me during an interview, after I queried him on the 2010-2015 coalition government's Big Society and push for local control: "Localism doesn't stack up to ideals. On the contrary, those with the most resources and most voice will consolidate. In contrast, with centralization, you can be visionary with resources and you can remove local oligarchies that have monopoly on power. Local empowerment is a big con."[59]

But, at least for now, in the United Kingdom major policy decisions about public safety *and the social policies that might mitigate crime* remain firmly in the hands of Parliament, a single venue where the controlling political party (or parties) can freely enact legislation. Whatever local needs are addressed through the PCCs reflects a prioritization of resources more than substantive decision-making about what actions to criminalize or whether imprisonment or "root cause" strategies (or some combination of both) are appropriate strategies for securing public safety. It is worth noting here that the relative *amount* of certain types of crime in different localities aside, there is nothing "local" about wanting to be secure from acts of violence of any kind.

In contrast to the United States, because so much social policy with respect to broad public goods and community safety in the United Kingdom are formulated in Parliament—education, poverty reduction, access to healthcare and mental health services, and so on—many of the social problems that form a penumbra around crime problems are dealt with in a more comprehensive manner than in the United States. The welfare floor, with respect to poverty, inequality, and health outcomes in the United Kingdom, for example, is much higher than in the United States.[60] The worst off in Britain generally fare better than their counterparts in the United States on many other measures as well, including predatory violence, which is substantially lower in the United Kingdom And while it is tempting to believe that the bundling of social welfare policies with tough-on-crime ones would be electoral suicide, the opposite appears to be true. In 1997 and 2001, the Labour party made crime a more substantial part of its party platform than it had previously, but compared to the Conservative Party it also included promises to increase spending on social welfare policy, in particular education, and it won both elections handily. The claim here is not that the public will necessarily *prefer* such "couplings," but that in political systems where winning parties have few obstacles to implementation of their platform, voters must choose between several sets of comprehensive policies. In the United States, by contrast, the many veto points allows political opponents, even if they are in the minority, to cherry-pick issues.[61] In the UK, the more equitable social welfare provisioning and greater opportunity for local police to tap into national policies and programs aimed at community safety allow a more holistic and comprehensive set of crime prevention policy goals and outcomes than in the United States.

Conclusion: Frustrated Majorities, Distrust, and Democratic Accountability

The overly democratic nature of the American constitutional system is more apparent than real. When stripped down to the realities of facilitating the production of social goods, including public safety, the US constitutional system—both in de jure and de facto terms—imposes many obstacles. The multiple pathways to power are more elusive for ordinary people than the institutional density would suggest because separation of powers and federalism facilitate the shunting of public goods provisions down the federalism ladder or off the political agenda entirely, and because the persistence of counterdemocratic institutions such as the Senate and the Supreme Court provide as much (or more) opportunity for blocking than for enacting. If a major purpose of modern democratic governments is to enhance the capacity of large groups of citizens to force government to act in their collective interests, the fragmentation and multilayered nature of the American system hardly facilitates such capacities.

Instead, the US constitutional system, in practice, divides and conquers by allowing minority parties in Congress to veto the policies of the winning party; pushing the provision of public safety, social welfare, and other protections down to levels of government with little capacity to provide them; and severing public debate and policy alternatives about a broad range of social goods into discreet units so that crime, police, and punishment, for example, become an isolated policy issue that is largely seen as a local problem, with little opportunity for connecting it to broader social welfare provisions.

Frustrating the will of the majority through institutional design has perhaps an even more insidious consequence, however. The thwarting of majority preference at the center, the challenges of producing adequate public goods at the state and local levels, and the highly constrained political choices offered by referenda can also *weaken the legitimacy of the state and increase mistrust in its capacity to address social problems.* Support for more policing and imprisonment because the citizenry lacks trust in the political system to lower serious crime rates by any other means (a well-earned view) is quite a different causal path to punitiveness than an unyieldingly mercurial majority.[62]

The United Kingdom certainly has its share of problems with trust and legitimacy. But at the foundational level of the political capacity of winning parties, expectations that a large portion of party policy commitments will be fulfilled, and the ability to produce and maintain a comprehensive policy system for social goods (including some measure of protection from housing, employment and health risks), however weakened it may be in the post-Thatcher era, contrasts sharply with the United States where each of these dynamic features of democratic accountability are frustrated. In addition to more punitive crime policies, for example, in 1998 New Labour also introduced Sure Start, a comprehensive effort to ensure that all parents of preschool children have access to childcare.

Where governments are broadly accountable to mass publics—where large groups of ordinary people can force government to impose costs on small groups and distribute collective goods—both violence and punishment may be lower. Where mass publics are hindered in their capacity to extract broad and universal public goods from political elites, it will be easier to fixate on punishment alone. Such constitutional arrangements do not result in more punishment because they are overly responsive to the public on crime but because they are *underresponsive* on collective goods. As a wide range of research suggests, while reliable, trustworthy, and swift policing can reduce crime, long-term reductions in violence and disorder are the result of much broader social, political, and economic policy decisions.[63]

Though routinely linked together in the politics of punishment literature, the United Kingdom looks much less like the US than we often assume. The United Kingdom still centralizes broad social policies, facilitates governance by the winning political party, minimizes veto opportunities for political "losers," and provides a minimum level of social welfare that exceeds that of the United States. Even recent developments, such as the election of PCCs and policing reform in Scotland, are unlikely to have dramatic effects on punishment practices so long as the major institutions of UK government remain responsive to democratically elected majorities.

Mass majorities may be punitive but they are also self-interested, and where public policies have demonstrably ameliorated social risks like unemployment, ill health, poor educational outcomes, communicable diseases, and so on, democratic systems that more readily translate public preferences into policy are likely to be more successful at actually reducing such risks. The United States is overflowing with political venues, but the effect is high political responsiveness but low levels of real accountability.

Notes

1. Frank R. Baumgartner and Bryan D. Jones, *Agendas and Instability in American Politics* (Chicago: University of Chicago Press, 2000).

2. Stuart Scheingold, *The Politics of Law and Order: Street Crime and Public Policy* (New York: Longman, 1984).

3. See, for example, David Jacobs and Richard Kleban, "Political Institutions, Racial Minorities and Punishment: A Cross-National Analysis of Imprisonment," *Social Forces* 82 (2)(2003): 755; Nicola Lacey, *The Prisoners' Dilemma: Political Economy and Punishment in Contemporary Democracies* (Cambridge: Cambridge University Press, 2008); Michael Tonry, "The Social, Psychological and Political Causes of Racial Disparities in the American Criminal Justice System," *Crime and Justice: A Review of Research* 39 (1)(2010): 273.

4. David Garland, *The Culture of Control: Crime and Social Order in Contemporary Society* (Chicago: University of Chicago, 2001); Nicola Lacey, "American Imprisonment in Comparative Perspective," *Daedalus* 139 (3) (2010): 102.

5. E.g., Tonry, "The Social, Psychological and Political Causes of Racial Disparities"; Jacobs and Kleban, "Political Institutions, Racial Minorities and Punishment"; for exceptions, see Albert W. Dzur and Rekha Mirchandani, "Punishment and Democracy: The Role of Public Deliberation," *Punishment and Society* 9 (2) (2007): 151; Ian Loader and Neil Walker, *Civilizing Security* (Cambridge: Cambridge University Press, 2007); Gerry Johnstone, "Penal Policymaking: Elitist, Populist or Participatory?" *Punishment and Society* 2 (2) (2002): 161.

6. John McCormick, "Control the Wealthy and Patrol the Magistrates: Restoring Elite Accountability to Popular Government," *American Political Science Review* 100 (2) (2006): 147.

7. Lisa L. Miller, "Power to the People: Violent Victimization, Inequality and Democratic Politics," *Theoretical Criminology* 17 (3) (2013): 283; on jurisdictional confusion, see Christopher Wlezien and Stuart N. Soroka, "Federalism and Public Responsiveness to Policy," *Publius* 41 (1) (2010): 31.

8. The term "political salience" refers to the relative level of political attention a given issue receives, compared to other policy areas. Salience is typically measured by policy scholars through issue mentions in political speeches, party documents, legislative hearings or bills, and so on. For an example, see Glen S. Krutz, "Issues and Institutions: "Winnowing in the U.S. Congress," *American Journal of Political Science* 49 (2) (2005): 313; for a broader discussion of issue salience, see Baumgartner, *Agendas and Instability.*

9. On how high-veto points contribute to lower social welfare spending, see Evelyne Huber, Charles Ragin, and John T. Stephens. "Social Democracy, Christian Democracy, Constitutional Structure and the Welfare State," *American Journal of Sociology* 99 (3) (1993): 711. See also Clem Brooks and Jeffrey Manza, *Why Welfare States Persist: The Importance of Public Opinion in Democracies* (Chicago: University of Chicago Press, 2007); Lorelei Moosbrugger, *The Vulnerability Thesis: Interest Group Influence and Institutional Design* (New Haven, CT: Yale University Press, 2012).

10. Miller, "Power to the People"; Lisa L. Miller, "What's Violence Got to Do With It? Inequality, Punishment and State Failure in American Politics," *Punishment and Society* 17 (2) (2005): 184.

11. Loader, *Civilizing Security.*

12. I am in very much in agreement with Stanley Cohen that crime, as a political issue, is a crucial part of how benefits and burdens are distributed in a democratic polity. See Stanley Cohen, *Folk Devils and Moral Panics* (Boulder, CO: Paladin, 1973).

13. James A. Fox and Marianne W. Zawitz, *Homicide Trends in the United States* (Washington, DC: Bureau of Justice Statistics, Office of Justice Programs, 2010); Office for National Statistics, *Crime Statistics: Annual Trend and Demographic Tables* 2011–12—*Crime in England and Wales, Quarterly First Release* (London: Office for National Statistics, 2012).

14. Long-term homicide data by race and gender are not readily available for England and Wales. Here I rely on a 2012 report that states that the male homicide rate in 2010–2011 was 1.6 per 100,000; see Kevin Smith, Sarah Osborne, Ivy Lau and Andrew Britton, *Homicides, Firearm Offences and Intimate Violence 2010/11: Supplementary Volume 2 to Crime in England and Wales 2010/11, Home Office Statistical Bulletin* (London: Home Office Statistics, 2012). Even accounting for the decline in homicides from the peak in

2002–2003, white homicide rates are lower than many racial and ethnic minority rates so the peak white male homicide rate in England and Wales was nowhere close to 11.0 murders per 100,000 for white males in the United States.

15. Ashley Nellis, "Throwing Away the Key: The Expansion of Life Without Parole Sentences in the United States," *Federal Sentencing Reporter* 23(1) (2010): 27.

16. For a general discussion, see Pablo Bermendi, "Federalism," in Susan C. Stokes and Charles Boix (eds.), *The Oxford Handbook of Comparative Politics* (Oxford: Oxford University Press, 2007): 752; For an analysis of the United States, see Malcolm Feeley and Edwin Rubin, *Federalism: Political Identity and Tragic Compromise* (Ann Arbor: University of Michigan Press, 2011).

17. Jorg Broschek, "Historic Institutionalism and the Varieties of Federalism in Germany and Canada," *Publius—The Journal of Federalism* 42 (4) (2012): 662.

18. Leslie McAra, "Crime, Criminology and Criminal Justice in Scotland," *European Journal of Criminology* 5 (4) (2008): 482.

19. For example race and sex discrimination (Civil Rights Act of 1964, Public Law 88-52), interstate commerce (Article I, Section 8).

20. E.g., *Gregory v. Ashcroft* 501 US 452 (1992).

21. See Amy Bridges, *A City in the Republic: Antebellum New York and the Origins of Machine Politics* (Ithaca, NY: Cornell University Press, 1987); Peter B. Evans, Dietrich Rueschemeyer, and Theda Skocpol (eds.), *Bringing the State Back In* (Cambridge: Cambridge University Press, 1985).

22. Gordon Silverstein, *Law's Allure: How Law Shapes, Constrains, Saves and Kills Politics* (Cambridge: Cambridge University Press, 2012).

23. For example, see Frank E. Zimring and Gordon Hawkins, *Crime Is Not the Problem: Lethal Violence Is* (Oxford: Oxford University Press, 1997).

24. On judicial elections and sentencing in criminal cases, see Greg Huber and Scott Gordon, "Accountability and Coercion: Is Justice Blind When it Runs for Office?" *American Journal of Political Science* 48 (2) (2004): 247.

25. On veto points, see William H. Riker, *Federalism: Origin, Operation and Significance* (New York: Little Brown, 1964); Brooks and Manza, *Why Welfare States Persist*. Indeed, federal systems are associated with lower social welfare spending (though it is not entirely clear that the two are causally related, see Alfred Stepan, *Arguing Comparative Politics* (New York: Oxford University Press, 2001).

26. See Malcolm Feeley and Edwin Rubin, *Federalism: Political Identity and Tragic Compromise* (Ann Arbor: University of Michigan Press, 2011).

27. Sarah A. Binder, *Stalemate: Causes and Consequences of Legislative Gridlock* (Washington, DC: Brookings Institution Press, 2003).

28. Data are from Mayhew's list of major legislative enactments in *Divided We Govern: Party Control, Lawmaking and Investigations* (New Haven, CT: Yale University Press, 1991 and 2002 editions), 52–73. See also http://campuspress.yale.edu/davidmayhew/datasets-divided-we-govern/.

29. See Saad, Lydia, "Americans Back Obama's Proposals to Address Gun Violence." Gallup Poll Politics, January 23, 2013www.gallup.com/poll/160085/americans-back-obama-proposals-address-gun-violence.aspx.

30. The Senate filibuster is a disruptive tactic used to prevent a measure from coming to the Senate floor for a vote. Sixty votes are needed to overcome the filibuster. Gregory

J. Wawro and Eric Schickler, *Filibuster: Obstruction and Lawmaking in the U.S. Senate* (Princeton, NJ: Princeton University Press, 2007). Total votes computed by taking the population of the states with two "yea" votes and half the population of states with divided votes. Only 25 percent of the population is represented by the seventeen states that had unified votes against the bill.

31. California, Colorado, Connecticut, Delaware, Hawaii, Illinois, Maine, Maryland, Massachusetts, Michigan, Minnesota, New Jersey, New Mexico, New York, Oregon, Pennsylvania, Rhode Island, Vermont, Virginia, Washington, and West Virginia.

32. House of Representatives bill HR 2122, 1999.

33. More than 31,000 people were killed by guns in the United States in 2009, with slightly more than half as suicides (there are about thirty times fewer murders with guns in Britain). An average of eight children and teens are killed by guns every day in the US. Current laws apply to only 60 percent of all guns sales. See the The Brady Campaign to Prevent Gun Violence, www.bradycampaign.org.

34. Gun Free School Zones Act 18 USC 921(a)(25). *U.S. v. Lopez* 514 (US) 549 (1995); *U.S. v. Morrison* 529 US 588 (2000).

35. *National Federation of Independent Businesses v. Sebelius.*567 US (2012)

36. With the exception of the Texas delegation, where Senators Ralph Yarborough and John Tower voted in favor of the Civil Rights Act.

37. The Supreme Court upheld the law in *Heart of Atlanta Motel v. U.S* 379 US 241 (1964).

38. Schlesinger, Traci. "The Failure of Race Neutral Policies: How Mandatory Terms and Sentencing Enhancements Contribute to Mass Racialized Incarceration. *Crime and Delinquency* 57 (1) (2008): 56. See *Harmelin v. Michigan* (501 US 957, 1991), severe and lengthy sentences do not violate the Eight Amendment; *Solemn v. Helm* (463 US 277 1983) on proportionality in Eight Amendment challenges; *Ewing v. California* (538 US 11, 2003), on the constitutionality of California's three-strikes-and-you're-out.

39. *McKlesky v. Kemp* 481 US 279, 1987; *U.S. v. Johnson* 309 US App. D.C. 180 1994; *U.S. v. Armstrong* 517 US 456; see also Doris Marie Provine, *Unequal Under Law: Race in the War on Drugs* (Chicago: University of Chicago Press, 2007); Naomi Murakawa and Katherine Beckett, "The Penology of Racial Innocence: The Erasure of Racism in the Study and Practice of Punishment," *Law and Society Review* 44 (3–4) (2010): 695; on racial profiling, see Milton Heumann and Lance Cassak, *Good Cop, Bad Cop: Racial Profiling and Competing Views of Justice* (New York: Peter Lang, 2007).

40. John Dinan, "Implementing Health Reform: Intergovernmental Bargaining and the Affordable Care Act," *Publius* 44 (3) (2014): 399.

41. Kansas City versus Kansas City is not the only rivalry going. South Dakota tries to woo Minnesota businesses, and Omaha (Nebraska) and Sioux City (Iowa) compete on similar grounds, see A. G. Sulzberger, "Businesses Stand to Gain Most in Rivalry of States," *New York Times*, April 7, 2011.

42. Rodden, Jonathan, *Hamilton's Paradox: The Promise and Pitfalls of Fiscal Federalism* (Cambridge: Cambridge University Press, 2007).

43. On the challenges to fiscal equality across the states, see Daniel Béland and André Lecours, "Fiscal Federalism and American Exceptionalism: Why Is There No Federal Equalization System in the United States?" *Journal of Public Policy* 34 (2) (2014): 303.

44. "Fitch Downgrades School District's Underlying Bond Rating," Kristen A. Graham, *Philadelphia Inquirer*, October 2, 2014.

45. "U.S. Department of Education Invests More Than $70 million To Improve School Climate and Keep Students Safe," Press Release, US Department of Education, September 23, 2014, www.ed.gov/news/press-releases/us-department-education-invests-more-70-million-improve-school-climate-and-keep-students-safe.

46. Nicola Lacey and David Soskice, "Crime, Punishment and Segregation in the United States: The Paradox of Local Democracy," *Punishment and Society* 17 (4) (2015): 454.

47. Paul Peterson, *City Limits* (Chicago: University of Chicago Press, 1981).

48. On cities and economies of scale, see Edward Glaeser, *Triumph of the City: How Our Greatest Invention Makes Us Richer, Smarter, Greener, Healthier, Happier* (New York: Penguin, 2010); on policing, see Ian Loader, "Why Do the Police Matter?," in Jennifer Brown (ed.), *Future of Policing* (London: Routledge 2013), 40–51.

49. Zimring, *Crime Is Not The Problem*.

50. On three-strikes policy, see Zimring, *Crime Is Not The Problem*; on the decline of jury trials, see Albert W. Dzur, *Punishment, Participatory Democracy, and the Jury* (New York: Oxford University Press, 2012).

51. On unemployment, lack of high school education, and crime, see Bruce Western, *Punishment and Inequality* (New York: Russell Sage, 2009); on plural policing, see Ian Loader, "Plural Policing and Democratic Governance," *Social and Legal Studies* 9 (3) (2000): 323.

52. Associate Justice Sandra Day O'Connor, *Gregory v. Ashcroft*, 111 S. Ct. 2395 (1991). See also D. Bruce La Pierre, *Political Accountability in The National Political Process—The Alternative* to *Judicial Review of Federalism Issues*, 80 Nw. U.L. REV. 577 (1985). Decentralization is used here to mean federalist arrangements.

53. Bureau of Justice Statistics, "Census of State and Local Law Enforcement Agencies," www.bjs.gov/index.cfm?ty=dcdetail&iid=249.

54. On a history of Operation Ceasefire in Boston, see David Kennedy, *Don't Shoot: One Man, a Street Fellowship, and the End of Vioelnce in Inner-City America* (New York: Bloomsbury, 2011).

55. The Sandy Hook shooting deaths of twenty elementary school children and seven teachers was among many mass shootings in the United States in the past decade. Mark Follman, Gavin Aronsen and Deanna Pan. "A Guide to Mass Shootings in America." *Mother Jones*, April 18, 2016 www.motherjones.com/politics/2012/07/mass-shootings-map; on fragmentation and policy, see also Miller, *The Perils of Federalism*.

56. My PCC, Frequently Asked Questions, www.gov.uk/government/news/mypcc-frequently-asked-questions.

57. Loader, "Why Do the Police Matter?" 5.

58. See Daniel Gilling Gordon Hughes, Matthew Bowden, Adam Edwards, Alistair Henry and John Topping, "Powers, Liabilities, and Expertise in Community Safety: Comparative Lessons for 'Urban Security' from the United Kingdom and the Republic of Ireland," *European Journal of Criminology* 10 (3) (2013): 326. "Problems of community safety are local in manifestation if not in causality," 355.

59. Interview (leader of a community activist group) by author, April 17, 2012. London, U.K.

60. The World Bank Gini index of inequality places the United Kingdom at 34.0 and the United States at 45.0 (higher numbers indicate higher inequality). For data on health outcomes, see Stephen Bezruchka, "The Deteriorating International Ranking of U.S. Health Status," *Annual Review of Public Health* 33 (2012): 157.

61. I refer to this as "lowest legislative common denominator" politics and elaborate on the concept in *The Myth of Mob Rule: Violent Crime and Democratic Politics* (New York: Oxford University Press, 2016).

62. Dzur, "Punishment and Democracy"; Randolph Roth, *American Homicide* (Cambridge, MA: Belknap Press, 2009); Frank E. Zimring and David T. Johnson, "Public Opinion and the Governance of Punishment in Democratic Political Systems," *Annals of the American Academy of Political and Social Sciences* 605 (2006): 265.

63. Roth, *American Homicide*; see also Ruth D. Peterson and Lauren J. Krivo, *Divergent Social Worlds: Neighborhood Crime and the Racial-Spatial Divide* (New York: Russell Sage, 2010); Robert J. Sampson, Jeffrey D. Morenoff, and Thomas Gannon-Rowley, "Assessing 'Neighborhood Effects': Social Processes and New Directions in Research," *Annual Review of Sociology* 28 (2002): 443.

CHAPTER 13 | Democracy All the Way Down

Deliberative Democracy and Criminal
Law: The Case of Social Protests

ROBERTO GARGARELLA

Introduction: Two Examples

Let me begin this presentation by introducing two judicial decisions, one
that was made in Argentina in 2002, in the *Schifrin* case;[1] the other that
was produced in England in 2009, in the *Austin and Saxby* case.[2]

The *Schifrin* decision, made by Argentina's High Court of Appeal,
condemned Marina Schifrin, a school teacher who had taken a leading
role in a blockade demanding for higher salaries.[3] In the central part of
its judgment, the Court made reference to a "democratic argument" in
order to condemn the teacher. Quoting Miguel Ekmedjián, a well-known
constitutional theorist, the Court maintained that according to Argentina's
Constitution there was "only one legitimate form for expressing the sovereign will of the people," which was periodical suffrage. Through this
means, it added, the people "accept or reject the alternatives that the political class poses to them." In December 2011, the Argentinean Congress—
in line with other Latin American countries—passed the Antiterrorist Law,
which has been regularly used in the region against demonstrators and
political activists.

The second case, which took place in England, was originated after a
mass rally organized against globalization.[4] Toward the end of the demonstration, police surrounded about three thousand people—some of them
had been involved in the demonstration, and some of them not—and refused to allow many of them to leave, a practice known as "kettling." As
a result, more than a thousand people were retained against their will for

around seven hours, without food, drink, or access to toilets. Geoffrey Saxby and protester Lois Austin were among those who were then retained by the police. None of them had been involved in the exercise of violence. They sought damages alleging deprivation of liberty, which was contrary to Article 5, European Convention of Human Rights and section 7 of the Human Rights Act. In the High Court, Tugendhat J claimed that the restriction of rights was justifiable, and that seven hours was well within what was legally permissible.[5] Later on, the Court of Appeal ratified that a police cordon was a lawful response to the particular circumstances of the May Day situation. The harsh attitude that the Judiciary adopted concerning public protests and popular mobilizations followed a renewed approach by the legislature in these matters, which began to take place in the mid-1980s. In fact, the English Parliament promoted a more repressive legislation at least since 1986, when it passed the Public Order Act. This wave of authoritarianism was extended and bolstered during the conservative period, and then reaffirmed with the New Labor government.[6]

These two examples pose crucial questions concerning democratic authority and democratic construction—particularly so in the face of judicial decisions that actually limit the scope of political participation, and legislative decisions that discourage rather than promote an active citizenry: Who has or should have the final say regarding the scope of our basic rights? How should we decide those fundamental questions about the meaning and content of our basic democratic rights?

In this chapter I will be interested in exploring some of these fundamental questions, which appear in the crossroad between democratic theory and criminal law. I will do this by focusing on a particular understanding of democracy, namely deliberative democracy. The aim of this chapter is twofold: partly descriptive and partly normative. In the first, descriptive part of this work, I want to give an account of the few but growing encounters between the two disciplines. More specifically, this descriptive part shall consist of the study of three examples showing existing and fruitful interactions between deliberative theory and criminal law: the first is related to criminal trials, the second is related to the sentencing process, and the third one is related to penal decision-making. The man interest of this chapter, however, is normative: I want to help strengthen the links between deliberative theories and criminal law. The chapter, and particularly its final part, should be understood as a contribution to the gradual democratization of the criminal law. I shall illustrate my normative view by reflecting on its implications concerning situations of social protests of the kind introduced in the pages above.

Deliberative Democracy and Criminal Law:
An Introduction

There are numerous reasons why we should strengthen the links between democratic theory and criminal law. First of all, for those of us who believe in the importance of democratic self-government, it seems clear that there are few problems more relevant than those related to the use of the State's coercive powers. Second, and more specifically, when we refer to the criminal law, we are referring to a very specific and worrisome aspect of the State's coercive powers. In fact, State violence may imply the infliction of pain and suffering, incarceration, and even death. It seems obvious, then, that for those who care about self-government, questions about the limits and scope of this particular kind of State violence cannot escape democratic reflection and control: what is at stake here is all too relevant. Finally, I should mention that in societies as the one in which I inhabit (namely Argentina, which I do not think is too different from other Western societies) the existence of profound and unjustified inequalities make the whole problem still more serious. In deeply unequal and unjust societies the risk of a biased, improper use of the most dangerous State's coercive powers seems to radically increase. In these contexts, privileged groups begin to use those coercive powers in defense of their own unfair advantages. This situation gives us additional reasons to care about how the State's coercive powers are used, and ensure that they are subjected to strict democratic regulation. It is at this point that the appeal to deliberative democracy becomes more attractive. We need that all decisions concerning the direst use of the State's coercive powers to be carefully debated: those decisions, in particular, need to be properly impartial, rather than biased toward or against certain groups.

Now, there is good and bad news regarding these possible and desired connections between deliberative democracy and the criminal law. The bad news is that the two disciplines have not frequently intersected. Political philosophers, in general, and democratic theorists, in particular, have not demonstrated a significant interest in basic questions of criminal law. This omission seems perplexing, given the tremendous public importance of what is at stake. Albert Dzur has made reference, in this respect, to the "*invisibility* of the problem of punishment," for democratic theory.[7] Following this view, Bernard Harcourt stated that "it remains the case that the prison is largely invisible to democratic theory or practice."[8] In a similar line, some years ago Pablo de Greiff asked: "What explains the reluctance on the part of Habermas and most other theorists of deliberative democracy to engage the topic of punishment directly, despite their interest in the coercive dimensions of the law?"[9] Take, for example, the case of three of the leading political philosophers of twentieth century, namely John Rawls in the Anglo-American world, Jurgen Habermas in continental Europe, and Carlos Nino in Latin America.[10] The three of them have been, in fact, deeply interested in fundamental questions related to the justification of State coercion—they took this justificatory problem as the most important problem faced by political philosophy. At the same time, they all clearly understood that a proper reflection about the justified use of the State coercive powers required also a reflection within democratic theory. More specifically, the three of them advocated a deliberative conception of democracy. Now, the fact is that even though they all recognized the need to say something more specific about criminal law, its justification, and its connection to democratic theory, none of them carried that reflection much further.

The reasons explaining this omission are not obvious.[11] Perhaps many deliberative democrats simply believed it was necessary to strengthen the theoretical basis of their theory (which faced numerous criticisms) before getting into the analysis of specific institutional issues; perhaps they considered it was necessary to first focus on issues of distributive justice before addressing the question of punishment.

Now the good news. In spite of what was just said, in recent times we find increasing theoretical efforts—promoted by sympathizers of deliberative democracy—trying to repair those serious omissions. First of all, we have seen, in the last few years, a growing theoretical interest in trying to establish the missing connections between Habermas's, Nino's, or Rawls's conceptions of democracy and justice, and basic issues of criminal law. Among other relevant writings, we find Dzur's and Mirchandani's work connecting Habermas's democratic theory and criminal law; Pablo de Greiff doing the same with Nino's democratic theory; and Sharon Dolovich pursuing a similar task by using John Rawls's theory of justice.[12] In addition to this, we find many other relevant writings trying to tie fundamental issues of criminal law together with central issues of political philosophy and democratic theory. Among many other important writings making these connections we can make reference to the work by John Braithwaite, Philip Pettit, and R. A. Duff.[13]

At this point, let me present the particular conception of democracy I will be taking as my standpoint in the following pages. This clarification may be relevant given the profound disagreements we have concerning the meaning of this *essentially contested* concept.[14] At the same time, and precisely as a result of the breadth and depth of the existing disagreements, I do not want and will not take as my standpoint a too demanding or too polemic view of democracy. So in what follows I will take as a regulative idea of democracy one that is basically in line with the one that Habermas, Rawls, or Nino had in mind, when they wrote about deliberative democracy. This view, at least, has the advantage of being shared—in one way or another—by numerous contemporary thinkers working with theories of democracy.[15]

I do not want or need to propose as a regulative ideal an oversophisticated or complex version of deliberative democracy, which would only accentuate the level of the existing disagreements. By contrast, I will be herein assuming a rather simple or standard version of deliberative democracy, based on the famous Habermasian *communicative approach to democracy*, according to which a justified public decision requires the deliberate agreement of *"all those potentially affected."* There are basically two fundamental notions in Habermas's claim, which I will take as the two basic requirements of a deliberative democracy. The first requirement relates to *public deliberation*, and the second to *social inclusion*. According to the regulative idea of democracy that I will be taking into account, a public decision will be in principle more justified, the more it represents the product of an inclusive debate—a debate among "all those potentially affected." In sum, for those who assume this deliberative view, legal norms should be the product of i) *a broad collective public discussion* in which ii) *all those potentially affected* by those legal norms take part. *Inclusiveness* and *public discussion* appear, then, as the two main requirements for a law to be considered a legitimate law. To put the same point differently, decisions that are the mere product of technocratic experts, or decisions that have not been properly discussed by the people at large, would not be here considered adequately justified.[16]

With these clarifications in mind, I will now proceed to examine three areas were we find promising attempts to integrate the criminal law and democratic theory.

Democracy and Criminal Trials

In the last few years, criminal law and democratic theory crossed their paths in different occasions, and these encounters were usually very rich. One of the most interesting areas of intersection is that of criminal trials, where the work of R. A. Duff, Carlos Nino, or Pablo de Greiff played a leading role. In different ways, they have all been advocating for communicative approaches that have strong implications for the criminal process. The communicative commitment aspect of their approach puts their theories together with other, more established expressive theories of punishment—they appear to be in a relationship of species and genus. However, and even though communicative theories and so-called expressive theories of punishment are clearly interrelated, it is important to differentiate one from the other.

In general terms, it could be said that the main purpose of expressive theories is communicative (rather than, for example, rehabilitation, suffering, or vengeance). What expressive approaches want is to communicate condemnation to the criminal for the wrongness of the act he committed: they "disavow that act as one which is not to be tolerated or condoned."[17] For example, according to Jean Hampton's particular approach to expressive punishment, punishment gains justification as a result of its (potential) service to moral education. Thus, punishment is justified "*as a good* for those who experience it," rather than as a "deserved evil."[18] Hampton compares this situation with the parent who punishes his beloved son, and states: "The infliction of pain by a parent on a beloved but naughty child, suggests to me that punishment should not be justified as a deserved evil, but rather as an attempt, by someone who cares, to improve a wayward person."[19] One may disagree with Hampton's view for different reasons (i.e., concerning the contribution of the deprivation of liberty to moral education), but still agree with the basic purpose of her enterprise, which is to approach the criminal law from a communicative perspective. We may say something similar regarding another well-known "expressive" view, such as the one advanced by Joel Feinberg. According to Feinberg, "punishment is a conventional device for the expression of attitudes of resentment and indignation, and of judgments of disapproval and reprobation, on the part either of the punishing authority himself or of those 'in whose name' the punishment is inflicted."[20] However, the fact is that expressive approaches to criminal law, like the ones that Joel Feinberg or Jean Hampton once offered, have only a thin connection with the central goals and ambitions of a deliberative democracy. In effect, expressive approaches seem to be mainly interested in "one-direction" communication, where the offender can only listen and finally accept the message that the others want to convey to him.

By contrast, communicative approaches of the kind I want to defend here see the criminal process in a different fashion, which seems more clearly related to the basic assumptions of a deliberative democracy. In effect, in Duff's, Nino's, or de Greiff's communicative approach, the criminal process is conceived of as a *dialogic* process, where the offender is not simply seen as a passive recipient of a public reproach. In other terms, in the kind of communicative approach that they advocate for, the criminal process is seen as a "two-way" process, where one part tries to actively address the other, resorting to his reason, rather than his fear. The entire point of the process is to engage in a *moral dialogue* with the offender, trying to appeal to his reason and his understanding.

With the support of Jurgen Habermas and Carlos Nino's work on democratic theory, de Greiff reads and interprets expressive theories of punishment in a "dialogic" manner. Based on those premises, he sees the criminal trial as a process where we engage with offenders as moral agents and do our best to appeal to their reason and understanding. For him, "the point is not merely that in blaming someone we simply claim that there *are* moral reasons why he should have avoided acting as he did, but that we offer those reasons to him. In blaming someone we engage him in a moral discussion whose aim is to get him to accept our judgment on his action."[21] Of course, the process may fail, because the offender remains unpersuaded by our arguments. Moreover, we need to be prepared to "be persuaded by *him* to modify [our] original judgment on his conduct."[22] But the final point is the same: "The aim of blaming is not merely to get people to change their behavior, but to do so for the right reasons."[23] At this point, de Greiff view on the criminal trial becomes indistinguishable from that of R. A. Duff.

R. A. Duff has developed a communicative approach to the criminal law over many years, but it was only recently when he overtly made a connection between that view and a deliberative idea of democracy. He explicitly endorsed "participatory and deliberative conceptions of democracy" in order to provide support for his view of the trial as a "process of calling to account, as just one of the various ways in which, as participants in the wide range of practices of reason that structure our lives, we hold each other responsible."[24] In recent years, Duff has provided us with what is probably the best and more influential account about dialogic criminal trials, and how they could look like. For Duff, "to put someone on trial, and to punish him for his wrongdoing, is to treat him as a member of the normative community under whose laws he is tried and punished." The accused has to be addressed as a fellow member of a normative community whose values he can be expected to understand and accept.[25] Moreover, he has to have a fair opportunity to be listened to, and his views have to be taken seriously and duly weighed.

In sum, despite their (partially) different theoretical backgrounds and goals, the work of Duff, Nino, or de Greiff provides us with interesting examples of how democratic theory could intersect with criminal law in order to renovate our thinking about criminal trials.[26]

Democracy and Sentencing

In the previous section we explored different suggestions coming from democratic theory in relation to the organization of criminal trials, and how they could be improved. Here we shall explore some proposals, also derived from democratic theory, concerning criminal justice sentencing. In general terms, as we shall see, advocates of deliberative theories of democracy (or similar) have shown an interest in changing the sentencing process, so as to make it more deliberative and, more significantly, more inclusive and open to civil society. In this way, they have challenged traditional legal approaches, which are distinguished by their individualized and juricentric features. In what follows, I will focus on two main alternatives to the prevalent sentencing process.

The first alternative that I want to explore relates to studies on restorative justice. More specifically, I will illustrate the first alternative through the innovative approach to restorative justice that was developed by John Braithwaite, particularly in collaboration with Philip Pettit. Inspired both by a republican political philosophy and also by the enormous theoretical and practical work on restorative justice that has been done in the last decades, John Braithwaite and Philip Pettit have developed a complete and renewed approach to criminal justice. Their theory was developed in its most complete form in their book *Not Just Deserts*, but they refined some of their basic ideas in numerous other essays that they wrote individually or together.[27]

For Braithwaite and Pettit, the criminal system should be designed "not primarily to punish offenders but, rather, out of community-based dialogue, to bring home to them the disapproval of others and the consequences for others of what they did."[28] The idea of fostering community-based dialogues seems an interesting proposal, which is very much in line with the principles and objectives of a deliberative democracy. Instead of conceiving the sentencing process as a process that is directed against an offender who has been singled out because of the fault he committed, here it is understood as a collective enterprise concerning a problem that, more or less directly, involves the entire community. The final goal of that process is not to obtain an individualized sentence against a particular individual who (most probably) will be then punished through a loss of liberty, which implies his being separated from the rest. Rather, the purpose of these community-based solutions is to create the conditions for making collective dialogue possible. The idea is to repair a crime that was committed against the entire community, so as to restore the previously existing situation, healing the social bonds that were damaged, and reintegrating the offender to the community.

In consonance with those assumptions, Braithwaite and Pettit have favored "a radical redesign of the criminal justice system," based on *community accountability conferences* as the ones that have taking place in New Zealand and Australia (and more recently in the United States, Canada, or the United Kingdom),[29] which have permitted deciding most criminal cases outside the courtrooms.[30] Community conferences are a restorative justice practice, designed to bring families and relatives of victims and offenders together, to find their own solutions to conflicts.[31] As Lode Walgrave has put it, the conference is an "inclusive process" aimed at finding solutions to "the problems and harms" caused by particular offenses.[32] Through its emphasis both on inclusion and deliberation, the conference-method seems particularly appropriate from those who care about deliberative democracy.[33] In sum, community conferences represent an attractive alternative to prevailing approaches to sentencing, which properly honor the main values of democratic deliberation, namely dialogue, inclusion, persuasion, and equality.[34]

Let me now examine a second alternative to traditional juricentric, top-down approaches to sentencing, which comes from academic works seeking to revitalize the institution of the jury. In particular, I want to focus my attention on recent works by Albert Dzur, who has been trying to explicitly reconnect his studies on the jury with basic issues of deliberative theory.

A harsh critic of both penal elitism and penal populism, Dzur demonstrates how, as a consequence of these theoretical influences, the dominant system of criminal justice tends to be organized around tribunals that "produce distance" from the public, "impede victims, offenders, and members of the public from recognizing the human suffering in both criminal offenses and in state punishment," and foster "segregation, separation, and ultimately, dehumanization."[35]

In addition, the prevalent situation seems to undermine the chances of alternative arrangements like the jury, which emphasizes the importance of public participation in penal sentencing: juries have thus been confined to the margins of the criminal justice system. According to

Dzur, in countries like Great Britain the jury has been limited to only the most serious criminal trials, while in America it "has been on the decline for decades as state and federal jury trials have shrunk in absolute members and as a percentage of total cases."[36] "Supplanted by plea agreements, settlements, summary judgements, and nontrial forums," Dzur adds, "juries in the United States hear a very small fraction— around 5 percent or lower—of all cases." As a consequence, he admits, commentators "now talk about the 'eclipse,' 'disappearance,' and inevitably, the 'extinction' of the jury."[37]

Facing these tendencies, the purpose of Dzur's recent work has been trying to strengthen support to the jury, restorative justice and other legal mechanisms that could contribute to "close social distances between offenders and victims, and between the people who commit offenses and the people who live near them and will live near them when the are done making amends."[38] These responses, Dzur assumes, can promote people's civic capacities, stressing our "interconnectedness" and "relationships that link us together." Again, what we have here is an approach to sentencing that is openly linked to deliberative approaches to democracy, and modeled on its fundamental principles of collective dialogue and social integration.

It is worth noting the way in which these more democratic alternatives promote a decentralized, open, horizontal, collective, discussed, case-sensitive way of producing sentences, which profoundly contrasts with the dominant model of top-down, vertical, juricentric decisions, epitomized by the system of sentencing guidelines that has gained increasing influence in the Anglo-American world.[39]

This exploration, I hope, helps us illustrate the ways in which democratic theory has intervened or can intervene in basic academic debates within the criminal law. The examples that I presented expose the richness and potential of the democratic approach, and at the same time demonstrate the capacity of democratic theory as a critical tool in the face of hardly justifiable dominant practices.

Democracy and Penal Decision-Making

So far we have explored possible connections between deliberative theory and the criminal trial and sentencing processes. Here I want to pay attention to the way in which deliberative democracy may help us challenge the two forces that have been driving penal decision-making in the last decades, namely *penal elitism* and *penal populism*. Democracy, I will maintain, requires all norms, but particularly criminal law norms (given the dramatic implications they have) to be fully discussed by all those who may be affected by their existence or their absence.

Although in principle penal elitism and penal populism are presented as opposed views, the two approaches seem to be closely connected in their actual, shared elitism. *Elitist views* appeal to *the people's interests*, without ever asking the people about their actual viewpoints. Meanwhile, *populist views* appeal to *the people's will*, without ever engaging with them in a fair conversation about their actual viewpoints. In the end, none of these views seems to take seriously the viewpoints of the actual people that they claim to represent. They both speak for the public.

From the perspective of a deliberative democracy, both approaches are unattractive because of the way they deal with democracy's two main requirements, namely *social inclusion* and *deliberation*. Elitist approaches to criminal justice—as I will understand them here—emphasize the role of technocratic experts in everything that concerns the criminal law (and consequently dismiss the importance of issues of social inclusion), while populist approaches have at least a rhetoric of social inclusion, while dismissing the value of fair public deliberation. Taking into account these very basic characteristics, one could also maintain that penal elitism is, for democrats, particularly flawed in what concerns social inclusion, while penal populism is particularly faulty in what concerns collective deliberation. Let me explore these two views separately.

Penal Elitism and Democracy

According to David Garland, *penal welfarism* dominated policymaking "in the decades following the Second World War."[40] During the years of its ascendancy, criminal law policies were created by governmental experts and professional practitioners. These policies were the product of "expert knowledge and empirical research," and they usually assumed that reform and social intervention were plausible responses to crime.[41] From a democratic perspective, penal welfarism can be seen as a clear example of elitism—in this case, elitism of the liberal type. As some criminologists have put it, it was the time of the "Platonic guardians": "We were the Platonic guardians; there was no question about that. We had a pretty good idea of what needed to be done, and we thought it was right."[42]

In the face of prevailing elitist policies (no matter the way they cover their elitism, or the rhetoric they employ in their defense), the responses coming from deliberative democracy must be clear: more inclusion and more discussion. On occasions, but not frequently, theorists of the criminal law have acknowledged the importance of these democratic requirements. Ian Loader, for example, has objected to the rule of the Platonic guardians in criminal justice, and suggested the promotion of democratic institutional reforms in the area. In his words, "we need to design institutional ways of living with, and seeking to make as inclusive and informed as is possible, the mediated public contests about crime and punishment that have become a recurrent feature of our time."[43] For him, "open public debate about crime and punishment is not something that democratic societies are or should be able to shy away from. Indeed, under the right conditions, such dialogue can buttress the public reason that Platonic guardians take to be fragile, and help counter the spontaneous convictions that they fear will ... run dangerously amok through the institutions of criminal justice."[44] We find similar democratic responses in the work of Loader and Sparks. According to them, "questions of crime, order and justice are—and should be—settled through political contest and debate."

In my view, these initial responses point to the right direction: penal decision-making has become an unjustifiable elitist practice; democracy needs to meet the criminal law even at this level; we should not be afraid of opening the discussion of crucial issues of public interest to the general public. Concerning these fundamental points, deliberative democrats cannot agree more with Loader, Sparks, and other theorists who have stressed the importance of insufflating democracy to the criminal law.[45] Now, and having said this, we still have to see what are the concrete practical implications of these initiatives. We know some of them, for instance in what concerns policing policies, and they seem very appropriate.[46] However, it is still not clear for me how much these proposals differ from other still elitist views that have been developed in this area, which I want to at least briefly explore in the following paragraphs.

Mainly, I am thinking about the more recent work of philosophers like Philip Pettit. Pettit has developed an interesting and novel approach to democracy and, particularly taking into account those attractive developments, the proposals that he presented in the face of increasingly punitive policies seem somehow surprising.[47] Pettit seems to be particularly concerned with what he calls "the outrage dynamic" that operates in the area of criminal justice.[48] The dynamic would take the following form: first, the State exposes to society a certain evil; second, the exposure of this evil leads, then, to popular outrage; and third, the popular outrage forces government to adopt new (and normally repressive) measures.[49] Taking into account this outrage dynamic, Pettit suggests taking the sentencing policy "out of the direct hands of parliament and given in the first instance to a body that operates at arm's length from parliament and government" (like a central bank). In this way, the area of sentencing policy would be totally removed "from the immediate pressures of popular outrage."[50] In my view, even if we accepted his descriptive presentation, as I do, we would still have no good reasons to advance proposals as the ones he advances. From the standpoint of a deliberative notion of democracy, one should at least make two objections to Pettit's view. The first objection has to do with the *deliberative* requirement of democracy. If we recognize with him that the main origins of the obnoxious outrage dynamic reside in the sensationalist media, or the people's lack of information, or the absence of adequate forum of debate, then the reaction should be the obvious one (which does not seem to be the obvious to Pettit), namely, to promote public discussions; open new forums for political debate; create new sources for the transmission of impartial information; reduce the influence of money in the media and in politics; and so forth.[51] Second, and concerning the *inclusive* requirement of a deliberative democracy, it seems clear that his proposal is problematic in its suggesting taking penal policy making away from the hands of the people, and proposing the adoption of new countermajoritarian institutions. Deliberative democracy does not propose inclusive discussions of public issues out of a preference for multitudinous meetings, but rather because it considers that well-designed collective deliberations favor impartiality.[52]

Penal Populism and Democracy

While penal elitism was particularly influential during the 1950s, and the years that followed the consolidation of Welfare State, the new experience of "law and order" appears as a more contemporary phenomenon, associated with neoconservative and neoliberal policies and, more specifically, to political phenomena as those that we knew as "Thatcherism" and "Reaganism."[53]

Initially, Antony Bottoms used the phrase "populist punitiveness" to "convey the notion of politicians tapping into, and using for their own purposes, what they believe to be the public's generally punitive stance."[54] For David Garland, penal populism refers to a "new experience" of law and order where experts are distrusted and legal decisions are greatly influenced by popular opinion and the media.[55] In fact, the term "populism" has became associated to politics of "tough on crime," and emotional responses usually following some horrific crimes that generate intense media attention.[56] The new populist formula represented an unbeatable and successful combination: it was a highly profitable political proposal that promised great achievements in terms of crime reduction, and which was, at the same time, highly justified and legitimized in democratic terms.

The profitable political character of these new policies seems to be beyond question. By contrast, their effectiveness and justification has been the object of much dispute. In terms of effectiveness, some authors maintained that, in balance, the costs imposed by these policies were excessively high, and some others suggested that the new tough on crime policies were, in actual practice, much less effective than announced.[57] In any case, and for the purposes of this chapter, I will here focus on the criticisms that were directed to the democratic justification of these sentencing policies.

Let me start this analysis by making three points, which are connected to the two main concerns of deliberative democracy, namely issues related to *inclusion* and issues related to *debate*. First of all, populists tend to appeal to the people's will, but in fact they frequently do not bother in actually consulting the people they refer to. Populists do not seem to be actually interested in engaging with those they constantly invoke. As John Pratt, one of the leading academics working with penal populism, put it, "penal populism" refers to those politicians and groups who *claim to speak* on behalf of "the people" in relation to the development of penal policies.[58] Populists usually require the adoption of tougher criminal policies as if it were simply obvious that such a policy was what the majority of the population demanded. This has been a typical populist attitude in Latin America, where policies of tough on crime have also acquired a growing relevance during the last decades. Clearly, this is also a typical case of populism failing to take the *inclusive* character of democracy seriously: thus, and in spite of its rhetoric, populism simply becomes another version of penal elitism.

The second point concerns populists who refer to opinion polls of one or another kind, in order to quickly extract punitive lessons from them (see Turner, this volume). In these cases, democratic theory would first recommend pausing for a while rather than using such polls to support a race toward punitivism. Authors such as Antony Bottoms, for example, have demonstrated the complexity of the people's attitudes to crime and punishment.[59] Writing against the unsophisticated assumptions and dramatic consequences of the new populist policies, Bottoms has established that "we cannot speak in any straightforward fashion about 'public opinion' on crime in a way that automatically equates it with a heavily punitive approach."[60] Reviewing the exiting literature on the topic, Gerry Johnston has also concluded that "a careful trawl through the results of surveys will turn up plenty of evidence" to the effect that public opinion is "more diverse, and less outrightly punitive than [is] usually supposed."[61]

The third point is, however, the most relevant one from the perspective of a deliberative democracy. It refers to the importance of distinguishing between "mere opinions" and "deliberative judgements," and invites us to resist trivializations concerning democracy and collective *debate*. For example, studies such as the one presented by David Green in the *British Journal of Criminology* in 2006 have been relevant in helping to distinguish between "public opinion and public judgment about crime."[62] In his work, Greene tried to build a case for more defensible assessments of informed public opinion on crime control and penal policy. Green's article, among others, came to provide support to one of the basic claims of deliberative democrats in this area, which actually explains their insistence about the importance of promoting actual democratic *debates*. For deliberative democrats, the idea is that collective public discussion is crucial for allowing each person to "launder" her own preferences.[63] Through public debates, it is here assumed, each person has the possibility to correct her own mistakes, incorporate new and relevant information to her reasoning, dilute unjustified prejudices, clarify ambiguities and contradictions in her thinking, and so forth. This is why deliberative democrats support institutional systems that do not take the people's preferences as given: they see people's declared preferences or "mere opinions" as endogenous outcomes of a process that often involved prejudice, resignations, and injustice. This is why, in the end, they make a clear separation between *the market and the forum*.[64]

Green's article—focused on the criminal law, and theoretically grounded on the work of deliberative democrats such as Jurgen Habermas—helps emphasize the previous point. In his view, "most typical conceptions of public opinion are not based on deliberation."[65] For him—and this is the main conclusion of his study—"public opinion" should be simply deemed as "uninformed, unconsidered opinion, tending to lack validity on contentious issues, measuring top-of-the-head reactions to questions about which little is known."[66] Other studies, also inspired by deliberative theories of democracy, such as the one by Dzur and Mirchandani, insist on a similar point, and present "punitive populism of three strikes laws as mere opinion."[67] Dzur and Mirchandani make an exhaustive analysis of neopunitive populist policies, and demonstrate the flaws of punitive polls from a democratic standpoint. For them, deliberative decisions require "*rational, open, ongoing and* ultimately *value pluralistic* [debates]," which cannot be found, in any significant way, behind the adoption of three-strikes laws.[68]

These studies, I believe, have been doing an important service, by urging us not to accept market polls as equivalent to democratic debates: there is a huge difference between them, which should always be taken into account, and most particularly at times of designing new public policies. These works have also come together with some interesting theoretical and practical efforts directed at the promotion of deliberative polls, which seem to be suitable mechanisms for measuring public views about criminal justice issues, certainly more promising than traditional polls.[69]

Democracy All the Way Down: Deliberative Democracy, Social Protests, and Authority

I now want to explore different forms in which the criminal justice system could be changed, in ways that strengthened and expanded its democratic character. Before doing that, let me briefly summarize our findings so far. First of all, we have explored how criminal trials could be reimagined and reorganized according to more robust democratic theories. Of course, to state this does not mean that things have changed or somehow improved in the direction of more democracy in the last few years. In fact, one could say that very little has changed, and the examples with which we began this exploration (*Austin and Saxby, Schifrin*) only confirm that uncomfortable news. However, it is still important to realize that democratic theory has demonstrated being well-equipped to deal with these issues, in ways that are both normatively attractive and practically plausible.

With regard to sentencing, again, we have seen that there are interesting proposals, also well-informed by democratic principles, which—ideally at least—could be used to replace the present practice or guide the elaboration of plausible reforms to it. The fact that changes are necessary seems to me obvious—and again, the actual practice in *Austin and Saxby* or *Schifrin* simply confirms this intuition. Protesters were reproached and finally condemned in ways that actually undermined the very practice of protesting that democrats consider vital for democracy. Certainly, such decisions—openly hostile to democratic contestation—may be explained by numerous reasons. However, it is difficult not to link them with the juricentric, top-down, individualized decision-making process that produced the final judicial decisions. Alternative processes, we can hypothesize, more sensitive to an inclusive process of deliberation, would at least be more sensitive to the demands of the less advantaged, which in many occasions seem to find it so difficult to present their views in public and thus enrich our democracies.

Finally, we paid attention to the penal decision-making process. It seems clear that, without the introduction of democratic changes at this stage, nothing could really change in the area: from the democratic perspective it is clear that we need better and fairer criminal trials, and also better sentencing process, but no improvements would be actually possible if the laws to be applied and interpreted in each case were unjust. According to our discussion so far, democratic theory has been very helpful in the area, by providing us with critical tools for objecting to both penal elitism and penal populism. The democratic critique of both these dominant penal currents is of primary importance. However, these objections are not enough for our purposes. We do not just need to object to the prevalent decision-making process in the area, which has been so dramatically elitist for so long, but also need to start thinking about democratic ways of replacing it. Again, our initial examples provide us with excellent illustrations to what I am saying. Of course, one may try to show that there are no reasons for applying the existing normative in such a restrictive way. But "finding ways out" is not the right answer to an unjust or repressive legislation: the problem starts from the very fact of having those laws, call them antiterrorist laws, like in England, Argentina, or Ecuador; or antisedition laws; or antisocial behavior laws. Under the light of these findings, my conclusion is that it is both possible and desirable to inform and shape the criminal law with democratic theory, all the way down.

In any case, it seems clear that in order to reach a full integration between the criminal law and democratic theory, there is still much theoretical and practical work to be done. For the purposes of this chapter, and given the space and time constraints that limit this exploration, I will concentrate my attention on three issues, concerning how this integration is being developed and could be improved. The first has to do with *consequences* of deliberation for the criminal law; the second has to do with the openness of deliberative democracy to *conflicts*, and social tensions in general; and the third has to do with issues of democratic *authority* and criminal law.

The Criminal Law and the Benign Consequences of Democratic Deliberation Title like all the others

Over many years, a simple (but empirically unsupported) assumption suggested the existence of a strong correlation between political participation and punitivism. The idea (central to the above-presented notion of penal populism) was that the vast majority of the people were motivated by revenge, and systematically defended more punishments and more severe punishments in what concerned the criminal law. This story had obvious implications in terms of public policy: one had to be careful before opening the Pandora box of political participation in the area of criminal law, given the dramatic consequences that tended to follow from it (i.e., impulses of revenge, stricter punishments). Assumptions of this kind played a crucial role in theoretical discussions about punishment and criminal law, and moved even criminal law theorists from the left to resist any aperture of the criminal law to democratic participation.[70]

Fortunately, in the last years we have seen the development of interesting empirical experiments that helped us to recognize that those alarming claims connecting democracy and punitivism were, to say the least, not obvious. The work of James Fishkin has been particularly helpful in this respect. The results of the first deliberative poll that was carried out in Great Britain for discussing the issue of rising crime and what to do about it, showed particularly interesting results. On the one hand, they offered "a picture of better informed and more thoughtful public opinion."[71] On the other hand, they also showed the emergence of less punitive attitudes among citizens, including a greater awareness regarding the implications of prison and long sentences.

These studies, related to the citizens' attitudes toward crime, have come together with other interesting empirical works, pointing toward other positive consequences of democracy (and deliberative democracy, in particular), in the area of criminal law. I am thinking about studies that presented "evidence of the virtues of [deliberative democracy] in reducing mass incarceration."[72] This new line of work came to provide empirical support to the idea that "civic engagement in a *deliberative* policymaking process can produce more equitable and less repressive public policies," and do so by closing the gap between "the public's demands for retribution and the criminal justice officials' technocratic responses to crime."[73] The idea is that "public participation" tends toward "penal moderation rather than law and order politics, contrary to conventional claims about too much democracy."[74] In addition, we have now better data about the importance of favoring the democratic integration of felons and former offenders.[75] In my view, the best case advanced by these empirical studies exploring connections between democracy and the criminal law is a negative one: they have helped us understand in what way the breakdown of democracy in many of our societies accounts (or partially accounts) for the massive rise in incarceration over the past three decades.[76]

All these empirical studies, of different type, have undoubtedly contributed to strengthen the case for deliberative democracy in the area of criminal law. They allow us to imagine the possibility of a fairer criminal justice system.

However, we do not need to appeal to these uncertain predictions in order to make my case for deliberative democracy. If "we" (meaning those of us who support deliberative democracy) make a case for this particular understanding of democracy, this is not *because* democracy tends to produce good consequences in issues related to crime, but for reasons of principle: we defend democratic mechanisms because we understand that they offer us the best way (this is to say, the most justified way) for dealing with our disagreements and uncertainties regarding issues of crime. When properly designed, they represent arrangements that we find to be fully respectful of our moral equality and equal dignity.[77] And we would defend these mechanisms even in the case that the empirical studies began to show different results. In other words, we do not base our case for deliberative democracy in the area of criminal law on the assumption that "more *deliberative* modes of criminal justice policymaking would be—or at least could be—conducive to moderate rates of punishment," as some authors have improperly suggested.[78] Even though I do not share this latter line of criticism, I do think that we should refine our approaches to democracy in this respect. We should extend and deepen our use of democratic theory; clarify what conception of democracy we support, and for what reasons; and recognize that the most important service that democracy can make to the criminal law comes not at the explanatory, but rather at the justificatory level: democracy can help us obtain a more justified criminal law (I will come back to this point below).

Democratic Deliberation and Disruptive Social Protests

The second clarification that is in order is the following. According to well-established approaches to deliberative democracy, democracy is basically about interchanging arguments. Now, if this were actually the case, then one of the main claims of this chapter would be severely affected.

In fact, I am here objecting to traditional approaches to the criminal law for many reasons, but also—and particularly—for being improperly hostile to political disruptions and social protests. More significantly, I am here using the theoretical apparatus of deliberative democracy for critically assessing those views. However, if it were true that deliberative democracy were only related to exchanging arguments, then such a view of democracy would help me to object different aspects of the dominant approaches to criminal law, but not some of the aspects I am most interested in objecting to.[79]

Clearly, there are good grounds for making this criticism to deliberative democracy, particularly if one takes into account Jurgen Habermas original definition of the concept, which ties it too closely to the "exchange of rational arguments." Having said this, however, I should clarify, first, that many other adherents of deliberative democracy have adequately criticized this approach for being improperly and unnecessarily narrow. Jane Mansbridge and Iris Marion Young, for example, maintained that through their emphasis on consensus the exchange of arguments and reasons, deliberative theories have inadequately relegated other forms of communication as rhetorical and strategic communication. For instance, Iris Young challenged Jurgen Habermas's view on deliberative democracy for considering arguing as the privileged and legitimate discourse in the public sphere. For her, prevailing deliberative theories improperly establish exclusionary norms of dispassionateness, orderliness, civility, and articulateness.[80] Contrary to Habermas's view, Young maintains that alternative forms of speech (which may include rhetoric, street demonstrations, and protest) should also be considered valuable forms of discourse. In her opinion, many of these acts are oriented toward inclusion. "[In] a deep democratic society," she affirms, "the presumption should be in favor of the protestors that their purpose is to persuade."[81] In an important article, trying to rethink and expand the notion of deliberative democracy, Jane Mansbridge and a group of distinguished (deliberative democracy) scholars maintained: "A deliberative democrat might, for example, justify strikes or the threat of strikes on . . . equalizing or neutralizing grounds. Any use of power to create the conditions for listening in situations of impeding inequality, would also qualify."[82]

I personally share this more expansive understanding of deliberative democracy, which I have tried to defend in other occasions, in connection with the criminal law.[83] Moreover, I consider this to be the only consistent and attractive approach to deliberative democracy, and the one that merits our closest attention. This approach suggests that the most crucial and attractive feature of democracy is precisely its capacity for taking the viewpoints of the dissidents—the viewpoints of those who disagree with the majority view—seriously. Without a serious consideration of those viewpoints, public decisions would lose the impartial character that should distinguish them—an impartial character that gives deliberative democracy its meaning and sense.

Now, given that in many occasions the expression of dissident voices and viewpoints assume disruptive and unpleasant forms (as in the particular cases of protests I am interested in considering), I will take some additional time trying to justify why (and how) deliberative democracy should (could) protect those demands.

First, someone may want to say that deliberative democracy should protect the dissidents' voices or words, but not necessary their actions. However, it is very important to recognize that some nontypically expressive behavior may contain expressive aspects. In those cases, we need to make additional efforts to preserve the *expressive component* of these actions, if that were possible.[84] The "flag burning" cases, among others, have forced legal scholars to think along these lines.[85] Doctrinaires have tended to conclude by saying that political messages can be conveyed in many different ways, which do not necessarily—and do not only—include words alone, written or spoken. Thus, the action of throwing an egg at a politician, which may be legally and morally condemned, usually conveys a strong message—actually a very strong critical message—in political terms. To neglect that part of the story is to neglect a crucial part of it.[86] We need to open up space for the consideration of the *illocutionary aspects* of nonverbal acts, particularly within a theory that emphasizes democratic deliberation.

Second, someone could object to what I just said, by adding that the dissident claims (either through their voices or actions) do not need to adopt disruptive or improper forms. However, my impression is that we cannot expect dissidents, still less demand them, to present their claims in a neat and quiet form, as if they were writing an op. ed. in a newspaper.[87] Usually, their demands take disruptive forms not because dissenters or protesters like to create conflict, but simply because they need to be heard. In modern societies, and particularly in those characterized by high levels of inequality and impoverished institutional systems, disadvantaged groups have an unjustified and disproportionally low opportunity to make their claims heard (our institutional systems seem to be much more permeable to the claims of the powerful few, than to the claims of the majority of the disadvantaged).

Third, the fact that some of these disruptions appear to be in conflict with the law (i.e., breaching peace and order) should not preclude further legal discussions and reflections on the topic ("you just broke the law"). By contrast, it is precisely in those cases when we need to begin a "theoretical ascent," as Ronald Dworkin put it.[88] At that point, we need to start wondering, for example, what different rights have been violated, and how to put them together, without simply assuming (as seems to be the rule in these cases) that protesters do not have the law on their side, or that they do not have fundamental rights to claim in their favor. To start with, protesters can claim to have on their side not only rights to free speech and rights to petition and manifest, as it was the case in *Austin and Saxby*,[89] but also more substantive rights, such as their social rights, as it was case in *Schifrin*.

Fourth, some people seem to accept the right to protest but at the same time allow significant curtailments of it when violence appears or is likely to appear (think, again, about the *Austin and Saxby* case). Against this view, one could assert the following: the fact that a particular protest comes together with acts of violence says nothing against the importance or the need to protect and preserve the protest.[90] We have a long experience dealing with these difficulties, for instance concerning the right of strike and situations of violence. That experience seems to be perfectly applicable in these circumstances. We know, for instance, that we may perfectly prevent or (once occurred) deal with acts of violence separately, without putting into question the right to strike. We may give full protection to the right to strike while taking care of those who create violence separately.

Finally, one could claim that democracy requires the limitation, rather than the protection of social protests, as I have suggested here. Notably, in fact, this is what many judges maintained, in their decisions about social protests. Remember, for example, the judicial response that I quoted regarding the *Schifrin* case. Judges of the Appeal Court then maintained that according to Argentina's Constitution there was "only one legitimate form for expressing the sovereign will of the people," which was suffrage. Now, against this important claim there is an obvious answer, which is, by the way, one that naturally and compellingly derives from the approach I tried to develop in this chapter. The answer could be, "Fine, but could you be more precise and tell me what conception of democracy you have in mind?" It seems clear to me (and this has been my argument so far) that a deliberative conception of democracy not only resists that restrictive judicial conclusion but also suggests a protective, rather than a hostile approach to social protests—particularly in the context of deep and unjustified inequalities, as the Argentine one. But I should say that I am also confident that less sophisticated or ambitious understandings of democracy would reach to similar outcomes (by the way, the same Argentine judges who were invoking the National Constitution's conception of democracy were not taking into account that that Constitution is strongly committed to numerous participatory mechanisms, for example. Against what they claimed, the National Constitution did not limit democracy to periodical suffrage).

Democratic Authority and Legitimacy of the Criminal Law

In the previous pages I maintained that the case for deliberative democracy did not derive from the supposed benefits that it generated, concerning penal moderation; or the way in which it could illuminate our approach to social protests. By contrast, I claimed that the virtues of deliberative democracy were connected to reasons of principle, namely the way in which it honored our equal moral dignity.

Concerning the foundations of the criminal law, this same democratic, principled approach may play a unique, necessary role by helping it to deal with the problem of political legitimacy. Nowadays, our criminal law theorists seem to have abandoned all serious reflections about the legitimacy of the law, as if the questions posed by those concerns had been already answered, or if the answers that were offered were obviously acceptable. But the fact is that our criminal law suffers from serious legitimacy problems. The origin of these problems seems clear: criminal norms imply involving the State in the imposition of severe pain, as a daily response to offenses committed by certain citizens against other citizens. But this public response is obviously problematic: How can we justify the imposition of severe pain to any person? Why are we presupposing that the imposition of pain represents a reasonable response to an offense? How do we justify the authority of public officers to distribute and impose punishments (more specifically, taking into account the way in which they routinely do it)? Why should someone simply assume that retribution is a better response than reparation? Why should someone accept that isolation in a prison is better (or a means to!) social reintegration?

As Sharon Dolovich has put it,

The punishment of criminal offenders can involve the infliction of extended deprivations of liberty, ongoing hardship and humiliation, and even death. Ordinarily, such treatment would be judged morally wrong, and roundly condemned, yet in the name of criminal justice, it is routinely imposed on members of society by state officials whose authority to act in these ways toward sentenced offenders is generally taken for granted.[91]

Undoubtedly, the task of justifying what the State does through its coercive powers is and will always be a difficult one, but those difficulties should not discourage us. The impossibility of finding the most perfect answer should not prevent us from trying to avoid the worst ones: the present situation is too dramatic to simple accept it as it stands. In the face of that drama, the democratic argument suggests that the task of thinking about the shape, contents and scope of our criminal law should be done collectively, through an inclusive process of discussion: What affects us all should be decided by all. More precisely, the idea is that all fundamental matters about issues of intersubjective morality should be decided by "all those potentially affected," so as to improve our chances of deciding impartially. This aim requires us to make a special effort for ensuring that the voices of all, and particularly the voices of the most affected by crime and punishment (particularly including the offenders and the offended), be heard.[92] I share, in this regard, Ian Loader's view, according to which an inclusive political deliberation is a good response, particularly in these difficult cases related to criminal justice: "The resulting opportunities for public communication about contested problems and social conflicts may thus help, not only to engender a sense of agency and political efficacy among (previously excluded) citizens and social groups, but also to introduce into debates on security greater knowledge and political experience, reflection on hitherto taken-for-granted positions, and the possibility of individual and collective learning."[93]

I understand that there are still numerous problems to deal with, related to the proposed connection between democracy and criminal law. For instance, how to organize this proposed democratic process? How to ensure that we consider and properly balance the viewpoints of all? How to avoid the risks of pure majoritarism (that penal populism promotes)? These are difficult tasks, but the seriousness of the present situation should inspire us to work for the introduction of immediate and profound reforms: for decades, the criminal law has been captured by small and privileged elites that seem to use the criminal law in their own favor, so as to preserve the unjust advantages that they presently enjoy. We live in unjust and unequal societies, and it is simply not acceptable to have our criminal norms created, applied and interpreted by an elite that benefits from this situation, and (quite obviously) is never affected by those coercive powers that they administer. Hopefully, in future, not-so-remote circumstances, things will be diverse. Perhaps, in such a desired scenario we will be able to decide cases such as *Schifrin* and *Austin and Saxby* differently. Expectantly, we will do so recognizing that democracy needs to preserve and protect as rich treasures the voices of those who dissent, voices that sometimes carry messages that we dislike, in forms that we dislike, but finally messages through which we learn how to live together.

Notes

I want to thank R. A. Duff, Albert Dzur, Elena Larrauri, Richard Sparks, and Ian Loader for comments on a previous version of this chapter. Also, I want to thank the Leverhulme Trust for a grant that allowed me to complete this research.

1. "Schifrin, Marina", Fallo de la Sala I de la Cámara Nacional de Casación Penal Tribunal: Cámara Nacional de Casación Penal, sala I Publishd in: LA LEY 2002-F, 53 – Sup. Penal 2002 (septiembre): 41.

2. *Austin v. Commissioner of the Police for the Metropolis*, [2009] UKHL 5.[2007] EWCA Civ 989, Times 29-Oct-2007, [2008] QB 660, [2008] 1 All ER 564, [2008] HRLR 1, [2008] 2 WLR 415, [2008] UKHRR 205

3. In 1997, the schoolteacher Marina Schifrin took part in a demonstration in the South of Argentina in demand for higher salaries. The demonstration was organized by schoolteachers, and included the participation of students and their parents. As it was common during those years, protesters decided to block roads in order to make their claims audible. Schifrin was then tried and found guilty, as one of the leaders of the protest, for breaching the law.

4. On May Day, 2001, there was a mass rally organized against globalization, at Oxford Circus, a commercial area in the City of London. The police had information about the meeting and assumed that there would be outbreaks of public disorder, as it had happened in previous demonstrations in the last two years.

5. In his view, "the court must allow for the fact that it may be very difficult for the police to identify the target or predict the scale of violent disorder."

6. The new legislation included the 1994 Criminal Justice and Public Order Act; the 1997 Harrasment Act (already with the New Labor in power); the 1998 Crime and Disorder Act; the 2003 Anti-Social Behaviour Act; the 2005 Serious and Organised Crime and Police Act; but also (like in Argentina) the Terrorism Act from 2000, which blurred the distinctions between terrorists and protesters.

7. See Albert Dzur, "An Introduction: Penal Democracy," *The Good Society* 23, no. 1 (2014): 1.

8. See Bernard Harcourt, "The Invisibility of the Prison in Democracy Theory," *The Good Society* 23 no. 1 (2014): 1. See also Ian Loader and Richard Sparks, "Criminology and Democratic Politics: A Reply to Critics," *British Journal of Criminology* 51, no. 1 (2011): 734–738.

9. Pablo de Greiff, "Deliberative Democracy and Punishment," *Buffalo Criminal law Review* 5, no. 2 (2002): 384.

10. See Jurgen Habermas, *Between Facts and Norms* (Cambridge, MA: MIT Press, 1996); Carlos Nino, *The Constitution of Deliberative Democracy* (New Haven, CT: Yale University Press, 1996); John Rawls, *Political Liberalism* (New York: Columbia University Press, 1991).

11. I think that the main problem at stake is the omission of democratic theorists to engage with the issue of punishment, rather than the more specific one, namely, the invisibility of the problem of mass incarceration for democratic theory. Deliberative democrats can simply say that they are against massive incarceration, and that no proper democratic theory would ever justify it.

12. See Albert Dzur, *Punishment, Participatory Democracy & The Jury* (Oxford: Oxford University Press, 2012); De Greiff, "Deliberative Democracy and Punishment"; Sharon Dolovich, "Legitimate Punishment in Liberal democracy," *Buffalo Criminal law Review* 7, no. 2 (2004): 307–442.

13. See John Braithwaite and Philip Pettit, "Republican Criminology and Victim Advocacy: Comment," *Law & Society Review* 28, no. 4 (1994): 765–776; John Braithwaite and Philip Pettit, "Republicanism and Restorative Justice: An Explanatory and Normative Connection," in Heather Strang and John Braithwaite (eds.), *Restorative Justice* (Burlington: Ashgate 2000), 145–163; John Braithwaite and Heather Strang, "Connecting Philosophy and Practice," in Heather Strang and John Braithwaite (eds.), *Restorative Justice* (Burlington: Ashgate, 2000); R. A. Duff, "Law, Language and Community: Some Preconditions of Criminal Liability," *Oxford Journal of Legal Studies* 18, no. 2 (1998): 189–206; R. A. Duff, *Punishment, Communication, and Community* (Oxford: Oxford University Press, 2001); R. A. Duff, "I Might me Guilty, But You Can't Try Me: Estoppel and Other Bars to Trial," *Ohio State Journal of Criminal Law* 1 (2004): 245–259; R. A. Duff, "Rethinking Justifications," *Tulsa Law Review* 39, no. 1 (2004): 829; R. A. Duff, "Punishment, Dignity and Degradation," *Oxford Journal of Legal Studies* 25, no. 1 (2005): 141–155; R. A. Duff, "Theorizing Criminal Law: A 25th Anniversary Essay," *Oxford Journal of Legal Studies* 25, no. 3 (2005): 353–367; R. A. Duff, "Who Is Responsible, for What, to Whom?" *Ohio State Journal of Criminal Law* 2 (2005) 441; R. A. Duff, "Blame, Moral Standing and the Legitimacy of the Criminal Trial," *Ratio* XXIII no. 2 (2010): 123–140; R. A. Duff, Linda Farmer, S. E. Marshall, and Victor Tadros, *The Trial on Trial: Towards a Normative Theory of the Criminal Trial* (Oxford: Hart Publishers, 2007); R. A. Duff and S. E. Marshall, *Penal Theory and Practice* (Manchester: Manchester University Press, 1996); Philip Pettit, "Republican Theory and Criminal Punishment," *Utilitas* 9, no. 1 (1997): 1; Philip Pettit, *Republicanism* (Oxford: Oxford University Press, 1997).

14. Jeremy Waldron, "Vagueness in Law and Language: Some Philosophical Issues," *California Law Review*. 82, no 1 (1994): 509.

15. Among many others, see James Bohman and William Rehg (eds.), *Deliberative Democracy* (Cambridge, MA: MIT Press, 1997); John Dryzek, *Deliberative Democracy and Beyond* (Oxford: Oxford University Press, 2002); Jon Elster, "The Market and the Forum," in Jon Elster and Aanud Hylland (eds.), *Foundations of Social Choice Theory* (Cambridge: Cambridge University Press, 1986), 103–132; Jon Elster, ed., *Deliberative Democracy* (Cambridge: Cambridge University Press, 1998); David Estlund, *Authority* (Princeton, NJ: Princeton University Press, 2009).

16. Of course, it is important to determine what kinds of decisions I am talking about. The issue is extremely complex and requires much additional work but, in principle,

I will be thinking about decisions on fundamental public questions or issues of intersubjective (rather than private) morality. See, for example, Carlos Nino, *Ética y derechos humanos* (Buenos Aires: Astrea, 1984). Also, there are issues related to the procedural and preconditions of democracy that cannot be simply delegated to a malfunctioning process of democratic discussion. See John Ely, *Democracy and Distrust* (Cambridge, MA: Harvard University Press, 1980); and also Habermas, *Between Facts and Norms*.

17. R. A. Duff, *Trials and Punishments* (Cambridge: Cambridge University Press, 1986), 235.

18. See Jean Hampton, "The Moral Education Theory of Punishment," *Philosophy and Public Affairs* 13, no. 3 (1984): 237.

19. Ibid.

20. See Joel Feinberg, "The Expressive Function of Punishment," *The Monist* 49, no. 3 (1965): 397–423.

21. De Greiff, "Deliberative Democracy and Punishment," 390–391.

22. Ibid.

23. Ibid.

24. Duff et al., *The Trial on Trial*, 220, 241.

25. Duff, *Trials and Punishments*.

26. To state this, however, does not mean that one could not favor such view on the trials from other different perspectives, not necessarily related to the democratic perspective that is here defended.

27. See, in particular, John Braithwaite and Philip Pettit, *Not just Deserts: A Republican Theory of Criminal Law* (Oxford: Clarendon Press, 1990).

28. Ibid., 767.

29. In these conferences, "a facilitator invites the offenders to nominate as participants the people most important in their lives ... Victim(s) also attend and are invited to nominate participants with a special relationship of care to support them." See Braithwaite and Pettit, *Not Just Deserts*, 770; Albert Dzur and Rekha Mirchandani, "Punishment and Democracy: The Role of Public Deliberation," *Punishment and Society* 9, no. 2 (2007): 152.

30. According to their study, "community accountability conferences have worked better than courts in conditions of the most extreme imbalance of power imaginable—cases in which the offenders were global corporations and victims were illiterate citizens of remote Aboriginal communities" (ibid.)

31. Estelle Zinsstag and Inge Vanfraechem, *Conferencing and Restorative Justice: International Practices and Perspectives* (Oxford: Oxford University Press, 2012).

32. Lode Walgrave, *Restorative Justice, Self-Interest and Responsible Citizenship* (Cullompton: Willan Publishing, 2008), 34.

33. However, it seems also clear that this conclusion depends on some additional normative premises, for instance related to (say, communitarian or republican) theories of justice, which some deliberative democrats may find unappealing.

34. Community conferences, so conceived, are very different from mediation processes: here we do not get "mediation between two individuals, but a problem-solving dialogue between two communities of care." Braithwaite and Pettit, *Not Just Deserts*, 772. See also Owen Fiss, "Against Settlement," *Yale Law Journal* 9 (1984) 1073. These

innovative practices confront obvious risks. Braithwaite and Mugford mention, for example, those of "re-professionalization, patriarchy, ritualistic proceduralism . . . and inappropriate net-widening), which tend to be compensated by some of its attractive virtues (they mention "the general direction of change is away from these pathologies; it is deprofessionalizing, empowering of women, oriented to flexible community problem-solving and, for the most part, narrowing nets of state control." See John Braithwaite and S. Mugford, "Conditions of Successful Reintegration Ceremonies," *British Journal of Criminology* 34, no. 2 (1994): 168.

35. See Albert Dzur, *Punishment, Participatory Democracy & the Jury*, 17–20.

36. Ibid., 5–6.

37. Ibid., 6.

38. Ibid., 5–6.

39. Andrew Ashworth and Julian Roberts (eds.), *Sentencing Guidelines: Exploring the English Model* (Oxford: Oxford University Press, 2013). To state this, however, does not mean that decentralized models simply manage to solve all the problems that the system of sentencing guidelines was directed at solving.

40. David Garland, *The Culture of Control* (Chicago: University of Chicago Press, 2001), 145–146.

41. Ibid.

42. Cited in Ian Loader, "Fall of the 'Platonic Guardians': Liberalism, Criminology and Political Responses to Crime in England and Wales," *British Journal of Criminology* 46, no. 4 (2006): 563. See also Mick Ryan, "Penal Policy Making Towards the Millennium: Elites and Populists; New Labour and the New Criminology," *International Journal of Sociology of Law* 27, no. 1 (1999): 16.

43. See Loader, "Fall of the 'Platonic Guardians'," 582.

44. Ibid.

45. Ian Loader and Richard Sparks, "Criminology and Democratic Politics."

46. See, for example, Ian Loader, "Thinking Normatively About Private Security," *Journal of Law and Society* 24, no. 3 (1997): 377–394; Ian Loader, "Plural Policing and Democratic Governance," *Social & Legal Studies* 9, no. 3 (2000): 323.

47. Philip Pettit, *On the People's Terms. A Republican Theory and Model of Democracy* (Cambridge: Cambridge University Press, 2012).

48. Philip Pettit, "Is Criminal Justice Politically Feasible?" *Buffalo Criminal Law Review* 5, no. 2 (2002): 427.

49. Ibid., 430.

50. Ibid, 442.

51. This is basically the same conclusion reached by Albert Dzur and Rekha Mirchandani, "Punishment and Democracy."

52. José L. Martí, "The Republican Democratization of Criminal law and Justice," in Samantha Besson and José L. Martí (eds.), *Legal Republicanism* (Oxford: Oxford University Press, 2009), 167–186.

53. Garland, *Culture of Control*, 145–146.

54. Antony Bottoms, "The Philosophy and Politics of Punishment and Sentencing," in C. Clarkson and R. Morgan (eds.), *The Politics of Sentencing Reform* (Oxford: Clarendon Press 1995), 40.

55. Garland, *Culture of Control*, 145–146.

56. One of the best-known recent cases of penal populism appeared during the early 1990s, after the state of California introduced its three-strikes-and-you're-out mandatory legislation for sentencing. See Frank Zimring, Franklin Hawkins, and Sam Kamin, *Punishment and Democracy: Three Strikes and You're Out in California* (Oxford: Oxford University Press, 2001). Following the Californian example, by the mid-1990s almost every US state, and also the federal government, had enacted some type of mandatory sentencing legislation. These events only confirmed the presence of a renewed populist trend in criminal law (we shall come back to this point later), which began to regain force in numerous Western countries, from England to Argentina. See Gerry Johnstone, "Penal Policy Making: Elitist, Populist or Participatory?" *Punishment & Society* 2, no. 2 (2000) 161; Mick Ryan, "Penal Policy Making Towards the Millennium"; Massimo Sozzo, "Transition to Democracy and Penal Policy: The Case of Argentina," Straus Working Paper 03/11, New York University, 2011.

57. Peter Benekos and Alida Merlo, "Three Strikes and You're Out: The Political Sentencing Game," *Fed. Probation* 59, no. 1 (1995): 3; Peter Greenwood, Peter Rydell, Allan Abrahamse, Jonathan Caulkins, James Chiesa, Karin Model, and Stephen Klein, "Three Strikes and You're Out: Estimated Benefits and Costs of California's New Mandatory-Sentencing Law" (Santa Monica, CA: RAND Corporation, 1994); Lisa Stolzenberg and Stewart D' Alessio, "Three Strikes and You' re Out: The Impact of California's New Mandatory Sentencing Law on Serious Crime Rates," *Crime and Delinquency* 43, no. 4 (1997): 457–469.

58. John Pratt, J. *Penal Populism: Key Ideas in Criminology* (London: Taylor & Francis, 2007).

59. Antony Bottoms, "The Philosophy and Politics of Punishment and Sentencing." See also Julian Roberts and Michael Hough, *Changing Attitudes to Punishment: Public Opinion, Crime and Justice* (Cullompton, Devon: Willan, 2002); Julian Roberts and Michael Hough, "Public Attitudes to Punishment: The Context," in Julian Roberts and Michael Hough (eds.), *Changing Attitudes to Punishment: Public Opinion, Crime and Justice* (Cullompton, Devon: Willan, 2002).

60. Antony Bottoms, "The Philosophy and Politics of Punishment and Sentencing," 40.

61. Gerry Johnstone, "Penal Policy Making," 146.

62. David Green, "Public Opinion Versus Public Judgement About Crime," *British Journal of Criminology* 46, no. 1 (2006): 131–154.

63. Robert Goodin, "Laundering Preferences," in Jon Elster and Aanud Hylland (eds.), *Foundations of Social Choice Theory* (Cambridge: Cambridge University Press, 1986).

64. Opinion polls may be useful to recognize the most immediate or urgent consumers' choices, but democracy is not about how to satisfy the consumption preferences of the majority, but rather about how to ensure profound and broad agreements on fundamental public issues about justice, freedom, or equality. Jon Elster, "The Market and the Forum," in Jon Elster and Aanud Hylland (eds.), *Foundations of Social Choice Theory* (Cambridge: Cambridge University Press, 1986); Amy Gutman and Dennis Thompson, *Why Deliberative Democracy?* (Princeton, NJ: Princeton University Press, 2004).

65. David Green, "Public Opinion Versus Public Judgement About Crime," 204.

66. Ibid.

67. Dzur and Mirchandani, "Punishment and Democracy," 163.

68. Ibid., 164.

69. David Green, "Public Opinion Versus Public Judgement About Crime." The Centre for Deliberative Democracy, from Stanford University, describes deliberative polls as "an attempt to use television and public opinion research in a new and constructive way. A random, representative sample is first polled on the targeted issues." After this baseline poll, members of the sample are invited to gather at a single place for a weekend in order to discuss the issues.

70. See Raúl Zaffaroni, *En busca de las penas perdidas* (Buenos Aires: Ediar, 2003). Also, see Luigi Ferrajoli, *Diritto e Ragione* (Roma: Laterza, 1989) and Luigi Ferrajoli, *Democracia y garantismo* (Madrid: Trotta, 2008). Also see this debate in Jesper Ryberg and Julian Roberts, *Popular Punishment* (Oxford: Oxford University Press, 2014).

71. Robert Luskin, James Fishkin, and Roger Jowell, "Considered Opinions: Deliberative Polling in Britain," *British Journal of Political Science* 32, no. 2 (2002): 484. See also Albert Dzur, *Punishment, Participatory Democracy & The Jury*, 110.

72. Andrew Taslitz, "The Criminal Republic: Democratic Breakdown as a Cause of Mass Incarceration," *Ohio State Journal of Criminal Law* 9, no. 1 (2011): 138. See also Vanessa Barker, "Deliberating Crime and Punishment: A Way Out of Get Tough Justice?" *Criminology and Public Policy* 5, no. 1 (2006): 37–44; and her *The Politics of Imprisonment: How the Democratic Process Shapes the Way American Punishes Offenders* (Oxford: Oxford University Press, 2009).

73. Vanessa Barker, "Prison and the Public Sphere: Toward a Democratic Theory of Penal Order," in David Scott (ed.), *Why Prison?* (Cambridge: Cambridge University Press, 2013), 41.

74. Ibid., 141. See also Lisa Miller, *The Perils of Federalism: Race, Poverty, and the Politics of Crime Control* (New York: Oxford University Press, 2008).

75. Christopher Uggen, Jeff Manza, and Melissa Thompson, "Citizenship, Democracy, and the Civic Reintegration of Criminal Offenders," *Annals of the American Academy of Political and Social Science* 605 (2006): 281–310.

76. The studies that I am taking into account are in most cases focused on the phenomenon of mass incarceration in the United States.

77. Alasdair Cochrane, "Prisons on Appeal. The idea of Communicative Incarceration," *Criminal Law and Philosophy* (forthcoming): 1–18.

78. Mike Rowan, "Democracy and Punishment: A Radical View," *Theoretical Criminology* 16, no. 1 (2012): 44.

79. John Medearis, "Social Movements and Deliberative Democratic Theory," *British Journal of Political Science* 35 (2004): 53–75.

80. Iris Young, *Inclusion and Democracy* (New York: Oxford Press 2000); 45. See also her "Activist Challenges to Deliberative Democracy," *Political Theory* 29, no. 5 (2001): 670–690.

81. Young, *Inclusion and Democracy*, 48.

82. Similarly, Jane Mansbridge tried to resist such restrictive approach to deliberative democracy. In her words, "good deliberation should also illuminate conflict. It should lead participants to a more nuanced understanding of their selves and their interests, ideally less influenced by hegemonic ideas, in a way that may put them in direct conflict with other participants." Jane Mansbridge, James Bohman, Simone Chambers, David Estlund,

Andreas Føllesdal, Archon Fung, Cristina Lafont, Bernard Manin and José luis Martí "The Place of Self-Interest and the Role of Power in Deliberative Democracy," *Journal of Political Philosophy* 18, no. 1 (2010): 82–83. Also, see Archon Fung, "Deliberation before the Revolution," *Political Theory* 33, no. 2 (2005): 379–419.

83. See my "Penal Coercion in Contexts of Social Injustice." *Criminal Law and Philosophy* 5, no. 1 (2011): 21–38. Also, see my "Law and Social Protests," *Criminal Law and Philosophy* 6, no. 2 (2012): 131–148..

84. In *NLRB v. Fruit Packers* (377 US 58, 1964), and examining the issue of picketing, Justice Black maintained that when the action of patrolling and that of speech were so intertwined, court should "weigh the circumstances" and "appraise the substantiality of the reasons advanced" for the regulation of the activity of picketing (ibid 77–78).

85. *Texas v. Johnson*, 491 US 397 (1989); *Tinker v. Des Moines Sch. Distr.* 393 US 503 (1969).

86. The Court could also invoke—as it sometimes did—the *clear and present danger* test to determine whether the actions in question afford constitutional protection or not. For example, see *Feiner v. New York* 340 US 315 (1951).

87. Against those who objected to those disruptive expressions maintaining that they could not be classified as "pure speech" but rather as "plus speech" (as the US Supreme Court has put it), Harry Kalven maintained that one could reject the "neat dichotomy" between "pure speech" and "plus speech." Harry Kalven, Jr. "The Concept of the Public Forum: Cox v. Louisiana." *The Supreme Court Review* (1965): 1–32; Harry Kalven "The Concept of the Public Forum: *Cox v. Louisiana*," *Supreme Court Review* 23, no. 1 (1965): 23. A similar view in Geoffrey Stone, "For Americana: Speech in Public Places," *Supreme Court Review* 233 (1974): 240.

88. Ronald Dworkin, *Justice in Robes* (Cambridge, MA: Harvard University Press, 2006), 25.

89. For Helen Fenwick, *Austin and Saxby* has confirmed that "the police have a very wide range of powers to use even against entirely peaceful protesters if a few protesters are or may be disorderly." Helen Fenwick, *Civil Liberties and Human Rights*, 771.

90. In addition, not all disruptions make a protest in the street unpeaceful. Thus, in recent cases, the European Court of Human Rights also recognized that disruptions incidental to holding an assembly do not render it "unpeaceful" (*Stankov and the United Macedonian Organisation Ilinden v. Bulgaria*, October 2, 2001), and also that the mere presence of a few agitators did not transform the assembly into a violent one.

91. Sharon Dolovich, "Legitimate Punishment in Liberal democracy," 310.

92. Vanessa Barker refers to the so-called participatory parity principle, namely the idea that "those most affected by crime control policies have an equal chance to impact the distribution of these public goods." Barker, "Prison and the Public Sphere," 131.

93. Loader, "Thinking Normatively About Private Security," 387.

INDEX

California (*cont.*)
 three-strikes law in, 145–146, 194,
  285–286
 violent crime levels in, 285–286
Canada, 195, 274, 306
capital punishment
 inequalities in implementation of, 201
 public opinion and, 130
 United Kingdom's prohibition of,
  130, 272
 in the United States, 272–273
Chesterston, G.K., 123, 125, 134
China, 140
Christie, Nils, 7, 144
citizen participation. *See also* citizenship
 advocacy for greater, 115, 120–124,
  126–136, 169–172, 200–201, 306–309
 civic schoolhouse thesis and,
  130–131, 307
 consultation in policymaking and, 222
 correction thesis and, 131–132
 criminal justice and, 9–10, 12–14, 36,
  114–124, 126–136
 criticism of and challenges to, 6, 115
 defusion thesis and, 127
 democratic institutions and, 122–123
 efficacy thesis and, 129–130
 fairness thesis and, 128–129
 juries and, 123, 127, 130–132,
  171–172, 222, 306–307
 legitimacy thesis and, 127–128
 mobilization *versus* organizing
  strategies for, 121–122
 the New Left and, 133–135
 penal severity lessened through, 84–85,
  221, 315
 rational disorganization and, 123
 reinvigorationism and, 166–167,
  171–172, 180
 rule of men not laws thesis and,
  132–133, 135
 sentencing and, 12, 14, 140–146,
  148–156, 207
 special role responsibility thesis and,
  133–135
citizenship. *See also* citizen participation
 civility and, 74

conditionality of, 53
constitutional rights and, 240, 245
consumerism and, 99–100, 107
convicted criminal offenders and, 46,
 48–50, 54, 67
crime victims and, 36, 112n65
criminal justice system and, 12, 35–36,
 44–46, 48–50, 52–55, 60–61, 123,
 134, 201
criminal offenders and, 39–41, 43,
 45–46, 48–50, 52–54, 67, 72, 76–77
ex-felons and, 28, 116
eyeball test and, 35
juries and, 36
political equality and, 90, 92–97,
 101–102, 104, 107
in prisons, 51, 89, 91–96, 99, 116
punishment and, 48–52, 54, 94, 96,
 102, 104, 107
self-government and, 134
sovereignty and, 90, 94, 96, 99, 104
suspension of, 85
citizens' juries, 13, 206, 208
City Limits (Peterson), 284
civic roles
 active *versus* passive dimensions
  of, 38, 40
 convicted criminal offenders and, 38,
  40, 46–51, 54
 criminal offenders and, 38–52, 54
 informal aspects of, 37
 normative aspects of, 38, 40
 punishment and, 11, 47–52, 55
civic schoolhouse thesis, 130–131, 307
civil liberty
 democracy and, 92–93, 105, 125
 political equality and, 90–93, 101, 103
 in prisons, 91–92, 105, 240, 245,
  320–321
Civil Rights Act of 1964, 280
Clinton, Bill, 193–194, 278–279
Columbine High School shootings
 (1999), 279
Commerce Clause (United States
 Constitution), 280–281
community accountability
 conferences, 306

Conservative Party (United Kingdom),
192–193, 290
Constitutional Reform Act of 2009
(United Kingdom), 275
constitutions
Argentina and, 298, 319–320
Commerce Clause (United States) and,
280–281
democratic accountability and, 269,
274, 276–285, 287–288, 290–292
due process clauses in, 281
inmate advisory councils and, 240
limits on powers set by, 202
rights of association and, 243–244
United Kingdom and, 267–268,
273–275, 290–292
United States and, 267–268, 273,
275–285, 290–292
Copson, Lynne, 12
crime
civic fellowship destroyed by, 53
confessing to, 42–45
control methods regarding, 14, 146,
288–290, 316
decreasing levels of, 2, 187, 205–206
determining what counts as, 75–76
fair play violated by, 64, 69, 75
mens rea concept and, 93–94, 102
moral *versus* political
understandings of, 88
negligence and, 94
normative responses to, 171
personhood and, 93
political equality's impact on,
104–105
politicians' discussions of, 189
poor disproportionally impacted by, 79,
104–105
public opinion on, 197–198, 267, 315
as public wrong concerning whole
polity, 53, 120, 149
rights denied through, 96–97, 100
social failure and structural causes of,
61, 70, 105, 146, 287
victims' standpoint in, 100
violation of game rules compared
to, 65, 68

criminal justice
citizenship and, 12, 35–36, 44–46,
48–50, 52–55, 60–61, 123, 134, 201
civic responsibility *versus* legal duty in,
42–44, 51–52, 55
civic roles and, 34–54
as coercion by a sovereign, 89
convicted criminal offenders' role in,
38, 40, 46–52
criminal offenders' roles in, 38–52
defendants and, 43–45, 56n16
deliberative democracy and, 14, 201,
299–322
democracy and, 14, 35, 78, 118–121,
201, 299–305
democratic deficit in, 120–121
in the democratic republic, 11, 35,
37–38, 41, 54
depoliticization of, 117, 127
discretionary judgments and, 42, 133
elections and, 72, 74, 98, 114,
116–117, 122
fair play principle and, 63, 67–70
Global Recession (2008-2009) and,
187–188
ideal theory of, 34–35, 41–43, 54–55
mistaken convictions in, 42–43, 51–52
personhood rights and, 92–93,
103, 105
political inequality and, 300
political theory and, 14, 35–36,
300–301
public opinion on, 12, 114, 116, 124,
216–221
public wrongs and, 38, 120
racial inequalities and, 18–19, 23,
25–26, 41, 188, 280
rule of law and, 133, 179
social solidarity reflected in, 169
state coercion and, 44–45, 300–301,
320–321
victims' role in, 36–38
witnesses' role in, 38
Criminal Justice Act of 2003 (United
Kingdom), 154
The Culture of Control (Garland), 115–116
Cuomo, Andrew, 27

Dagger, Richard, 11
D'Amato, Alfonse, 194
death penalty. *See* capital punishment
de Greiff, Pablo, 300–305
deliberative democracy
  criminal justice and, 14, 201, 299–322
  criminal trials and, 304–305, 313
  democratic accountability and, 206
  juries and, 222, 306–307
  just ordering and, 206
  liberalism and, 189, 201–204, 207–208
  majoritarianism contrasted with, 204
  penal decision-making and,
    307–308, 314
  penal elitism and, 308–310, 314
  penal populism and, 190, 204–205,
    308, 310–314
  political equality and, 202, 219–220
  public deliberation and, 302, 310
  public opinion methods and, 230
  punishment and, 9, 190, 303–304
  reasonable pluralism and, 203–204
  sentencing and, 305–307, 313–314
  social inclusion and, 302, 310
  social protests and, 313–314,
    317–320, 322
  state coercion and, 300–301, 320–321
deliberative polls
  penal policy and, 79, 206, 313
  public opinion nuances and, 13, 224–225
democracy. *See also* deliberative
    democracy; the democratic republic
  civility and, 74–75
  civil liberty and, 92–93, 105, 125
  as cooperative enterprise, 71–78
  criminal justice and, 35, 78, 118–121,
    299–305
  definitions of, 301–302
  delegation of powers and, 117–120,
    129, 134
  democratic deficit and, 120–121, 267
  elections and, 72, 74, 98, 114, 116–117,
    122, 127–128
  fair play and, 70–79
  ideals of, 2–3, 8
  institutions' role in, 122–123

  liberalism and, 167, 169, 189, 200–208
  mass incarceration and, 7–8, 10, 18,
    60–61, 63, 73, 101, 164, 175
  measures of, 124–125
  penal populism and, 60, 63, 71, 73,
    79, 84, 114, 116–117, 121–122,
    190–196, 204–205, 207, 215, 308,
    310–314, 321
  personhood and, 93, 103
  political equality and, 72–73, 78, 85,
    89–91, 93, 95, 97, 101–107, 109n21,
    118, 125, 128, 201
  political participation declines and,
    84, 98–99, 101–102, 106–107, 121,
    166, 175
  preference-aggregation model of,
    72–74, 78
  in prisons, 13, 50–51, 239–262
  prisons' place within, 2–10, 20, 28, 73,
    84–86, 89–90, 95, 97–98, 105–107
  protective *versus* developmental
    conceptions of, 125–126, 128, 133
  punishment and, 7–10, 84–86, 88, 94–99,
    102–107, 116–136, 201, 300–301
  regulative ideal of, 302
  as self-government, 78, 89, 97, 99, 102,
    104–107, 130, 300
  social change and, 175–176
  "tyranny of the majority" and, 202
democratic accountability
  constitutional system design and, 269,
    274, 276–285, 287–288, 290–292
  definition of, 267–268
  deliberative democracy and, 206
  gun control legislation and, 278–280
  "local control" advocacy and, 286–290
  penal policies and, 267–268, 277,
    280–281, 283–284, 287–288, 290–292
  in the United Kingdom, 267, 290–292
  in the United States, 267, 277–285,
    287–288, 290–292
  veto points as obstacle to, 13, 269,
    278–280, 290–291
democratic decrementalism, 95–98, 107
Democratic Party (United States), 19,
    23, 193

the democratic republic
civic roles in, 38
criminal justice and, 11, 35,
37–38, 41, 54
definition of, 11, 35
imprisonment and, 49
inclusionary spirit and, 39, 46, 53–54
democratic retributive abolitionism,
106–107
deregulation in American governance, 23
deterrence
punishment and the goal of, 8, 47, 62
restorative justice and, 155
sentencing and, 129, 146
utilitarianism and, 86
dialectical utopianism (Harvey), 174
DiIulio, John, 239, 249
"doing good by stealth," 190, 193,
196–199
Dolovich, Sharon, 301, 320–321
Doob, Anthony, 194–195, 223, 225
Drakeford, Mark, 190, 193, 196
drug laws
justifiability of, 41
mandatory minimum sentences
and, 22, 41
marijuana laws and, 27
mass incarceration and, 61–62, 76, 188
reduction of penalties in, 27–28
unequal enforcement of, 71
Dryzek, John, 228
Dubber, Markus, 101
Duff, R. A., 11, 301–305
Dukakis, Michael, 193
Dworkin, Ronald, 35, 319
Dzur, Albert W.
on Chesterton, 123, 125
citizen participation in criminal justice
encouraged by, 115, 120–124, 126,
129, 132, 134–135, 169–172, 201,
306–307
on deliberative forms of
participation, 171
on democracy's moral
dimension, 60–61
on democratic institutions, 122–123

developmental view of democracy
and, 125
Habermas and, 301
on juries and jury trials, 123, 171–172,
207, 306–307
on laws' unequal burdens on different
citizens, 78
on mobilization *versus* organization
strategies, 121–122
on nonevasion, 134
penal populism criticized by, 312–313
on "the invisibility of punishment" in
democratic theory, 300
on thick populism, 97, 201
on thin populism, 198–199

Eason, John, 19
Ecuador, 314
Eisenhower, Dwight D., 278
Ekmedjián, Miguel, 298
elitism. *See* penal elitism
El Reno Federal Correction Facility
(Oklahoma), 1–2
England. *See also* United Kingdom
British Parliament and, 274
homicide rates in, 268, 271
incarceration rates in, 79, 100,
140, 268
Police and Crime Commissioners
(PCC) in, 274, 284, 289, 292
The Enlightenment, 6
European Convention of Human
Rights, 299
European Court of Human Rights, 275
expertise in criminal justice. *See also*
penal elitism
advocacy for relying on, 117–119,
128–129, 166–171
democracy curtailed by reliance on, 4,
114–115, 120, 171
desensitization and, 131
establishing relevance of, 165
insulationism and, 166–171, 175,
179–180
skepticism regarding, 114, 116–117,
120, 169–172, 175

Jackson, "Shoeless" Joe, 67
Johnston, Gerry, 312
Jones, Peter, 176
Jones v. North Carolina Prisoner Union,
    239, 244–245, 260
juries
    citizen juries and, 13, 206, 218
    citizen participation and, 123, 127,
        130–132, 171–172, 222
    citizenship and, 36
    collective deliberation and, 131
    episodic nature of, 130
    experts contrasted with, 131
    legitimacy and, 127
    passive spectatorship and, 172
    random selection and, 127
    rational disorganization and, 123
just ordering, 169, 205–207

Kansas City (Kansas) and Kansas City
    (Missouri), 282
Kennedy, John F., 278

Labour Party (United Kingdom)
    "doing good by stealth" policies and,
        193, 196–197
    education policies and, 291
    penal policies and, 192–193,
        196–197, 290
Lacey, Nicola
    on democracy's competing values, 118
    Dzur's critique of, 120
    penal elitism advocated by, 117–120,
        124, 126, 129, 135
    protectionist view of democracy and,
        125–126
    United States and United Kingdom as
        focus of study for, 268
Latinos, 18, 20–21, 25, 254
Law, John, 214, 222, 227–228
legitimacy
    citizen participation and, 127–128
    of the criminal justice system, 127–128,
        190, 207, 214, 320–322
    of deliberative methods of public
        opinion gathering, 223–224, 226
    democracy and, 9, 189

of elected officials, 189, 198, 206
elections and, 127–128
of expert-driven technocratic
    approaches, 169
of imprisonment for public protection
    (IPP) sentences, 54
inmate advisory councils' role in
    promoting, 248–249
just ordering and, 206
mass incarceration and, 165
of police actions, 188, 205
of prison policies, 240, 245–246,
    248–249
of punishment, 47, 169
sentencing and, 127–128
stakeholding and, 151
of the state, 191, 200, 277
Leib, Ethan, 207
Lerman, Amy, 8, 13
Levitas, Ruth, 164, 178–179, 181
liberalism
    democracy and, 167, 169, 189,
        200–208
    of fear, 180, 203–205
    individual dignity and rights in, 7,
        86–87, 89, 167–168, 179–180,
        202, 205
    just ordering and, 205
    majoritarianism contrasted with, 204
    mass incarceration and, 164
    penal theory and, 85–89, 106, 162–163,
        179, 189
    personhood and, 167
    social change and, 168, 180
    utopia and, 168, 180
    welfare state and, 3
Loader, Ian
    on deliberative democracy and criminal
        justice, 321
    on just ordering, 205–206
    penal elitism critiqued by, 309
    on penal populism and the unpopularity
        of politics, 98–99
    on the state's responsibility to prevent
        violence, 270
"local control" advocacy, 286–290
Locke, John, 203

penal elitism. *See also* expertise
  advocacy for, 117–118, 124, 140–141,
    162, 201, 310
  definition of, 4
  deliberative democracy and,
    308–310, 314
  skepticism regarding, 114, 120, 127,
    141, 308–309
penal populism
  assumptions regarding, 5, 12,
    15–16n13, 169–170, 200, 315
  calculus of, 189–191, 193–201, 207, 214
  citizen participation contrasted with,
    120–122, 135, 166–167, 171, 181,
    206–207
  criminology's contribution to, 163
  criticisms of, 115–117, 162–163,
    165–166, 190–191, 310–311, 321
  definition of, 191
  deliberative democracy as means of
    addressing, 190, 204–205, 308,
    310–314
  democracy and, 60, 63, 71, 73,
    79, 84, 114, 116–117, 121–122,
    190–196, 204–205, 207, 215, 308,
    310–314, 321
  doing good by stealth and, 193, 196–199
  financial costs of, 311
  high-roading and, 193–198, 200
  insulationist responses to, 169–170,
    179–180
  lexical neutrality of, 191–192
  loud high-roading and, 195, 196
  loud low-roading and, 194–195,
    196–198, 204
  low-roading and, 194–198, 200, 204
  political participation declines and,
    84, 98–99, 101–102, 106–107, 121,
    166, 175
  public knowledge and, 170, 175, 197,
    199–200, 217
  quiet high-roading and, 196–198, 200
  quiet low-roading and, 195–196, 204
  spaces of hope challenges to, 163,
    175, 181
  victims and, 116

penal theory
  Hegel and, 88–89
  liberalism and, 85–89, 106, 162–163,
    179, 189
  minimalism and, 86–88
  offenders' rights and, 39–40
  proportionality and, 86–88
  utilitarianism and, 86
penal welfarism, 308
personhood rights, 92–95, 101, 103,
    105, 167
Peterson, Paul, 284
Pettit, Philip
  on citizenry and vigilance, 78
  "eyeball test" of, 35
  on "the outrage dynamic," 309–310
  on punishment and
    proportionality, 87
  on restorative justice, 305–306
PGA Tour, Inc. v. Martin, 81–82n18
Philadelphia (Pennsylvania), 283
Philosophy of Right (Hegel), 88
plea bargaining, 6, 45
Police and Crime Commissioners
    (PCC; United Kingdom), 274, 284,
    289, 292
political equality
  citizenship and, 90, 92–97, 101–102,
    104, 107
  civil liberty and, 90–93, 101, 103
  crime and, 104–105
  deliberative democracy and, 202,
    219–220
  democracy and, 72–73, 78, 85, 89–91,
    93, 95, 97, 101–107, 109n21, 118,
    125, 128, 201
  democratic sovereignty and, 89
  as emergent property, 103
  incarceration and, 11–12, 85, 90–91,
    94–95, 99
  normative commitments regarding,
    90–91, 98, 102, 104
  punishment and, 95–96,
    102–104, 106
  self-government and, 90, 98,
    102–104, 107

on rehabilitation, 199
on restorative justice, 145–146, 148, 155
science and technology studies (STS)
and, 214, 226–227
Public Order Act (United Kingdom,
1986), 299
Public Safety Realignment initiative
(California), 27
public welfare offenses, 94, 100–101
punishment. *See also* penal theory
citizenship and, 48–52, 54, 94, 96, 102,
104, 107
civic duty and, 11, 47–52, 55
collateral consequences of, 54
communicative approaches to, 303–304
community service and, 71
in cooperative enterprises, 63–64
deliberative democracy and, 9, 190,
303–304
democracy and, 7–10, 84–86, 88, 94–99,
102–107, 116–136, 201, 300–301
deterrence and, 8, 47, 62
dialogic approach to, 304
expressive approaches to, 303
fair play concept as justification for, 11,
60, 63–64, 67, 69, 71–72, 77
humiliation and, 48, 57n33
ideal theory of, 34–35
incapacitation and, 100
justification for, 11, 60, 63–64, 67, 69,
71–72, 77, 189, 303
legitimacy of, 47, 169
local control ethos and, 286–290
noncitizens and, 102
participatory nature of some forms
of, 49–51
political equality and, 95–96,
102–104, 106
political rhetoric regarding, 12, 23,
187, 189
political theory and, 7–9, 88, 96,
102, 167
poor disproportionally impacted by, 104
postdemocracy and, 98–99, 106–107
proportionality and, 86–88, 94–95,
97, 105

public opinion regarding, 11–13,
28, 116, 130, 166, 169, 191,
199, 213–218, 221, 224, 267,
311–313, 315
racial disparities regarding, 18–19, 23,
41, 188, 280
right to resist, 44
social justice and, 102–103
unified theories of, 154–155, 160n61
utilitarian approaches to, 86
varieties of, 47, 62, 71
*Punishment, Participatory Democracy
and the Jury* (Dzur), 120–123
punitive restoration
citizen participation and, 148–152,
155–156
community's role in, 148
conference format of, 148–150, 159n40
criminal offenders' role in, 148–153, 155
definition of, 141
general public's role in, 149–151
hard treatment and, 149, 151–155
justification for, 141–142
objections to, 154
stakeholding and, 141–142,
149–151, 154
victimless crimes and, 151
victims' role in, 148–151

Ramsay, Peter, 11, 202
Rawls, John
deliberative democracy and, 302
on justice as fairness, 189, 202
on the natural duty of civility, 74
on the polity as cooperative
enterprise, 63
on the reasonable *versus* the rational,
202–204
state coercion and, 301
recidivism
democratic failure and, 72
high prison rates and, 140
in New York State, 21
restorative justice and, 144–145, 148, 154
short-term incarceration and, 152
in the United Kingdom, 70

rehabilitation
    decline in practices of, 115
    formal ceremonies and, 54
    public opinion on, 199
    as punishment goal, 8, 62
    restorative justice and, 152–155
    sentencing and, 12, 53–54
    short-term incarceration and, 152–154
    structural obstacles to, 22
    utilitarianism and, 86
reinvigorationism, 166–167, 171–172, 180
reparation, 40–41, 46–48, 54
Republican Party (United States),
    18–19, 188
Resident Government Council (RGC;
    Washington State Penitentiary), 243
restorative justice
    as alternative to mainstream criminal
        justice, 12, 53, 142, 145, 147, 150,
        155, 305–306
    citizen participation and, 9, 130,
        142–152, 155–156, 171
    community accountability conferences
        and, 306
    community definition questions and,
        147–148
    conventional criminal justice system's
        hegemony over, 174
    criminal offenders' role in, 52,
        143–145, 148–153, 155, 206–207
    deliberative democracy and, 7, 10,
        305–307
    diversity of approaches in, 141–143,
        145, 148
    financial costs of, 144–145, 148, 153
    hard treatment and, 146–147, 149,
        151–155
    limits of, 145–148
    process-oriented nature of, 143, 306
    public confidence in, 148, 151, 155
    public opinion regarding, 145–146,
        148, 155
    punitive restoration and, 141–142,
        148–156
    recidivism and, 144–145, 148, 154
    rehabilitation and, 152–155

retributivism and, 52, 106
    sentencing and, 141, 143–146, 305–307
    stakeholding and, 141–143,
        149–151, 154
    substance abuse treatment and, 144,
        152–153, 155
    training and, 144, 152
    victimless crimes and, 151
    victims' roles in, 143–145, 148–151
Restorative Justice Council, 143
retributivism
    criticisms of, 85–86, 102–104
    democratic retributive abolitionism and,
        106–107
    democratic retributivism and, 85–86,
        92–95, 102–106
    fair play concept and, 64
    legal retributivism and, 102–103, 105
    political equality and, 106
    proportionality of punishment
        and, 87–88
    punishment and, 47, 100
    restorative justice and, 52, 106
    social justice and, 103–104
    stereotypes and, 122
Ristroph, Alice, 44
Roberts, Julian, 170, 191, 217, 223, 225
Rose, Nikolas, 227
Rowan, Mike, 203
Royal Society for the Arts (United
    Kingdom), 70
rule of law *versus* rule of men,
    132–133, 135
rural America
    economic decline in, 19–20, 24
    prison development in, 11,
        19–20, 23–28
    social welfare system decline and, 24
Russell, Michael, 176–177
Russia, 140

Sanders, Bernie, 188
Sandy Hook school shooting (2012), 278
Scheingold, Stuart, 266
Schifrin case (Argentina), 298, 313,
    319, 322

Schudson, Michael, 197
Schumpeter, Joseph, 72
science and technology studies (STS), 214, 226–227
Scotland
  devolution of powers to, 273–274
  homicide rate in, 271
  incarceration rates in, 140, 268
  independence referendum (2014) in, 163, 176–177, 181
  life sentences without parole (LWOP) in, 272
  Parliament in, 273
  policing reform in, 292
Second Chance Act of 2007 (United States), 199
security
  citizens' perception of, 100
  inmate advisory councils' impact on prisons and, 239, 243–244, 246–247, 250–261
  "local control" and, 288
  police's role in providing, 74
  prison classification levels and, 252–256
  in prisons, 239–240, 243–249, 252–261
  state's role in providing, 13, 191, 267, 270–271, 277, 285, 287–289
segregation, 20–22, 26, 201–202
sentencing
  citizen participation and, 12, 14, 140–146, 148–156, 207
  community service and, 34
  criminal justice expertise and, 120, 127, 129, 135
  deliberative democracy and, 305–307, 313–314
  deterrence and, 129, 146
  juvenile offenders and, 272–273
  legitimacy and, 127–128
  life sentences without parole (LWOP) and, 53, 272–273
  mandatory minimums and, 1, 22, 41, 62, 71, 199, 272
  parole provisions and, 22
  public confidence in, 140, 155

  public opinion regarding, 170, 216–217, 224
  recidivism and, 140
  rehabilitation and, 12, 53–54
  restorative justice and, 141, 143–146, 305–307
  stakeholding and, 149
  suspended sentences and, 12, 153
  three strikes laws and, 22, 62, 71, 116, 145–146, 285–286
  truth-in-sentencing mindset and, 195, 199
  victim impact statements and, 116
Shklar, Judith, 179, 184n32, 203
Simon, Jonathan, 1, 7, 99, 135, 165
Skarbek, David, 249
social protests
  in Argentina, 298, 319–320
  deliberative democracy and, 313–314, 317–320, 322
  expressive component of, 318
  illocutionary aspects of, 318
  "kettling" and, 298–299
  socially disadvantaged groups and, 318
  strikes and, 319
  in the United Kingdom, 298–299
  violence and, 319
Society of Captives (Sykes), 249
Socrates, 33
solitary confinement, 34
"spaces of hope," 163, 173–177, 181
Sparks, Richard, 205–206, 229, 309
stakeholding, 12, 141–143, 149–151, 154
Supreme Court (United States). *See also specific cases*
  on the Affordable Care Act, 280
  on associational rights within prisons, 13, 239, 244–245
  on federalism and states' rights, 275
  on gun control legislation, 280
  on jury trials, 44
  on penal policies, 280
  substantial powers of, 276, 291
Sure Start, 291
Survey of Inmates in State and Federal Correctional Facilities, 1997 (Bureau of Justice Statistics), 251

suspended sentences, 153
Sykes, Gresham, 249

Ten Points/Operation Ceasefire
    Project, 288
thick populism, 97, 201, 203
thick populism (Dzur), 97
thin populism, 198, 201, 206–207
Thorpe, Rebecca, 11
Three-Fifths Clause, 26
three strikes laws. *See under* sentencing
Tocqueville, Alexis de, 63, 77–78,
    262, 276
Truman, Harry S., 278
Trump, Donald, 188
Turner, Elizabeth, 12–13, 169–170, 311
Tyler, Tom, 198

undocumented immigrants, 27
unemployment
    among African Americans, 21–22
    "local control" and, 287
    prisons as response to, 21
    social welfare system decline and, 24
    spatial dimensions of, 19
United Kingdom. *See also* England;
    Scotland; Wales
    anti-globalization protests in, 298–299
    anti-recidivism efforts in, 70
    anti-terrorism laws in, 314
    British Parliament in, 268, 273–275,
        290, 299
    capital punishment prohibited in,
        130, 272
    community accountability conferences
        in, 306
    community service sentences in, 34
    constitutional system in, 267–268,
        273–275, 290–292
    decentralization in, 273–274
    deliberative polls on crime in, 315
    democratic accountability in, 267,
        290–292
    electoral discussions of penal policy in,
        192–193
    federalism in, 274

homicide rates in, 268, 271
imprisonment for public protection
    (IPP) sentences in, 53–54
incarceration rates in, 79, 140
inmate advisory groups in, 246, 248
judicial review in, 273, 275
jury trials in, 307
life sentences without parole (LWOP)
    in, 272
"local control" advocacy in, 287, 289
mass incarceration in, 7, 84, 117, 268
minority populations' vulnerability
    violent crime in, 272
Police and Crime Commissioners
    (PCC) in, 274, 284, 289, 292
Scotland independence referendum
    (2014) in, 163, 176–177, 181
sentencing in, 100
social welfare system in, 290–291
Supreme Court in, 275–276
voter turnout levels in, 273
United States
    capital punishment in, 272–273
    community accountability conferences
        in, 306
    Congress in, 276, 278–281, 291
    constitutional system in, 267–268, 273,
        275–285, 290–292
    crime level declines in, 2, 187,
        205–206
    decentralization in, 5, 275
    democratic accountability in, 267,
        277–285, 287–288, 290–292
    democratic ideals in, 8
    drug laws in, 61–62, 71, 76, 188
    economic inequality in, 79–80, 188
    electoral system in, 79–80
    federalism in, 268, 273, 275–277,
        281–285, 287–288, 291
    Great Recession (2008-2009) and,
        187–188
    gun control legislation in, 278–280
    homicide rates in, 268, 271, 285–286
    incarceration rates in, 18, 21, 27,
        60–62, 79, 140, 238, 262, 272
    judicial elections in, 276